LOGIC DESIGN WITH PASCAL
Computer-Aided Design Techniques

LOGIC DESIGN WITH PASCAL
Computer-Aided Design Techniques

Thomas Downs

Mark F. Schulz

Department of Electrical Engineering
University of Queensland
Brisbane, Australia

VNR VAN NOSTRAND REINHOLD
New York

Copyright © 1988 by Van Nostrand Reinhold
Library of Congress Catalog Card Number 87-6233
ISBN 0-442-21889-3

Printed in the United States of America

Van Nostrand Reinhold
115 Fifth Avenue
New York, New York 10003

Van Nostrand Reinhold (International) Limited
11 New Fetter Lane
London EC4P 4EE, England

Van Nostrand Reinhold
480 La Trobe Street
Melbourne, Victoria 3000, Australia

Macmillan of Canada
Division of Canada Publishing Corporation
164 Commander Boulevard
Agincourt, Ontario M1S 3C7, Canada

16 15 14 13 12 11 10 9 8 7 6 5 4 3 2 1

Library of Congress Cataloging-in-Publication Data

Downs, Thomas, 1946–
  Logic Design with Pascal: Computer-aided Design Techniques

  Includes index.
  1. Logic circuits—Design and construction—Data
processing. 2. Computer-aided design. 3. PASCAL
(computer program language) I. Schulz, Mark F.,
1951–   . II. Title. III. Series.
TK7888.4.D68 1988   621.39'5'0285   87-6233
ISBN 0-442-21889-3

D
621·3819'582
DOW

To Our Wives
TANYA AND SHAUNA

PREFACE

The basic aim of this book is to provide an introductory course on the design of logic circuits and systems and further to provide some computer aids which should be of particular assistance in laboratory work associated with the course. The book is organized as follows.

Following the introductory material in Chapter 1, the subject of Chapters 2 and 3 is combinational logic design. Chapter 2 covers the traditional material on simplification of combinational logic by Boolean algebra, Karnaugh maps and tabular methods. Chapter 3 details methods which are suitable for implementation on a computer and provides a set of Pascal listings that are based on these methods. Chapters 4 and 5 are concerned with sequential logic, Chapter 4 introducing basic flip-flop types and the standard material on synchronous sequential design, including state minimization and state assignment; Chapter 5 describes methods suitable for computer implementation and provides a set of Pascal listings. Chapters 6 and 7 are concerned with MSI devices and their use in the design of synchronous digital systems. Chapter 6 introduces the multiplexer, read-only memory and programmable logic array and illustrates their use in digital system design. Chapter 7 describes a computer-aided approach to the top-down design of digital systems and illustrates the use of further Pascal programs provided in this chapter to assist with the top-down design process. An Appendix on the TTL and MOS logic families is also provided.

In summary, Chapters 1, 2, 4 and 6 make up a basic course in the design of logic circuits and systems and Chapters 3, 5 and 7 provide a set of computer design aids along with some more advanced material which the instructor may select from as he or she wishes.

We point out that the later chapters, particularly Chapters 6 and 7, have been written so as to encourage consultation of manufacturers' catalogs. We add that we did not have sufficient space to provide a fully integrated software-design package, but we feel that the development of such a package from the listings given in this book could be achieved by means of student projects.

We wish to thank Keith Burston, Philip McCrea and Peter Maxwell for helpful comments during the development of the manuscript. In addition, Keith

Burston deserves special thanks for carefully debugging the more complex of our design examples. Also, we thank Larry Skattebol for providing the two particularly colorful exercises at the end of Chapter 4. Finally we thank Natalie Nikitin for assistance with some of the manuscript drawings and, above all, June Martin for her excellent typing and for assisting with some of the manuscript drawings.

Tom Downs
Mark Schulz

CONTENTS

LOGIC DESIGN WITH PASCAL
Computer-Aided Design Techniques

1

INTRODUCTION

1.1. DIGITAL VERSUS ANALOG

The scientific and engineering community currently uses three kinds of computers. First there is the *digital* computer, which is by far the most widely used of the three and which has recently been finding very general applications, not only in commerce and industry, but also in the home. The digital computer operates according to a set of instructions called a *program* which is provided by a computer programmer. In scientific and engineering problems, the program is very often a set of instructions detailing a step-by-step procedure for the solution of a mathematical problem. A second type of computer is the *analog* computer, which finds application in the study of systems whose behavior is very difficult to analyze mathematically (implying that it would be difficult or impossible to write a program to analyze such systems on a digital computer). For many systems of this kind it is possible to build electrical circuits whose behavior provides the required information. Without going into details, we point out that this is achieved by building circuits in which voltages at certain points behave in a manner *analogous* to parameters of a system under study. This is the idea underlying the analog computer whose name obviously derives from the analogous behavior that its circuits can provide. The third type of computer is called a *hybrid* computer which, as its name implies, is a combination of the digital and analog types. The hybrid computer finds its main applications in systems simulation and process control.

When an analog computer is used to represent a given system, it is possible to vary an input over a continuous range, usually by varying an input voltage. Such action will normally lead to a continuous change in each of the parameters of interest and these continuous changes can be observed by means of voltmeters. Continuous variations in parameter values are not possible in a digital computer because all information stored in a digital computer is *discretized*, i.e., stored in the form of arithmetical digits. The number of digits used to represent a given numerical quantity obviously has to be finite and this is why continuous variation is impossible. To illustrate this point, consider the representation of ordinary real numbers by four arithmetical digits. In this represen-

1

tation, the number zero is represented by 0.000 and the number one is represented by 1.000. Clearly, this representation does not allow a continuous variation from zero to one. The variation has to go in discrete steps starting at 0.000, moving to 0.001, then to 0.002 and so on, up to 1.000. This fact illustrates a most important difference between analog and digital computers. The analog computer works with continuous variables and the digital computer works with discrete variables. This fact has led to the adjective "analog" being used to describe any quantity that can be continuously varied, e.g., the term "analog signal" which means "continuously-varying signal." Similarly, the adjective "digital" is used to describe quantities that have been discretized, e.g., the digital watch, which displays the passage of time in a sequence of discrete jumps.

In the real world, most quantities are analog, i.e., they vary continuously. Typical examples are temperature, pressure, speed and rate of flow. Computers are very often used to control these kinds of quantities and the computers employed are most often digital. In order for a digital computer to control an analog quantity, it must be able to measure the quantity and to send out appropriate control signals. An *analog-to-digital (A/D) converter* is required to convert an analog quantity into a digital signal that can be interpreted by a digital computer. Similarly, when the computer decides to take a particular control action, it sends out a digital control signal which must be fed through a *digital-to-analog (D/A) converter* before the appropriate control action can take place.

In spite of the need for A/D and D/A converters, digital computers are by far the most widely used for monitoring and controlling analog systems. A major reason for this is that much greater precision is possible with a digital computer than with an analog computer. The accuracy of the analog computer depends entirely upon the accuracy of the components from which its circuits are built. And even if high-quality components with tight tolerances† are employed, it is not uncommon for errors of the order of 1% to occur. In a digital computer, on the other hand, accuracy can be made as high as one likes without the need to use components with tight tolerances. The reason tight tolerances are unnecessary arises from the fact that, as we shall see, the digital computer works with a number system which uses only two arithmetical digits, namely 0 and 1. These two digits are usually represented within the computer by voltage

---

†Components are usually manufactured in batches and, because of unavoidable fluctuations in the manufacturing process, no two components are precisely the same. Thus, for instance, if a batch of 100 Ω resistors is being produced, each resistor will have a value close to 100 Ω and, depending on the care exercised during manufacture, the spread of values around 100 Ω may be narrow or wide. If the manufacturing process has not been carefully controlled, values as far away as 80 Ω or 120 Ω might be obtained; if these values represent the extremes, the resistors would be said to have a 20% tolerance. If greater care is exercised in manufacture, a tighter tolerance, say 1% could be obtained. It should be obvious to the reader that components with tighter tolerances are more expensive.

levels and in most cases a low voltage represents 0 and a high voltage level represents 1. The system will usually recognize any voltage below a certain level as a 0 and any voltage above a certain level as a 1. Thus there is plenty of leeway in what constitutes a 0 and what constitutes a 1. This is why components in a digital computer need not have tight tolerances. The fact that accuracy can be made as high as we like in a digital computer can be seen by considering a computation which involves a sequence of arithmetic operations. If a 4-digit representation is employed for all numbers, a 4-digit solution will be obtained, and this may not be considered sufficiently accurate. Greater accuracy could be achieved by using an 8-digit representation for each number and repeating the computation. There is no limit, in principle, to the number of digits that can be used in digital computations and hence the accuracy of a computation can be made as high as we like.

Because accuracy can be made as high as we like without going to great expense, digital computers possess an enormous advantage over analog computers for most applications. This advantage provided a major impetus for the development of digital technology and in the last 20 years or so this technology has advanced by leaps and bounds. Techniques for designing logic circuits, which are the elementary building blocks of digital systems, were devised before the advent of integrated circuits (IC's), but as IC technology developed, so did the techniques for design. Some of these techniques are the subject of the following chapters.

We have introduced the concepts of digital and analog systems in terms of computer systems, but both, of course, have wide applications elsewhere. The important point to note is that with the rapid developments that have taken place in IC technology (and these have been almost entirely in the digital area), many of the electrical systems that traditionally depended on analog techniques are now converting to digital. The most spectacular example of this is in telecommunications: most of the world's communication networks are currently being converted from analog to digital. A major reason is that the effects of noise and interference are much easier to combat when signals are digital rather than analog. This is largely because a substantial disturbance is required to convert a 0 to a 1 and vice-versa, whereas even a small disturbance imposes distortion on an analog signal. There are many other good reasons for converting the telecommunications system from analog to digital, but the main point we wish to make here is that in all areas where digital systems are employed, i.e., in telecommunications, computers or anywhere else, the basic design techniques on which those systems are based are essentially the same, and those design techniques are the subject of this book.

It was mentioned above that the digital computer works with a number system that uses only two digits, 0 and 1. Before we proceed with our description of the theory and techniques underlying the design of digital systems, it is important that we devote some attention to number systems and related matters.

1.2. NUMBER SYSTEMS

In our everyday lives, the number system we use is the *decimal* system, so-called because it has ten distinct digits 0, 1, 2, . . . , 9. This system represents numbers greater than 9 in the familiar fashion. For instance, 7463 represents the number equal to 7 thousands, 4 hundreds, 6 tens, and 3; i.e.,

$$7463 = 7 \times 10^3 + 4 \times 10^2 + 6 \times 10^1 + 3 \times 10^0 \qquad (1.1)$$

The representation extends to fractional numbers:

$$21.73 = 2 \times 10^1 + 1 \times 10^0 + 7 \times 10^{-1} + 3 \times 10^{-2} \qquad (1.2)$$

A more general example will help with the following discussion. Consider the decimal number $a_3 a_2 a_1 a_0 . a_{-1} a_{-2}$ in which the a_i represent digits from the set $(0, 1, 2, . . . , 9)$. As above, this number can be written

$$a_3 \times 10^3 + a_2 \times 10^2 + a_1 \times 10^1 + a_0 \times 10^0$$
$$+ a_{-1} \times 10^{-1} + a_{-2} \times 10^{-2} \qquad (1.3)$$

In the decimal system, the number 10 is called the *base* or *radix*. The base-10 number system has evolved simply because we happen to have 10 fingers and they provide useful aids to counting. In computer systems, the number 10 is less convenient as a base and the number 2 is generally employed (although other bases, particularly 8 and 16 are sometimes used). Before we go on to consider different number systems, we must introduce a notation that will allow us to distinguish between numbers with different bases. The notation normally used encloses a number in parentheses and appends a subscript equal to the base. Thus, the base-10 number in Equation (1.2) is written $(21.73)_{10}$.

Recall again that the base-10 number system has 10 digits 0, 1, 2, . . . , 9. A number system with some other base, say base r, will have r digits 0, 1, 2, . . . , $r - 1$. An arbitrary number in the base r system, say $b_2 b_1 b_0 . b_{-1} b_{-2}$, has the meaning indicated by the following expression:

$$(b_2 b_1 b_0 . b_{-1} b_{-2})_r = b_2 \times r^2 + b_1 \times r^1$$
$$+ b_0 \times r^0 + b_{-1} \times r^{-1} + b_{-2} \times r^{-2} \qquad (1.4)$$

where the b_i represent digits from the set $(0, 1, 2, . . . , r - 1)$. If the addition on the right-hand side of Equation (1.4) is carried out using normal decimal arithmetic then the result obtained is the decimal equivalent of the base r number. Thus for example:

$$(10101.1101)_2 = 1 \times 2^4 + 0 \times 2^3 + 1 \times 2^2 + 0 \times 2^1 + 1 \times 2^0$$

$$+ 1 \times 2^{-1} + 1 \times 2^{-2} + 0 \times 2^{-3} + 1 \times 2^{-4}$$

$$= (16 + 0 + 4 + 0 + 1 + 0.5 + 0.25 + 0 + 0.0625)_{10}$$

$$= (21.8125)_{10} \tag{1.5}$$

and

$$(372.24)_8 = 3 \times 8^2 + 7 \times 8^1 + 2 \times 8^0 + 2 \times 8^{-1} + 4 \times 8^{-2}$$

$$= (192 + 56 + 2 + 0.25 + 0.0625)_{10}$$

$$= (250.3125)_{10} \tag{1.6}$$

If we wish to use a system with base greater than 10 we need more than 10 symbols to represent all the digits. In such a case, letters are usually used to represent digits greater than 9. Thus A is used to represent 10, B is used to represent 11, and so on. As an example, the hexadecimal (base-16) number F43C has the meaning below.

$$(F43C)_{16} = 15 \times 16^3 + 4 \times 16^2 + 3 \times 16^1 \times 12 \times 16^0$$

$$= (61440 + 1024 + 48 + 12)_{10}$$

$$= (62524)_{10} \tag{1.7}$$

In this book we shall be concerned primarily with the base 2 or *binary* number system. The binary system is almost universally used in computer systems and in digital systems generally. The reason for this is that the base-2 system involves only two digits and these can be very easily represented by electronic devices. As stated above, this representation usually takes the form of two voltages, one high and one low. The high voltage represents one digit and the low voltage represents the other digit. In such a system it is very easy for digits to be transferred from device to device because electronic devices can be made to distinguish very readily between high voltages and low voltages. If, however, we wanted to work in a number system with a base greater than 2, devices would have to be constructed that could distinguish between more than two voltage levels and this would make system construction more difficult.

Equations (1.5) through (1.7) indicate that conversion of a number from any base r to base 10 is very easy. Conversion the other way, i.e., from base 10 to base r, is slightly more involved, but the principle on which it is based is quite simple. In general, the base-10 number requiring conversion will have an integer part and a fractional part. See, for instance, the base-10 number on the right-hand side of Equation (1.6) in which the integer part is 250 and the fractional part is .3125. It turns out that the conversion from base 10 to base r is most easily carried out if we treat the integer part and the fractional part separately. Thus, suppose we are given a base-10 number whose integer part is N and whose fractional part is F. We will consider the integer part first.

We can write

$$(N)_{10} = \left(a_m a_{m-1} \cdots a_2 a_1 a_0\right)_r \qquad (1.8)$$

where the a_i's are the digits of the base r representation for $(N)_{10}$. These are the unknowns in the conversion problem; i.e., we wish to find the a_i. Now note that we can write

$$\left(a_m a_{m-1} \cdots a_2 a_1 a_0\right)_r$$
$$= a_m r^m + a_{m-1} r^{m-1} + \cdots + a_2 r^2 + a_1 r^1 + a_0 \qquad (1.9)$$

Equations (1.8) and (1.9) give

$$(N)_{10} = a_m r^m + a_{m-1} r^{m-1} + \cdots + a_2 r^2 + a_1 r^1 + a_0 \qquad (1.10)$$

If we now divide both sides of Equation (1.10) by r, we obtain

$$\frac{(N)_{10}}{r} = a_m r^{m-1} + a_{m-1} r^{m-2} + \cdots + a_2 r^1 + a_1 + \frac{a_0}{r} \qquad (1.11)$$

That is, we obtain an integer part and a fractional part. The fractional part is equal to the unknown digit a_0 divided by the radix r. Thus, by this means, we can identify one of the unknowns, viz., a_0.

If we denote the integer part of (1.11) by N_1, we have

$$N_1 = a_m r^{m-1} + a_{m-1} r^{m-2} + \cdots + a_2 r^1 + a_1 \qquad (1.12)$$

and, dividing again by r, we obtain

$$\frac{N_1}{r} = a_m r^{m-2} + a_{m-1} r^{m-3} + \cdots + a_2 + \frac{a_1}{r} \qquad (1.13)$$

Again we obtain an integer part and a fractional part. This time the fractional part is equal to the unknown digit a_1 divided by the radix r. Hence, we can now identify the unknown a_1.

Proceeding in this way, the full set of digits in the base-r representation of $(N)_{10}$ can be obtained. As an example, we will convert $(21)_{10}$ to binary; the reverse of this conversion process has already been carried out and appears as the integer part of Equation (1.5). Thus, we will be able to check our result.

The conversion of $(21)_{10}$ to binary is as follows:

	Integer		Fraction	Binary Coefficient
$\dfrac{21}{2} =$	10	+	$\dfrac{1}{2}$	$a_0 = 1$
$\dfrac{10}{2} =$	5	+	0	$a_1 = 0$
$\dfrac{5}{2} =$	2	+	$\dfrac{1}{2}$	$a_2 = 1$
$\dfrac{2}{2} =$	1	+	0	$a_3 = 0$
$\dfrac{1}{2} =$	0	+	$\dfrac{1}{2}$	$a_4 = 1$

Thus, $(21)_{10} = (a_4 a_3 a_2 a_1 a_0)_2 = (10101)_2$.

Clearly, then, conversion of the integer part of a base-10 number to some other base is quite straightforward. Conversion of the fractional part is equally straightforward, as the following discussion shows.

If the fractional part of a decimal number is F, we can write

$$(F)_{10} = (.a_{-1}a_{-2}a_{-3} \cdots a_{-n})_r \qquad (1.14)$$

where the a_{-i} are the digits of the base r representation for $(F)_{10}$.

We can write

$$(a_{-1}a_{-2}a_{-3} \cdots a_{-n})_r$$
$$= a_{-1}r^{-1} + a_{-2}r^{-2} + a_{-3}r^{-3} + \cdots + a_{-n}r^{-n} \qquad (1.15)$$

Equations (1.14) and (1.15) give

$$(F)_{10} = a_{-1}r^{-1} + a_{-2}r^{-2} + a_{-3}r^{-3} + \cdots + a_{-n}r^{-n} \qquad (1.16)$$

If we now multiply both sides of Equation (1.16) by r we obtain

$$r(F)_{10} = a_{-1} + a_{-2}r^{-1} + a_{-3}r^{-2} + \cdots + a_{-n}r^{-n+1} \qquad (1.17)$$

In Equation (1.17), there is an integer part equal to the unknown digit a_{-1}, and a fractional part which will be denoted by F_1. Then

$$F_1 = a_{-2}r^{-1} + a_{-3}r^{-2} + \cdots + a_{-n}r^{-n+1} \qquad (1.18)$$

and multiplication by r gives

$$rF_1 = a_{-2} + a_{-3}r^{-1} + \cdots + a_{-n}r^{-n+2} \qquad (1.19)$$

The unknown digit a_{-2} is now available as the integer part of Equation (1.19). The process continues until either the process terminates or sufficient digits for the required accuracy have been obtained.

As an example, we will convert $(.8125)_{10}$ to binary; this is the reverse of the conversion carried out on the fractional part in Equation (1.5). We proceed as follows:

	Integer		Fraction	Binary Coefficient
$2(.8125) =$	1	+	.625	$a_{-1} = 1$
$2(.625) =$	1	+	.25	$a_{-2} = 1$
$2(.25) =$	0	+	.5	$a_{-3} = 0$
$2(.5) =$	1	+	0	$a_{-4} = 1$

Thus $(.8125)_{10} = (.a_{-1}a_{-2}a_{-3}a_{-4})_2 = (.1101)_2$, which agrees with the fractional part of Equation (1.5).

As a formal example, we will carry out the reverse of the conversion process in Equation (1.6).

Example 1.1. Convert $(250.3125)_{10}$ to octal (i.e., base 8).

Solution. Commence with the integer part of the decimal number:

	Integer		Fraction	Octal Coefficient
$\dfrac{250}{8} =$	31	+	$\dfrac{2}{8}$	$a_0 = 2$
$\dfrac{31}{8} =$	3	+	$\dfrac{7}{8}$	$a_1 = 7$
$\dfrac{3}{8} =$	0	+	$\dfrac{3}{8}$	$a_2 = 3$

Thus, $(250)_{10} = (372)_8$.

For the fractional part we have

	Integer	Fraction	Octal Coefficient
$8(.3125)$	2	+ .5	$a_{-1} = 2$
$8(.5)$	4	+ .0	$a_{-2} = 4$

so that $(.3125)_{10} = (.24)_8$ and putting the integer and fractional parts together, we have

$$(250.3125)_{10} = (372.24)_8 \qquad (1.20)$$

which agrees with Equation (1.6). □

1.3. BINARY ARITHMETIC

Logic circuits that carry out arithmetic are fairly easily constructed and are widely used in computer systems. For reasons given in the previous section, these circuits perform the basic operations of arithmetic in binary.

Binary addition is carried out in much the same way as decimal addition, the only difference being that there are two symbols (0 and 1) in binary and ten symbols in decimal. As a consequence, the rules of addition in binary are

$$0 + 0 = 0, \quad 0 + 1 = 1, \quad 1 + 1 = 10$$

The third of the above is simply stating in base 2 the fact that in base 10 we have $1 + 1 = 2$.

Using these rules we can readily add any pair of binary numbers.

Example 1.2. Add $(21)_{10}$ and $(19)_{10}$ in binary.

Solution

Decimal		Binary	
1	← carry	1 111	← carries
21		10101	
19 +		10011 +	
40		101000	

□

Note the carries in the addition process for both systems.

The example shows how binary addition is a very similar procedure to decimal addition. Binary subtraction can also be carried out in the well-known elementary-school fashion. As an illustration, consider the subtraction of 43 from 61 in both decimal and binary:

	Decimal			Binary	
1		← borrow	1		← borrow
	61			111101	
	43 −			101011 −	
	18			010010	

In the decimal subtraction, following the elementary-school procedure, we start with the right-hand column and attempt to subtract 3 from 1. The only way that this can be achieved is by "borrowing" a 1 from the left-hand column and subtracting 3 from 11. In the binary case, the same principle is applied, with the borrowed digit being equal to $(100)_2$.

Multiplication and division can also be carried out in the familiar way. As an illustration we show below the binary multiplication of $(12)_{10}$ by $(11)_{10}$ and the division of $(132)_{10}$ by $(12)_{10}$.

```
                                      1011
                   1100        1100 | 10000100
                   1011               1100
                _____              ____
                   1100              10010
                  1100                1100
                 0000                 ____
                1100                  1100
              _____                1100
              10000100                ____
                                      0000
```

We will return to binary multiplication in Section 7.2 where a circuit will be designed for carrying out the multiplication operation.

1.3.1. Two's Complement

The above discussion has illustrated how the familiar techniques of decimal arithmetic can be employed in carrying out arithmetic in binary. The techniques employed in computer circuits for carrying out binary arithmetic differ some-what from those described above, chiefly because the subtraction operation can be very easily converted into an addition operation, thereby allowing the same circuitry to be employed for each of these fundamental operations.

The basic idea involved in converting a subtraction operation into an addition operation can be seen by considering an arbitrary subtraction in decimal, say $61 - 43 = 18$. Another way that we can arrive at this answer is to carry out the *addition* $61 + 57 = 118$. The fact that we can obtain the required result from this addition operation can be seen by noting that $61 + 57 = 61 + (100$

$- 43$) which indicates that $61 + 57$ should give us the result of $61 - 43$, but with one hundred added. Hence, to get the result, we must discard the one hundred in 118 to obtain the required answer, 18.

The number 57 is known as the *10's complement* of 43. The 10's complement of an n-digit decimal number N is defined as $10^n - N$. In general, a decimal subtraction operation $A - B$ can be replaced by an addition $A + B'$, where B' is the 10's complement of B; the required result is obtained by discarding the most significant digit (which is always a 1). As a second example, evaluate the difference $792.63 - 324.17$. The 10's complement of 324.17 is 675.83 so we can obtain the difference by evaluating the sum $792.63 + 675.83 = 1468.46$. We then discard the most significant digit to obtain the required result: 468.46.

This method is not of much value in decimal computations because a subtraction has to be carried out in order to calculate the 10's complement (thus defeating the object of the exercise, which is to replace subtraction by addition). However, for binary arithmetic, the technique can be very profitably employed. In binary, the method requires use of the 2's complement in place of the 10's complement. For an n-digit binary number N, the 2's complement is defined as $2^n - N$. The method works well in binary because the 2's complement of a binary number can be obtained very simply, without the need to compute the subtraction implicit in the definition. We shall come to this aspect a little later. First let us repeat one of the examples given above, this time in binary. The subtraction $(61 - 43)_{10}$ becomes $111101 - 101011 = 010010$. Following the definition, the 2's complement of 101011 is $1000000 - 101011 = 010101$. Then, adding the 2's complement of 101011 to 111101 gives 1010010 and, discarding the most significant digit, we obtain the required result, 010010, which is the 6-digit binary representation of $(18)_{10}$.

As mentioned above, the 2's complement of a binary number can be obtained without the need to carry out any subtraction. The procedure is carried out on a digit-by-digit basis. We start with the right-hand (least significant) digit and then scan to the left, looking for the first non-zero digit. All digits scanned, up to and including the first non-zero digit, are left unchanged. All remaining digits have their values changed; that is, in the remaining digits, all zeros are changed to ones and all ones are changed to zeros. To illustrate this, let us form again the 2's complement of 101011. We start with the least-significant digit, which is a one. The digit is left unchanged, and all other digits are changed. Thus, the 2's complement is 010101, as before. As a second example, the 2's complement of 101000 is 011000.

In actual computations carried out using logic circuits, some means of representing the sign of a number is required. If n digits are used to represent numbers in a given system, only $n - 1$ of the digits are used to represent the magnitude of the number, and the remaining digit is used to indicate the sign. The usual convention is to use a 0 to indicate a positive number and a 1 to indicate a negative number. The sign digit is located in the left-hand (most significant) digit position.

To illustrate, we consider again the subtraction $(61 - 43)_{10}$. If this subtraction operation were to be carried out by logic circuitry, an addition circuit (an adder) would be used and the two numbers would be presented to the inputs of the adder, one as a positive number and the other as a negative number in 2's complement form. If we were using an 8-digit adder, the positive number $(61)_{10}$ would be represented by 00111101, where the left-hand digit indicates that the number is positive and the remaining digits are the 7-bit† representation of $(61)_{10}$. The negative number, $(-43)_{10}$ would be represented by 11010101; the first bit indicates the sign, and the remaining seven digits are the 2's complement of 0101011. Adding the two numbers gives

$$
\begin{array}{r}
00111101 \\
\underline{11010101} \\
00010010
\end{array}
$$

and the sign bit is 0 indicating that the result is a positive number (namely $(18)_{10}$ in binary).

To see how the method works when a negative result is obtained, let us consider evaluation of the subtraction $(43 - 61)_{10}$ in binary. The 2's complement of $(-61)_{10}$ in binary (with sign attached) is 11000011 so that the subtraction can be evaluated as

$$
\begin{array}{r}
00101011 \\
\underline{11000011} \\
11101110
\end{array}
$$

Here the sign bit is negative and the remaining digits constitute the 2's complement of 0010010 (i.e., $(-18)_{10}$ in binary). Note that the negative number obtained from this calculation is in a form suitable for future, similar, calculations. As a consequence, if this calculation were part of a sequence of calculations being carried out by a computer, the computer would store this number in the 2's complement form obtained above. Negative numbers are generally stored in 2's complement form in digital systems, and positive numbers are stored in the "normal" form. This form of representation allows all four basic arithmetic operations (add, subtract, multiply and divide) to be carried out by means of an adder. We have seen how it allows subtraction to be carried out this way, and the examples given earlier indicate how binary multiplication can be evaluated as a series of additions, and binary division as a series of subtractions. Thus, signed addition is the basic arithmetical operation in most digital systems.

---

† The word "bit" is a widely-used abbreviation of "binary digit."

1.4. BINARY CODES

We have seen how digital systems carry out their internal processes using binary numbers. If a digital system provides a visual output (a digital voltmeter is a typical example), the user of the system would far prefer to have the output displayed in decimal rather than in binary. Similarly, when the user has to supply numerical inputs to the system (as in the case of a pocket calculator), the decimal system is preferable to binary. Thus, although digital systems operate in binary, they very frequently have to be able to communicate with the external world in decimal. This implies that some means of converting from decimal to binary and back again is often required. The range of decimal numbers requiring conversion to binary is normally very large and for this reason it has been found preferable to implement the conversion from decimal separately for each digit in a given decimal number, rather than converting the decimal number as a whole. The advantage of this is that conversion circuitry is only required for ten different conversions, i.e., to convert each of the decimal digits 0 through 9.

The most straightforward way of carrying out the conversion is to convert each decimal digit to its binary equivalent. Note that the binary representations of the decimal digits 8 and 9 are 1000 and 1001 respectively. That is, each requires four bits for its representation. The other decimal digits have binary representations involving fewer bits. However, the problem of designing circuitry for conversion between the two number systems is vastly simplified if each decimal digit is represented by the same number of bits. Thus, rather than represent the decimal digits 0, 1, 2, 3, etc. by 0, 1, 10, 11, etc., all are given a four-bit representation. This representation is called *binary-coded-decimal* or the "BCD code" and is listed in Table 1.1.

The BCD code is also sometimes referred to as the 8421 code because of the manner in which the conversion from BCD to decimal is carried out. When this conversion is made, the most significant bit is multiplied by 2^3 ($=8$), the next bit by 2^2 ($=4$), and so on. That is, if $a_3 a_2 a_1 a_0$ is an arbitrary BCD codeword, the decimal digit N that it represents is given by

$$N = w_3 a_3 + w_2 a_2 + w_1 a_1 + w_0 a_0$$

where $w_3 = 8$, $w_2 = 4$, $w_1 = 2$ and $w_0 = 1$. The w_i's are known as the *weights* of the code. Codes other than the 8421 code are sometimes used because in certain types of computation they offer particular advantages. Examples are the 7421 code and the 6311 code shown in Table 1.2. The weights can even be negative (see the $74-2-1$ code in Table 1.2).

Note that there are only 16 possible 4-bit codewords, and each of the weighted codes is made up of an ordered set of 10 codewords out of the 16. The ordering can be quite important in some applications. One type of ordering, known as *Gray* code, is organized in such a way that in the list of codewords adjacent

Table 1.1. Binary-coded-decimal.

Decimal digit	BCD codeword
0	0000
1	0001
2	0010
3	0011
4	0100
5	0101
6	0110
7	0111
8	1000
9	1001

codewords differ in only one bit position. A Gray code for the decimal digits is shown in Table 1.3. Gray codes are chiefly used in situations where analog signals are to be converted into digital form. The main reason is that if any type of code is employed, undesirable behavior can occur. For instance, let us suppose that an analog system is being controlled digitally. Assume that the digital controller is to monitor a particular analog signal which will rise continuously

Table 1.2. Weighted codes.

Decimal digit	7421 codeword	6311 codeword	74-2-1 codeword
0	0000	0000	0000
1	0001	0001	0111
2	0010	0011	0110
3	0011	0100	0101
4	0100	0101	0100
5	0101	0111	1010
6	0110	1000	1001
7	1000	1001	1000
8	1001	1011	1111
9	1010	1100	1110

Table 1.3. Gray code.

Decimal digit	Gray codeword	BCD codeword
0	0000	0000
1	0001	0001
2	0011	0010
3	0010	0011
4	0110	0100
5	0111	0101
6	0101	0110
7	1101	0111
8	1100	1000
9	1000	1001

in value from zero. For simplicity, assume that the range of possible values of the signal has been split into ten levels, and that the controller input is a 4-bit codeword which indicates signal level. Thus, if the signal level is 5, the controller input will be 0101 if BCD coding is employed. Now suppose that the main purpose of the controller is to monitor the analog signal up to the point it reaches level 7 and, when this level is reached, the controller is to initiate some action (say to open a valve). Notice that a problem could occur if BCD coding is employed. As the signal level goes from 3 to 4, the codeword fed to the controller would have to change from 0011 to 0100. Each bit in the codeword is provided by some electronic device and it is in the nature of digital circuits that the devices will not all change their bit values at precisely the same time. Consequently, it is possible that the second bit from the left in the codeword will change first, leading to the controller momentarily having the input 0111 (i.e., decimal 7). This could lead to the valve being opened prematurely. With Gray code, no such problems could arise. Note that Gray codes are *not* weighted codes and no simple formula exists for calculating the decimal value of a Gray-coded number.

This discussion of binary codes was introduced through consideration of the need for digital systems to be able to communicate with the external world in decimal rather than binary. The codes we have so far looked at are suitable for communicating *numerical* information. In many applications of digital systems, data to be processed may contain not only numbers, but also alphabetic and other symbols. An example is a computer system with a VDU, keyboard and printer. In order for communication to take place between the user and computer system, *all* necessary symbols must be represented by a binary code. Codes which represent numerical, alphabetic and other symbols are called *alphanumeric* codes. One commonly used alphanumeric code is the ASCII code (ASCII stands for American Standard Code for Information Interchange and is pronounced "ass-key"). Because of the need to represent both upper- and lower-case alphabetic symbols, along with the decimal numbers and a range of punctuation and control symbols, the total number of characters is greater than 64 (but less than 128) so that the ASCII and similar codes require seven bits to represent each character. The number of bits normally employed in implementing these codes is actually eight in practice because an extra digit is almost always employed in order to assist with error detection.

1.4.1. Use of Parity Bit for Error Detection

Binary data can be transferred from one digital system to another by means of a communications medium such as cable or radio waves. Whatever medium is used, it will occasionally be subjected to disturbances called electrical noise. These disturbances are often sufficient to change a transmitted 0 into a 1 and vice-versa. For obvious reasons, it is important that transmission errors of this sort be detected. One very simple and widely used method of detecting bit errors involves the use of *parity* bits. By adding an extra bit (the parity bit) to each codeword, the presence of a single bit error in any codeword can be detected. The procedure is very simple and can be carried out either as an *even-parity* scheme or an *odd-parity* scheme.

In the even-parity scheme, the value of the parity bit to be added to each codeword is chosen in such a way that the number of 1's in the codeword is an *even* number. Then, if electrical noise causes a single bit error to occur in the transmission of a codeword, that codeword would be received with an odd number of 1's and the presence of an error would be evident. To illustrate this, part of the ASCII code has been listed in Table 1.4 with a parity bit (even parity) added in the most-significant-bit position of each codeword. Suppose some information containing the word "BEGIN" is being transmitted using the ASCII code in Table 1.4. The word "BEGIN" would be coded as

01000010   11000101   01000111   11001001   01001110

B   E   G   I   N

Suppose noise imposed a bit error on two of the codewords, say E and G, so that the message is received as

01000010   11100101   00000111   11001001   01001110

The receiver would check each codeword for even parity and would find that two codewords have odd parity, indicating that each of these codewords contains an error. Depending on circumstances the receiver might ask for a retransmission.

Table 1.4.   ASCII code for upper-case literals with an even parity bit.

A	01000001	J	11001010	S	01010011
B	01000010	K	01001011	T	11010100
C	11000011	L	11001100	U	01010101
D	01000100	M	01001101	V	01010110
E	11000101	N	01001110	W	11010111
F	11000110	O	11001111	X	11011000
G	01000111	P	01010000	Y	01011001
H	01001000	Q	11010001	Z	01011010
I	11001001	R	11010010		

Obviously if two bit errors occur in a single codeword, their presence would not be detected by this scheme (although the presence of any odd number of errors would be detected). In practice the scheme is only used where bit errors occur very infrequently.

Some schemes use odd parity, where the parity bit is chosen so that each codeword contains an odd number of 1's. In the odd parity scheme the receiver detects the presence of an error when a codeword arrives with an even number of 1's.

Bit errors occur not only in transmission but also in the storage of binary data. Errors can occur when the storage medium (say a disk or integrated circuit) has slight imperfections, and parity checking provides some protection against this source of errors also.

Exercises

1.1. Convert the following decimal numbers to binary:

(a) 73
(b) 27.5
(c) 129.6875
(d) 11.7

1.2. Verify the results obtained in Exercise 1.1 by carrying out the reverse conversion, from binary to decimal.

1.3. Convert the decimal numbers in Exercise 1.1 to

(a) octal
(b) hexadecimal

1.4. Verify the results obtained in Exercise 1.3 by carrying out the reverse conversions.

1.5. Convert the following binary numbers to decimal:

  (a) 111011
  (b) 100101101
  (c) 11011.0111
  (d) 101.00011

1.6. Verify the results obtained in Exercise 1.5 by carrying out the reverse conversion.

1.7. Convert the binary numbers in Exercise 1.5 to

  (a) octal
  (b) hexadecimal.

1.8. Verify the results obtained in Exercise 1.7 by carrying out the reverse conversions.

1.9. Perform the following binary subtractions using (i) the ''ordinary'' subtraction technique; (ii) the two's complement method.

  (a) 11011 − 10101
  (b) 11100 − 1001
  (c) 1001 − 11011
  (d) 1000 − 1101

1.10. Perform the following binary division operations and in each case verify your answer by carrying out the reverse operation (i.e., multiplication followed by addition of the remainder term):

  (a) 111100011 ÷ 1011
  (b) 10001110 ÷ 1100
  (c) 100000111 ÷ 1001

1.11. Convert the following decimal numbers to BCD:

  (a) 327
  (b) 9415

1.12. Construct a 6321 code for the decimal digits.

1.13. Explain why it is not possible to construct a 7411 code.

1.14. Use Table 1.4 to decode the following message, which has been constructed from 7-bit ASCII codewords (i.e., ASCII codewords without a parity bit). Note that the ASCII codeword for a space is 0100000.

              1001000100000110101101000101010000001000001
              0100000100111010010011000011100010101000000
              1000100100000011011001

2

COMBINATIONAL CIRCUITS

2.1. INTRODUCTION

The fundamental building blocks of digital computers and other digital systems are *binary* digital circuits. In these circuits only two voltage levels are recognized; a voltage measured at any terminal within the circuit is interpreted as being either "high" or "low". The analysis and design of these circuits is carried out using a mathematical technique that has been specially developed for the manipulation of variables which can take on only two values. The technique, which is known as Boolean algebra, was first developed by George Boole in the middle of the nineteenth century as a means of manipulating logical propositions. In 1938, Claude E. Shannon [1] observed how Boole's work could be applied to the analysis of switching systems employed in telephone networks. Since the publication of Shannon's paper, Boolean algebra has become the cornerstone of digital systems design.

Much of the terminology which Boole employed in his manipulation of logical propositions is now freely used in relation to digital circuits. Thus, digital circuits themselves are widely referred to as logic circuits and the names of the basic logical operators employed by Boole are now used to describe some of the basic building blocks of digital circuits.

Boole's logical propositions could take on two values: TRUE or FALSE. These logical propositions are represented by symbols; for instance, the proposition "this switch is closed" might be the represented by the symbol A. A is then a Boolean variable capable of taking on either of the *truth values* TRUE or FALSE. A will have the value TRUE if the switch referred to in the proposition is indeed closed and will have the value FALSE if the switch is open.

For convenience in the use of his algebra, Boole represented the truth values in his equations by numerical quantities; thus the value TRUE was represented by 1 and the value FALSE was represented by 0. This convention is still in general use today and will be used throughout this book.

2.1.1. The Basic Operations

We have seen that logical propositions constitute the variables in Boole's algebra. Another essential requirement for an algebra is a set of operations that can be carried out on the variables. In Boolean algebra there are three basic operations: NOT, AND and OR; these operations are commonly called *connectives*.

The NOT Connective.   The NOT connective is a negation operation. As an example of its use, consider again the Boolean variable A representing ''this switch is closed''. If we apply the NOT connective to this variable we obtain the variable NOT A which represents the proposition ''this switch is not closed''. From this we see that if A has the value TRUE then NOT A has the value FALSE and if A has the value FALSE then NOT A has the value TRUE.

It is general practice to employ an abbreviated notation for the application of the NOT connective. Thus, in this text, instead of NOT A we shall write $\overline{A}$; some other texts use other representations of NOT A.

Recall that in binary digital circuits only two voltage levels are recognized, namely ''high'' and ''low''. Let us associate the high-voltage level with logic value 1 (TRUE) and the low-voltage level with logic value 0 (FALSE)†. Then, a circuit device which carries out the NOT operation is one that converts a high-voltage level into a low-voltage level and vice-versa. Such a circuit is very easily constructed and is referred to as an *inverter*. The circuit symbol for an inverter is shown in Figure 2.1(a).

A common method of illustrating the logical behavior of a digital circuit employs a table showing the value of the output for each possible value of the input. A table of this sort is known as a *truth table* and the values of the inputs and outputs are usually entered in such a table in the form of 1's and 0's. The truth table for an inverter is shown in Figure 2.1(b). This table shows that if the input, A, to an inverter has the value 0, then the output, $\overline{A}$, has the value 1; and if the input has the value 1 then the output has the value 0. The Boolean symbol 0 is often referred to as the *complement* of the symbol 1 (similarly 1 is referred to as the complement of 0); consequently the NOT operation is often called the *complementation operation*.

The AND Connective.   If A and B are two logical propositions, then the proposition $Z = A$ AND B is TRUE if and only if both propositions A and B are TRUE. Application of the AND connective is usually represented in shorthand form. Students of logic usually write the proposition $Z = A$ AND B in the

---

†This is known as the positive logic convention. We could, if we wished, adopt the other alternative and associate the low voltage with logic 1 and the high voltage with logic 0. This is the negative logic convention, which is less commonly used than the positive convention. Throughout this book, the positive convention will be employed.

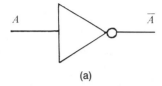

(a)

Figure 2.1. Inverter: (a) symbol; (b) truth table.

A	$\overline{A}$
0	1
1	0

(b)

form $Z = A \wedge B$; designers of computer hardware usually use a representation which is identical to that generally employed for algebraic multiplication, i.e., they write the proposition $Z = A$ AND B in the form $Z = A.B$ or $Z = AB$. In this text, we shall make use of both forms.

A circuit that carries out the AND operation is called an *AND gate* and the symbol for an AND gate is shown in Figure 2.2(a). Recalling our convention of assigning the numerical value 1 to the logical value TRUE and 0 to the logical value FALSE, we see that the Boolean function $Z = AB$ can have the value 1 if and only if both the variables A and B have the value 1. This is indicated in the truth table for the AND gate shown in Figure 2.2(b).

The reader should note that the AND connective can be applied to more than two variables simultaneously. For instance, the function $Z = A$ AND B AND C AND D is TRUE if and only if the variables A, B, C, D are all TRUE; otherwise, it is FALSE.

The OR Connective. If A and B are two logical propositions, then the proposition $Z = A$ OR B is TRUE if A or B or both are TRUE; Z is FALSE only if A and B are both FALSE. Students of logic usually write the proposition $Z =$

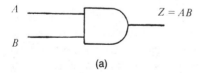

(a)

A	B	Z = AB
0	0	0
0	1	0
1	0	0
1	1	1

(b)

Figure 2.2. AND gate: (a) symbol; (b) truth table.

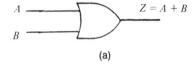

(a)

A	B	Z = A+B
0	0	0
0	1	1
1	0	1
1	1	1

(b)

Figure 2.3. OR gate: (a) symbol; (b) truth table.

A OR B in the form $Z = A \vee B$ but hardware designers more commonly use a representation that is identical to that employed for algebraic addition, i.e., $Z = A + B$. This is the notation we shall use in this book.

A circuit that carries out the OR operation is called an *OR gate* and the symbol for an OR gate is shown in Figure 2.3(a). The truth table in Figure 2.3(b) indicates that the Boolean function $Z = A + B$ takes on the value 1 if A or B or both have the value 1 and takes on the value 0 only if both A and B have the value 0.

The OR connective can be applied to more than two variables simultaneously. As an example, the function $Z = A$ OR B OR C OR D is FALSE only if all the variables A, B, C, D are FALSE; otherwise it is TRUE.

A Note on the Application of the Connectives.   In the above, we showed how the NOT connective can be applied to single Boolean variables and how the AND and OR connectives can be applied to two or more variables. The connectives can be applied to functions of Boolean variables in a similar fashion. For instance, given the proposition $Z = A + B + C$, we can negate the proposition and write NOT $Z =$ NOT $(A + B + C)$ or, simply, $\overline{Z} = \overline{A + B + C}$.

We often use brackets (as in algebraic multiplication) to denote application of the AND connective to functions of Boolean variables. Thus, given the propositions $Z = A + B$ and $Y = C + D$, the proposition Z AND Y can be written $ZY = (A + B)(C + D)$. As we shall see below, this expression can be expanded in the manner of multiplication to read $ZY = AC + AD + BC + BD$.

2.1.2 The Fundamental Rules

We have pointed out that in this text the algebraic symbols for addition and multiplication will be employed in writing Boolean expressions to represent OR and AND respectively. This is perfectly normal practice, but it can lead to confusion among those unfamiliar with the implementation of Boolean algebra.

The main reason for the confusion stems from the use of the numerical values "1" and "0" as representations of TRUE and FALSE respectively.

As an example, consider the proposition $Z = A$ OR B which we will normally write as $Z = A + B$. We know that Z is TRUE if either A or B or both are TRUE. Thus, if both A and B are TRUE, Z is also TRUE; assignment of the numerical value "1" (for "TRUE") to each term in the expression $Z = A + B$ gives $1 = 1 + 1$. This equation highlights the source of confusion; it is very important that the beginner bear in mind that the numerical values "1" and "0" actually represent *truth values* and that the algebraic symbols for multiplication and addition represent *logical* connectives.

With this cautionary note having been sounded, we can now state the basic rules of Boolean algebra which will be frequently drawn upon in the remainder of the text. We begin with the basic rules for the connectives:

(i) NOT: $\bar{0} = 1$; $\quad\quad \bar{1} = 0$

(ii) AND: $0.0 = 0$; $\quad 0.1 = 0$
$\quad\quad\quad\quad 1.0 = 0$; $\quad 1.1 = 1$

(iii) OR: $\quad 0 + 0 = 0$; $\quad 1 + 0 = 1$
$\quad\quad\quad\quad 0 + 1 = 1$; $\quad 1 + 1 = 1$

We now state a further set of rules which involve Boolean variables; these variables (A, B, C below) can take only the two values 0, 1. That these rules must hold true is quite easy to prove and some examples of proof are given below.

1. Properties of 0 and 1 $\quad 0 + A = A; 0.A = 0$
$\quad\quad\quad\quad\quad\quad\quad\quad\quad\quad 1 + A = 1; 1.A = A$

2. Complementation laws $\quad A + \bar{A} = 1; A.\bar{A} = 0$

3. Involution $\quad\quad\quad\quad (\overline{\bar{A}}) = A$

4. Commutative laws $\quad\quad A + B = B + A; AB = BA$

5. Associative laws $\quad\quad A + (B + C) = (A + B) + C$
$\quad\quad\quad\quad\quad\quad\quad\quad\quad A(BC) = (AB)C$

6. Distributive laws $\quad\quad A(B + C) = AB + AC$
$\quad\quad\quad\quad\quad\quad\quad\quad\quad A + BC = (A + B)(A + C)$

7. Idempotence laws $\quad\quad A + A = A; A.A = A$

8. Absorption laws $\quad\quad A + AB = A; A(A + B) = A$
$\quad\quad\quad\quad\quad\quad\quad\quad\quad A + \bar{A}B = A + B; A(\bar{A} + B) = AB$

9. De Morgan's laws $\quad\quad \overline{(A + B)} = \bar{A}.\bar{B}$
$\quad\quad\quad\quad\quad\quad\quad\quad\quad \overline{AB} = \bar{A} + \bar{B}$

A	A.A
0	0
1	1

Figure 2.4. Truth table for idempotence law.

The reader will note that several of these rules are quite different to those which govern ordinary algebra. We emphasize again that this is because the symbols in Boolean algebra represent truth values rather than ordinary numerical quantities.

Each rule consists of two expressions which are claimed to be equivalent. One obvious approach to the proof of these rules is to draw up the truth table for each expression and show that the value of the two expressions is the same for every possible set of values of the variables involved.

Thus, for the idempotence law $A.A = A$, we construct the truth table shown in Figure 2.4. Comparison of the entries in the two columns of the table shows that for each of the possible values of A, the expression $A.A$ assumes an identical value. Hence the law is proved.

As a slightly more complex example, consider the absorption law $A + AB = A$. To prove the validity of this relationship, we construct the truth table shown in Figure 2.5. Note that in constructing a truth table for a complex expression it is a good idea to list the values of subexpressions as well. Thus, to assist in determining the truth values of $A + AB$ we have listed the values of the sub-expression AB; this allows the entries in the fourth column of the table to be written down directly, using columns one and three. Comparison of the entries in the first and last columns of Figure 2.5 indicates that the expression $A + AB$ is indeed equal to A for all possible combinations of values of the variables A and B; hence the rule is proved.

The above two examples indicate the simplicity of the truth table approach to the proof of the basic rules of Boolean algebra. In the later sections of this book, we shall often be dealing with expressions involving many Boolean variables. It is not usually feasible to attempt to prove (by hand) the equivalence of two such expressions by means of the truth-table method. The reason for this is quite simple; the truth-table approach requires listing of all possible combinations of values of the variables involved in the two expressions. If there are n variables involved, the number of combinations is 2^n. This indicates that as the number of variables increases, the truth table rapidly becomes impractical as a hand-calculation tool.

A	B	AB	A + AB
0	0	0	0
0	1	0	0
1	0	0	1
1	1	1	1

Figure 2.5. Truth table for absorption law.

One approach, which is often useful, attempts to demonstrate the equivalence of two Boolean expressions by algebraic deduction. Given two expressions, this approach attempts to prove their equivalence by using results that have been previously proved. In relation to proving the basic rules of Boolean algebra listed above, a fundamental limitation of this approach is immediately apparent. One could not hope to prove *all* the rules in this way because, at the outset, there would be no previously proven results upon which to draw. This is a problem common to all algebras and it is overcome for a given algebra by agreement on a set of fundamental rules upon which the algebra is to be based. These fundamental rules, usually referred to as postulates (or axioms), constitute a minimal set of rules from which all other rules can be deduced. The minimal nature of the set is guaranteed by ensuring that the postulates are independent, i.e., no postulate can be deduced from any other postulate. A suitable set of postulates for Boolean algebra was published by Huntington in 1904 [2].

We will not detail Huntington's postulates here, but simply point out that the basic rules of Boolean algebra listed above consist of many more relationships than do the postulates. This implies that many of the basic rules can be deduced from other basic rules. We will use this fact to illustrate the technique of algebraic deduction as it applies to Boolean algebra.

Consider, for instance, the two distributive laws in the above list. The first of these appears self-evident, but the second does not. We can prove the validity of the second distributive law by assuming the validity of the first one (i.e., by accepting it as a postulate), by accepting the commutative laws as postulates and by drawing upon the two rules proved by the truth tables above.

Thus, we have

$$(A + B)(A + C) = AA + AC + BA + BC \quad \text{(first distributive law)}$$
$$= A + AC + BA + BC \quad \text{(idempotence law } A.A = A\text{)}$$
$$= A + BA + BC \quad \text{(absorption law } A + AC = A\text{)}$$
$$= A + AB + BC \quad \text{(commutative law)}$$
$$= A + BC \quad \text{(absorption law } A + AB = A\text{)}$$

as required.

As a second example, let us deduce one of De Morgan's laws by assuming the validity of all the laws numbered 1–8. The technique employed below indicates that application of the method of algebraic deduction often requires a considerable degree of ingenuity. The proof given here relies upon the fact that a Boolean variable Z is the complement of another variable Y if and only if the two complementation laws $Z + Y = 1$ and $ZY = 0$ are satisfied.

We wish to prove the validity of the relationship

$$\overline{(A + B)} = \overline{A}.\overline{B} \qquad (2.1)$$

If this equality is true, then $(A + B)$ is the complement of $\overline{A}.\overline{B}$ and we can prove the validity of Equation (2.1) by showing that $(A + B)$ and $\overline{A}.\overline{B}$ satisfy the two complementation laws.

We have

$$
\begin{aligned}
\overline{A}\overline{B} + (A + B) &= (\overline{A}\overline{B} + A) + B && \text{(associative law)} \\
&= (\overline{B} + A) + B && \text{(absorption law)} \\
&= A + (\overline{B} + B) && \text{(commutative and associative laws)} \\
&= A + 1 && \text{(complementation law)} \\
&= 1 && \text{(property of 0 and 1)}
\end{aligned}
$$

Secondly

$$
\begin{aligned}
(\overline{A}\overline{B})(A + B) &= \overline{A}\,\overline{B}A + \overline{A}\,\overline{B}B && \text{(distributive law)} \\
&= \overline{A}A\overline{B} + \overline{A}\,\overline{B}B && \text{(commutative law)} \\
&= 0\overline{B} + \overline{A}0 && \text{(complementation law)} \\
&= 0 + 0 && \text{(property of 0 and 1)} \\
&= 0 && \text{(basic rule of OR connective)}
\end{aligned}
$$

Thus, $(A + B)$ and $\overline{A}.\overline{B}$ do indeed satisfy the two complementation laws, and hence $(A + B)$ is the complement of $\overline{A}.\overline{B}$. This is written

$$\overline{A + B} = \overline{A}.\overline{B}$$

which is the relationship we wished to prove.

The Principle of Duality. The reader will have noticed that all the rules of Boolean algebra stated above (excepting involution) are given in the form of two or four equations. These sets of equations are manifestations of an important and useful property which is known as the *principle of duality*. This principle states that, given a Boolean identity (in the form of an equation in one or more variables) a second identity can be obtained by (i) replacing each OR operation by an AND and each AND by an OR and (ii) replacing each 0 by a 1 and each 1 by a 0.

For example, in the list of rules above, we have the identity $0 + A = A$. Using the principle of duality, we obtain the second identity $1.A = A$.

Similarly, the first of the distributive laws states $A(B + C) = AB + AC$; applying the principle of duality we obtain the second of these laws: $A + BC = (A + B)(A + C)$.

The reader should check that in all the rules stated above (excepting involution) each identity is stated with its dual.

2.2. REALIZATION OF BOOLEAN FUNCTIONS

2.2.1. Minimization and AND/OR Realizations

The design of a logic circuit, like that of any other type of engineering system, commences with a specification. The specification for a logic circuit includes a statement of the required logical behavior of the circuit with many practical requirements such as maximum power dissipation, maximum allowable switching times, voltage levels representing "0" and "1", and so forth. For the moment, we will ignore the fact that a range of practical requirements usually have to be satisfied and concentrate on the single problem of producing a circuit that provides the logical behavior required. We will refer to this problem as *the basic logic design problem.*

A very straightforward approach to the basic logic design problem commences with the construction of a truth table to represent the required logical behavior. From this table, a Boolean function, which also represents required behavior, can be obtained directly. A logic circuit that provides the logical behavior described by the Boolean function can then be drawn up immediately. This logic circuit is called a *realization* of the Boolean function.

As we shall see, logic circuits obtained in this simple and straightforward way are usually very wasteful in the number of logic gates that they employ. In other words, we shall see that it is usually possible to obtain realizations that require far fewer gates than those obtained using this straightforward approach. The main objective of this section (and much of this book) is to present techniques that produce realizations requiring the minimum number of gates.

Example 2.1. As an illustrative example, suppose we require a logic circuit to control the operation of a photo-copying machine in a typical university department. The required logical behavior is specified as follows:

> Operability of the machine depends upon the type of user. If students wish to use the machine, they are required to supply 5 cents per copy; faculty members are provided with a key which, when inserted in the machine, allows operation free of charge. In addition, the machine will only operate if there is blank paper at the machine inlet.†

Solution. This is a typical written statement describing required behavior. From this statement, the designer must identify those quantities which will act as inputs to the logic circuit and establish the relationships between these quantities which determine the required output (or outputs) from the circuit.

In this case, the operability of the machine depends upon the presence or absence of three quantities: money (M), the key (K) and blank paper (P).

---

† A further requirement is, of course, that the electric power for the machine be turned on. We will assume that the user is expected to attend to this.

Assume that suitable transducers are available to indicate the presence or absence of these quantities by voltage levels corresponding to logic "1" or "0" respectively. These voltage levels will then provide the inputs to the logic circuit. The circuit will have a single output, which the designer would require to be at the voltage level corresponding to logic "1" whenever conditions for operability of the machine are met; a logic "0" output is required otherwise. The output could then be used to operate a switch controlling operability of the machine.

We can now construct a truth table which describes the required behavior of the logic circuit. The truth table is shown in Figure 2.6, where the output symbol F has been used to represent the output function.

The reader will note that the truth table requires an output function for the unlikely case where the key is inserted (presumably by a faculty member) and money is also supplied. We will ignore the question of the intelligence of faculty members and assume that the machine is required to operate if both key and money are supplied.

From the truth table, we can obtain a Boolean expression for the output function F in two distinct ways. First of all, we can use the fact that F is equal to 1 if any one of three conditions is satisfied. The first of these conditions is given by row 4 of the table where $M = 0$, $K = 1$, and $P = 1$; this condition can be written algebraically as $\overline{M}KP = 1$. The other two conditions can be written $M\overline{K}P = 1$ and $MKP = 1$. Since F is 1 if any of these conditions is satisfied, we can write

$$F = \overline{M}KP + M\overline{K}P + MKP \qquad (2.2)$$

If we assume that each variable and its complement is available† then Equation (2.2) can be realized directly by the circuit shown in Figure 2.7.

Equation (2.2) was derived from the truth table in Figure 2.6 by noting that F takes on the value 1 if any one of three conditions is satisfied. The truth table also shows that F takes on the value 0 if any one of five conditions is satisfied.

M	K	P	F
0	0	0	0
0	0	1	0
0	1	0	0
0	1	1	1
1	0	0	0
1	0	1	1
1	1	0	0
1	1	1	1

Figure 2.6. Truth table for Example 2.1.

---

†If complements of variables were not available they could be easily obtained by use of inverters.

Under any of these five conditions, the complement of F will have the value 1 so that we can write

$$\bar{F} = \overline{M}K\overline{P} + \overline{M}\,\overline{K}P + \overline{M}K\overline{P} + M\overline{K}\,\overline{P} + MK\overline{P}$$

We can now use De Morgan's laws (number 9 in the list of rules) to obtain an expression for F which leads to a rather different circuit realization:

$$F = \overline{\overline{M}K\overline{P} + \overline{M}\,\overline{K}P + \overline{M}K\overline{P} + M\overline{K}\,\overline{P} + MK\overline{P}}$$
$$= \overline{\overline{M}K\overline{P}}.\overline{\overline{M}\,\overline{K}P}.\overline{\overline{M}K\overline{P}}.\overline{M\overline{K}\,\overline{P}}.\overline{MK\overline{P}}$$
$$= (M + \overline{K} + P)(M + K + \overline{P})(M + \overline{K} + P)$$
$$\cdot (\overline{M} + K + P)(\overline{M} + \overline{K} + P) \qquad (2.3)$$

Equation (2.3) can be realized directly by the circuit shown in Figure 2.8.

Note that in Equation (2.2) F is expressed in the form of a "sum of products" of the variables and that in Equation (2.3) F is expressed as a "product of sums" (these two terms are discussed in more detail in Section 2.2.2). Boolean functions can always be expressed in these two ways and we shall have more to say about this fact a little later.

Each of the realizations we have obtained involves AND and OR gates and the logical operations in both circuits take place in two stages. In Figure 2.7, the first stage consists of three AND gates whose outputs are fed to a single OR gate making up the second stage. In Figure 2.8, the first stage consists of five OR gates with their outputs feeding to a single AND gate. Each of these realizations is referred to as a *two-level* network.

An example of a three-level network is easily obtained by writing Equation (2.2) in the form

$$F = (\overline{M}K + M\overline{K} + MK)P$$

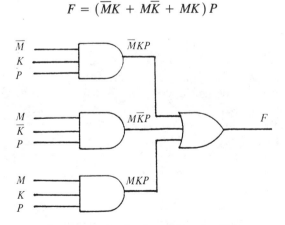

Figure 2.7. Realization of Equation (2.2).

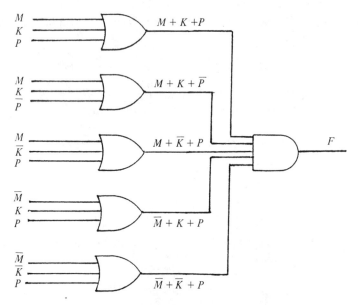

Figure 2.8. Realization of Equation (2.3).

which is realized by the network shown in Figure 2.9. In the three-level realization, because of the extra level of gating, the effects of the signals M and K
take longer to propagate from input to output than in the two-level case. In
many applications, speed of operation is crucial to overall system performance
so that in most situations, the minimum number of gating levels is preferred.†

Except in the most trivial cases it is not possible to realize a Boolean function
with fewer than two levels, but two levels are always sufficient. It should be
clear to the reader that if a Boolean function is expressed in the form of a sum
of products (as in Equation (2.2)) or a product of sums (as in Equation (2.3))
a two-level circuit realization can always be obtained directly. The sum-of-
products form leads to a circuit in which the first level consists of several AND
gates (one for each product) and the second level consists of a single OR gate
(to carry out the sum). The product-of-sums form leads to a circuit in which
the first level consists of several OR gates (one for each sum) and the second
level consists of a single AND gate (to carry out the product).

The realizations shown in Figures 2.7, 2.8 and 2.9 are all very wasteful in
the number of gates they require. By drawing upon the basic rules of Boolean
algebra we can reduce both Equations (2.2) and (2.3) to a form which requires
the minimum amount of hardware for the realization of F.

---

† There are, of course, situations where speed is not particularly important and in such situations
a realization with more than two levels of gating may offer advantages. For instance, it sometimes
happens that the realization requiring the minimum number of gates involves three (or an even
higher number of) levels.

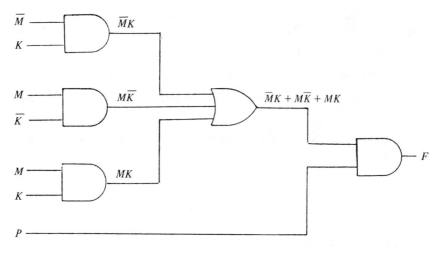

Figure 2.9. A three-level realization of Equation (2.2).

Commencing with Equation (2.2) we have

$$F = \overline{M}KP + M\overline{K}P + MKP$$
$$= \overline{M}KP + M(\overline{K} + K)P \quad \text{(distributive law)}$$
$$= \overline{M}KP + MP \quad \text{(complementation law)}$$
$$= (\overline{M}K + M)P \quad \text{(distributive law)}$$
$$= (K + M)P \quad \text{(absorption law)}$$

This reduced expression for F allows the required logical behavior to be realized using circuit shown in Figure 2.10.

Reduction of Equation (2.3) to minimum form requires considerably more ingenuity. We have

$$F = (M + K + P)(M + K + \overline{P})(M + \overline{K} + P)$$
$$\cdot (\overline{M} + K + P)(\overline{M} + \overline{K} + P) \qquad (2.4)$$

We begin by drawing upon the fact that $A.A = A$, where A is any logical expression. We use this fact initially to make Equation (2.4) apparently more complex:

$$F = (M + K + P)(M + K + \overline{P})(M + K + P)(M + \overline{K} + P)$$
$$\cdot (\overline{M} + K + P)(\overline{M} + \overline{K} + P)$$

To reduce this expression, we rely heavily on the identity $(A + B)(A + \overline{B})$

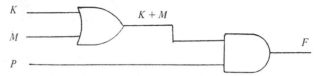

Figure 2.10. A realization requiring minimum hardware.

$= A$; the reader should verify this identity. Using this identity we may write immediately

$$F = (M + K)(M + P)(\overline{M} + P)$$
$$= (M + K)P$$

which is also realized by the circuit in Figure 2.10.

The function F could not be realized by a circuit requiring less hardware than the circuit in Figure 2.10. Consequently the circuit in Figure 2.10 is termed a *minimal realization* of F. □

The steps employed in the simplification of Equations (2.2) and (2.3) indicate that as long as we know the basic rules and identities of Boolean algebra, we should always be able to obtain a minimal realization for a given function. Though this statement is true in principle, the minimization of Boolean functions in this way often requires considerable resourcefulness and skill, as was perhaps indicated by the technique used to simplify Equation (2.4). This fact renders the algebraic manipulation approach to function minimization rather unattractive and other, more systematic, approaches to the problem have been developed. Before describing some of these more systematic approaches, we will deal with a few other items pertinent to the current discussion.

2.2.2. Minterms and Maxterms

In the previous section an example was given in which a Boolean function was obtained in two distinct ways from a truth table. For convenience, the truth table is redrawn here in Figure 2.11. In this figure, we have added an extra column which provides an enumeration of the rows in the table.

Note that the various combinations of input variables in the truth table can be interpreted as 3-digit binary numbers. For instance, the combination $M = 1$, $K = 0$ and $P = 1$ provides the entry 101 in the table; the binary number 101 is equivalent to the decimal number 5. The entry 101 lies in the row numbered 5 in the table and as the reader should check, each row in the table has been assigned a number which is the decimal equivalent of the combination of input variables in that row.

Row No.	M	K	P	F
0	0	0	0	0
1	0	0	1	0
2	0	1	0	0
3	0	1	1	1
4	1	0	0	0
5	1	0	1	1
6	1	1	0	0
7	1	1	1	1

Figure 2.11. Truth table for Example 2.1.

One of the two Boolean functions obtained (in the previous section) from the truth table was

$$F = \overline{M}KP + M\overline{K}P + MKP \qquad (2.2)$$

This equation consists of a sum of products and each product corresponds to a row in the truth table in which the function F has the value 1. Thus, the function F takes on the value 1 whenever one of the products in Equation (2.2) has the value 1. Consider the first of the products in Equation (2.2), viz, $\overline{M}KP$. This product has the value 1 if and only if $M = 0$, $K = 1$ and $P = 1$. Each of the other products similarly indicates a combination of input variable values which causes F to take on the value 1. Each product involves all three input variables and such products are known as *minterms*.

Every row of the truth table has an associated minterm. The minterms associated with the truth table of Figure 2.11 are listed in Figure 2.12.

The notation for minterms allows us to write Equation (2.2) in the shorthand form

$$F = m_3 + m_5 + m_7$$

Row No.	M	K	P	Minterm
0	0	0	0	$m_0 = \overline{M}\,\overline{K}\,\overline{P}$
1	0	0	1	$m_1 = \overline{M}\,\overline{K}P$
2	0	1	0	$m_2 = \overline{M}K\overline{P}$
3	0	1	1	$m_3 = \overline{M}KP$
4	1	0	0	$m_4 = M\overline{K}\,\overline{P}$
5	1	0	1	$m_5 = M\overline{K}P$
6	1	1	0	$m_6 = MK\overline{P}$
7	1	1	1	$m_7 = MKP$

Figure 2.12. Minterms associated with Example 2.1.

This is often written in the form

$$F = \Sigma m(3, 5, 7)$$

This very useful notation, which is said to express the function F in *minterm list form*, is frequently employed later in this book.

Figure 2.12 indicates that there are 8 ($=2^3$) minterms associated with a problem involving three input variables. It should be obvious that for problems involving n input variables, the number of minterms is 2^n.

The truth table of Figure 2.11 allows a second form of Boolean function to be obtained as a representation of the function F. In the previous section it was shown that the function F can be written

$$F = (M + K + P)(M + K + \overline{P})(M + \overline{K} + P)$$
$$\cdot (\overline{M} + K + P)(\overline{M} + \overline{K} + P) \qquad (2.4)$$

This equation consists of a product of sums with each sum corresponding to a row in the truth table in which the function F has the value 0. Thus, the function F takes on the value 0 whenever one of the sums in Equation (2.4) has the value 0. Consider the first of the sums in Equation (2.4), viz, $M + K + P$. This sum has the value 0 if and only if $M = 0$, $K = 0$ and $P = 0$. Each of the other sums similarly indicates a combination of input variable values which causes F to take on the value 0. Each sum involves all three input variables and such sums are known as *maxterms*.†

Every row of the truth table has an associated maxterm. The maxterm associated with row number i is given the symbol M_i. The maxterms associated with the truth table of Figure 2.11 are listed in Figure 2.13.

Row No.	M	K	P	Maxterm
0	0	0	0	$M_0 = M + K + P$
1	0	0	1	$M_1 = M + K + \overline{P}$
2	0	1	0	$M_2 = M + \overline{K} + P$
3	0	1	1	$M_3 = M + \overline{K} + \overline{P}$
4	1	0	0	$M_4 = \overline{M} + K + P$
5	1	0	1	$M_5 = \overline{M} + K + \overline{P}$
6	1	1	0	$M_6 = \overline{M} + \overline{K} + P$
7	1	1	1	$M_7 = \overline{M} + \overline{K} + \overline{P}$

Figure 2.13. Maxterms associated with Example 2.1.

---

†The reason for the terminology *minterm* and *maxterm* will become clear later.

The notation for maxterms allows us to write Equation (2.4) in the shorthand from .

$$F = M_0 M_1 M_2 M_4 M_6$$

This is often written in the form

$$F = \Pi M(0, 1, 2, 4, 6)$$

and is referred to as the *maxterm list form*.

In the previous section, Equation (2.4) was obtained by application of De Morgan's law to a sum of products representing $\overline{F}$. Now that we know about maxterms, we have no need to use De Morgan's law to obtain a product-of-sums expression for F; we can write it down directly from the truth table.

When a Boolean function is expressed as a sum of minterms (as in Equation (2.2)), or as a product of maxterms (as in Equation (2.4)) it is said to be written in *standard form*. The sum of minterms is referred to in this text as the *standard sum-of-products* form and the product of maxterms is referred to here as the *standard product-of-sums* form.

Example 2.2. A lighting system is to be designed for a large gymnasium. It is required that the lights can be switched on or off from any of four switching points. Set up a truth table for the problem and hence obtain a Boolean function which represents the required behavior. Express this function in both the minterm list and the maxterm list forms.

Solution. For this problem, we require a Boolean function F to represent the required logical behavior. Let F take on the value 1 for all conditions under which the lights are to be on and let it take on the value 0 otherwise. Let us represent the position (on or off) of switch i ($i = 1, 2, 3, 4$) by the Boolean variable x_i. Let x_i have the value 1 when switch i is on and let it have the value 0 when switch i is off.

In order to derive a truth table for F, let us assume to begin with that all four switches are in the "off" position. In such a case, we do not want the lights to be on and so, for this case, we require $F = 0$. This gives the first row in the truth table shown in Figure 2.14. If any switch is now put into the "on" position, we require the lights to be on. This gives us the rows numbered 1, 2, 4 and 8 in the truth table and these represent the situation where the lights are on with one switch in the "on" position and the others all "off". Lighting systems of this kind are usually arranged so that, from this situation, the pressing of any one switch will result in the lights being turned off again. That is, to turn off the lights from the current situation, we can either return the "on" switch to the "off" position, or we can put some other switch into the "on" position. The latter action would result in two switches being in the "on" position and

Row No.	x_1	x_2	x_3	x_4	F
0	0	0	0	0	0
1	0	0	0	1	1
2	0	0	1	0	1
3	0	0	1	1	0
4	0	1	0	0	1
5	0	1	0	1	0
6	0	1	1	0	0
7	0	1	1	1	1
8	1	0	0	0	1
9	1	0	0	1	0
10	1	0	1	0	0
11	1	0	1	1	1
12	1	1	0	0	0
13	1	1	0	1	1
14	1	1	1	0	1
15	1	1	1	1	0

Figure 2.14. Truth table for Example 2.2.

indicates that when any two switches are on, we require the lights to be out, i.e., $F = 0$. The reader should be able to work out the remaining details. The complete truth table for the problem is shown in Figure 2.14.

From the truth table we see that the function F can be written in the standard sum-of-products form as

$$F = \bar{x}_1\bar{x}_2\bar{x}_3x_4 + \bar{x}_1\bar{x}_2x_3\bar{x}_4 + \bar{x}_1x_2\bar{x}_3\bar{x}_4 + \bar{x}_1x_2x_3x_4 + x_1\bar{x}_2\bar{x}_3\bar{x}_4$$
$$+ x_1\bar{x}_2x_3x_4 + x_1x_2\bar{x}_3x_4 + x_1x_2x_3\bar{x}_4 \qquad (2.5)$$

or as a minterm list as

$$F = \Sigma m(1, 2, 4, 7, 8, 11, 13, 14) \qquad (2.6)$$

which is clearly a more concise form.

The function F can also be written in the standard product-of-sums form as

$$F = (x_1 + x_2 + x_3 + x_4)(x_1 + x_2 + \bar{x}_3 + \bar{x}_4)(x_1 + \bar{x}_2 + x_3 + \bar{x}_4)$$
$$\cdot (x_1 + \bar{x}_2 + \bar{x}_3 + x_4)(\bar{x}_1 + x_2 + x_3 + \bar{x}_4)(\bar{x}_1 + x_2 + \bar{x}_3 + x_4)$$
$$\cdot (\bar{x}_1 + \bar{x}_2 + x_3 + x_4)(\bar{x}_1 + \bar{x}_2 + \bar{x}_3 + \bar{x}_4) \qquad (2.7)$$

or as a maxterm list

$$F = \Pi M(0, 3, 5, 6, 9, 10, 12, 15) \qquad (2.8)$$

The realization of these equations is considered in the next section. □

2.2.3. NAND and NOR Realizations

Up to now, the various realizations we have presented have all been implemented using AND and OR gates. In actual practice, two other types of realizations are almost universally employed. These types of realizations employ *NAND* and *NOR gates* and the reason these gates are more widely used is that they are more easily fabricated (and hence are cheaper) than AND and OR gates.

The NAND Gate.   The NAND function is the complement of the AND function; its truth table is given in Figure 2.15(a). The most common symbol for the NAND gate is shown in Figure 2.15(b); This symbol is simply an AND gate with a small circle attached to indicate complementation.†

Another symbol is sometimes employed for the NAND gate, and this symbol arises from the following observation. Application of the NAND operation to two Boolean variables A and B gives the function $Z = \overline{AB}$; one of De Morgan's laws implies that this function can be equivalently written $Z = \overline{A} + \overline{B}$. This equivalent form indicates that the NAND operation can be carried out by forming the complement of each input variable and then passing the result through an OR gate. This leads to the alternative symbol for a NAND gate (sometimes called the invert-OR) shown in Figure 2.16.

The NOR Gate.   The NOR function is the complement of the OR function and its truth table is shown in Figure 2.17(a). The most common symbol for the NOR gate is shown in Figure 2.17(b); this symbol is simply an OR gate symbol with a small circle attached to indicate complementation.

Another symbol is sometimes employed for the NOR gate and, as was the case with the NAND gate, we can arrive at this alternative symbol by drawing upon one of De Morgan's laws.

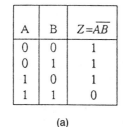

A	B	$Z=\overline{AB}$
0	0	1
0	1	1
1	0	1
1	1	0

(a)

Figure 2.15. NAND gate: (a) truth table; (b) symbol.

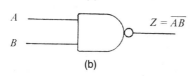

$Z = \overline{AB}$

(b)

---

†The small circle is generally used for this purpose.

$$Z = \overline{A} + \overline{B} = \overline{AB}$$

Figure 2.16. Invert-OR representation of NAND gate.

Application of the NOR operation to two Boolean variables A and B gives the function $Z = \overline{A + B}$; one of De Morgan's laws implies that this function can be equivalently written $Z = \overline{A}.\overline{B}$. This equivalent form indicates that the NOR operation can be carried out by forming the complement of each input variable and then passing the resulting variables through an AND gate. This leads to the alternative symbol for a NOR gate (sometimes called the invert-AND) shown in Figure 2.18.

NAND-Gate Realizations. The NAND gate is said to be a *universal gate* because any Boolean function can be realized using NAND gates alone. That this is true can be seen by noting that the AND, OR and NOT functions can all be implemented by NAND gates.

An implementation of a NOT gate using a 2-input NAND gate is shown in Figure 2.19(a). (The reader can check that the gate in Figure 2.19(a) is indeed an inverter by referring to the truth table in Figure 2.15(a)). The gate in Figure 2.19(a) provides a single-input device and it is usually drawn as in Figure 2.19(b).

The NAND-gate implementation of an AND gate is simple and is shown in Figure 2.20(a). A method of realizing an OR gate using NAND gates can be seen from De Morgan's rule:

$$A + B = \overline{\overline{A}.\overline{B}}$$

The implementation of this rule is shown in Figure 2.20(b).

A	B	$Z=\overline{A+B}$
0	0	1
0	1	0
1	0	0
1	1	0

(a)

Figure 2.17. NOR gate: (a) truth table: (b) symbol.

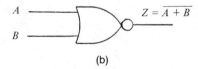

$$Z = \overline{A + B}$$

(b)

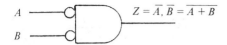

Figure 2.18. Invert-AND representation of NOR gate.

As an example of the realization of a Boolean expression using NAND gates only, consider the expression:

$$Z = AB + CDE \qquad (2.9)$$

This is a sum-of-products expression, and such expressions are particularly easily realized using NAND gates.

First let us realize the function using AND and OR gates as shown in Figure 2.21(a). Then replace these gates by their NAND implementations as shown in Figure 2.21(b). Now note that the signals travelling between the AND gates and the OR gates in Figure 2.21(b) are inverted just before leaving the AND gates and are inverted again as soon as the reach the OR gate. Thus, the effect of the inverters in the AND gates is cancelled by the inverters in the OR gate. Clearly, if we remove all four inverters from the circuit, this will have no effect on the output. This leads to the NAND-gate realization shown in Figure 2.22.

It is useful to note the similarity between the circuits of Figure 2.21(a) and Figure 2.22. Clearly the NAND realization of the Boolean function given in Equation (2.9) can be obtained directly from the AND/OR realization by simply replacing the AND and OR gates by NAND gates. Indeed, whenever a sum-of-products expression is realized as a 2-level AND/OR circuit we can always obtain an equivalent circuit by replacing all gates (both AND and OR) with NAND gates.

This simple property does not, unfortunately, extend to realizations that involve AND and OR gates in other configurations. For instance, if we realize a product-of-sums expression as a 2-level circuit we obtain an OR/AND realization and the equivalent NAND-gate realization is a 4-level circuit.

As an example, consider the function

$$Y = (A + B)(C + D + E)$$

The OR/AND realization of this function is shown in Figure 2.23(a) and the circuit obtained by replacing AND and OR gates by their NAND implementa-

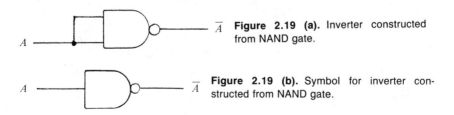

Figure 2.19 (a). Inverter constructed from NAND gate.

Figure 2.19 (b). Symbol for inverter constructed from NAND gate.

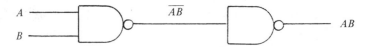

Figure 2.20 (a). AND gate constructed from NAND gates.

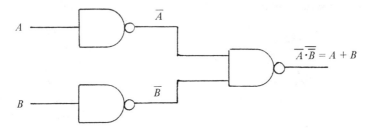

Figure 2.20 (b). OR gate constructed from NAND gates.

tions is shown in Figure 2.23(b). There is no obvious way in which this NAND-gate realization can be simplified.

NOR-Gate Realizations. Any Boolean function can be realized using only NOR gates so that the NOR gate is also said to be a universal gate.

The implementation of a NOT gate using a 2-input NOR gate is shown in Figure 2.24(a). This arrangement provides a single-input device which is usually represented as in Figure 2.24(b).

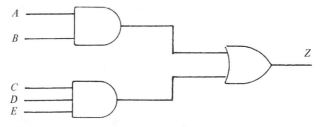

Figure 2.21 (a). AND/OR realization of Equation (2.9).

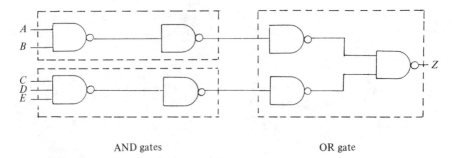

AND gates   OR gate

Figure 2.21 (b). NAND realization of Equation (2.9).

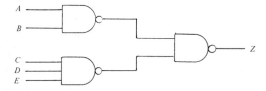

Figure 2.22. Simplified NAND realization of Equation (2.9).

The NOR-gate implementation of an OR gate is simple and is shown in Figure 2.25(a). A method of realizing an AND gate using NOR gates can be seen from De Morgan's rule:

$$AB = \overline{\overline{A} + \overline{B}}$$

The implementation of this rule is shown in Figure 2.25(b).

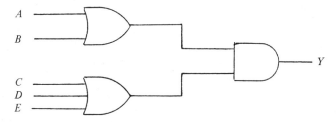

Figure 2.23 (a). OR/AND circuit.

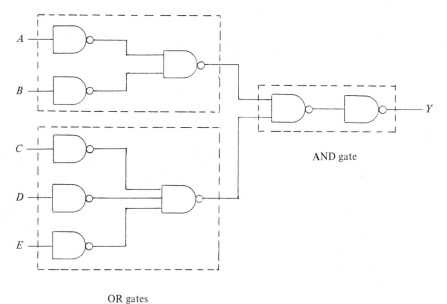

AND gate

OR gates

Figure 2.23 (b). NAND realization of OR/AND circuit.

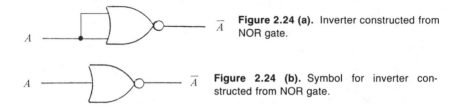

Figure 2.24 (a). Inverter constructed from NOR gate.

Figure 2.24 (b). Symbol for inverter constructed from NOR gate.

Boolean expressions in the product-of-sums form can be realized using 2-level NOR networks. As an example, consider the expression

$$Y = (A + B)(C + D + E) \qquad (2.10)$$

First let us realize the expression using AND and OR gates, as shown in Figure 2.26(a). Then replace these gates by their NOR implementations, as shown in Figure 2.26(b).

The inverters in Figure 2.26(b) are clearly redundant and can be removed to give the realization shown in Figure 2.27. Thus we see that a NOR-gate realization of the Boolean function given in Equation (2.10) can be obtained directly from the OR/AND realization in Figure 2.26(a) by simply replacing all gates by NOR gates. And in fact, whenever a product-of-sums expression is realized as a 2-level OR/AND circuit we can always obtain an equivalent circuit by replacing all gates with NOR gates.

This property does not extend to realizations that involve AND and OR gates in other configurations.

Example 2.3. Realize a logic circuit for the lighting system discussed in Example 2.2 using

(i) NAND logic, and
(ii) NOR logic.

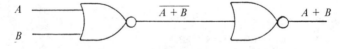

Figure 2.25 (a). OR gate constructed from NOR gates.

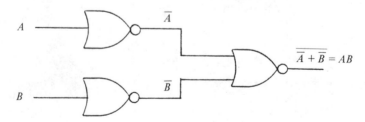

Figure 2.25 (b). AND gate constructed from NOR gates.

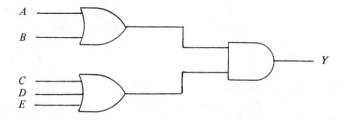

Figure 2.26 (a). OR/AND realization of Equation (2.10).

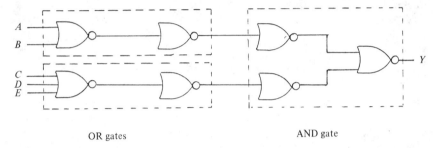

OR gates   AND gate

Figure 2.26 (b). NOR realization of Equation (2.10).

In each case, use a 2-level realization which employs the minimum amount of hardware.

Solution.

(a) A NAND-logic realization can be drawn immediately from the standard sum-of-products expression

$$F = \bar{x}_1\bar{x}_2\bar{x}_3x_4 + \bar{x}_1\bar{x}_2x_3\bar{x}_4 + \bar{x}_1x_2\bar{x}_3\bar{x}_4 + \bar{x}_1x_2x_3x_4 \qquad (2.11)$$
$$+ x_1\bar{x}_2\bar{x}_3\bar{x}_4 + x_1\bar{x}_2x_3x_4 + x_1x_2\bar{x}_3x_4 + x_1x_2x_3\bar{x}_4$$

However, we are asked to produce a 2-level realization which requires the minimum amount of hardware. This implies that we must attempt to reduce Equation (2.11) to a minimum sum-of-products form.

One could spend some considerable time attempting to reduce the expression

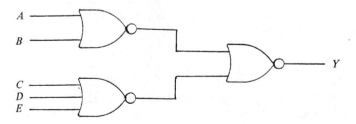

Figure 2.27 Simplified NOR realization of Equation (2.10).

in Equation (2.11). In fact, the expression cannot be reduced to a simpler sum-of-products form, and this draws attention to a major difficulty in attempting to reduce Boolean expressions by applying the basic rules: in general, one can never be sure that a given expression is reducible and, if it is, and some reduction is carried out, one can never be sure that a minimal form has been attained. The more systematic techniques to be described in the following sections of this chapter and in later chapters provide the user with a much more reliable approach to the minimization process. It will be shown in the next section, in a very simple way, that the expression in Equation (2.11) is, indeed, not reducible.

The NAND-gate realization of Equation (2.11) can be obtained by first drawing up an AND/OR realization and then replacing all gates by NAND gates. With a little practice, the reader will be able to dispense with the first step. The 2-level NAND-gate realization of Equation (2.11) is shown in Figure 2.28.

This example emphasizes that 2-level realizations often require gates with many inputs. In 2-level NAND realizations, this occurs when the function to be realized is a sum of many products. The function in Equation (2.11) is a sum of eight products, so that a NAND gate with eight inputs is required. NAND gates with up to 13 inputs are available from most manufacturers, but if a 2-level realization requires a NAND gate with more than 13 inputs, the designer has to look to other alternatives. One possibility is to use a programmable logic array; this is an MSI device that allows 2-level realizations involving sums of very many products (see Chapter 6). Another alternative is often available if speed is not crucial. It is usually possible to modify a given sum of products by collecting terms into factors. Factored expressions generally require more than two levels of logic (thus reducing speed of operation) but they also require gates with less inputs than are required by unfactored expressions. For example, the function in Equation (2.11) can be factored into the form:

$$F = \bar{x}_1\left[\bar{x}_2(\bar{x}_3 x_4 + x_3\bar{x}_4) + x_2(\bar{x}_3\bar{x}_4 + x_3 x_4)\right]$$
$$+ x_1\left[\bar{x}_2(\bar{x}_3\bar{x}_4 + x_3 x_4) + x_2(\bar{x}_3 x_4 + x_3\bar{x}_4)\right]$$

which can be realized directly as a 6-level circuit using AND gates and OR gates, each with two inputs. The function can also be realized as a 6-level circuit using 2-input NAND gates only (see Exercise 2.11). Since this example concerns a lighting system, the increased delay caused by the extra levels of gating would be quite irrelevant.

(b) As will be shown in the next section, the product-of-sums expression for F (Equation (2.7)) is also irreducible. The reader should be able to draw a 2-level NOR-gate realization for the product-of-sums expression (if necessary, drawing the OR/AND realization as an intermediate step). □

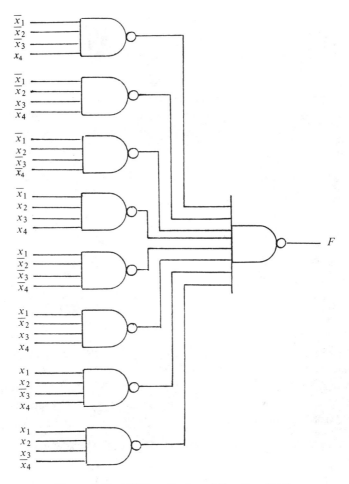

Figure 2.28. NAND realization of Equation (2.11).

2.2.4. The Exclusive-OR and Exclusive-NOR gates

The exclusive-OR gate is a 2-input gate that proves very useful in certain circumstances. The circuit symbol for the gate is shown in Figure 2.29(a) and the truth table in Figure 2.29(b). The truth table shows that the output of the gate takes on the value 1 when either A or B (but not both) has the value 1. The behavior of the gate is obviously similar to that of the conventional OR gate, the difference being that the cases for which the output takes the value 1 exclude the case $A = B = 1$ (and hence the name exclusive-OR). The exclusive-OR operation is indicated by the symbol $\oplus$ so that the output of the gate in Figure 2.29(a) is written $Z = A \oplus B$.

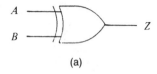

(a)

A	B	Z
0	0	0
0	1	1
1	0	1
1	1	0

(b)

Figure 2.29. Exclusive-OR gate: (a) symbol; (b) truth table.

From the truth table we see that the exclusive-OR operation (which is usually abbreviated to XOR) can be written

$$Z = A \oplus B = \bar{A}B + A\bar{B} \qquad (2.12)$$

As an example of the use of the XOR gate, we can return again to the problem of the lighting system discussed in Example 2.2.

Example 2.4. Realize a logic circuit for the lighting system discussed in Example 2.2 using XOR gates.

Solution. The sum-of-products expression for the lighting system is

$$F = \bar{x}_1\bar{x}_2\bar{x}_3x_4 + \bar{x}_1\bar{x}_2x_3\bar{x}_4 + \bar{x}_1x_2\bar{x}_3\bar{x}_4 + \bar{x}_1x_2x_3x_4$$
$$+ x_1\bar{x}_2\bar{x}_3\bar{x}_4 + x_1\bar{x}_2x_3x_4 + x_1x_2\bar{x}_3x_4 + x_1x_2x_3\bar{x}_4$$

which can be factored into the form

$$F = (\bar{x}_1\bar{x}_2 + x_1x_2)(\bar{x}_3x_4 + x_3\bar{x}_4) + (\bar{x}_1x_2 + x_1\bar{x}_2)(\bar{x}_3\bar{x}_4 + x_3x_4) \qquad (2.13)$$

We recognize two of the factors in this expression, namely $(\bar{x}_3x_4 + x_3\bar{x}_4)$ and $(\bar{x}_1x_2 + x_1\bar{x}_2)$, as being realizable directly using XOR gates (see Equation 2.12). What about the other two factors? They are, in fact, very closely related to the first two factors. To see this, write

$$X = \bar{x}_1x_2 + x_1\bar{x}_2$$

Then, it is easy to verify, by means of a truth table (and the reader is urged to do so) that

$$\overline{X} = \overline{x}_1\overline{x}_2 + x_1x_2$$

Similarly, if we write $Y = \overline{x}_3x_4 + x_3\overline{x}_4$, we have $\overline{Y} = \overline{x}_3\overline{x}_4 + x_3x_4$ so that Equation (2.13) can be written

$$F = \overline{X}Y + X\overline{Y}$$

Thus, F can be realized by carrying out the XOR operation on the variables X and Y. But the variables X and Y themselves are also available through the XOR operation, so that the logic required for the lighting system can be realized as shown in Figure 2.30. □

The circuit shown in Figure 2.30 is obviously much simpler than the realization obtained earlier using NAND gates (Figure 2.28). It is shown in the next section that this XOR realization could be implemented using a single IC package, whereas five IC packages would be required to implement the NAND realization.

The circuit shown in Figure 2.30 forms part of a circuit that is widely used in a rather different application. The nature of this application is fairly evident from the truth table for the lighting system problem (Figure 2.14). Notice that the function F is required to take on the value 1 when an odd number of input variables have the value 1; F is required to be zero otherwise. Recall our discussion of parity bits in Chapter 1. The circuit in Figure 2.30 obviously provides a simple means of obtaining parity bits (even parity) for codewords of 4 bits. In practice, codewords with 8 bits are more common. An example is the ASCII code in which 7 bits are used for symbol representation and the eighth bit is used as a parity bit (See Table 1.4). A generalization of the circuit in Figure 2.30 can be used as both a parity checker and a parity-bit generator for codes such as ASCII. The generalized circuit is shown in Figure 2.31.

As with the circuit of Figure 2.30, this circuit gives an output of 1 if an odd number of input variables have the value 1. To demonstrate, suppose the code-

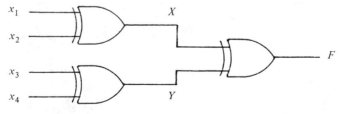

Figure 2.30. XOR gate realization of Equation (2.13).

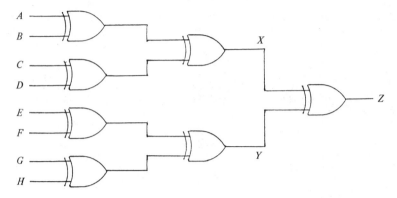

Figure 2.31. 8-bit parity-checker circuit.

word at the input is $A = 1, B = 0, C = 0, D = 1, E = 0, F = 0, G = 0, H = 1$. Then

$$Z = X \oplus Y$$
$$= ((A \oplus B) \oplus (C \oplus D)) \oplus ((E \oplus F) \oplus (G \oplus H))$$
$$= ((1 \oplus 0) \oplus (0 \oplus 1)) \oplus ((0 \oplus 0) \oplus (0 \oplus 1))$$
$$= (1 \oplus 1) \oplus (0 \oplus 1)$$
$$= 0 \oplus 1$$
$$= 1$$

If this circuit is employed in a receiver in a data communication system using even-parity codewords, a transmission error is indicated when the output Z takes the value 1. The use of this circuit also as a parity-bit *generator* is discussed in Exercise 2.12 at the end of this chapter.

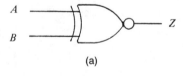

(a)

A	B	Z
0	0	1
0	1	0
1	0	0
1	1	1

(b)

Figure 2.32. Exclusive-NOR gate: (a) symbol; (b) truth table.

Besides the exclusive-OR-gate, there is also an exclusive-NOR (XNOR) which is occasionally useful. The circuit symbol and truth table for the XNOR are shown in Figure 2.32. From the truth table, we see that the output Z takes the value 1 when the inputs have identical values and takes the value 0 otherwise. For this reason the XNOR is sometimes called the *equivalence gate*. Comparison of the truth tables in Figures 2.29 and 2.32 shows that the XNOR can be constructed by means of an XOR and an inverter and this is implied in the circuit symbol in Figure 2.32.

2.2.5. Integrated-Circuit Packages

The fact that arbitrary logic functions can be realized using a single type of gate (either NAND or NOR) has led to the widespread use of integrated circuits (IC's) with several identical gates on a single chip. Typical examples can be found in the series of IC's whose designation commences with the number 74. These IC's are produced by a range of manufacturers and are based upon TTL (transistor-transistor logic—see the Appendix at the end of this book). The layout of the 7400 chip is shown in Figure 2.33. This chip contains four separate 2-input NAND gates and is referred to in the manufacturers' catalogs as a quad 2-input NAND gate. Pins 7 and 14 on the package are for power supply connections.

Other IC's in this series include the 7402 (a quad 2-input NOR gate), the 7410 (a triple 3-input NAND gate) and the 7404, which contains 6 inverters. The series of IC's from which these examples are drawn is known as the 7400 series and includes a very extensive range of circuits. If the reader consults a manufacturer's catalog, the variety of the 7400 series range will be evident. For instance, the 7400 chip depicted in Figure 2.33 is also available as 74H00, 74L00, 74S00, 74LS00 and 74C00. Each has exactly the same layout as de-

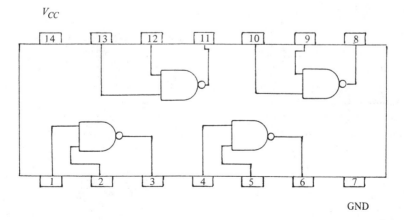

Figure 2.33. The layout of the 7400.

picted in Figure 2.33, but the gates in each are constructed in different ways. The method of construction is indicated by the letter inserted in the numerical designation. All but one of these different types of gate are varieties of TTL; the other, designated by the letter C, is based upon a quite different technology called CMOS. Each type has particular properties that are useful in certain applications. More details are given in the Appendix at the end of the book.

In this book, when referring to different IC's in the 7400 series, we shall give only the numerical designation and not concern ourselves with specific types. We point out here, however, that the LS variety (low-power Schottky) is currently the most widely used. Reasons why this is so are given in the Appendix.

The discrete gate types available in the 7400 series are not confined to NAND gates and NOR gates. AND gates and OR gates are also available (e.g., the 7408, a quad 2-input AND gate, and the 7432, a quad 2-input OR gate). Also available are XOR and XNOR gates, for example, the 7486 (a quad XOR).

The fact that the 7486 contains four XOR gates indicates that the XOR realization of the lighting system logic (Figure 2.30) can be implemented using a single 7486 chip. In contrast, the 2-level NAND realization of the same logic function (Figure 2.28) would require five IC packages: one 8-input NAND (a 7430) and four dual 4-input NAND's (i.e., four 7420's). The XOR realization offers enormous savings in space, chip cost and wiring cost. In most applications it is important to try and keep the number of IC packages in a design (i.e., the "package count") to a minimum.

2.2.6. Fan-Out and Fan-In

When interconnecting packages of logic gates, it is very common for the output of a gate to be connected to the inputs of several other gates. For instance, in Figure 2.28, the variable x_1 is fed to the inputs of each of the bottom four gates. If the variable x_1 is the output of some other gate then, for the correct operation of the circuit in Figure 2.28, it is essential that the gate providing variable x_1 is able to "drive" the inputs to four gates simultaneously. A gate that is able to drive four other gates (but no more than four) is said to have a *fan-out* of four. Thus, the fan-out of a gate specifies the maximum number of other gates that the gate can drive. Standard TTL gates have a fan-out of 10, while CMOS gates, because of the very high impedances of the transistors involved, have a fan-out of 50.

Occasionally the term *fan-in* is used. For a given gate, the fan-in is simply the number of inputs that the gate has. For instance, the fan-in of a 3-input NAND gate is 3.

2.2.7. Scales of Integration

The integrated circuit chip depicted in Figure 2.33 is an example of *small-scale integration* (SSI). The term small-scale integration is normally used in reference to IC packages containing up to 10 logic gates. For IC's containing between 10 and 100 logic gates, the term *medium-scale integration* (MSI) is used. The term *large-scale integration* (LSI) is applied to IC's with more than 100 gates and VLSI (*very-large-scale integration*) is applied to IC's with many thousands of gates. This chapter, and the next three chapters of this book, are chiefly concerned with the design of logic circuits using SSI chips. In Chapters 6 and 7 we look specifically at design using MSI chips.

2.3. SYSTEMATIC TECHNIQUES FOR THE MINIMIZATION OF SWITCHING FUNCTIONS

In the previous section, the possibility of reducing switching functions to minimal form by means of algebraic manipulation was demonstrated. It was pointed out that in applying the direct algebraic approach, considerable ingenuity and skill is often required. The main reason such ingenuity can be necessary lies in the fact that the algebraic approach to function minimization does not have a systematic framework within which to work. In other words, when the algebraic approach is applied, there are no specific rules to guide the reduction process from one step to the next. If we wish to write a computer program to carry out the reduction process for us, a systematic approach is essential.

The first technique that we shall describe in this section is not sufficiently systematic for computer implementation but has proved of great value as an aid to the reduction of Boolean functions involving a small number of variables (not more than 6). This technique, known as the *map method*, is based upon a rearrangement of the truth table and relies heavily upon the human ability to detect patterns in diagrammatic representations of data. The basic ideas underlying this approach were first proposed by Veitch [3], and a little later Karnaugh [4] described a slightly modified method which has been very widely used; it is known as the *Karnaugh-map method*.

2.3.1. Karnaugh Maps

The manner in which the Karnaugh map constitutes a rearrangement of the truth table will be illustrated in terms of two basic 2-variable switching functions. (In what follows we will, for brevity, simply write K-map instead of Karnaugh map).

Consider the function $F = AB$. The truth table for this function is shown in Figure 2.34(a) and the corresponding K-map is shown in Figure 2.34(b). The K-map has two rows (one for each possible value of the variable A) and two columns (one for each of the two possible values of the variable B). The possible values of A are marked at the left of each row and the possible values of B are marked above each column. Each little "box" within the map therefore corresponds to a particular pair of values of the variables A and B and, for each such pair of values, the value of the function $F = AB$ is marked in the appro-

A	B	F = AB
0	0	0
0	1	0
1	0	0
1	1	1

(a)

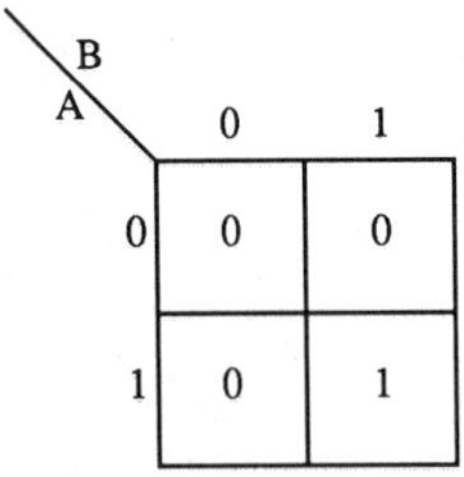

Figure 2.34. $F = AB$: (a) truth table; (b) K-map.

(b)

priate box. Thus, the bottom right-hand box, which corresponds to the values $A = 1$, $B = 1$, contains the entry "1" while the other three boxes contain the entry "0". Now consider the function $F = A + B$. The truth table for this function is given in Figure 2.35(a) and the corresponding K-map is shown in Figure 2.35(b).

K-maps for functions involving more variables are formed in a similar way.

A	B	F=A+B
0	0	0
0	1	1
1	0	1
1	1	1

(a)

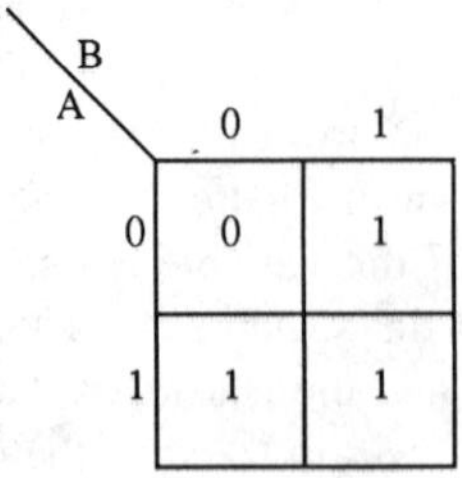

Figure 2.35. $F = A + B$: (a) truth table; (b) K-map.

(b)

Consider, for instance, the 3-variable function which arose in relation to the problem of the photo-copying machine in Section 2.2.1; the function is

$$F = \overline{M}KP + M\overline{K}P + MKP \qquad (2.2)$$

This function is in the standard sum-of-products form; it contains three products and these indicate the three combinations of values of the variables M, K, P for which the function takes on the value 1. The truth table for the function is given in Figure 2.11 and the corresponding K-map is shown in Figure 2.36. In this K-map, there is one row for each possible value of the variable M and one column for each possible pair of values of the variables K and P. The perceptive reader will have noticed that these pairs of values have been ordered in a rather special way (00, 01, 11, 10 instead of the usual 00, 01, 10, 11). The reason for this will become clear shortly.

The 4-variable case now follows directly. Consider the function

$$F = \overline{A}\,\overline{B}\,\overline{C}\,\overline{D} + \overline{A}\,\overline{B}\,\overline{C}D + \overline{A}BCD + ABCD \qquad (2.14)$$

This function is in the standard sum-of-products form. It is not necessary to consult the truth table of such a function in order to determine the entries in a K-map (indeed, as will become clear in what follows, it is never necessary to consult the truth table of a function in order to draw up its K-map representation). In Equation (2.14) the function F takes on the value 1 for four different combinations of the variables A, B, C, D. The first product tells us that F has the value "1" if $A = B = C = D = 0$; this implies that we should place a 1 in the top left-hand box of the K-map in Figure 2.37. The other non-zero entries are similarly determined.

We shall now turn to the question of using K-maps to minimize switching functions; 5-variable and 6-variable switching functions will be briefly considered at the end of the section.

Using the K-Map for Function Minimization.   As a first illustration of the use of K-maps for function minimization, consider the map in Figure 2.37. The two non-zero entries in the top row (which represent the first two products in

KP M	00	01	11	10
0	0	0	1	0
1	0	1	1	0

Figure 2.36. K-map for Equation (2.2).

CD AB	00	01	11	10
00	1	1	0	0
01	0	0	1	0
11	0	0	1	0
10	0	0	0	0

Figure 2.37. K-map for Equation (2.14).

Equation (2.14)) indicate that the function F in Equation (2.14) takes on the value 1 if $A = B = C = D = 0$ or if $A = B = C = 0$ and $D = 1$. Note that this implies that if $A = B = C = 0$, then F takes on the value 1 regardless of whether D is 0 or 1. In other words, when $A = B = C = 0$, the function F is 1 independently of the value of D. This is simply a manifestation of the fact that the first two products in Equation (2.14) can be combined as follows:

$$\overline{A}\,\overline{B}\,\overline{C}\overline{D} + \overline{A}\,\overline{B}\,\overline{C}D = \overline{A}\,\overline{B}\,\overline{C}(\overline{D} + D) = \overline{A}\,\overline{B}\,\overline{C}$$

The other two products making up the function F in Equation (2.14) can be similarly combined:

$$\overline{A}BCD + ABCD = (\overline{A} + A)\,BCD = BCD$$

Thus the expression for F in Equation (2.14) simplifies to the form

$$F = \overline{A}\,\overline{B}\,\overline{C} + BCD$$

This type of simplification is very easily detected by means of K-maps. That the first two products in Equation (2.14) can be combined is evident in the K-map from the fact that the two non-zero entries in the top row of the map are next to one another. These two non-zero entries occur in boxes corresponding to $A = B = C = 0$, with $D = 0$ in one box and $D = 1$ in the other. The function F being 1 in both cases indicates that the two products can be combined (to give $\overline{A}\,\overline{B}\,\overline{C}$) and this is indicated on the K-map by means of a loop drawn around the two entries as shown in Figure 2.38. The other two entries can similarly be looped, as shown in the figure. These two entries lie next to one another in the third column; they occur in boxes corresponding to $B = C = D = 1$ with $A = 0$ in one box and $A = 1$ in the other. Since the function F is 1

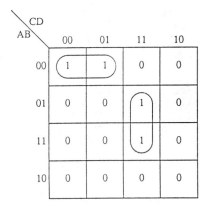

Figure 2.38. K-map for $F = \overline{A}\,\overline{B}\overline{C} + BCD$.

in both cases, the two products corresponding to these entries can be combined to give BCD.

This example helps explain why the pairs of variable values are arranged in the order 00, 01, 11, 10 on the K-map. With this ordering, *any* two boxes lying next to one another in any row or column of the map represent products in which all variables *except one* have the same value. If a K-map has a 1 in any two such adjacent boxes, they can be "looped" as in Figure 2.38 and the resulting loop represents a single product containing one less variable.

Note that the ordering 00, 01, 11, 10 also ensures that boxes lying at the two ends of any row or column also represent products in which all variables except one have the same value. If a K-map has a 1 in any two such boxes, they can also be looped. As an example, consider the function

$$F = \overline{A}B\overline{C}\overline{D} + \overline{A}BC\overline{D} + \overline{A}\,\overline{B}CD + A\overline{B}CD \qquad (2.15)$$

This function obviously reduces to the form

$$F = \overline{A}B\overline{D} + \overline{B}CD$$

and this form is obtained by the looping carried out in Figure 2.39(a).

It is important to understand that a pair of 1's in boxes that are adjacent diagonally do not provide any simplification. Thus, addition of the product term $ABCD$ to the function F in Equation (2.15) leads to the map shown in Figure 2.39(b). The loops drawn on Figure 2.39(a) can again be drawn on Figure 2.39(b), but the additional 1 in the new K-map cannot be looped with any other 1 to provide further simplification. The reason is that the variables in the product $ABCD$ always differ from the variables in the products in Equation (2.15) in at least two values. A 1 which cannot be looped with any other 1 in a K-map is given its own individual loop as shown in Figure 2.39(b).

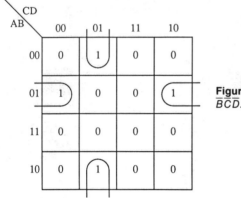

Figure 2.39 (a). K-map for $F = \overline{A}B\overline{D} + \overline{B}\overline{C}D$.

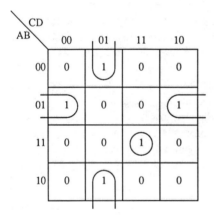

Figure 2.39 (b). K-map for $F = \overline{A}B\overline{D} + \overline{B}\overline{C}D + ABCD$.

The K-Map Displays Minterms. We have seen that if a function is expressed in the standard sum-of-products form, it is a straightforward matter to represent the function on a K-map; each product term provides a 1 entry in one of the boxes in the map. Recall that the products in a standard sum-of-products expression are called minterms. Thus we see that when a function is expressed as a minterm list, the K-map can be drawn up directly.

In a 4-variable map, the minterms are arranged as shown in Figure 2.40. The function F in Equation (2.15) can be written as a minterm list:

$$F = \Sigma m(1, 4, 6, 9)$$

indicating agreement between Figures 2.39(a) and 2.40.

CD	00	01	11	10
AB				
00	m_0	m_1	m_3	m_2
01	m_4	m_5	m_7	m_6
11	m_{12}	m_{13}	m_{15}	m_{14}
10	m_8	m_9	m_{11}	m_{10}

Figure 2.40. Arrangement of minterms on 4-variable map.

Looping More Than Two Entries in the Map. Consider the 4-variable function

$$F = \Sigma m(2, 6, 8, 9, 10, 12, 13, 14)$$

displayed on the map in Figure 2.41.

If the reader were to write out this expression in full, he or she would find that combining various terms reduces the expression to

$$F = C\overline{D} + A\overline{C} \qquad (2.16)$$

This minimal form can be obtained directly from the K-map by looping the two groups of four 1s, as shown in the figure.

The right-hand column of 1s indicates that if $C = 1$ and $D = 0$, the function F will take on the value of 1 for all possible values of the variables A and B.

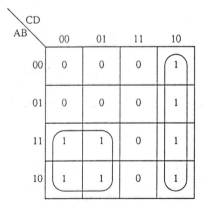

Figure 2.41. 4-variable K-map for $F = C\overline{D} + A\overline{C}$.

Thus, when $C = 1$ and $D = 0$, the function F is 1 independently of the values of A and B; this gives the first term in Equation (2.16).

Similarly the other grouping of four 1s looped in Figure 2.41 indicates that if $A = 1$ and $C = 0$, the function F takes on the value 1 whatever the values of the variables B and D; this gives the second term in Equation (2.16).

Note that the looping of four 1's produces a product containing two fewer variables than the total number of variables in the given function.

As a further example note that the function

$$F = \Sigma m(2, 3, 4, 5, 10, 11, 12, 13)$$

reduces to

$$F = B\overline{C} + \overline{B}C$$

as indicated in Figure 2.42.

Observe also that the four corners of a 4-variable map can be looped, as indicated in Figure 2.43, which represents the function

$$F = \Sigma m(0, 2, 8, 10)$$

and which reduces to

$$F = \overline{B}\,\overline{D}$$

It is also possible to loop eight entries in the map, as is indicated by the example

$$F = \Sigma m(0, 1, 4, 5, 8, 9, 12, 13)$$

which reduces to $F = \overline{C}$ as should be clear from Figure 2.44.

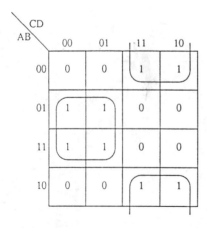

Figure 2.42. 4-variable K-map for $F = B\overline{C} + \overline{B}C$.

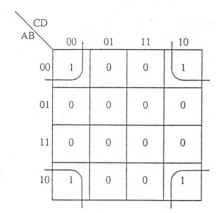

Figure 2.43. 4-variable K-map for $F = \overline{B}\overline{D}$.

If every box in a K-map contains a 1, this indicates that the function F represented by the map is equal to 1 regardless of the values of the variables. That is, the function F is simply equal to 1 and the whole K-map can be looped.

Overlapping of Loops. In many situations a minimal form for a switching function can be obtained only by including some of the K-map entries in more than one loop.

As an example, consider the 3-variable map for the photo-copying machine problem (shown in Figure 2.36 and reproduced here as Figure 2.45). This map represents the function

$$F = \overline{M}KP + M\overline{K}P + MKP \qquad (2.2)$$

and the overlapping of the loops indicates that the term MKP can be combined with either of the other two terms to produce a reduced term. The loop on the

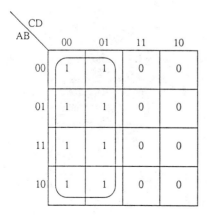

Figure 2.44. 4-variable K-map for $F = \overline{C}$.

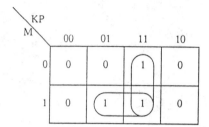

Figure 2.45. K-map for Equation (2.2).

bottom row tells us that F takes on the value 1 if $M = 1$ and $P = 1$ (regardless of the value of K) and the loop in the third column tells us that F also takes on the value 1 if $K = 1$ and $P = 1$ (regardless of the value of M). Thus we may write

$$F = MP + KP$$

which agrees with the reduced form obtained in Example 2.1 by algebraic reduction.

Very often a switching function does not have a unique minimal form. This occurs when the looping of map entries can be carried out in several ways, each leading to a reduced form of the same complexity. As an example, consider the K-map shown in Figure 2.46. Four different loopings are shown, each leading to a minimal sum-of-products form. Each of these expressions can be used to obtain a 2-level logic realization requiring the minimum number of gates. In this book, unless otherwise stated, such realizations are the objective of the function minimization process.

Implicants, Prime Implicants, and Essential Prime Implicants.
When a switching function is expressed in the sum-of-products form, each product is referred to as an *implicant*. This terminology stems from the fact that if a given product in the sum has the value 1, this *implies* that the function itself has the value 1. When such a function is reduced to a minimal sum-of-products form (not necessarily unique) the products in the sum are referred to as *prime implicants*. Thus, in each of the expressions for the function F in Figure 2.46, the product terms are prime implicants.

That four minimal sum-of-products expressions for F exist can be seen to be due to the alternative looping schemes that are available on the map of this function. However, note that although each map contains a different set of loops, two loops are common to all maps. These are the loop around the four inner squares and the loop "enclosing" the four corner squares. The entries in these two sets of squares cannot be looped in any other way without producing a non-minimal expression for the function F. The loop around the inner squares produces the product BD and the loop enclosing the corner squares produces the

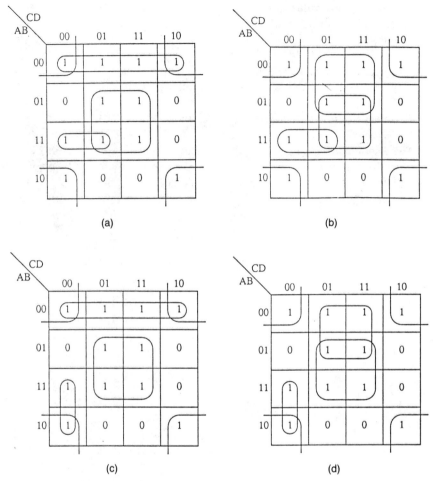

Figure 2.46. Four equivalent minimum forms for the function F:
(a) $F = BD + \overline{A}\overline{B} + AB\overline{C} + \overline{B}\overline{D}$ (b) $F = BD + AB\overline{C} + \overline{B}\overline{D} + \overline{A}D$
(c) $F = BD + \overline{A}\overline{B} + \overline{B}\overline{D} + A\overline{C}\overline{D}$ (d) $F = BD + \overline{B}\overline{D} + \overline{A}D + A\overline{C}\overline{D}$

product $\overline{B}\overline{D}$. These two products appear in all four expressions for F and are
referred to as *essential prime implicants*. This term indicates that no minimal
sum-of-products expression for F can be formed without including the prime
implicants BD and $\overline{B}\overline{D}$.

The Basic Rules for Function Minimization using K-Maps.

The loop-
ing process is used to combine products to form prime implicants. The basic
rules underlying this process are:

1. Every square containing a 1 must be included in at least one loop.

2. The largest possible groups of squares are looped.
3. The minimum possible number of loops is employed in order to avoid duplication.

There is an exception to rule (2) which the reader should be aware of. It is readily accounted for if the following extra rule is observed:

4. Always start with the essential prime implicants (EPI's).

The importance of rule (4) can be seen by considering the map in Figure 2.47(a). In this map one would undoubtedly be tempted to draw a loop around the group of four 1's in the bottom right-hand corner, but this would lead to a non-minimal expression. To see this, note that if we start with the EPI's (rep-

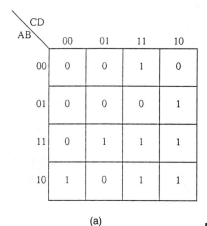

(a)

Figure 2.47. Example illustrating need to commence with EPI's: (a) K-map prior to looping; (b) best choice of looping.

(b)

resented by those groups of squares that can only be looped in one way) we obtain the arrangement shown in Figure 2.47(b). This figure shows that looping the EPI's has resulted in all the 1's in the map being looped. This means that the function represented by the map in Figure 2.47(a) is completely defined by the set of EPI's. But by definition every EPI must appear in a minimal sum-of-products expression and hence the set of EPI's provides the minimal sum-of-products form for the function. Thus looping the four 1's in the bottom right-hand corner of Figure 2.47(a) would simply generate a redundant implicant.

Drawing Up the Map for a Function Which Is Not in Standard Form. So far, all the switching functions for which we have drawn K-maps have been expressed in the standard sum-of-products form. If a K-map representation is required for a function which is not in the standard sum-of-products form, the most straightforward approach is to convert the function to standard form and then draw the map directly.

Example 2.5. Minimize the 4-variable function

$$F = \overline{A}\,\overline{B}\,\overline{C} + BCD + B\overline{C} \qquad (2.17)$$

Solution. This function can be written

$$F = \overline{A}\,\overline{B}\,\overline{C}\,(\overline{D} + D) + (\overline{A} + A)\,BCD + (\overline{A} + A)\,B\overline{C}\,(D + \overline{D}) \qquad (2.18)$$

Multiplying out gives an expression in standard sum-of-products form whose K-map representation is shown in Figure 2.48.

The minimum form for the function is clearly

$$F = \overline{A}\,\overline{C} + B\overline{C} + BD \qquad \qquad \square$$

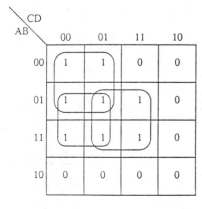

Figure 2.48. Minimization of Equation (2.18).

With a little practice the reader will be able to directly draw the K-map for a switching function such as Equation (2.17) without any need to go through the intermediate step indicated by Equation (2.18).

Don't-Care Conditions.   In some systems, only a subset of all possible values of the input variables is ever used. As an example, consider a system which is required to transmit decimal digits (0 to 9) in binary code. In order to accommodate the ten decimal digits involved, a 4-bit binary code is necessary. In addition, as was explained in Chapter 1, it is common practice to provide such a system with some ability to check for errors in transmission. This can be done by adding an extra bit (a parity bit) to each of the 4-bit coded decimal numbers prior to transmission. In such a system, each decimal number is transmitted as a combination of five binary digits.

Suppose we are required to produce a combinational circuit which will output the required parity bit when any binary coded decimal number is applied to its input terminals. If we employ an even-parity scheme, then the truth table for the required system is as shown in Figure 2.49. Clearly six of the possible combinations of input variables will never arise and we express this in the output column by writing a "d" to indicate that we don't care what would happen to the output of our circuit under these circumstances. The six combinations of input values are referred to as *don't-care conditions*.

Note that the don't-care conditions have arisen because this problem only

Decimal Number	Binary Code				Parity Bit
	x_1	x_2	x_3	x_4	P
0	0	0	0	0	0
1	0	0	0	1	1
2	0	0	1	0	1
3	0	0	1	1	0
4	0	1	0	0	1
5	0	1	0	1	0
6	0	1	1	0	0
7	0	1	1	1	1
8	1	0	0	0	1
9	1	0	0	1	0
	1	0	1	0	d
	1	0	1	1	d
	1	1	0	0	d
	1	1	0	1	d
	1	1	1	0	d
	1	1	1	1	d

Figure 2.49. Truth table for parity bit generator.

specifies required behavior for 10 out of the 16 possible combinations of input variables. In cases such as this, the required switching function is termed an *incompletely specified function*. Don't-care conditions can often be profitably employed in the minimization of incompletely specified functions, although some care is required in their use.

To see this, consider the K-map for the problem in hand (Figure 2.50). The "d" entries in the map can be treated as 0's or 1's as we please; we don't care which because the corresponding input combinations will never occur.

If we set each "d" entry to 0, we would not be able to carry out any simplifications on the map and the switching function would be

$$P = \bar{x}_1\bar{x}_2\bar{x}_3x_4 + \bar{x}_1\bar{x}_2x_3\bar{x}_4 + \bar{x}_1x_2\bar{x}_3\bar{x}_4 + \bar{x}_1x_2x_3x_4 + x_1\bar{x}_2\bar{x}_3\bar{x}_4 \quad (2.19)$$

If we set each "d" entry to 1, considerable simplification appears possible, as indicated in Figure 2.51. However, the function obtained from the map in Figure 2.51 is

$$P = \bar{x}_1\bar{x}_2\bar{x}_3x_4 + \bar{x}_2x_3\bar{x}_4 + x_2\bar{x}_3\bar{x}_4 + x_2x_3x_4 + x_1x_2 + x_1x_3 + x_1\bar{x}_3\bar{x}_4$$

$$(2.20)$$

which requires more gates for a 2-level realization than the function obtained by setting all the d's to 0.

The best solution is usually obtained by setting some d's to 0 and some to 1. This has been done in Figure 2.52 and leads to the function

$$P = \bar{x}_1\bar{x}_2\bar{x}_3x_4 + \bar{x}_2x_3\bar{x}_4 + x_2\bar{x}_3\bar{x}_4 + x_2x_3x_4 + x_1\bar{x}_4 \quad (2.21)$$

This function provides only a slight improvement over that obtained by setting all the d's to 0. However, the example does make the point that care should

x_1x_2 \ x_3x_4	00	01	11	10
00	0	1	0	1
01	1	0	1	0
11	d	d	d	d
10	1	0	d	d

Figure 2.50. K-map for parity bit generator.

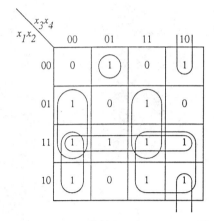

Figure 2.51. K-map with all "d's" set to 1.

be taken in allocating values to the don't-care entries in a K-map. In some of the exercises at the end of this chapter, considerable simplifications can be achieved by appropriately choosing the values of the don't-care entries.

Minimal Product-of-Sums Expressions.   So far we have used the K-map reduction technique to produce switching functions in minimal sum-of-products form. This is achieved by looping the "1" entries in the K-map, these entries indicating the minterms making up the given switching function.

In order to generate minimal product-of-sums expressions, we need to work with the maxterms of a given switching function, and these are given by the "0" entries in a K-map.

In case the reader is in any doubt about this statement, let us consider again the photo-copying machine problem. The truth table for this problem is given in Figure 2.11, the K-map is given in Figure 2.45 (and reproduced here as Figure 2.53) and the switching function in the form of a product of sums was

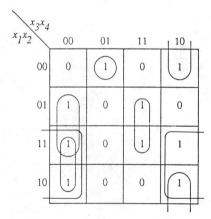

Figure 2.52. K-map with best choice of "d" values.

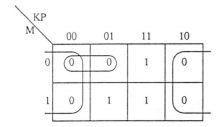

Figure 2.53. Using the K-map for a product-of-sums realization.

given as Equation (2.4) and is reproduced below:

$$F = (M + K + P)(M + K + \overline{P})(M + \overline{K} + P)$$
$$\cdot (\overline{M} + K + P)(\overline{M} + \overline{K} + P) \qquad (2.4)$$

Each sum in this product is a maxterm (see Figure 2.13) and each corresponds to a zero of F in the truth table. Consequently, each corresponds to a zero in the K-map and by looping the zeros as shown, the minimal product-of-sums form is obtained.

The two zeros that have been looped in the top row indicate that the function F is zero when either $M = 0$, $K = 0$ and $P = 0$ or $M = 0$, $K = 0$ and $P = 1$. Thus $F = 0$ when $M = 0$ and $K = 0$ regardless of the value of P. This is simply a manifestation of the fact that

$$(M + K + P)(M + K + \overline{P}) = M + K$$

which follows from the identity $(A + B)(A + \overline{B}) = A$.

The looping of four zeros in the left- and right-hand columns of the map indicates that F is 0 when P is 0, regardless of the values of M and K.

Thus, the minimal product-of-sums expression for Equation (2.4) is

$$F = (M + K)P$$

which agrees with the result obtained earlier.

We are now in a position to see how the K-map method allows us to detect effortlessly that the switching function for the lighting problem in Example 2.2 cannot be reduced. The switching function was stated in Equation (2.8) as the maxterm list below:

$$F = \Pi\, M(0, 3, 5, 6, 9, 10, 12, 15)$$

This function is plotted on the K-map of Figure 2.54 and it is immediately clear that the function cannot be reduced.

Note that the minterm expression for F (Equation (2.6)) is also represented on the map (by the "1" entries) and it is clear that this, too, cannot be reduced.

x_1x_2 \ x_3x_4	00	01	11	10
00	0	1	0	1
01	1	0	1	0
11	0	1	0	1
10	1	0	1	0

Figure 2.54. K-map for Example 2.2.

Multiple-Output Circuits. So far we have only considered the use of K-maps for the simplification of single-output systems. A simple example of a multiple-output system is one which takes binary-coded decimal digits and converts them into some other code, say the Gray code. The truth table for this conversion is shown in Figure 2.55; clearly a combinational circuit with four outputs is necessary to do the job.

One obvious approach to the design of such a combinational circuit is to treat the problem as four separate single-output problems. Thus, we might draw up a separate K-map for each of the four outputs g_1, g_2, g_3, g_4, reduce each output function to a minimal form and then produce a separate realization for each.

This is certainly a feasible approach, but in most cases it leads to circuits requiring more hardware than is strictly necessary. This is because very often hardware can be shared by different output functions; this possibility is totally ignored when each output function is realized separately. Of course, output functions obtained in this way may contain common terms, allowing some hard-

BCD				Gray Code			
x_4	x_3	x_2	x_1	g_4	g_3	g_2	g_1
0	0	0	0	0	0	0	0
0	0	0	1	0	0	0	1
0	0	1	0	0	0	1	1
0	0	1	1	0	0	1	0
0	1	0	0	0	1	1	0
0	1	0	1	0	1	1	1
0	1	1	0	0	1	0	1
0	1	1	1	0	1	0	0
1	0	0	0	1	1	0	0
1	0	0	1	1	1	0	1
				d	d	d	d

Figure 2.55. Truth table for a multiple-output function.

ware sharing, but because the method is not fully directed toward taking advantage of the possibility of hardware sharing, any common terms that occur among the different output functions do so largely due to chance.

We will not pursue this question any further in this chapter, except to point out that it is possible to develop a K-map technique for multiple-output systems which takes fuller account of the possibility of hardware sharing [5]. Furthermore, in Chapter 3, a fully automated technique is described which allows the design of multiple-output systems using minimal hardware and for which a set of program listings is provided.

Five- and Six-Variable K-Maps. For K-maps representing functions with up to 4 variables, the process of function minimization is very easy. If working with a minterm expression, one simply looks for 1's in adjacent squares; if working with a maxterm expression, one looks for 0's in adjacent squares. For functions involving more than 4 variables, it is impossible to order the squares in such a way that all simplifying combinations of 1's (or 0's) appear in neighboring positions in the map.

The most usual way of representing a 5-variable map is as shown in Figure 2.56. It is simply two 4-variable maps placed side-by-side. Each map represents the first four variables in the usual way while the fifth variable is incorporated by being assigned the value 0 for one map and 1 for the other. Within each map, entries can be combined in the usual way. For instance, the two looped entries in the left-hand map represent the combination of the two terms $\overline{A}B\overline{C}D\overline{E}$ and $\overline{A}BCD\overline{E}$ to give $\overline{A}BD\overline{E}$. Terms in identical positions in the two separate maps can also be combined. Thus, the entries shown in the bottom row of each

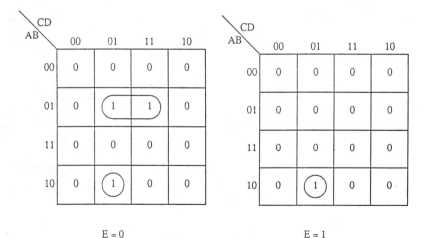

$$E = 0 \qquad\qquad\qquad E = 1$$

Figure 2.56. A 5-variable K-map.

map represent the terms $A\bar{B}\bar{C}D\bar{E}$ and $A\bar{B}\bar{C}DE$ and can be combined to give $A\bar{B}CD$.

A similar technique can be developed to deal with 6-variable problems, but this requires four separate 4-variable maps and "adjacencies" are rather more difficult to recognize. Maps for problems involving 7 or more variables are quite impractical to use.

The difficulties associated with the application of K-maps to problems involving more than 5 or 6 variables need not concern us any further here because other methods for dealing with such problems are available. These methods are usually implemented on a computer and, before we can describe them in detail, some new notation and terminology must be introduced. This is the subject of the next section.

2.3.2 The Cube Notation

As explained at the end of the previous section, we must introduce some new notation and terminology before proceeding to the description of more systematic techniques for the reduction of Boolean expressions.

From now on, we will represent the variables of an n-variable problem by the symbols x_i, $i = 1, 2, \ldots, n$. As an illustration, for a 3-variable problem, the list of possible values of the variables and their associated minterms is shown in Figure 2.57. A convenient way of representing these minterms is obtained by associating each with a vertex of a cube. This is indicated in Figure 2.58 where the vertex labelled 000 corresponds to minterm m_0, the vertex labelled 001 corresponds to minterm m_1, and so forth. (The various m_i's are marked on this diagram, but will be omitted in future diagrams). The 3-variable function

$$F_1 = \Sigma m(0, 3, 6, 7) \tag{2.22}$$

x_1	x_2	x_3	Minterm
0	0	0	$m_0 = \bar{x}_1\bar{x}_2\bar{x}_3$
0	0	1	$m_1 = \bar{x}_1\bar{x}_2x_3$
0	1	0	$m_2 = \bar{x}_1x_2\bar{x}_3$
0	1	1	$m_3 = \bar{x}_1x_2x_3$
1	0	0	$m_4 = x_1\bar{x}_2\bar{x}_3$
1	0	1	$m_5 = x_1\bar{x}_2x_3$
1	1	0	$m_6 = x_1x_2\bar{x}_3$
1	1	1	$m_7 = x_1x_2x_3$

Figure 2.57. The 3-variable minterms.

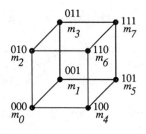

Figure 2.58. Minterms displayed on a cube.

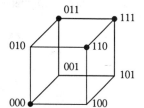

Figure 2.59. Cube representation of $F_1 = \Sigma m(0, 3, 6, 7)$.

can be represented on the cube as shown in Figure 2.59. Thus, the vertices representing the minterms in F are marked on the cube by the heavy black dots.

This form of representation is also easily applied to 2-variable problems, for which a 2-dimensional cube (i.e., a square) is required. For instance, the 2-variable function

$$F_2 = \Sigma m(2, 3) \qquad (2.23)$$

is represented as shown in Figure 2.60.

Single-variable problems can be represented as a 1-dimensional cube (i.e., a straight line). In such problems we have the single variable x_1 and, as an example, the function representing the behavior of an inverter is $F = \overline{x_1}\,(=m_0)$. This function is depicted on the 1-dimensional cube in Figure 2.61.

For n-variable problems with $n > 3$, this form of diagrammatic representa-

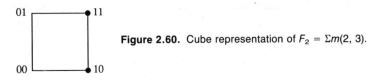

Figure 2.60. Cube representation of $F_2 = \Sigma m(2, 3)$.

Figure 2.61. Cube representation of $F = \overline{x}_1$.

tion becomes rather difficult to draw (an example of the case $n = 4$ is shown in Figure 2.62). This need not concern us here because, in the remainder of this book, we will represent cubes using a notation which can be introduced by considering problems in no more than 3 variables; extension to problems involving a greater number of variables will be seen to occur in a quite obvious and natural fashion.

We will now show how the cube representation of Boolean functions can be used as an aid to function minimization. Our main purpose in so doing is to introduce a number of useful ideas associated with the cube concept and also some new terminology. As a first item of terminology, we point out that in future we will refer to n-dimensional cubes simply as *n-cubes*.

Reduction of Boolean functions by means of the cube representation is carried out in a very similar fashion to that employed in using K-maps. This similarity stems from the manner in which the vertices of the cube are labelled. Note that in each of the cubes depicted in Figures 2.59–2.62, the two vertices belonging to any edge represent minterms that differ in only one variable. As a consequence, we are able to see at a glance that the function represented on the 2-cube in Figure 2.60 can be reduced. The function represented in this figure is $F_2 = x_1\bar{x}_2 + x_1x_2$ which of course simplifies to $F_2 = x_1$. We represent this simplification on the 2-cube by thickening the line joining the two vertices; this is shown in Figure 2.63. The line joining the two vertices is a 1-cube and is

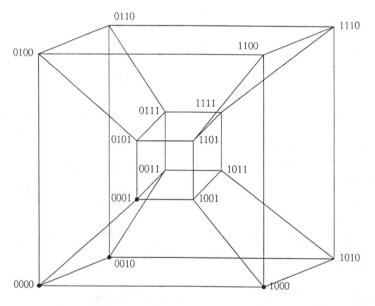

Figure 2.62. A 4-dimensional cube.

Figure 2.63. Simplification of $F_2 = \Sigma m(2, 3)$.

given a symbol to indicate the simplification that it represents. The symbol is $1x$, as marked on Figure 2.63. In this symbol, the 1 indicates that x_1 has the value 1 at both vertices of the 1-cube and the x indicates that x_2 disappears in the simplification. We say that the 1-cube $1x$ *covers* the vertices 10 and 11.

It is general practice in logic design to refer to the vertices of cubes as 0-cubes. Thus, we can also say that the 1-cube $1x$ in Figure 2.63 covers the 0-cubes 10 and 11.

As a second example, consider the function represented on the 3-cube in Figure 2.59. We can see at a glance that the 1-cube $11x$ covers the 0-cubes 111 and 110 and that the 1-cube $x11$ covers the 0-cubes 111 and 011. The resulting simplification is indicated in Figure 2.64.

Consider now the function

$$F_3 = \Sigma m(0, 2, 3, 6, 7)$$

which differs from F_1 (in Figure 2.64) by the addition of the extra minterm, m_2, corresponding to the 0-cube 010. Adding this extra 0-cube will provide a further three 1-cubes, covering the pairs of 0-cubes (010, 011), (010, 110) and (010, 000); this is shown in Figure 2.65. The alert reader may suspect that Figure

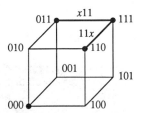

Figure 2.64. Simplification of $F_1 = \Sigma m(0, 3, 6, 7)$.

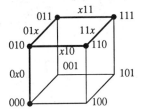

Figure 2.65. Partial simplification of $F_3 = \Sigma m(0, 2, 3, 6, 7)$.

2.65 indicates that a further simplification can be carried out. In the figure, the four vertices making up the top face of the cube are covered by 1-cubes. These four vertices represent the (sub)function

$$F = \bar{x}_1 x_2 \bar{x}_3 + \bar{x}_1 x_2 x_3 + x_1 x_2 x_3 + x_1 x_2 \bar{x}_3$$

$$= \bar{x}_1 x_2 + x_1 x_2$$

$$= x_2$$

Thus, the top face of the cube represents the single term x_2. This fact is represented as shown in Figure 2.66(a). The top face of the cube is a 2-cube and it is given the symbol $x1x$ to indicate that on this face, the variable x_2 has the value 1 while the pair of variables (x_1, x_3) takes on all possible values. In case the reader has any difficulty understanding the meaning of a 2-cube, we have represented the function F_3 on a K-map in Figure 2.66(b). The 2-cube $x1x$ clearly corresponds to the four 1's that are looped together in the map. Note also that the 1-cube $0x0$ corresponds to the other looping (of two 1's). It should also be evident that 0-cubes correspond to individual "1" entries in the K-map.

Thus, the loopings in a K-map correspond to the combining of 0-cubes to form higher-dimensional cubes. In this example, the function F_3 reduces to the

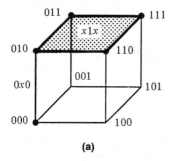

(a)

Figure 2.66. Complete simplification of F_3 = $\Sigma m(0, 2, 3, 6, 7)$: (a) cube representation; (b) K-map representation.

(b)

expression $\bar{x}_1\bar{x}_3 + x_2$. In cube notation, the first term in this reduced form is represented by the 1-cube $0x0$ and the second term by the 2-cube $x1x$ (refer again to Figure 2.66(a)).

In the remainder of this chapter we will develop methods for the reduction of Boolean functions that are based entirely upon the idea of combining 0-cubes to form higher-dimensional cubes. As an aid to this development, we will now introduce a method of representing cubes using arrays.

Array Representation. The concepts associated with n-cubes, discussed above, provide a basis for the development of the more systematic methods for the reduction of Boolean functions that will be discussed in the next section and in Chapter 3. A problem with n-cubes is that they become rather difficult to draw for $n > 3$, but this difficulty can be completely overcome by representing the vertices of n-cubes in an array form.

Consider the function F_3 which is depicted on the 3-cube of Figure 2.65 above. We have

$$F_3 = \Sigma m(0, 2, 3, 6, 7) \qquad (2.24)$$

The 0-cubes corresponding to the minterms in this list are marked with heavy black dots in Figure 2.65. The 0-cubes indicate those sets of values of the input variables for which F_3 takes on the value 1. If we list these 0-cubes in an array, we say that we are forming the *ON-array* for F_3 (the array contains those 0-cubes for which F_3 is "ON"). Thus, the *ON* array for F_3 is

$$ON = \left\{ \begin{matrix} 000 \\ 010 \\ 011 \\ 110 \\ 111 \end{matrix} \right\} \qquad (2.25)$$

At the other vertices of the 3-cube in Figure 2.65 the function F_3 takes on the value "0". Listing the 0-cubes corresponding to these vertices gives the *OFF-array* for F_3:

$$OFF = \left\{ \begin{matrix} 001 \\ 100 \\ 101 \end{matrix} \right\} \qquad (2.26)$$

We are assuming here that there are no don't-care conditions associated with F_3 (i.e., that F_3 is a completely specified function). In this case, the *ON* and *OFF* arrays contain all eight 0-cubes on the 3-cube of Figure 2.65. We can represent this fact mathematically by writing

$$ON \cup OFF = U_3$$

where the symbol $\cup$ represents the operation of *union* employed in set theory; the symbol U_3 represents the set of eight 0-cubes making up the complete 3-cube. (We refer to such ''complete'' cubes as *universal cubes* and represent the universal n-cube by the symbol U_n.)

The *ON* array in Equation (2.25) is simply a list of the 0-cubes corresponding to the minterms listed in Equation (2.24). We already know that the function F_3 can be reduced, and that the reduced form can be represented by the 1-cube and 2-cube indicated on Figure 2.66(a). Thus, in reduced form, the ON array for F_3 can be written

$$ON = \begin{Bmatrix} 0x0 \\ x1x \end{Bmatrix}$$

In the next section, a systematic method for carrying out such array reductions is described; the method is based entirely upon the array representation.

Before leaving this introduction to array representations we must consider the case of incompletely specified functions. In order to represent such functions, we have to introduce a third array which contains the 0-cubes corresponding to don't-care conditions. This array is referred to as the *DC-array*.

An example involving don't-cares was discussed in Section 2.3.1 and the truth table associated with the example is depicted in Figure 2.49. The example concerned the problem of generating parity check bits for binary coded decimals. The *ON*, *OFF*, and *DC* arrays for this problem can be written down directly from Figure 2.49:

$$ON = \begin{Bmatrix} 0001 \\ 0010 \\ 0100 \\ 0111 \\ 1000 \end{Bmatrix} ; \; OFF = \begin{Bmatrix} 0000 \\ 0011 \\ 0101 \\ 0110 \\ 1001 \end{Bmatrix} ; \; DC = \begin{Bmatrix} 1010 \\ 1011 \\ 1100 \\ 1101 \\ 1110 \\ 1111 \end{Bmatrix} \quad (2.27)$$

Note that the *ON*, *OFF* and *DC* arrays contain, in total, all 16 0-cubes making up the universal 4-cube. This can be written mathematically as

$$ON \cup OFF \cup DC = U_4 \quad (2.28)$$

It should be clear to the reader that the array representation extends naturally and easily to n-variable problems, where $n > 4$. For such problems, in the incompletely specified case, Equation (2.28) becomes

$$ON \cup OFF \cup DC = U_n$$

and, in the completely specified case, where the DC array is null (empty), we have

$$ON \cup OFF = U_n$$

2.3.3. The Quine-McCluskey Method

We pointed out at the end of Section 2.3.1 that the K-map method for the reduction of a Boolean function becomes progressively more difficult to implement as the number of variables in the function increases beyond four. The K-map technique relies upon the human ability to recognize patterns and as a consequence is not readily implemented in the form of a computer algorithm. The Quine-McCluskey method [6], [7] is a systematic tabular procedure which can be easily implemented on a computer.

The method commences with the minterm list of the function to be reduced. The minterms are entered in a table in the form of 0-cubes and the 0-cubes are ordered in a way that assists the reduction process (i.e., the process of combining 0-cubes to form cubes of higher dimension).

The procedure is most easily presented in terms of examples; we will commence with the completely-specified case and assume that we wish to reduce the following function

$$F = \Sigma m(1, 5, 7, 8, 9, 10, 11, 14, 15) \tag{2.29}$$

The ON-array for this function is

$$ON = \begin{Bmatrix} 0001 \\ 0101 \\ 0111 \\ 1000 \\ 1001 \\ 1010 \\ 1011 \\ 1110 \\ 1111 \end{Bmatrix}$$

To assist in the explanation of the procedure, we show the K-map of the function in Figure 2.67.

The first step in the procedure is to find all possible 1-cubes. Recall that 1-cubes correspond to the looping of adjacent pairs of 1 entries in a K-map. All possible pairs of loopings in this case are shown in Figure 2.68. Each looped pair in the K-map corresponds to a pair of 0-cubes in the ON array which differ in only one variable. For example, the pairs (0001, 0101) and (0111, 1111) are looped. This fact implies that we can find all possible 1-cubes by searching

x_1x_2 \ x_3x_4	00	01	11	10
00	0	1	0	0
01	0	1	1	0
11	0	0	1	1
10	1	1	1	1

Figure 2.67. K-map for Equation (2.29).

the *ON* array for all pairs of entries that differ in only one variable value. The search procedure is greatly simplified by noting that a pair of 0-cubes that can be combined to form a 1-cube is distinguished by a particular property: the number of 1's in one 0-cube differs from the number of 1s in the other 0-cube by unity. (As examples, consider again the pairs (0001, 0101) and (0111, 1111)). The Quine-McCluskey method takes advantage of this fact by ordering the 0-cubes in the *ON* array according to the number of 1's they contain. This ordering, for our example, has been carried out in the table of Figure 2.69(a). This table allows us to determine very easily those pairs of 0-cubes that can be combined to form 1-cubes. Note that the decimal equivalent of each 0-cube is also listed in the table. As will become clear, these decimal equivalents provide a simple way of keeping track of the 0-cubes covered by higher-order cubes.

The 0-cubes in the top group in the table (i.e., those containing a single 1) cannot possibly combine with those containing 3 or more 1's. Thus, only those 0-cubes in the second group down need be considered for combination with the 0-cubes in the top group. Hence, in carrying out the procedure, each 0-cube in the top group is compared with each 0-cube in the second group down to form

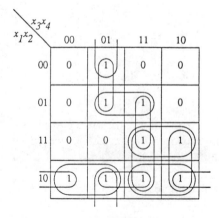

Figure 2.68. All possible pairings of 1's in the K-map.

No. of 1s	0-cubes	Decimal Equivalents
1	0001√	1
	1000√	8
2	0101√	5
	1001√	9
	1010√	10
3	0111√	7
	1011√	11
	1110√	14
4	1111√	15

(a)

1-cubes	Combining 0-cubes
0x01	1, 5
x001	1, 9
100x√	8, 9
10x0√	8, 10
01x1	5, 7
10x1√	9, 11
101x√	10, 11
1x10√	10, 14
x111	7, 15
1x11√	11, 15
111x√	14, 15

(b)

Figure 2.69. Tables generated by Quine-McCluskey method: (a) 0-cubes; (b) 1-cubes; (c) 2-cubes.

2-cubes	Combining 1-cubes.
10xx	8, 9, 10, 11
1x1x	10, 11, 14, 15

(c)

1-cubes. If a pair of 0-cubes is found which differ in only one variable value, the corresponding 1-cube is obtained by placing an x in the position of the variable value which differs in the two 0-cubes. A list of 1-cubes is formed, and alongside each 1-cube is written the decimal equivalent of the two 0-cubes that it covers. This is illustrated in Figure 2.69(b).

Thus the procedure commences by comparing the 0-cube 0001 with the three 0-cubes in the next group down. We see that this 0-cube can be combined with both 0101 and 1001 to form the 1-cubes $0x01$ and $x001$ respectively. (Note that it does not combine with 1010). These 1-cubes are entered in the list of 1-cubes (Figure 2.69(b)) along with the decimal equivalents of the combining 0-cubes. A check mark is placed (in Figure 2.69(a)) against each of the three 0-cubes involved.

Next, the second 0-cube in the top group (1000) is compared with the three 0-cubes in the next group down. This 0-cube can be combined with 1001 and 1010 to form $100x$ and $10x0$ respectively. These 1-cubes are added to the list and a check mark placed against each 0-cube involved (except for 1001, which has already been checked).

We have now found all the 1-cubes that can be formed with the 0-cubes in the top group. A line is drawn under these 1-cubes (listed in Figure 2.69(b)) in order to distinguish them from the 1-cubes that will be formed next.

The next set of 1-cubes is formed by comparing 0-cubes in the group second from the top (in Figure 2.69(a)) with those in the third group from the top. The procedure is exactly the same as for the first two groups and results in four more 1-cubes.

In the general application of the Quine-McCluskey procedure, this process of comparison of pairs of successive groups is continued until the last pair of groups has been accounted for. In this particular example, the next pair of groups is in fact the last pair requiring consideration and leads to three more 1-cubes.

Figure 2.69(b) shows that several 0-cubes are used more than once in forming the 1-cubes and emphasizes the fact that the procedure is aimed at identifying *all* possible 1-cubes. Note that the 1-cubes obtained correspond exactly to the looped pairs in the K-map of Figure 2.68. Note also that all the 0-cubes in Figure 2.69(a) have been checked; this fact implies that *every* 0-cube can be combined with at least one other 0-cube to form a 1-cube and, consequently, that the minimal sum-of-products form of the function F (defined in Equation (2.29)) does not contain any minterms.

The next stage of the procedure consists of a search through Figure 2.69(b) to find pairs of 1-cubes that can be combined to form 2-cubes. The 1-cubes in Figure 2.69(b) have been split into three groups (by the horizontal lines) and, as before, the search is commenced by comparing those cubes in the top group with those in the group second from the top. As before also, the cubes in each group need only be compared with those in the next group below.

In this case, however, cubes need only be compared if they have their x in the same position (the reason for this will be explained below). Thus, the first entry in Figure 2.69(b), viz, $0x01$, need only be compared with the cube $1x10$ and, since these cubes differ in three positions, they cannot be combined. Thus we conclude that the 1-cube $0x01$ cannot be combined with any other 1-cube. The next 1-cube in the list is $x001$ and, since there are no cubes in the second group that have an x in the first position, we conclude that this cube also cannot be combined with any other 1-cube. The third 1-cube in the list, viz, $100x$, differs from the 1-cube $101x$ in only one position, so the two *can* be combined to form the 2-cube $10xx$. These two 1-cubes are checked and the 2-cube is entered in a new list, Figure 2.69(c). The final 1-cube in the first group, $10x0$, is compared to both $01x1$ and $10x1$ (each has an x in the third position). $10x0$ cannot be combined with the first of these, but it does combine with the second, to give the 2-cube $10xx$. However, we have already entered this 2-cube in Figure 2.69(c); we do not repeat this entry, but we do check the two 1-cubes to indicate that they are covered by the 2-cube. This completes the comparison procedure for the first two groups of 1-cubes in Figure 2.69(b); a line is drawn under the 2-cube in Figure 2.69(c) to distinguish it from any further 2-cubes which might be formed from future comparisons.

The 1-cubes in the second group (in Figure 2.69(b)) are now compared with those in the third group in order to determine any other pairs that combine to form 2-cubes. These comparisons provide one more 2-cube (viz $1x1x$) which can be formed by combining the pair $(101x, 111x)$ and also by combining the pair $(1x10, 1x11)$.

For this example the process of combining cubes to form cubes of higher dimension now terminates because the 2-cubes in Figure 2.69(c) cannot be combined (in order to combine they would have to have their x's in the same position and differ in only one variable value). In the general case (with a problem in n variables), one would continue the process in the obvious manner, producing cubes of higher and higher dimension until no further combining of cubes is possible.

For this example then, Figure 2.69 indicates the state of the tables of cubes at the termination of the process of combining cubes.

Before we describe how the contents of the tables in Figure 2.69 are employed in establishing a minimal form for the function F we will briefly indicate, by means of an example, the reason why in comparing 1-cubes (for possible combination to form a 2-cube) it is only necessary to consider those pairs of 1-cubes that have an x in the same position.

Example 2.6. Consider the formation of the 2-cube $10xx$ in Figure 2.69(c). From the figure, we see that this 2-cube was formed from the 0-cubes 8, 9, 10 and 11. In other words, 2-cube $10xx$ was formed by combining the minterms m_8, m_9, m_{10} and m_{11}. Writing out the combination process algebraically, we have

$$m_8 + m_9 + m_{10} + m_{11} = x_1\bar{x}_2\bar{x}_3\bar{x}_4 + x_1\bar{x}_2\bar{x}_3x_4 + x_1\bar{x}_2x_3\bar{x}_4 + x_1\bar{x}_2x_3x_4$$

$$= x_1\bar{x}_2\bar{x}_3(\bar{x}_4 + x_4) + x_1\bar{x}_2x_3(\bar{x}_4 + x_4) \quad (2.30)$$

$$= x_1\bar{x}_2\bar{x}_3 + x_1\bar{x}_2x_3 \quad (2.31)$$

$$= x_1\bar{x}_2(\bar{x}_3 + x_3) \quad (2.32)$$

$$= x_1\bar{x}_2 \quad (2.33)$$

The two products in Equation (2.31) represent the two 1-cubes $100x$ and $101x$. In each of these 1-cubes, the x indicates the fact that the variable x_4 has been eliminated. By definition, for any given problem, a 1-cube represents a product in which one of the variables of the problem is missing (having been eliminated by the combination of two 0-cubes). A moment's thought should convince the reader that it is not possible for two 1-cubes to combine (as in Equation (2.32)) unless they each represent a product with the same missing variable. This, of course, implies that we can combine only 1-cubes which have an x in the same position.

It is for the same reason that 2-cubes (such as the one represented by Equation (2.33)) can only combine if they have their (two) x's in the same positions. In general, k-cubes can combine only if they have all k x's in the same positions. □

Returning to the problem of minimizing the function F, the reader should note that the 2-cubes in Figure 2.69(c) correspond exactly to the two available loopings of four 1's in the K-map representation of the problem in Figure 2.67. These loopings are shown in Figure 2.70. Clearly the 2-cubes only cover a subset of the minterms making up the given function F. However, comparison with Figure 2.68 shows that these 2-cubes *do* cover seven 1-cubes (looping of two 1's) and this is further indicated by the checks placed against seven 1-cubes in Figure 2.69(b). The two 2-cubes will appear in the minimal form for F, but the seven 1-cubes will not. Recalling our earlier terminology, the two 2-cubes are prime implicants and the seven 1-cubes are not. We are now in a position to define more formally the concept of a prime implicant:

Definition
A prime implicant *is any cube of a switching function which is not completely covered by a higher-dimensional cube of that function.*

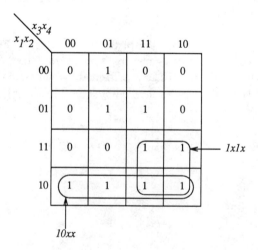

Figure 2.70. 2-cubes represented on a K-map.

The four 1-cubes which are not checked in Figure 2.69(b) are all prime implicants of F. However, a glance at Figure 2.70 indicates that only two of these 1-cubes are actually required to complete the cover of F. In applying the Quine-McCluskey method we would not normally have a K-map to guide us in this way, and so a procedure for completing the cover of a given function directly from the final tables of cubes (as in Figure 2.69) is required.

The procedure that is usually adopted involves the setting up of a table of prime implicants. The table for this example is shown in Figure 2.71(a). Each row of the table corresponds to one of the prime implicants and each column corresponds to one of the minterms (0-cubes) in F.

The prime implicants are arranged in the table according to cube dimension. The highest-order† cubes, which cover the most minterms, are entered first. In this case, there are only two types of cubes (2 cubes and 1-cubes) to be entered, but in the general case, there would be several types, from which the highest-order cubes would be entered first, those of second highest order entered second, and so on. The prime implicants are entered in the column second from the left and represented by the minterms that they cover. Thus, in this example, each prime implicant has been assigned a row in the table in Figure 2.71(a). In the row corresponding to each prime implicant, a check is placed in the column corresponding to each minterm covered by that prime implicant.

The search for a minimum cover‡ now commences with a search through the columns of the table to find any columns that contain only one check. In this example, two such columns can be found, namely columns 8 and 14. A single check in column 8 implies that the 2-cube $10xx$ (which cover minterms 8, 9, 10 and 11) is the only prime implicant covering minterm 8. This being the case, any minimum cover for the given function F must include the 2-cube $10xx$; in other words, $10xx$ is an essential prime implicant. Similarly, the 2-cube $1x1x$ is an essential prime implicant because it is the only prime implicant covering minterm 14. That we will be including these two prime implicants in our cover for F is indicated by placing an asterisk (*) in the left-hand column of the table. The minterms covered by the essential prime implicants are indicated by checks in the bottom row of the table.

At this point in the procedure, the table of prime implicants has the form shown in Figure 2.71(b). Since the essential prime implicants do not provide a complete cover for F, we must now complete the cover by use of some of the remaining prime implicants. We see from the table that there are three possible choices of pairs of 1-cubes that can be used to complete the cover. These are (1, 5, and 5, 7) (1, 5, and 7, 15) and (1, 9 and 5, 7); if any other pair is chosen, it will require a third 1-cube to complete the cover and hence will not provide a minimum cover (this fact is elaborated upon a little later).

Since each of the possible choices of prime implicants for completion of the

---

† The term "highest order cube" has the same meaning as the term "highest-dimension cube".

‡ A minimum cover for a function F is a minimum set of cubes necessary to cover the minterms making up F.

Minterms covered by PI	1	5	7	8	9	10	11	14	15
8, 9, 10, 11				√	√	√	√		
10, 11, 14, 15						√	√	√	√
1, 5	√	√							
1, 9	√				√				
5, 7		√	√						
7, 15			√						√

(a)

	Minterms covered by PI	1	5	7	8	9	10	11	14	15
*	8, 9, 10, 11				√	√	√	√		
*	10, 11, 14, 15						√	√	√	√
	1, 5	√	√							
	1, 9	√				√				
	5,7		√	√						
	7,15			√						√
					√	√	√	√	√	√

(b)

Figure 2.71. Table of prime implicants: (a) initial table; (b) table after identification of EPI's.

cover will have the same hardware cost (because each possible choice consists of a pair of 1-cubes) it is immaterial which pair we choose. Thus, we will arbitrarily choose the pair 1, 5, and 5, 7. These two 1-cubes and the two 2-cubes which were earlier identified as essential prime implicants provide a minimum cover for the given function F.

The final step in the procedure is to write out the minimal cover in sum-of-products form. The products associated with each of the cubes making up the cover are as follows:

$$8, 9, 10, 11 \rightarrow 10xx \rightarrow x_1\bar{x}_2$$

$$10, 11, 14, 15 \rightarrow 1x1x \rightarrow x_1x_3$$

$$1, 5 \rightarrow 0x01 \rightarrow \bar{x}_1\bar{x}_3x_4$$

$$5, 7 \rightarrow 01x1 \rightarrow \bar{x}_1x_2x_4$$

The minimal form obtained for F is therefore ·

$$F = x_1\bar{x}_2 + x_1x_3 + \bar{x}_1\bar{x}_3x_4 + \bar{x}_1x_2x_4$$

Note that this is a minimal sum-of-products form and that it is not unique. There were two other pairs of 1-cubes that we could have employed that would have provided an equivalent solution. It should now be quite clear that if we had employed three 1-cubes to complete the cover for F (instead of two) our expression for F would have consisted of a sum of five products; it would not have been in minimal form and would have required more hardware for its realization than does the expression above.

The Incompletely Specified Case. In the foregoing, the basics of the Quine-McCluskey method were explained in terms of an example. This example involved the reduction of a completely specified function (i.e., one without don't-cares). The Quine-McCluskey method is very easily modified to account for don't-cares. All that is required is that the initial table of 0-cubes be extended to include don't-cares. Then, at the completion of the process, the prime implicant table exposes any simplifications that are offered by the presence of don't-cares. This is best demonstrated by means of an example: we will once gain employ the function whose truth table is given in Figure 2.49 and which, as a minterm list, may be written

$$F = \Sigma m(1, 2, 4, 7, 8) + d(10, 11, 12, 13, 14, 15)$$

The ON array and DC array for this function are given in Equation (2.27) and repeated here for convenience.

$$ON = \left\{ \begin{matrix} 0001 \\ 0010 \\ 0100 \\ 0111 \\ 1000 \end{matrix} \right\} ; DC = \left\{ \begin{matrix} 1010 \\ 1011 \\ 1100 \\ 1101 \\ 1110 \\ 1111 \end{matrix} \right\}$$

As before, we draw up a table of 0-cubes ordered according to the number of 1's they contain. Since we are here concerned with an incompletely specified function, we include the 0-cubes from both the ON array and the DC array, as shown in Figure 2.72(a).

The method proceeds in exactly the same way as for the completely specified case. A list of 1-cubes, obtained by combining 0-cubes, is formed and a list of 2-cubes is obtained by combining 1-cubes, as shown in Figure 2.72. The process of combining cubes terminates at this point and the prime implicant table

No. of 1s	0-cubes	Decimal Equivalents
1	0001 0010√ 0100√ 1000√	1 2 4 8
2	1010√ 1100√	10 12
3	0111√ 1011√ 1101√ 1110√	7 11 13 14
4	1111√	15

(a)

1-cubes	Combining 0-cubes
x010 x100 10x0√ 1x00√	2,10 4,12 8,10 8,12
101x√ 1x10√ 110x√ 11x0√	10,11 10,14 12,13 12,14
x111 1x11√ 11x1√ 111x√	7,15 11,15 13,15 14,15

(b)

Figure 2.72. Quine-McCluskey method in incompletely specified case: (a) 0-cubes; (b) 1-cubes; (c) 2-cubes.

2-cubes	Combining 1-cubes
1xx0	8,10,12,14
1x1x	10,11,14,15
11xx	12,13,14,15

(c)

is now constructed, as shown in Figure 2.73. Note that the columns of this table represent only the minterms of the given function; the don't-cares are *not* included because we are interested in finding a cover for the minterms only.

The prime implicant table shows that two of the 2-cubes obtained do not provide any cover for the minterms in the given function F. Also, each column in the table contains only one check, indicating that each of the prime implicants

	Minterms covered by PI	1	2	4	7	8
*	8,10,12,14 10,11,14,15 12,13,14,15					√
* * *	2,10 4,12 7,15		√	√	√	
*	1	√				
		√	√	√	√	√

Figure 2.73. Table of prime implicants.

that *does* contribute to F is an essential prime implicant. Consequently, the minimal sum-of-products form for F is unique. The products making up this minimal form are given by

$$8, \ 10, \ 12, \ 14 \ \rightarrow \ 1xx0 \ \rightarrow \ x_1\bar{x}_4$$

$$2, \ 10 \ \rightarrow \ x010 \ \rightarrow \ \bar{x}_2x_3\bar{x}_4$$

$$4, \ 12 \ \rightarrow \ x100 \ \rightarrow \ x_2\bar{x}_3\bar{x}_4$$

$$7, \ 15 \ \rightarrow \ x111 \ \rightarrow \ x_2x_3x_4$$

$$1 \ \rightarrow \ 0001 \ \rightarrow \ \bar{x}_1\bar{x}_2\bar{x}_3x_4$$

so that the minimal form for F is given by

$$F = x_1\bar{x}_4 + \bar{x}_2x_3\bar{x}_4 + x_2\bar{x}_3\bar{x}_4 + x_2x_3x_4 + \bar{x}_1\bar{x}_2\bar{x}_3x_4$$

which agrees with the solution (Equation (2.21)) obtained using K-maps.

The reader should note that the Quine-McCluskey algorithm has given the minimal form for F in a straightforward fashion. In attempting to find a solution from the K-map for the problem (in Figure 2.50) the true minimal form (which is obtained only by setting some d's to 0 and others to 1) could easily be missed.

Additional Remarks. Although the Quine-McCluskey method may, in comparison to the K-map method, appear rather laborious in its implementation, the reader should bear in mind that the K-map method cannot be easily applied to problems involving more than 5 variables. The Quine-McCluskey method, on the other hand, is directly applicable to problems in any number of variables. The main drawback to its implementation is that, when applied to problems involving many variables, the lists of cubes involved tend to become inordinately long. The method can, of course, be implemented on a computer, but for problems in many variables, the lengths of the lists of cubes can lead to unacceptable memory requirements.

In the next chapter, techniques are described which build upon the ideas developed in this treatment of the Quine-McCluskey method. These techniques are rather less susceptible to problems associated with memory requirements and are generally more efficient with regard to computational requirements.

In our discussion of the Quine-McCluskey method, we have avoided mention of some the difficulties which can be encountered in attempting to obtain the "absolute" minimum cover for a given function. These difficulties arise when, after identification of essential prime implicants, there is no obvious choice of cubes that will clearly lead to a minimum cover. Questions of this nature are reserved for the next chapter. Also reserved for the next chapter is the problem of obtaining a realization of a multiple-output function which employs the minimum amount of hardware.

REFERENCES

[1] C. E. Shannon, *A symbolic analysis of relay and switching circuits*, Trans. AIEE, Vol. 57, pp. 713–723, 1938.

[2] E. V. Huntington, *Sets of independent postulates for the algebra of logic*, Trans. Amer. Math. Soc., Vol. 5, pp. 288–309, 1904.

[3] E. W. Veitch, *A chart method for simplifying truth functions*, Proc. ACM, May 1952, pp. 127–133.

[4] M. Karnaugh, *The map method for synthesis of combinational logic circuits*, Trans. AIEE, Vol. 72, Part I, pp. 593–598, 1953.

[5] D. L. Dietmeyer, *Logic design of digital systems*, 2nd Edition, Allyn and Bacon, 1978.

[6] W. V. Quine, *The problem of simplifying truth functions*, Amer. Math. Monthly, Vol. 59, pp. 521–531, 1952.

[7] E. J. McCluskey, *Minimization of Boolean functions*, Bell System Tech. J., Vol. 35, pp. 1417–1444, 1956.

Exercises

2.1. Verify the following identities by the truth table method:

(a) $A + \overline{A}B = A + B$

(b) $(A + B)(A + \overline{B}) = A$

(c) $\overline{AB}(A + B) = \overline{A}B + A\overline{B}$

(d) $A + BC = (A + B)(A + C)$

2.2. Use the basic rules for the connectives and rules 1–9 given at the beginning of Section 2.1.2 to verify the following identities:

(a) $(ABC + \overline{C})(\overline{A} + C) = ABC + \overline{A}\,\overline{C}$

(b) $(A + B)(\overline{B} + C) = A\overline{B} + BC$

(c) $AB + \overline{A}B + \overline{B}C = B + C$

(d) $(A + B)(A + C)(\overline{B} + C) = (A + B)(\overline{B} + C)$

2.3. Observe that each of the following functions has been expressed in product-of-sums form and hence that each can be realized as a two-level OR/AND circuit. Use this information to obtain a realization for each function which uses NOR gates only:

(a) $F_1 = (A + C)(\bar{B} + D)(A + \bar{B})(A + E)$

(b) $F_2 = (A + \bar{D})(B + \bar{E})(\bar{A} + C + D)$

(c) $F_3 = (\bar{A} + B + D)(\bar{A} + C + D)(\bar{B} + D)$

2.4. Express each of the functions in Exercise 2.3 in sum-of-products form and hence obtain a realization of each function which uses NAND gates only.

2.5. Use De Morgan's laws to express each of the following in sum-of-products form:

(a) $\overline{\bar{A}(B + \bar{C})}$

(b) $\overline{(A + \overline{BC})(A + \bar{C})}$

(c) $\overline{(A + E)(B + \overline{\overline{AE}})(DC + \overline{DC})}$

2.6. Write a Boolean expression for F in Figure E2.6 in terms of the inputs A, B, C, D, E.

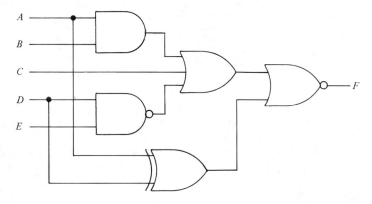

Figure E2.6. Combinational logic circuit.

2.7. Draw a circuit that realizes the Boolean function

$$F = B(A\bar{C} + \bar{A}C) + D(\overline{\overline{EAC} + B})$$

2.8. Suppose the waveforms shown in Figure E2.8 are applied to a 2-input AND gate. Draw the resulting output. Repeat for 2-input OR, NAND, NOR and XOR gates.

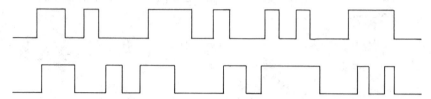

Figure E2.8. Two input waveforms.

2.9. Suppose that a combinational circuit is required which will receive a 4-bit number at its input terminals and give an output of 1 if the number received is binary-coded decimal (i.e., if the decimal equivalent of the number lies in the range 0–9). The circuit is required to output a 0 if the number received is not BCD. Write out a Boolean expression for the logic function that the circuit is required to carry out and simplify it as much as possible. Draw a logic circuit that realizes the simplified expression you obtain.

2.10. A 4-input logic circuit is required which will output a 1 only when three or more of the inputs have the value 1. Write out a Boolean expression for the required logic function and simplify it so as to produce a circuit which requires the minimum number of gates.

2.11. In the solution to Example 2.3, a factored expression for the required switching function was derived. Factoring in this way provides a means of reducing the numbers of inputs necessary on individual gates in a realization. In Example 2.3, the factored expression was

$$F = \bar{x}_1 [\bar{x}_2 (\bar{x}_3 x_4 + x_3 \bar{x}_4) + x_2 (\bar{x}_3 \bar{x}_4 + x_3 x_4)] \\ + x_1 [\bar{x}_2 (\bar{x}_3 \bar{x}_4 + x_3 x_4) + x_2 (\bar{x}_3 x_4 + x_3 \bar{x}_4)]$$

Realize this expression as an AND/OR circuit. Hence obtain a 6-level NAND-gate realization. Compare your NAND realization with the one given in Figure 2.28. Observe that gates with no more than two inputs are required and that the price paid for the reduction in gate input is a three-fold decrease in circuit speed.

2.12. Verify that the circuit in Figure 2.31 can be used as an even-parity-bit generator (for 7-bit codewords) by setting one bit permanently at 0.

2.13. (a) Plot the following function of a K-map:

$$F(A, B, C, D) = \Sigma m(0, 1, 2, 3, 8, 10, 13, 15)$$

(b) Find the minimum sum-of-products and hence produce a NAND-gate realization.

(c) Find the minimum product-of-sums and hence produce a NOR-gate realization.

2.14. **(a)** Plot the following function on a K-map:

$$F(A, B, C, D) = AB\overline{C} + \overline{A}BD + BCD$$

(b) Determine the minimum sum-of-products representation for this function.

2.15. **(a)** Plot the following function on a K-map:

$$F(A, B, C, D) = \Pi M(1, 3, 6, 9, 11, 12, 14)$$

(b) Determine the minimum sum-of-products representation of F.

2.16. **(a)** Plot the following function on a K-map:

$$F(A, B, C, D) = \Sigma m(0, 5, 10, 11, 15) + \Sigma d(6, 7, 8)$$

(b) Identify the essential prime implicants and determine the minimum sum-of-products representation of F.

2.17. Plot the following function on a 5-variable K-map and hence find the minimum sum-of-products form:

$$F(A, B, C, D, E) = \Sigma m(0, 2, 7, 8, 10, 11, 15, 16, 18, 23, 24, 26, 27, 31)$$

2.18. Use the Quine-McCluskey method to verify the result obtained in Exercise 2.17.

2.19. **(a)** Use the Quine-McCluskey method to identify the prime implicants and essential prime implicants of the function

$$F(A, B, C, D) = \Sigma m(0, 4, 7, 9, 12, 14) + \Sigma d(2, 8, 11)$$

(b) Realize the resulting function under the assumption that the only logic gates available are NAND gates with 3 inputs.

2.20. Use the Quine-McCluskey method to simplify the following function:

$$F(A, B, C, D, E) = \Sigma m(1, 4, 7, 14, 17, 20, 21, 22, 23) + \Sigma d(0, 3, 6, 19, 30)$$

2.21. Use the Quine-McCluskey method to simplify the following functions:

(a) $F(A, B, C, D, E, F, G) = \Sigma m(0, 8, 32, 64, 72, 73, 96, 104)$

(b) $F(A, B, C, D, E, F, G) = \Sigma m(1, 17, 33, 51, 65, 81, 83) + \Sigma d(19, 68, 97)$

(c) $F(A, B, C, D, E, F, G, H) = \Sigma m(32, 96, 160, 161, 169, 224, 225, 233, 241)$

2.22. The code shown in Figure E2.22 is to be employed for the transmission of a stream of integers in the range 0–15. Observe that no codeword contains more than two 1's. You are required to design a combinational logic circuit that receives codewords of this type and outputs a 1 whenever a 5-bit word is received which is not one of the codewords in the Figure. Assume that a NAND gate realization is required which uses as few gates as possible.

Integer	Codeword				
	A	B	C	D	E
0	0	0	0	0	0
1	0	0	0	0	1
2	0	0	0	1	0
3	0	0	1	0	0
4	0	1	0	0	0
5	1	0	0	0	0
6	0	0	0	1	1
7	0	0	1	0	1
8	0	1	0	0	1
9	1	0	0	0	1
10	0	0	1	1	0
11	0	1	0	1	0
12	1	0	0	1	0
13	0	1	1	0	0
14	1	0	1	0	0
15	1	1	0	0	0

Figure E2.22. Codeword representation of integers.

2.23. A combinational circuit is required to act as an encoder to convert binary coded decimal numbers into Gray code. The required encoding operation is summarized in Figure E2.23. Determine minimum sum-of-products expressions for the output functions W, X, Y and Z.

2.24. A combinational circuit is required to act as an encoder to convert binary-coded decimal numbers to the 6311 code shown in Figure E2.24. Determine minimum sum-of-products expressions for the output functions W, X, Y and Z.

Binary Coded Decimal				Gray Code			
A	B	C	D	W	X	Y	Z
0	0	0	0	0	0	0	0
0	0	0	1	0	0	0	1
0	0	1	0	0	1	0	1
0	0	1	1	0	1	0	0
0	1	0	0	1	1	0	0
0	1	0	1	1	1	1	0
0	1	1	0	1	0	1	0
0	1	1	1	1	0	1	1
1	0	0	0	1	0	0	1
1	0	0	1	1	0	0	0

Figure E2.23. Conversion of BCD to Gray code.

Binary Coded Decimal				6311 Code			
A	B	C	D	W	X	Y	Z
0	0	0	0	0	0	0	0
0	0	0	1	0	0	0	1
0	0	1	0	0	0	1	1
0	0	1	1	0	1	0	0
0	1	0	0	0	1	0	1
0	1	0	1	0	1	1	1
0	1	1	0	1	0	0	0
0	1	1	1	1	0	0	1
1	0	0	0	1	0	1	1
1	0	0	1	1	1	0	0

Figure E2.24. Conversion of BCD to 6311 code.

3

COMPUTER TECHNIQUES FOR COMBINATIONAL LOGIC DESIGN

3.1 INTRODUCTION

We have so far discussed two basic methods for the minimization of switching functions, viz, the Karnaugh map method and the Quine-McCluskey method. Neither of these methods is really suitable for computer implementation. We have already discussed the limitations of the Karnaugh map method and although the Quine-McCluskey method constitutes a much more systematic procedure which could be readily programmed, it suffers from the disadvantage that the lists of minterms involved in its implementation can become inordinately long, requiring an excessive amount of computer memory.

In this chapter we will develop a systematic approach which avoids the possibility of generating long lists of minterms. In this approach, the prime implicants of a given switching function are generated directly; from these the essential prime implicants are determined and finally a minimal or near-minimal cover is selected. The method will be first explained in terms of single-output functions and then extended to the multiple-output case. Program listings of all the required procedures are given at the end of the chapter.

We commence with an explanation of the "sharp" operation which is widely used in the ensuing discussion.

3.2 THE SHARP OPERATION

Suppose we are dealing with a 3-variable problem and are given the *OFF* array as

$$OFF = \left\{ \begin{matrix} 001 \\ 101 \\ 111 \end{matrix} \right\} = \left\{ \begin{matrix} x01 \\ 1x1 \end{matrix} \right\}$$

Suppose further that the *OFF* array completely specifies the problem (i.e., the *DC* array is null).

In this case, a minimal form for the *ON* array can be obtained by consulting the cube representation in Figure 3.1. In this figure, all vertices except those representing the *OFF* array are marked with heavy black dots. The marked vertices indicate the 0-cubes making up the *ON* array and these may be combined in the manner shown in the figure to give

$$ON = \left\{ \begin{matrix} 01x \\ xx0 \end{matrix} \right\}$$

Essentially what we have done is to remove from the universal cube U_3 ($= xxx$) those cubes that belong to the *OFF* array and combine the remaining 0-cubes so as to represent the *ON*-array in terms of cubes of the highest possible dimension. This is an example of the sharp operation. We say that we have "sharped away" the *OFF* array from U_3 to leave the *ON*-array. In symbols we write

$$ON = U_3 \ \# \ OFF$$

In general, the sharp operation may be defined as follows:

Definition
If A and B are two arrays of cubes, then A # B is made up of all 0-cubes that belong to A and not to B with these 0-cubes combined to form cubes of the highest possible dimension.

We will illustrate this definition by means of two examples, one using the cube representation and the other using Karnaugh maps.

Example 3.1.
(i) The arrays

$$A = \left\{ \begin{matrix} 0xx \\ x00 \end{matrix} \right\} \quad B = \left\{ \begin{matrix} x10 \\ 1x0 \\ 11x \end{matrix} \right\}$$

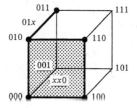

Figure 3.1. Cube representation of ON array.

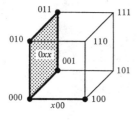

(a) Array A

Figure 3.2. Cubes in Example 3.1(i): (a) array A; (b) array B.

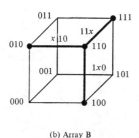

(b) Array B

are depicted on separate cubes in Figure 3.2. To obtain $A \# B$ we must remove from A all 0-cubes which are common to A and B; in other words we must remove from A the intersection of A and B. This intersection is depicted in Figure 3.3. The result of removing $A \cap B$ from A is shown in Figure 3.4(a) and, combining the remaining 0-cubes, we have

$$A \# B = \begin{Bmatrix} 0x1 \\ 00x \end{Bmatrix}$$

Similarly, $B \# A$ is given by removing $A \cap B$ from B and, as shown in Figure 3.4(b) we have

$$B \# A = \{11x\}$$

(ii) The arrays

$$A = \begin{Bmatrix} xx00 \\ x0x0 \\ x111 \end{Bmatrix} \quad B = \begin{Bmatrix} 0x0x \\ 01xx \end{Bmatrix}$$

are depicted on Karnaugh maps in Figure 3.5.

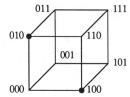

Figure 3.3. Cube representation of $A \cap B$ in Example 3.1(i).

The intersection $A \cap B$ is shown in Figure 3.6. Removing $A \cap B$ from array A and combining gives $A \mathbin{\#} B$ as shown in Figure 3.7(a). Thus

$$A \mathbin{\#} B = \begin{cases} 1x00 \\ 1111 \\ 10x0 \\ x010 \end{cases}$$

Similarly, removal of $A \cap B$ from array B and combining gives

$$B \mathbin{\#} A = \begin{cases} 0x01 \\ 0110 \end{cases}$$

as depicted in Figure 3.7(b). $\square$

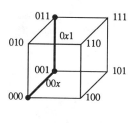

(a) $A \mathbin{\#} B$

Figure 3.4. The sharp operation in Example 3.1(i): (a) $A \mathbin{\#} B$; (b) $B \mathbin{\#} A$.

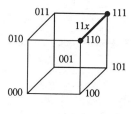

(b) $B \mathbin{\#} A$

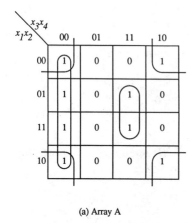

(a) Array A

Figure 3.5. K-map for arrays in Example 3.1(ii): (a) array A; (b) array B.

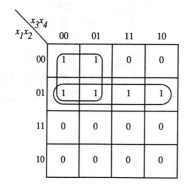

(b) Array B

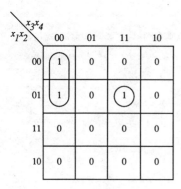

Figure 3.6. K-map representation of A ∩ B in Example 3.1(ii).

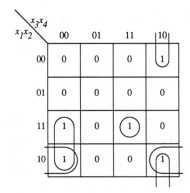

(a) A # B

Figure 3.7. The sharp operation in Example 3.1(ii) (a) A # B (b) B # A.

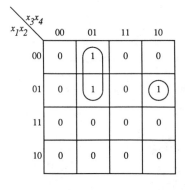

(b) B # A

The second of the above examples brings out the fact that after removal of common 0-cubes a substantial amount of work is often required to combine the remaining cubes. For problems in many variables, evaluation of the sharp operation by hand can be a very tedious exercise. However, this fact need not concern us here because a Pascal procedure which carries out the sharp operation is listed at the end of the chapter.

Before we proceed with the development of an algorithm for the generation of prime implicants, we introduce two further items of terminology that will prove useful in what follows.

Consider the 3-variable switching function

$$F = x_1 \bar{x}_2 \bar{x}_3 + x_1 \bar{x}_3$$

In this function, the term $x_1 \bar{x}_2 \bar{x}_3$ is redundant because $x_1 \bar{x}_3 = x_1 \bar{x}_2 \bar{x}_3 + x_1 x_2 \bar{x}_3$. We say that $x_1 \bar{x}_2 \bar{x}_3$ *subsumes* $x_1 \bar{x}_3$. The function F can therefore be simplified, and we can write $F = x_1\bar{x}_3$. In carrying out this simplification, we say that the term $x_1\bar{x}_2\bar{x}_3$ is *absorbed* by the term $x_1\bar{x}_3$.

3.3 GENERATION OF PRIME IMPLICANTS

3.3.1. Iterative Consensus

We now turn to an approach to the generation of the prime implicants of a switching function which is based upon a concept that we have not yet discussed, namely the *consensus* of implicants. The consensus operation is much simpler to carry out than it is to explain in words; accordingly our explanation of the operation is followed by several illustrative examples. When the reader has studied the examples he or she should have no difficulty in understanding the concept.

Definition
The consensus *of two implicants can be formed only if the implicants contain one and only one variable (say x_i) which is complemented in one implicant and not in the other. In such a case, the consensus is obtained by deleting the variable x_i from each implicant and forming the product of the variables remaining in each implicant. Any repetitions of variables in the resulting product are eliminated.*

Example 3.2

  (i) x_1x_3 is the consensus of x_1x_2 and $\bar{x}_2x_3$
  (ii) $x_1x_3x_4$ is the consensus of $x_1x_2x_3$ and $\bar{x}_2x_3x_4$
  (iii) $x_2\bar{x}_3$ is the consensus of x_1 and $\bar{x}_1x_2\bar{x}_3$

   Note also the special case:
  (iv) x_1 is the consensus of x_1x_2 and $x_1\bar{x}_2$ □

In the above examples we used the subscripted variable notation, which allows the consensus idea to be much more readily appreciated than does the cube notation. We shall employ the subscripted variable notation to explain the *iterative* consensus method also.

The iterative consensus method works by repeatedly forming consensus terms from the terms in the expression defining a given switching function; each consensus term is added to the switching function expression. The expression is reduced to a set of prime implicants by deletion of subsuming terms.

Application of the method to a given switching function takes place in two basic steps:

1. Delete all subsuming terms from the expression and combine the remaining terms into cubes of the highest possible dimension.

2. Check each pair of terms in the remaining expression to see if a consensus exists. All consensus terms found are added to the expression.

After completion of step 2 the procedure returns to step 1 and the whole process is repeated. Further repeats are required until no new consensus terms can be found.

The name *iterative consensus*, by which this particular procedure is usually known, derives from the fact that in general the two steps of the procedure have to be applied several times, implying repeated use of the consensus operation.

Example 3.3. Use the iterative consensus method to generate all prime implicants of the switching function

$$F = \bar{x}_2\bar{x}_3\bar{x}_4 + \bar{x}_1\bar{x}_2x_3 + \bar{x}_1x_2x_3 + x_1\bar{x}_3x_4 + x_1\bar{x}_2x_3\bar{x}_4 + x_1\bar{x}_2\bar{x}_3x_4.$$

Solution

Step 1: $x_1\bar{x}_2\bar{x}_3x_4$ subsumes $x_1\bar{x}_3x_4$ and is deleted. $\bar{x}_1\bar{x}_2x_3$ and $\bar{x}_1x_2x_3$ are combined to form $\bar{x}_1x_3$. The function F now has the form

$$F = \bar{x}_2\bar{x}_3\bar{x}_4 + \bar{x}_1x_3 + x_1\bar{x}_3x_4 + x_1\bar{x}_2x_3\bar{x}_4$$

Step 2: Each pair of remaining terms is now checked for consensus:

$\bar{x}_2\bar{x}_3\bar{x}_4$ and $\bar{x}_1x_3$ have consensus $\bar{x}_1\bar{x}_2\bar{x}_4$

$\bar{x}_2\bar{x}_3\bar{x}_4$ and $x_1\bar{x}_3x_4$ have consensus $x_1\bar{x}_2\bar{x}_3$

$\bar{x}_2\bar{x}_3\bar{x}_4$ and $x_1\bar{x}_2x_3\bar{x}_4$ have consensus $x_1\bar{x}_2\bar{x}_4$

$\bar{x}_1x_3$ and $x_1\bar{x}_3x_4$ have no consensus

$\bar{x}_1x_3$ and $x_1\bar{x}_2x_3\bar{x}_4$ have consensus $\bar{x}_2x_3\bar{x}_4$

$x_1\bar{x}_3x_4$ and $x_1\bar{x}_2x_3\bar{x}_4$ have no consensus

Now add the consensus terms to those remaining in the expression for F at the end of Step 1. This gives

$$F = \bar{x}_2\bar{x}_3\bar{x}_4 + \bar{x}_1x_3 + x_1\bar{x}_3x_4$$
$$+ x_1\bar{x}_2x_3\bar{x}_4 + \bar{x}_1\bar{x}_2\bar{x}_4 + x_1\bar{x}_2\bar{x}_3 + x_1\bar{x}_2\bar{x}_4 + \bar{x}_2x_3\bar{x}_4$$

The two steps are now repeated.

Step 1:

$x_1\bar{x}_2x_3\bar{x}_4$ subsumes $x_1\bar{x}_2\bar{x}_4$ and is deleted

$\bar{x}_2\bar{x}_3\bar{x}_4$ and $\bar{x}_2x_3\bar{x}_4$ are combined to form $\bar{x}_2\bar{x}_4$

$\bar{x}_1\bar{x}_2\bar{x}_4$ subsumes $\bar{x}_2\bar{x}_4$ and is deleted

$x_1\bar{x}_2\bar{x}_4$ subsumes $\bar{x}_2\bar{x}_4$ and is deleted

This gives

$$F = \bar{x}_2\bar{x}_4 + \bar{x}_1x_3 + x_1\bar{x}_3x_4 + x_1\bar{x}_2\bar{x}_3$$

Step 2: Check for consensus among pairs not previously checked:

$\bar{x}_2\bar{x}_4$ and $\bar{x}_1x_3$ have no consensus

$\bar{x}_2\bar{x}_4$ and $x_1\bar{x}_3x_4$ have consensus $x_1\bar{x}_2\bar{x}_3$

$\bar{x}_2\bar{x}_4$ and $x_1\bar{x}_2\bar{x}_3$ have no consensus

$\bar{x}_1x_3$ and $x_1\bar{x}_2\bar{x}_3$ have no consensus

$x_1\bar{x}_3x_4$ and $x_1\bar{x}_2\bar{x}_3$ have no consensus

The consensus term obtained here already exists in the expression for F obtained at the end of Step 1. Thus, this consensus term is redundant and need not be added to F. F therefore remains unchanged:

$$F = \bar{x}_2\bar{x}_4 + \bar{x}_1x_3 + x_1\bar{x}_3x_4 + x_1\bar{x}_2\bar{x}_3 \qquad (3.1)$$

If steps 1 and 2 are applied again, no new consensus terms will be generated, indicating that the four implicants in Equation (3.1) constitute the complete set of prime implicants for the given switching function. □

To see how the consensus operation may be described in terms of cube notation, let us look back at Example 3.2. In terms of 4-dimensional cubes, the the four cases given in this example can be written:

(i) $1x1x$ is the consensus of $11xx$ and $x01x$

(ii) $1x11$ is the consensus of $111x$ and $x011$

(iii) $x10x$ is the consensus of $1xxx$ and $010x$

(iv) $1xxx$ is the consensus of $11xx$ and $10xx$

The manner in which consensus is formed in terms of cube notation is not immediately obvious from these examples, but is, in fact, quite simple, once understood.

Remember that the consensus of two terms can only exist if one and only one variable is complemented in one term and not in the other. If we have two cubes $a_1a_2..a_n$ and $b_1b_2..b_n$, we can check for the existence of consensus by checking each pair of variables a_i and b_i; consensus exists if, for one and only one value of i, a_i is the complement of b_i.

More concisely, a consensus exists between two cubes $a_1a_2..a_n$ and $b_1b_2..b_n$ if and only if for some r, $1 \le r \le n$

$$a_r = \bar{b}_r$$

and

$$a_i \ne \bar{b}_i \quad i \ne r$$

In such a case, if the consensus cube is represented by $c_1c_2..c_n$, we have $c_r = x$ and $c_i = a_i \cap b_i$, $i \ne r$. To see this, consider case (ii) above. We have

$$a_1a_2a_3a_4 = 111x \quad b_1b_2b_3b_4 = x011$$

In this case $a_2 = \bar{b}_2$ and $a_i \ne \bar{b}_i$ for $i = 1, 3, 4$; this indicates the existence of a consensus.

The consensus $c_1c_2c_3c_4$ is formed by writing $c_2 = x$ and $c_i = a_i \cap b_i$ for $i = 1, 3, 4$; thus

$$c_1 = 1 \cap x = 1 \quad c_3 = 1 \cap 1 = 1 \quad c_4 = x \cap 1 = 1 \qquad (3.2)$$

and

$$c_1c_2c_3c_4 = 1x11$$

The reader should evaluate the remaining examples above using this approach.

In future, we will use a simplified notation; the series of intersections in Equation (3.2) is written

$$c_1c_3c_4 = a_1a_3a_4 \cap b_1b_3b_4 = 11x \cap x11 = 111$$

3.3.2 Generalized Consensus

The iterative consensus algorithm is rather inefficient because it requires checks for consensus on every pair of cubes involved. The generalized consensus approach avoids many of these time-consuming checks. The method is based upon the following very simple observation.

A switching function can be represented as an array A of cubes. The first column of A in general contains 0s, 1s and xs. Let us now split array A into three new arrays as follows. Let A_1^0 be an array made up of the cubes in A which have a 0 in column 1. Similarly, let A_1^1 and A_1^x be arrays made up of the cubes in A which have a 1 and x respectively in column 1 of array A. Let one of the cubes in A_1^0 be $0a_2a_3 \cdots a_n$ and let one of the cubes in A_1^1 be $1b_2b_3 \cdots b_n$.

Then, a consensus will only exist between these cubes if $a_i \neq \bar{b}_i$ for $i = 2$, $3, \cdots, n$. This fact forms the basis of the generalized consensus algorithm which will be best explained by means of an example.

Example 3.4. Consider again the example of the previous section, where the switching function may be written in array form as

$$A = \begin{Bmatrix} x000 \\ 001x \\ 011x \\ 1x01 \\ 1010 \end{Bmatrix} \tag{3.3}$$

Solution. Note that we have ignored the cube 1001 which subsumes $1x01$. In applying the generalized consensus method it is not essential to delete subsuming terms until the end of the procedure, but greater efficiency is achieved if they are deleted whenever possible.

Note also that the cubes $001x$ and $011x$ could be combined to form the cube $0x1x$. We could, if we wished, combine the two cubes in this way before implementing the generalized consensus procedure, but this is not necessary; the procedure itself takes care of such combinations.

The first step of the procedure is to split the array A into the three arrays

$$A_1^0 = \begin{Bmatrix} 001x \\ 011x \end{Bmatrix} \quad A_1^1 = \begin{Bmatrix} 1x01 \\ 1010 \end{Bmatrix} \quad A_1^x = \{x000\}$$

We now wish to compare the cubes in A_1^0 and A_1^1 for consensus. In this case, if we take any cube $0a_2a_3a_4$ from A_1^0 and any cube $1b_2b_3b_4$ from A_1^1, consensus will exist if $a_i \neq \bar{b}_i$ for $i = 2, 3, 4$.

Another way of stating this (which simplifies the presentation considerably) is to say that consensus will exist so long as the intersection $a_2a_3a_4 \cap b_2b_3b_4$ is non-empty.

Evaluation of this intersection for each pair of cubes gives

$$01x \cap x01 = \phi$$
$$01x \cap 010 = 010 \tag{3.4}$$
$$11x \cap x01 = \phi$$
$$11x \cap 010 = \phi$$

where ϕ represents the empty set. Equation (3.4) indicates that only one consensus term exists between A_1^0 and A_1^1. This term is the consensus of $001x$ and

1010 and hence is equal to $x010$. We say that the generalized consensus of array A with respect to column 1 is $x010$.

The cube $x010$ is now added to array A to give

$$
A = \left\{
\begin{array}{l}
x000 \\
001x \\
011x \\
1x01 \\
\cancel{1010} \\
x010
\end{array}
\right\}
$$

We note that the cube 1010 subsumes cube $x010$ so that 1010 is deleted.

Having found the consensus of array A with respect to column 1 we should now proceed to find the consensus terms with respect to the remaining columns. However, before proceeding further we would like to point out that Equations (3.4) can be written in the shorthand form

$$
\left\{
\begin{array}{l}
01x \\
11x
\end{array}
\right\} \cap \left\{
\begin{array}{l}
x01 \\
010
\end{array}
\right\} = \{010\} \tag{3.5}
$$

and in the future we will write equations such as Equation (3.4) in the form of Equation (3.5).

Now, to find the consensus terms with respect to column 2, we split array A into the three arrays A_2^0, A_2^1, and A_2^x to obtain

$$
A_2^0 = \left\{
\begin{array}{l}
x000 \\
001x \\
x010
\end{array}
\right\} \quad A_2^1 = \{011x\} \quad A_2^x = \{1x01\}
$$

The splitting of array A in this way is referred to as "splitting about column 2." Consensus with respect to column 2 is obtained by forming the intersection

$$
\left\{
\begin{array}{l}
x00 \\
01x \\
x10
\end{array}
\right\} \cap \{01x\} = \left\{
\begin{array}{l}
01x \\
010
\end{array}
\right\}
$$

so that the generalized consensus of array A with respect to column 2 is

$$
\left\{
\begin{array}{l}
0x1x \\
0x10
\end{array}
\right\}
$$

Note, however, that the cube $0x10$ subsumes the cube $0x1x$ so that we need only add the latter cube to array A. With this addition array A becomes

$$A = \left\{ \begin{array}{c} x000 \\ \cancel{001x} \\ \cancel{011x} \\ 1x01 \\ x010 \\ 0x1x \end{array} \right\}$$

Now note that the cubes $001x$ and $011x$ subsume the cube $0x1x$ so they are deleted. Splitting about column 3 then gives

$$A_3^0 = \left\{ \begin{array}{c} x000 \\ 1x01 \end{array} \right\} \quad A_3^1 = \left\{ \begin{array}{c} x010 \\ 0x1x \end{array} \right\} \quad A_3^x = \phi$$

Consensus with repect to column 3 is then obtained from the intersection

$$\left\{ \begin{array}{c} x00 \\ 1x1 \end{array} \right\} \cap \left\{ \begin{array}{c} x00 \\ 0xx \end{array} \right\} = \left\{ \begin{array}{c} x00 \\ 000 \end{array} \right\}$$

Thus, the generalized consensus of array A with respect to column 3 is

$$\left\{ \begin{array}{c} x0x0 \\ 00x0 \end{array} \right\}$$

The cube $00x0$ subsumes $x0x0$ so that only the latter cube need be added to array A. With this addition we obtain

$$A = \left\{ \begin{array}{c} \cancel{x000} \\ 1x01 \\ \cancel{x010} \\ 0x1x \\ x0x0 \end{array} \right\}$$

The cubes $x000$ and $x010$ subsume the cube $x0x0$ and are deleted. Splitting about column 4 then gives

$$A_4^0 = \{x0x0\} \quad A_4^1 = \{1x01\} \quad A_4^x = \{0x1x\}$$

Consensus with respect to column 4 is then obtained from the intersection

$$\{x0x\} \cap \{1x0\} = \{100\}$$

so that the generalized consensus with respect to column 4 is $100x$. Adding this to array A completes the procedure and gives

$$A = \left\{ \begin{array}{c} 1x01 \\ 0x1x \\ x0x0 \\ 100x \end{array} \right\} \tag{3.6}$$

which agrees with the result obtained using iterative consensus (see Equation 3.1). □

With such a small example it is not possible to demonstrate the advantages of the generalized consensus procedure. However, the reader is invited to try Exercise 3.11 at the end of the chapter, which is designed to illustrate how generalized consensus avoids the large number of time-consuming cube comparisons that are required when applying iterative consensus to a problem of practical size. Another significant point is that the iterative consensus procedure can only establish, by carrying out a further time-consuming set of cube comparisons, that all the prime implicants have been generated; this is in contrast to the generalized consensus procedure which terminates in an obvious manner.

Statement of Procedure. Suppose we are given an array A of n-variable cubes which we wish to reduce to an array of prime implicants using generalized consensus. Then, for $i = 1, 2, \ldots, n$, the following procedure is carried out.

1. Delete all subsuming terms.
2. Split array A into the three arrays A_i^0, A_i^1 and A_i^x.
3. Delete column i from A_i^0 and A_i^1; denote the resulting arrays by B_i^0 and B_i^1 respectively.
4. Form the intersection $C = B_i^0 \cap B_i^1$.
5. Insert an x after entry $i - 1$ in each row of C; denote the resulting array by D.
6. Add the cubes in D to array A. If $i \neq n$, return to step 1. If $i = n$, stop.

3.4 DETERMINATION OF ESSENTIAL PRIME IMPLICANTS

In the previous section, the problem of reducing a given switching function to a set of prime implicants was considered and the generalized consensus method was developed. Reduction of a switching function to a set of prime implicants is, of course, only an intermediate step in the derivation of a minimum cover. In this section, we turn our attention to the determination of essential prime implicants.

We will first give an illustration of the procedure by applying it to the example of the previous section. This will be followed by a more general description.

3.4.1. Illustration of the Procedure

The generalized consensus algorithm was employed in the previous section to reduce a given switching function (represented by array A in Equation (3.3)) to a set of prime implicants (represented by array A in Equation (3.6)). We shall here refer to the array in Equation (3.3) as the *ON* array (it is the *ON* array for the given switching function) and we shall refer to the array of prime implicants as the *PI* array. Thus we write

$$ON = \left\{ \begin{array}{c} x000 \\ 001x \\ 011x \\ 1x01 \\ 1010 \end{array} \right\} \quad PI = \left\{ \begin{array}{c} 1x01 \\ 0x1x \\ x0x0 \\ 100x \end{array} \right\} \tag{3.7}$$

Before proceeding with the example, we introduce one further item of notation: the ith prime implicant in the *PI* array in Equation (3.7) is denoted by p^i.

The procedure for determining the essential prime implicants in this example now commences with the selection of the first prime implicant p^1 ($= 1x01$) from the *PI* array and formation of the intersection $ON \cap p^1$. This intersection is, in general, an array of cubes. We will use the symbol A to represent this array; i.e., we write

$$A = ON \cap p^1$$

This intersection gives us all the cubes in the *ON* array that are covered by p^1. In this case

$$A = \left\{ \begin{array}{c} x000 \\ 001x \\ 011x \\ 1x01 \\ 1010 \end{array} \right\} \cap \{1x01\} = \{1x01\}$$

Thus, p^1 covers two 0-cubes in the *ON* array and will be an essential prime implicant if it provides the only cover for one or both of these 0-cubes. We can test for this by sharping away the remaining prime implicants from A. Thus we form

$$B = A \mathbin{\#} (PI - p^1)$$

where $PI - p^1$ represents an array containing all the entries in PI except p^1.

B consists of all cubes in A that are covered by p^1 and not covered by any other prime implicant. Since A consists of all cubes in the *ON* array that are covered by p^1, we see that B consists of all cubes in the *ON* array for which p^1 provides the only cover. Thus, if B is non-empty, p^1 is an essential prime implicant. In this case

$$B = \{1x01\} \mathbin{\#} \begin{Bmatrix} 0x1x \\ x0x0 \\ 100x \end{Bmatrix} = \{1101\}$$

Thus, p^1 provides the sole cover for the 0-cube 1101 and hence p^1 is an essential prime implicant. p^1 is now placed in an array E which will eventually contain all the essential prime implicants.

The next prime implicant in the *PI*-array will be tested in exactly the same way, but prior to carrying out the test, we carry out two minor bookkeeping operations.

First, we remove from the *ON* array those cubes that are covered by p^1 (in this case we simply remove $1x01$) and second, we delete p^1 from the *PI*-array.

Now we can take the second prime implicant p^2 ($= 0x1x$) and form the intersection

$$A = ON \cap p^2 = \begin{Bmatrix} x000 \\ 001x \\ 011x \\ 1010 \end{Bmatrix} \cap \{0x1x\} = \begin{Bmatrix} 001x \\ 011x \end{Bmatrix}$$

We see that p^2 covers four 0-cubes in the *ON* array and now we must check to see if it provides the only cover for any of these 0-cubes. As before, we sharp away the remaining prime implicants from A; i.e., we form

$$B = A \mathbin{\#} (PI - p^2) = \begin{Bmatrix} 001x \\ 011x \end{Bmatrix} \mathbin{\#} \begin{Bmatrix} x0x0 \\ 100x \end{Bmatrix} = \begin{Bmatrix} 0011 \\ 011x \end{Bmatrix}$$

Thus, p^2 provides the sole cover for three 0-cubes and hence is essential. We add p^2 to array E, remove from the ON array those cubes that are covered by p^2, and finally delete p^2 from the PI array.

Now take the third prime implicant p^3 ($= x0x0$) and form the intersection

$$A = ON \cap p^3 = \left\{ \begin{matrix} x000 \\ 1010 \end{matrix} \right\} \cap \{x0x0\} = \left\{ \begin{matrix} x000 \\ 1010 \end{matrix} \right\}$$

Sharp away the remaining prime implicants from A; i.e., form

$$B = \left\{ \begin{matrix} x000 \\ 1010 \end{matrix} \right\} \# \{100x\} = \left\{ \begin{matrix} 0000 \\ 1010 \end{matrix} \right\}$$

which tells us that p^3 provides the sole cover for two 0-cubes in the ON-array.

Thus, we add p^3 to array E and remove from the ON array those cubes that are covered by p^3. Here the procedure terminates because p^3 covers all the remaining cubes in the ON array. We have therefore found that the ON array in Equation (3.7) is completely covered by the first three prime implicants in the PI array in Equation (3.7). Thus, the final prime implicant, p^4 ($= 100x$) must be nonessential. This can be verified by noting that p^4 is covered by p^1 and p^3.

The non-essential nature of p^4 in this example was determined without subjecting p^4 to the test procedure. The reader is advised to reorder the entries in the PI array in Equation (3.7) so that the prime implicant $100x$ is placed in some other position and then work through the example again in order to observe how the procedure determines that $100x$ is non-essential.

3.4.2. A More General Statement and Explanation of the Procedure

Suppose the PI array contains n prime implicants; let these be numbered p^1, $p^2, \ldots, p^n$. Then, for $i = 1, 2, \cdots, n$, the following procedure is carried out.

Step 1: Form the intersection

$$A = ON \cap p^i \tag{3.8}$$

If this intersection is empty (i.e., if $A = \phi$), this means that p^i does not cover any cubes in the ON array; this occurs if p^i covers only don't-care's and/or cubes covered by prime implicants already selected as essential. Thus, if $A = \phi$ in Equation (3.8), the prime implicant p^i can be discarded; it is simply deleted from the PI array and given no further consideration. If $i < n$, we increase i by unity and return to the beginning of step 1. If $i = n$, the procedure terminates.

If $A \neq \phi$ in Equation (3.8), then A consists of the cubes in the ON array that are covered by p^i. In such a case we carry out step 2.

Step 2: Compute

$$B = A \,\#\, (PI - p^i) \qquad (3.9)$$

where $PI - p^i$ represents an array containing all the entries currently in PI excepting p^i.

In Equation (3.9) we are sharping away from A those cubes that are covered by prime implicants other than p^i in the PI array. Clearly, if the outcome is an empty set (i.e., if $B = \phi$), p^i is not essential because the cubes that it covers in the ON array are also covered by other prime implicants. Nevertheless, we cannot simply discard p^i in this case because, as will be discussed in Section 3.5, it may yet be required to form part of the minimum cover. Thus, in this case, if $i < n$, we simply move on to consideration of the next prime implicant, leaving p^i for possible further consideration as discussed in Section 3.5. That is, if $i < n$, we increase i by unity and return to step 1; if $i = n$, the procedure terminates.

If $B \neq \phi$ in Equation (3.9), then p^i provides the only cover for at least one 0-cube in the ON array; it is added to the array E, which contains the essential prime implicants. Those cubes in the ON array that are covered by p^i are then deleted (this is done by sharping away p^i from the ON array) and p^i itself is deleted from the PI array. Finally, if $i < n$ and the ON array is still non-empty, we increase i by unity and return to Step 1; if $i = n$ or the ON array is empty, the procedure terminates.

A Pascal listing of the procedure (named EPI) is given at the end of the chapter.

Example 3.5. In order to illustrate the above procedure let us find the essential prime implicants of the switching function

$$F = \Sigma m(0, 1, 2, 3, 4, 6, 8, 9, 12) + d(11, 13) \qquad (3.10)$$

Solution. The ON and DC arrays for this switching function can be written

$$ON = \left\{ \begin{array}{c} 00xx \\ 0xx0 \\ xx00 \\ x00x \end{array} \right\} \qquad DC = \left\{ \begin{array}{c} 1011 \\ 1101 \end{array} \right\}$$

and, from Exercise 3.8 at the end of the chapter, we have

$$PI = \begin{cases} 1: \ 00xx \\ 2: \ 0xx0 \\ 3: \ xx00 \\ 4: \ x00x \\ 5: \ x0x1 \\ 6: \ 1x0x \end{cases}$$

The left-hand column of integers has been introduced into the *PI* array so that individual prime implicants may be readily identified as the example proceeds.

In order to determine the essential prime implicants, we compute Equations (3.8) and (3.9) for each of the entries in the *PI* array. Thus, we proceed as follows:

1. Consider p^1.

$$A = ON \cap \{00xx\} = \begin{cases} 00xx \\ 00x0 \\ 0000 \\ 000x \end{cases} = \{00xx\}$$

(the last equality arises because we include the deletion of subsuming terms in our definition of intersection).

$$B = \{00xx\} \ \# \ (PI - p^1) = \phi$$

Thus, p^1 is not essential.

2. Consider p^2.

$$A = ON \cap \{0xx0\} = \begin{cases} 00x0 \\ 0xx0 \\ 0x00 \\ 0000 \end{cases} = \{0xx0\}$$

$$B = \{0xx0\} \ \# \ (PI - p^2) = \{0110\}$$

Thus, p^2 is essential and the various arrays are modified according to the procedure given above, so that we now have

$$PI = \begin{cases} 1: 00xx \\ 3: xx00 \\ 4: x00x \\ 5: x0x1 \\ 6: 1x0x \end{cases} \quad E = \{0xx0\}$$

$$ON = \begin{cases} 00xx \\ 0xx0 \\ xx00 \\ x00x \end{cases} \# \{0xx0\} = \begin{cases} 00x1 \\ 1x00 \\ x001 \\ 100x \end{cases}$$

3. Consider p^3.

$$A = ON \cap \{xx00\} = \begin{cases} 1x00 \\ 1000 \end{cases} = \{1x00\}$$

$$B = \{1x00\} \# (PI - p^3) = \phi$$

Therefore, p^3 is non-essential.

4. Consider p^4.

$$A = ON \cap \{x00x\} = \begin{cases} 0001 \\ 1000 \\ x001 \\ 100x \end{cases} = \begin{cases} x001 \\ 100x \end{cases}$$

$$B = \begin{cases} x001 \\ 100x \end{cases} \# (PI - p^4) = \phi$$

Therefore, p^4 is non-essential.

5. Consider p^5.

$$A = ON \cap \{x0x1\} = \begin{Bmatrix} 00x1 \\ x001 \\ 1001 \end{Bmatrix} = \begin{Bmatrix} 00x1 \\ x001 \end{Bmatrix}$$

$$B = \begin{Bmatrix} 00x1 \\ x001 \end{Bmatrix} \# (PI - p^5) = \phi$$

Therefore, p^5 is non-essential.

6. Consider p^6.

$$A = ON \cap \{1x0x\} = \begin{Bmatrix} 1x00 \\ 1001 \\ 100x \end{Bmatrix} = \begin{Bmatrix} 1x00 \\ 100x \end{Bmatrix}$$

$$B = \begin{Bmatrix} 1x00 \\ 100x \end{Bmatrix} \# (PI - p^6) = \phi$$

Therefore, p^6 is non-essential. Thus, the procedure terminates with

$$PI = \begin{Bmatrix} 1:\ 00xx \\ 3:\ xx00 \\ 4:\ x00x \\ 5:\ x0x1 \\ 6:\ 1x0x \end{Bmatrix} \quad E = \{0xx0\} \quad ON = \begin{Bmatrix} 00x1 \\ 1x00 \\ x001 \\ 100x \end{Bmatrix}$$

The given switching function has only one essential prime implicant. The fact that the ON array is non-empty tells us that array E does not contain a complete cover for the given function. In order to find a complete cover, we must now turn to the non-essential prime implicants which remain in the PI array. Finding a minimum cover using the non-essential prime implicants is the subject of the next section. $\square$

3.5 FINDING A MINIMUM COVER

Implementation of the procedure developed in the previous section results in the transference of all essential prime implicants from the PI array to the array E. In addition, the procedure deletes from the ON array all cubes that are covered by the essential prime implicants. When the procedure terminates, the *ON* array may or may not be empty. If it is empty, we need proceed no further because in such a case array *E* contains a non-redundant cover for the given switching function. If the *ON* array is not empty (and this is the more common case in practice), those cubes that remain in the *ON* array can only be covered by nonessential prime implicants. And, as was demonstrated by the example at the end of the last section, the required non-essential prime implicants are to be found in the *PI* array.

Our problem now is to add to array *E* sufficient of the non-essential prime implicants to provide a complete cover for the switching function. We wish to do this in such a way that the cost of realizing the switching function in digital hardware is kept to a minimum.

We will refer to the 0-cubes of the switching function that remain to be covered as *outstanding vertices*. Note that each outstanding vertex is covered by two or more prime implicants in the *PI* array. (If this were not so, there would still be one or more essential prime implicants in the *PI* array).

There are two basic steps in our procedure for determining a minimum cost cover.

Step 1: Elimination of Non-Contributing Cubes. In the first step we search the *PI* array for cubes that can be immediately identified as *not* contributing to a minimum-cost cover.

For each entry p^i in the *PI* array, we form the intersection $p^i \cap ON$; this intersection gives the outstanding vertices that are covered by p^i and is used to determine whether or not p^i can contribute to a minimum cover. Non-contributing cubes fall into two basic types.

Type 1: Redundant cubes. If $p^i \cap ON$ is empty, then p^i does not cover any outstanding vertices. In such a case p^i is redundant and is deleted from the *PI* array.

Type 2: Less-than cubes. If $p^i \cap ON$ is non-empty, then it is made up of those outstanding vertices that are covered by p^i. Now each outstanding vertex is covered by two or more prime implicants, so there is a possibility that the outstanding vertices covered by p^i are also covered by some other prime implicant p^j. In such a circumstance, we *may* be able to delete p^i from the *PI* array and give it no further consideration.

This situation is probably best illustrated by means of an example.

In Figure 3.8, where each Z represents an outstanding vertex and X represents a don't-care, we see that p^j covers two essential vertices including the one outstanding vertex covered by p^i. Note that $p^j = 0x00$ and $p^i = x100$ which indicates that in a two-level AND/OR realization, both cubes would require a 3-input AND gate for their realization. Thus the hardware cost of each cube is the same. But p^j covers two outstanding vertices, including the one

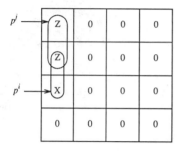

Figure 3.8. An illustration of less-than cubes.

outstanding vertex covered by p^i. Hence, we can conclude that p^i cannot in this case contribute to a minimum-cost cover.

Contrast this situation with the one depicted in Figure 3.9 where $p^j = 0x00$ and $p^i = x10x$. As before, p^j covers two outstanding vertices including the one covered by p^i, but in this case, p^i requires a 2-input AND gate for its realization. In other words, p^i is cheaper to realize than p^j. In a situation such as this (bearing in mind that there are usually many cubes in the *PI* array) we cannot, without further investigation, conclude that p^i will not contribute to a minimum-cost cover.

Hence, at this stage, we proceed as follows. If a cube p^j covers all the outstanding vertices that are covered by another cube p^i and if p^j costs no more to realize than does p^i, we conclude that p^i cannot contribute to a minimum cost cover; thus p^i can be deleted.

More formally, p^i is deleted from the *PI* array if the array contains another cube p^j such that

$$(\text{i})\quad (p^i \cap ON) \,\#\, p^j = \phi$$

and

$$(\text{ii})\quad cost(p^i) \geq cost(p^j)$$

Condition (i) is simply a statement of the fact that p^j covers all the outstand-

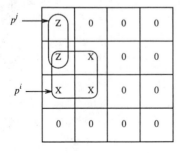

Figure 3.9. A second illustration of less-than cubes.

ing vertices covered by p^i. In condition (ii), cube cost is measured in terms of the number of inputs required for an AND-gate realization.

If two cubes p^i and p^j satisfy the conditions (i) and (ii) above, the cube p^i is said to be *less-than* cube p^j; this is a widely used terminology with *less-than* apparently being an abbreviation of "less desirable than." When a less-than cube is located, it is deleted from the *PI*-array and the procedure moves on to step 2.

Step 2: Determination of Essential Prime Implicants. Recall that prior to step 1, each outstanding vertex is covered by two or more prime implicants. Deletion of a less-than cube from the *PI* array will generally leave one or more outstanding vertices with a single cover. Those prime implicants which provide the sole cover for these outstanding vertices are now identified and added to array E. Since the one important property of these prime implicants is that they provide the sole cover for one or more 0-cubes in the *ON* array, they can now be treated as essential prime implicants and identified using the procedure developed in Section 3.4.

When these essential prime implicants have been located, the procedure returns to step 1 in order to search again for non-contributing cubes. And so the process continues, alternating between searches for essential prime implicants and non-contributing cubes.

The procedure terminates when one of the following conditions is met:

(i) The *ON* array becomes empty (recall that the procedure of Section 3.4 involves deletion of cubes from the *ON* array).

(ii) The *ON* array is non-empty, but no more less-than cubes can be found.

The first condition implies that a minimum-cost cover has been found (and is located in array E).

The second condition implies that a *cyclic* cube structure has been located; special action is required to deal with this situation, and this is the subject of the next section.

We will now illustrate the procedure as developed so far by application to the example that was incompletely solved at the end of the last section.

Example 3.6. The example at the end of the last section terminated with

$$PI = \begin{Bmatrix} 1: 00xx \\ 3: xx00 \\ 4: x00x \\ 5: x0x1 \\ 6: 1x0x \end{Bmatrix} \quad E = \{0xx0\} \quad ON = \begin{Bmatrix} 00x1 \\ 1x00 \\ x001 \\ 100x \end{Bmatrix}$$

Step 1: Elimination of Non-Contributing Cubes. We commence the test for non-contributing cubes by forming the intersection

$$p^1 \cap ON = 00x1$$

The intersection is non-empty and indicates that p^1 covers the outstanding vertices 0001 and 0011. We now proceed to check whether p^1 is less-than any other cube in the *PI* array. Since the cost of each cube in the *PI* array is the same, we simply need to check whether *PI* contains a cube p^j such that $(p^1 \cap ON) \# p^j = \phi$. Thus, we form

$$(p^1 \cap ON) \# p^3 = 00x1 \# xx00 = 00x1$$
$$(p^1 \cap ON) \# p^4 = 00x1 \# x00x = 0011$$
$$(p^1 \cap ON) \# p^5 = 00x1 \# x0x1 = \phi$$

This tells us that p^1 is less-than p^5. In other words, the outstanding vertices covered by p^1 are also covered by p^5. But p^5 costs no more to realize than does p^1 and so p^1 is not required for a minimum cost cover and is deleted from the *PI* array.

We now have

$$PI = \begin{cases} 3: xx00 \\ 4: x00x \\ 5: x0x1 \\ 6: 1x0x \end{cases}$$

Step 2: Determination of Essential Prime Implicants. We now employ the procedure of Section 3.4 to check whether any of the prime implicants in the *PI* array have become essential following the deletion of a less-than cube in Step 1.

p^3:

$$A = ON \cap xx00 = \begin{cases} 1x00 \\ 1000 \end{cases} = 1x00$$
$$B = 1x00 \# (PI - p^3) = \phi$$

Therefore, p^3 is not essential.

p^4:

$$A = ON \cap x00x = \left\{ \begin{array}{c} 0001 \\ 1000 \\ x001 \\ 100x \end{array} \right\} = \left\{ \begin{array}{c} x001 \\ 100x \end{array} \right\}$$

$$B = \left\{ \begin{array}{c} x001 \\ 100x \end{array} \right\} \# (PI - p^4) = \phi$$

Therefore, p^4 is not essential.

p^5:

$$A = ON \cap x0x1 = \left\{ \begin{array}{c} 00x1 \\ x001 \\ 1001 \end{array} \right\} = \left\{ \begin{array}{c} 00x1 \\ x001 \end{array} \right\}$$

$$B = \left\{ \begin{array}{c} 00x1 \\ x001 \end{array} \right\} \# (PI - p^5) = 0011$$

Thus, p^5 is now an essential prime implicant. p^5 is added to the E array, deleted from the PI array and sharped away from the ON array. The various arrays now become

$$PI = \left\{ \begin{array}{c} 3: xx00 \\ 4: x00x \\ 6: 1x0x \end{array} \right\} \quad E = \left\{ \begin{array}{c} 0xx0 \\ x0x1 \end{array} \right\}$$

$$ON = \left\{ \begin{array}{c} 00x1 \\ 1x00 \\ x001 \\ 100x \end{array} \right\} \# x0x1 = \{1x00\}$$

p^6:

$$A = ON \cap 1x0x = 1x00$$

$$B = 1x00 \# (PI - p^6) = \phi$$

Therefore, p^6 is not essential.

This completes Step 2. At the end of Step 2 we have

$$PI = \left\{ \begin{array}{l} 3: xx00 \\ 4: x00x \\ 6: 1x0x \end{array} \right\} \quad E = \left\{ \begin{array}{l} 0xx0 \\ x0x1 \end{array} \right\} \quad ON = \{1x00\}$$

Step 1: Elimination of Non-Contributing Cubes. Again we note that the cost of each cube in the *PI* array is the same. Then we form the intersection $A = ON \cap p^3 = 1x00$. Since $A \neq \phi$, we proceed to the less-than test. Thus, we proceed as before and commence by forming

$$(p^3 \cap ON) \# p^4 = 1x00 \# x00x = 1100$$
$$(p^3 \cap ON) \# p^6 = 1x00 \# 1x0x = \phi$$

Thus p^3 is less than p^6 and is deleted from the *PI* array. We now have

$$PI = \left\{ \begin{array}{l} 4: x00x \\ 6: 1x0x \end{array} \right\}$$

Step 2: Determination of Essential Prime Implicants.

p^4:

$$A = ON \cap x00x = 1000$$
$$B = 1000 \# (PI - p^4) = \phi$$

Therefore, p^4 is not essential.

p^6:

$$A = ON \cap 1x0x = 1x00$$
$$B = 1x00 \# (PI - p^6) = 1100$$

Thus p^6 is essential; p^6 is added to the E array, deleted from the *PI* array and sharped away from the *ON* array. This gives

$$PI = \{x00x\} \quad E = \left\{ \begin{array}{l} 0xx0 \\ x0x1 \\ 1x0x \end{array} \right\} \quad ON = \phi$$

The *ON* array is now empty, so array *E* contains a minimum cost cover for the switching function (given in Equation (3.10)). □

3.6 BREAKING A CYCLIC STRUCTURE

In the previous section a method of finding a minimum cover was described and it was stated that the method would fail to terminate if the given switching function contained a cyclic structure.

An example of a cyclic structure is shown in Figure 3.10. Clearly there are no essential prime implicants in this example. In addition, each prime implicant covers two 0-cubes in the *ON* array, but no prime implicant is completely covered by another. Thus, there are no less-than cubes in this example, so that the procedure of the previous section cannot help us in deciding which of the non-essential prime implicants we should delete first.

In fact, the problem of determining a minimum cost cover for a function containing a cyclic structure can become quite complex (see [1] for example) but fortunately a very simple strategy has been found to give satisfactory results.

To break away from a cyclic structure, we simply search the *PI* array for the least-costly prime implicant. Having found it,† we delete it from the *PI* array, add it to the *E* array, and sharp it away from the *ON* array. As an example, the function depicted in Figure 3.11 has a cyclic structure with prime implicant p^i costing less to realize than any other.

Having broken the cyclic structure we can then call upon the procedure of the previous two sections to set about determining a minimum-cost cover for those cubes that remain in the *ON* array. Although this simple approach is not guaranteed to provide a minimum-cost cover for a given switching function, it very often does so. In other cases, it provides a cover which is very nearly

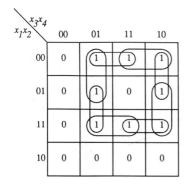

Figure 3.10. An illustration of a cyclic structure.

---

†There may be several prime implicants having the same (minimum) cost, e.g., the function depicted in Figure 3.10; in such a case, any one of them will do.

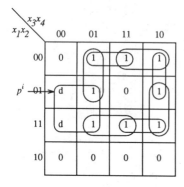

Figure 3.11. An opportunity to break a cyclic structure.

minimum-cost, so we refer to our overall procedure as one of determining a *near-minimum cover*. The complete algorithm is summarized in the next section.

3.7 THE OVERALL PROCEDURE FOR DETERMINING A NEAR-MINIMUM COVER

The complete procedure is obtained by putting together the techniques described in the previous four sections.

The procedure may be stated in the form of an algorithm, called the *extraction algorithm* as follows:

1. Use generalized consensus to compute the prime implicants of $A = ON \cup DC$.
2. Determine the essential prime implicants. Each time an essential prime implicant is found it is added to the E array, deleted from the PI array and sharped away from the ON array. If, at the completion of this step, the ON array is empty, the process terminates.
3. Search the PI array for non-contributing cubes. Delete any redundant cubes found. If a less-than cube is found, delete it from the PI array and go to step 2; if not, go to step 4.
4. Find the least costly cube in the PI array. Add it to the E array, delete it from the PI array and sharp it away from the ON array. Go to step 3.

3.8. MINIMIZATION OF MULTIPLE-OUTPUT SWITCHING FUNCTIONS

In this chapter we have up to now restricted our attention to single-output systems. In actual practice, a designer is far more likely to be required to produce a system with several outputs rather than a single output. In order to deal with a multiple-output system, the designer could take the easy way out and produce several single-output systems, each one of which provides one of the outputs for the required system. By adopting this approach, the designer would be able to employ the techniques described earlier in this chapter. Unfortunately, this "easy" approach often leads to realizations that are far from minimal.

To see why this is so, note that any given output can be represented by a set of prime implicants (for convenience we will refer to this set as a *representation* of the given output). Note also that in a 2-level AND/OR configuration, each prime implicant is realized by means of an AND gate. Now, in multiple output systems, any given prime implicant which appears in the representation of one output might well appear in the representation of another output. In such a case, the AND gate realizing the given prime implicant can be shared by the two outputs. In this section, a systematic technique suitable for programming is developed for the sharing of gates among outputs in order that a minimal or near-minimal realization can be obtained. A Pascal listing of a procedure implementing these techniques is given at the end of this chapter.

To assist in the explanation of the required concepts, we will now give an example of a multiple-output function. Consider a 3-output function defined by the equations

$$z_1 = \Sigma\, m(0, 5, 7, 14, 15) + d(1, 6, 9)$$

$$z_2 = \Sigma\, m(13, 14, 15) + d(1, 6, 9)$$

$$z_3 = \Sigma\, m(0, 1, 5, 7) + d(9, 13, 14)$$

It can be seen quite clearly that some of the implicants and don't-cares are common to two or three outputs. Our objective is to develop a procedure for taking full advantage of this fact.

Karnaugh maps for the three output functions are shown in Figure 3.12.

For single output functions the Karnaugh-map method provides a straightforward method of identifying optimum or near optimum combinations of implicants. Our three output example, however, indicates that for multiple output systems, the required combinations of implicants are far less easily identified using the map method.

The method we shall develop is a generalization of the technique developed in the preceding sections of this chapter.

We begin by drawing up a *function array* for the given three output function. This array is rather like a truth table; it lists the inputs that correspond to *ON* values or *DC* values in the outputs and displays the values of the outputs along-

x_1x_2 \ x_3x_4	00	01	11	10
00	1	d	0	0
01	0	1	1	d
11	0	0	1	1
10	0	d	0	0

z_1

x_1x_2 \ x_3x_4	00	01	11	10
00	0	d	0	0
01	0	0	0	d
11	0	1	1	1
10	0	d	0	0

z_2

Figure 3.12. K-maps for a 3-output function.

x_1x_2 \ x_3x_4	00	01	11	10
00	1	1	0	0
01	0	1	1	0
11	0	d	0	d
10	0	d	0	0

z_3

side. Thus, in this case, the function array is given by

$$
F = \begin{Bmatrix} 0000 \ 101 \\ 0001 \ xx1 \\ 01x1 \ 101 \\ 0110 \ xx0 \\ 1001 \ xxx \\ 1101 \ 01x \\ 1110 \ 11x \\ 1111 \ 110 \end{Bmatrix} \tag{3.11}
$$

The first four columns of F contain the inputs and the remaining three columns show the corresponding values of the outputs z_1, z_2, and z_3 (in that order). Note that in drawing up the function array, advantage has been taken of the fact that minterms 5 and 7 are both required for the same set of outputs ($z_1 = 1$, $z_2 = 0$, $z_3 = 1$) and that the 0-cubes corresponding to these two minterms can be combined to form the 1-cube $01x1$. No other simplification of this kind is possible.

We now wish to develop a procedure similar to the generalized consensus method described earlier for single output systems. The objective of such a procedure in application to our example is to generate all the prime implicants for the three outputs. Before we can do this, there is a minor problem which we must overcome.

Consider the inputs $01x1$ and 1111 that appear in the third and last rows of F. These terms have consensus $x111$, but this consensus applies only to output z_1 because the other two outputs are not allowed to be "on" for *both* of these inputs. Clearly, if we are to use a consensus algorithm, it must be capable of indicating the outputs to which consensus terms apply. We are very fortunate that a simple modification to the function array F ensures this capability.

If we replace all the 1's in the "output" columns of F by x's, the consensus of two complete rows of F gives us the required information. For example, if we consider again the third and last rows of F, the consensus of $01x1 \ x0x$ and $1111 \ xx0$ is $x111 \ x00$; the x in column 5 of the consensus term indicates that the consensus applies to output z_1 only.†

With this simple modification to the function array F, the generalized con-

---

†The fact that the modification to array F is necessary can be seen by noting that without it the terms in the third and last rows of F ($01x1 \ 101$ and $1111 \ 110$) do not have a consensus.

sensus procedure can be applied to multiple-output systems in exactly the same way as it was applied earlier to single-output systems.

3.8.1. Determining Prime Implicants by Generalized Consensus

We will now apply the generalized consensus procedure to find the prime implicants of the three output functions considered earlier in the section. We commence by carrying out the required modification to the function array in Equation (3.11). That is, all the 1's in the last three columns (the ''output'' columns) are changed to x's. This gives

$$
F = \begin{cases}
0000 \ x0x \\
0001 \ xxx \\
01x1 \ x0x \\
0110 \ xx0 \\
1001 \ xxx \\
1101 \ 0xx \\
1110 \ xxx \\
1111 \ xx0
\end{cases}
$$

To find the generalized consensus of array F with respect to column 1, we now split it into three arrays:

$$
F_1^0 = \begin{cases}
0000 \ x0x \\
0001 \ xxx \\
01x1 \ x0x \\
0110 \ xx0
\end{cases}
\qquad
F_1^1 = \begin{cases}
1001 \ xxx \\
1101 \ 0xx \\
1110 \ xxx \\
1111 \ xx0
\end{cases}
\qquad
F_1^x = \phi
$$

Consensus with respect to column 1 is then given by

$$
\begin{cases}
000 \ x0x \\
001 \ xxx \\
1x1 \ x0x \\
110 \ xx0
\end{cases}
\cap
\begin{cases}
001 \ xxx \\
101 \ 0xx \\
110 \ xxx \\
111 \ xx0
\end{cases}
=
\begin{cases}
001 \ xxx \\
101 \ 00x \\
111 \ x00 \\
110 \ xx0
\end{cases}
$$

and the consensus terms are

$$\left\{\begin{matrix} x001\ xxx \\ x101\ 00x \\ x111\ x00 \\ x110\ xx0 \end{matrix}\right\}$$

These consensus terms are now added to the function array F and subsuming terms are deleted, as below. We will call the resulting array S_1.

$$S_1 = \left\{\begin{matrix} 0000\ x0x \\ \cancel{0001\ xxx} \\ 01x1\ x0x \\ \cancel{0110\ xx0} \\ \cancel{1001\ xxx} \\ 1101\ 0xx \\ 1110\ xxx \\ 1111\ xx0 \\ x001\ xxx \\ x101\ 00x \\ x111\ x00 \\ x110\ xx0 \end{matrix}\right\}$$

The reader should be able to see by inspection that consensus with respect to column 2 of S_1 is given by the intersection

$$\left\{\begin{matrix} 000\ x0x \\ x01\ xxx \end{matrix}\right\} \cap \left\{\begin{matrix} 0x1\ x0x \\ 101\ 0xx \\ 110\ xxx \\ 111\ xx0 \\ x01\ 00x \\ x11\ x00 \\ x10\ xx0 \end{matrix}\right\} = \left\{\begin{matrix} 001\ x0x \\ 101\ 0xx \\ x01\ 00x \end{matrix}\right\}$$

We add the resulting consensus terms to array S_1 to obtain S_2:

$$S_2 = \begin{Bmatrix} 0000 & x0x \\ 01x1 & x0x \\ \cancel{1101} & \cancel{0xx} \\ 1110 & xxx \\ 1111 & xx0 \\ x001 & xxx \\ \cancel{x101} & \cancel{00x} \\ x111 & x00 \\ x110 & xx0 \\ 0x01 & x0x \\ 1x01 & 0xx \\ xx01 & 00x \end{Bmatrix}$$

Subsuming terms are deleted as shown.

The procedure is continued in the same way with consensus about columns 3 and 4 resulting in arrays S_3 and S_4.

$$S_3 = \begin{Bmatrix} 0000 & x0x \\ 01x1 & x0x \\ 1111 & xx0 \\ 1110 & xxx \\ x001 & xxx \\ x111 & x00 \\ x110 & xx0 \\ 0x01 & x0x \\ 1x01 & 0xx \\ xx01 & 00x \\ 11x1 & 0x0 \\ 01x1 & x00 \end{Bmatrix} \qquad S_4 = \begin{Bmatrix} \cancel{0000} & \cancel{x0x} \\ 01x1 & x0x \\ \cancel{1111} & \cancel{xx0} \\ 1110 & xxx \\ x001 & xxx \\ \cancel{x111} & \cancel{x00} \\ x110 & xx0 \\ 0x01 & x0x \\ 1x01 & 0xx \\ xx01 & 00x \\ 11x1 & 0x0 \\ 111x & xx0 \\ \cancel{011x} & \cancel{x00} \\ x11x & x00 \\ 000x & x0x \end{Bmatrix}$$

Array S_4 is the required array of prime implicants.

3.8.2. Determining Essential Prime Implicants

The procedure we use for determining essential prime implicants for multiple-output functions is almost identical to the one employed in the single-output case. We can best explain the method by continuing the example from the previous section.

As in Section 3.4, the procedure for determining essential prime implicants requires that we commence with the ON and PI arrays. In our example, the PI array is equal to the array S_4 obtained at the end of the last section and the ON array can be determined directly from the function array F in Equation (3.11); the ON array is obtained by removing the don't-care entries from the last three columns (the output columns) of F. Thus, we have

$$
ON = \left\{ \begin{matrix} 0000 \;\; 101 \\ 0001 \;\; 001 \\ 01x1 \;\; 101 \\ 1101 \;\; 010 \\ 1110 \;\; 110 \\ 1111 \;\; 110 \end{matrix} \right\} \quad
PI = \left\{ \begin{matrix} 1:\; 01x1 \;\; x0x \\ 2:\; 1110 \;\; xxx \\ 3:\; x001 \;\; xxx \\ 4:\; x110 \;\; xx0 \\ 5:\; 0x01 \;\; x0x \\ 6:\; 1x01 \;\; 0xx \\ 7:\; xx01 \;\; 00x \\ 8:\; 11x1 \;\; 0x0 \\ 9:\; 111x \;\; xx0 \\ 10:\; x11x \;\; x00 \\ 11:\; 000x \;\; x0x \end{matrix} \right\} \quad (3.12)
$$

If we attempt to apply the method of Section 3.4 directly to these two arrays, we might encounter some difficulty. To illustrate this difficulty, suppose that prime implicant p^8 is the first to be determined as essential.† The procedure of Section 3.4 would require us to delete from the ON array those cubes that are covered by p^8 before proceeding to consideration of the next prime implicant. In Section 3.4, this deletion operation was carried out by means of the sharp operator. In the example we are considering, we cannot apply the sharp operation directly because the ON array in Equation (3.12) contains not only a list of cubes but also a list of the outputs to which each cube applies. The prime implicant p^8 covers cubes 1101 010 and 1111 010, but the latter cube cannot be deleted by the sharp operation because it has been combined with a similar cube to form 1111 110.

The difficulty is easily overcome by rearranging the ON array so that the

---

†p^8 is not, in fact, essential in the example, but it is the most suitable entry in PI to illustrate the difficulty which could occur.

outputs are treated separately. Thus, in our example we rewrite the *ON* array in the form

$$ON = \begin{cases} 0000\ 100 \\ 01x1\ 100 \\ 111x\ 100 \\ 11x1\ 010 \\ 111x\ 010 \\ 000x\ 001 \\ 01x1\ 001 \end{cases} \tag{3.13}$$

The reader should verify that the *ON* arrays in Equation (3.12) and Equation (3.13) have the same meaning.

With the *ON* array as in Equation (3.13) and the *PI* array as in Equation (3.12) we can now proceed exactly as in Section 3.4 in order to determine the essential prime implicants. We take the prime implicants one at a time from the *PI* array and form the intersection

$$A = ON \cap p^i \tag{3.14}$$

where p^i is the ith prime implicant selected from the *PI* array. If $A = \phi$, the prime implicant p^i does not cover any cubes in the *ON* array and can therefore be discarded; it is deleted from the *PI* array and given no further consideration. If $A \neq \phi$, we compute

$$B = A \,\#\, (PI - p^i) \tag{3.15}$$

If $B = \phi$, we conclude that p^i is not essential and move on to consideration of the next prime implicant. We allow p^i to remain in the *PI* array because it may yet be required to form part of the minimum cover.

If $B \neq \phi$, then p^i provides the sole cover for at least one cube in the *ON* array; it is therefore added to the minimal cover array E and those cubes in the *ON* array that are covered by p^i are deleted by application of the sharp operation in the form $ON \,\#\, p^i$.

Thus, in terms of our example, the procedure runs as follows:

We begin by defining the minimum cover array E to be an empty array. Then, in order to determine the essential prime implicants, we compute Equations (3.14) and (3.15) for each of the entries in the *PI* array.

Considering p^1:

$$A = ON \cap \{01x1\ x0x\} = \begin{Bmatrix} 01x1\ 100 \\ 01x1\ 001 \end{Bmatrix}$$

$$B = A \# (PI - p^1) = \{0111\ 001\}$$

Thus, p^1 provides the sole cover for the 0-cube 0111 required by output z_3. (This 0-cube is also required by output z_1, but for z_1, cover for this 0-cube is provided not only by p^1 but also by p^{10}).

Since p^1 provides the only cover for a 0-cube required by one of the outputs, it is an essential prime implicant and is added to the array E. Thus we have

$$E = \{01x1\ x0x\}$$

We now sharp away p^1 from the ON array (this simply has the effect of deleting $01x1\ 100$ and $01x1\ 001$ from the array in Equation (3.13)) and we also delete p^1 from the PI array.

Considering p^2:

$$A = ON \cap \{1110\ xxx\} = \begin{Bmatrix} 1110\ 100 \\ 1110\ 010 \end{Bmatrix}$$

$$B = A \# (PI - p^2) = \phi$$

which indicates that p^2 is not essential; the arrays ON, PI, and E are left unchanged.

The next eight prime implicants are similarly found to be non-essential. Only the final entry in the PI array turns out to be an essential prime implicant. For p^{11} we find

$$A = ON \cap \{000x\ x0x\} = \begin{Bmatrix} 0000\ 100 \\ 000x\ 001 \end{Bmatrix}$$

$$B = A \# (PI - p^{11}) = \begin{Bmatrix} 0000\ 100 \\ 0000\ 001 \end{Bmatrix}$$

Thus, p^{11} provides the sole cover for the 0-cube 0000 for both output z^1 and output z^3; p^{11} is therefore added to array E, sharped away from the ON array and deleted from the PI array.

At the completion of the procedure for determining essential prime implicants, we therefore have

$$
ON = \left\{ \begin{array}{l} 111x\ 100 \\ 11x1\ 010 \\ 111x\ 010 \end{array} \right\} \quad PI = \left\{ \begin{array}{l} 2:\ 1110\ xxx \\ 3:\ x001\ xxx \\ 4:\ x110\ xx0 \\ 5:\ 0x01\ x0x \\ 6:\ 1x01\ 0xx \\ 7:\ xx01\ 00x \\ 8:\ 11x1\ 0x0 \\ 9:\ 111x\ xx0 \\ 10:\ x11x\ x00 \end{array} \right\} \quad E = \left\{ \begin{array}{l} 01x1\ x0x \\ 000x\ x0x \end{array} \right\}
$$

Our procedure has identified two essential prime implicants and these are contained in array E. The fact that the ON array is non-empty tells us that array E does not contain a complete cover for the given switching function. In order to find a minimum cover for the function, we must now follow a procedure similar to that employed in Section 3.5.

3.8.3. Finding a Minimum Cover

Having determined the essential prime implicants of a given switching function, the next task, if the ON array is non-empty, is to add to array E sufficient of the non-essential prime implicants (which are stored in the PI array) to provide a complete cover. As in the case of single output systems, we wish to do this at minimum cost.

The procedure for multiple-output systems is virtually identical to that employed for single-output systems (detailed in Section 3.5). There are two basic steps to the procedure:

Step 1: Elimination of Non-Contributing Cubes. In this step, we search the PI array for cubes that can be immediately identified as *not* contributing to a minimum-cost cover. As in the single-output case, these cubes fall into two basic types. Each entry in the PI array is checked to see if it belongs to one of these two types by forming the intersection $p^i \cap ON$. This intersection gives the outstanding vertices that are covered by p^i.

If $p^i \cap ON = \phi$, then p^i does not cover any outstanding vertices. Thus p^i is redundant and is deleted from the PI array.

If $p^i \cap ON \neq \phi$, we check to see if p^i is less-than any other cube in the PI array. If p^j is some other cube in the PI array, then p^i is less-than p^j if the following two conditions are satisfied:

$$(i) \quad (p^i \cap ON) \, \# \, p^j = \phi$$

$$(ii) \quad cost \, (p^i) \geq cost \, (p^j)$$

These conditions are exactly the same as those pertaining to the single output case; condition (i) states that p^j covers all the outstanding vertices covered by p^i and in condition (ii) cube cost is again measured in terms of the number of inputs required for an AND gate realization.† The examples given below should clarify the procedure.

Step 2: Determination of Essential Prime Implicants. As in the single-output case, deletion of a less-than cube may leave one or more outstanding vertices with a single cover. Those prime implicants that provide the sole cover for any such vertices can now be identified and added to the minimum cover array E using the procedure for determining essential prime implicants developed in Section 3.8.2.

The procedure then returns to step 1 to search for non-contributing cubes. The process continues, alternating between steps 1 and 2 until either the ON array becomes empty (implying that a minimum cost cover has been found), or no more less-than cubes can be found. In the latter case a cyclic cube structure has been found; the method we use to "break the cycle" is identical to that employed in the single-output case and is very briefly discussed in the next section.

We will now illustrate the procedure described in this section by continuing the example that we have used in the last two sections. At the end of Section 3.8.2, the essential prime implicants had been identified and placed in the E array. The three arrays of interest were as below.

$$
ON = \begin{pmatrix} 111x \ 100 \\ 11x1 \ 010 \\ 111x \ 010 \end{pmatrix}
\quad
PI = \begin{cases} 2: \ 1110 \ xxx \\ 3: \ x001 \ xxx \\ 4: \ x110 \ xx0 \\ 5: \ 0x01 \ x0x \\ 6: \ 1x01 \ 0xx \\ 7: \ xx01 \ 00x \\ 8: \ 11x1 \ 0x0 \\ 9: \ 111x \ xx0 \\ 10: \ x11x \ x00 \end{cases}
\quad
E = \begin{pmatrix} 01x1 \ x0x \\ 000x \ x0x \end{pmatrix}
$$

---

† More complicated cost measures, which take account of both inputs and outputs, can be formulated, but these have not been found to offer any significant advantages over the simple approach adopted here [1].

Step 1: Elimination of Non-Contributing Cubes. We begin by selecting the first prime implicant p^2 ($= 1110\ xxx$) from the *PI* array and forming the intersection

$$p^2 \cap ON = \begin{Bmatrix} 1110\ 100 \\ 1110\ 010 \end{Bmatrix}$$

Thus, p^2 covers two outstanding vertices and we now proceed to check whether p^2 is less-than any other cube in the *PI* array. We commence by forming

$$(p^2 \cap ON)\ \#\ p^3 = \begin{Bmatrix} 1110\ 100 \\ 1110\ 010 \end{Bmatrix} \#\ \{x001\ xxx\} = \begin{Bmatrix} 1110\ 100 \\ 1110\ 010 \end{Bmatrix}$$

This shows that p^3 does not cover any of the outstanding vertices covered by p^2 so that p^2 is *not* less-than p^3. We next form

$$(p^2 \cap ON)\ \#\ p^4 = \begin{Bmatrix} 1110\ 100 \\ 1110\ 010 \end{Bmatrix} \#\ \{x110\ xx0\} = \phi$$

Since p^4 covers the outstanding cubes covered by p^2, we now wish to compare the costs of realization of p^2 and p^4. Recall that we measure cost in terms of the number of inputs required for an AND gate realization; p^2 requires four inputs and p^4 requires only three. Thus p^2 is less-than p^4 and is deleted from the *PI* array. Having deleted a less-than cube, we proceed to step 2.

Step 2: Determination of Essential Prime Implicants. In the search for essential prime implicants, each prime implicant in the *PI* array is subjected to two operations. Consider an arbitrary prime implicant p^i. The first operation carried out on p^i is the formation of its intersection with the *ON* array. This tells us the cubes in the *ON* array that p^i covers; these cubes are stored in an array A. Secondly, all prime implicants except p^i are sharped away from array A; if the outcome is non-empty, this tells us that p^i is essential.

It can happen that the array A is found to be empty, implying that p^i is a redundant cube. This can happen because the search for redundant prime implicants in step 1 terminates as soon as a less-than cube is found. If a redundant prime implicant is located in this step, it is simply deleted from the *PI* array.

We will not give any more details of the implementation of step 2 at this stage† because the algorithm terminates without locating any essential prime implicants. (This implies that each of the outstanding vertices is still covered

---

†A detailed implementation of step 2 is given immediately after the next implementation of step 1.

by two or more prime implicants in the *PI* array.) In this circumstance, we return to step 1.

Before returning to step 1, we point out that in this instance, step 2 identifies one redundant prime implicant, *viz.* p^5. (Note that $p^5 \cap ON = \phi$.) Thus, the next implementation of step 1 is carried out with p^5 deleted from the *PI* array.

Step 1: Determination of Non-Contributing Cubes. We now select the first prime implicant in the *PI* array (viz. $p^3 = x001\ xxx$) and form the intersection

$$p^3 \cap ON = \phi$$

Thus, p^3 is redundant and is deleted from the *PI* array.

Next we choose $p^4 = x110\ xx0$ and form

$$p^4 \cap ON = \left\{ \begin{matrix} 1110\ 100 \\ 1110\ 010 \end{matrix} \right\}$$

We must now proceed to check if p^4 is less-than any other cube in the *PI* array. We form

$$(p^4 \cap ON) \# p^6 = \left\{ \begin{matrix} 1110\ 100 \\ 1110\ 010 \end{matrix} \right\} \# \{1x01\ 0xx\} = \left\{ \begin{matrix} 1110\ 100 \\ 1110\ 010 \end{matrix} \right\}$$

This shows that p^6 does not cover either of the outstanding vertices covered by p^4. In the same way we find that p^7 and p^8 do not cover either of these outstanding vertices. However, when we come to p^9 we find

$$(p^4 \cap ON) \# p^9 = \left\{ \begin{matrix} 1110\ 100 \\ 1110\ 010 \end{matrix} \right\} \# \{111x\ xx0\} = \phi$$

and we see that p^9 *does* cover the outstanding vertices covered by p^4. We also note that the cost of p^9 is equal to the cost of p^4 so that p^4 is declared less-than p^9 and is deleted from the *PI* array. Having deleted a less-than cube we proceed to step 2.

Step 2: Determination of Essential Prime Implicants. Since p^2 through p^5 have already been deleted, we commence with p^6.

$$A = ON \cap \{1x01\ 0xx\} = \{1101\ 010\}$$
$$B = \{1101\ 010\} \# (PI - p^6) = \phi$$

Therefore, p^6 is not essential.

In a similar fashion p^7 and p^8 are found to be non-essential.
Consider now p^9:

$$A = ON \cap \{111x\,xx0\} = \begin{Bmatrix} 111x\ 100 \\ 1111\ 010 \\ 111x\ 010 \end{Bmatrix} = \begin{Bmatrix} 111x\ 100 \\ 111x\ 010 \end{Bmatrix}$$

$$B = \begin{Bmatrix} 111x\ 100 \\ 111x\ 010 \end{Bmatrix} \# (PI - p^9) = \{1110\ 010\}$$

Thus, p^9 is now an essential prime implicant. It is added to the E array, deleted from the PI array and sharped away from the ON array. The three arrays become

$$PI = \begin{Bmatrix} 6:\ 1x01\ \ 0xx \\ 7:\ xx01\ \ 00x \\ 8:\ 11x1\ \ 0x0 \\ 10:\ x11x\ \ x00 \end{Bmatrix} \quad E = \begin{Bmatrix} 01x1\ x0x \\ 000x\ x0x \\ 111x\ xx0 \end{Bmatrix}$$

$$ON = \begin{Bmatrix} 111x\ 100 \\ 11x1\ 010 \\ 111x\ 010 \end{Bmatrix} \# \{111x\,xx0\} = \{1101\ 010\}$$

The algorithm now moves on to a consideration of p^{10}, the last cube in the PI array.

$$A = ON \cap \{x11x\,x00\} = \phi$$

Thus, p^{10} is now redundant and is deleted from the PI array.

Step 1: Elimination of Non-Contributing Cubes. We select the first prime implicant in the PI array (i.e., $p^6 = 1x01\ 0xx$) and form the intersection

$$p^6 \cap ON = \{1101\ 010\}$$

which shows that p^6 covers the one remaining outstanding vertex. Following the algorithm, we now check to see if p^6 is less-than any other cube in the PI array. We form

$$(p^6 \cap ON)\,\#\,p^7 = \{1101\ 010\}$$

indicating that p^6 is *not* less-than p^7. Now form

$$(p^6 \cap ON) \# p^8 = \phi$$

which indicates that p^8 also covers the remaining outstanding vertex. We note that the cost of p^6 is equal to the cost of p^8 so that p^6 is declared less-than p^8 and deleted from the *PI* array. Having deleted a less-than cube we return to step 2.

Step 2: Determination of Essential Prime Implicants. The first entry in the *PI* array is now p^7 and we proceed as follows

$$A = ON \cap \{xx01\ 00x\} = \phi$$

indicating that p^7 is redundant; p^7 is deleted from the *PI* array.
Consider p^8:

$$A = ON \cap \{11x1\ 0x0\} = \{1101\ 010\}$$
$$B = \{1101\ 010\} \# (PI - p^8) = \{1101\ 010\} \# \phi = \{1101\ 010\}$$

so that p^8 is identified as an essential prime implicant. It is added to the *E* array, deleted from the *PI* array and sharped away from the *ON* array.

The *ON* array is now empty so the procedure terminates. A minimum cover for the given switching function is now to be found in array *E*; thus the minimum cover obtained is

$$E = \begin{Bmatrix} 01x1\ x0x \\ 000x\ x0x \\ 111x\ xx0 \\ 11x1\ 0x0 \end{Bmatrix}$$

3.8.4. Breaking Cyclic and Similar Structures

As in the case of the single-output systems, if a cyclic structure is encountered, we break the cycle by extracting the least-costly prime implicant from the *PI* array. If several prime implicants in the array have the same minimum cost, we can choose any one of them for deletion.

In the multiple-output case, a situation reminiscent of the cyclic structure is sometimes encountered due to the manner in which the outputs are stored in the *PI* array. This situation is explained in the example of the next section; the problem is overcome by taking action similar to that employed in breaking a cyclic structure.

3.8.5. A Further Illustrative Example

The example in this section illustrates the application of the techniques described in the previous four sections. We are to find a minimum cover for the switching function defined by the function array

$$F = \begin{cases} 0001\ 001 \\ 0010\ 101 \\ 0011\ 001 \\ 0100\ 110 \\ 0101\ 010 \\ 1010\ 111 \\ 1011\ 111 \\ 1100\ 101 \\ 1101\ 110 \end{cases}$$

Derivation of the *PI* array for this example requires the use of the generalized consensus method described in Section 3.8.1. This derivation appears as Exercise 3.9 at the end of the chapter. The *PI* array is given below, along with the *ON* array which is obtained directly from the given function array *F*.

$$PI = \begin{cases} 1:\ 00x1\ 00x \\ 2:\ 0100\ xx0 \\ 3:\ 101x\ xxx \\ 4:\ 1100\ x0x \\ 5:\ 1101\ xx0 \\ 6:\ x010\ x0x \\ 7:\ x100\ x00 \\ 8:\ x101\ 0x0 \\ 9:\ 110x\ x00 \\ 10:\ x01x\ 00x \\ 11:\ 010x\ 0x0 \end{cases} \quad ON = \begin{cases} 0001\ 001 \\ x01x\ 001 \\ 1100\ 001 \\ 010x\ 010 \\ 101x\ 010 \\ 1101\ 010 \\ 0010\ 100 \\ 0100\ 100 \\ 101x\ 100 \\ 110x\ 100 \end{cases} \qquad (3.16)$$

Note that the outputs in the *ON* array have been separated; the reader should verify that the *ON* and *F* arrays have the same meaning.

The essential prime implicants are now determined using the procedure of Section 3.8.2 and assembled in the minimum-cover array E. The resulting arrays are given by Exercise 3.10 and are

$$
PI = \left\{ \begin{array}{l} 2: 0100\ xx0 \\ 5: 1101\ xx0 \\ 7: x100\ x00 \\ 8: x101\ 0x0 \\ 9: 110x\ x00 \\ 11: 010x\ 0x0 \end{array} \right\} \quad
ON = \left\{ \begin{array}{l} 010x\ 010 \\ 1101\ 010 \\ 0100\ 100 \\ 1101\ 100 \end{array} \right\} \quad
E = \left\{ \begin{array}{l} 1100\ x0x \\ 00x1\ 00x \\ 101x\ xxx \\ x010\ x0x \end{array} \right\}
$$

Having determined the essential prime implicants, we now move on to the application of the procedure detailed in Section 3.8.3 which commences with a search for redundant and less-than cubes. In this particular case, no such cubes are found. In a multiple-output problem, this does not necessarily imply that a cyclic structure has been found. The problem can arise simply because the multiple output columns are included in the PI array. For instance, in this particular case, no cube in the PI array covers any other cube *for all required outputs* (e.g., p^2 in the PI array is covered by p^7 in relation to output z_1 and by p^{11} in relation to output z_2, but no cube in PI provides a complete cover for p^2). Therefore no less-than cubes can be found in this case. This extra little difficulty is a price we have to pay for wanting a true multiple-output solution rather than a collection of single-output solutions.

When this situation arises, we proceed in exactly the same way as when a cyclic structure is encountered; we simply choose the least costly cube in the PI array and transfer it to the minimum-cover array E.

Examination of the PI array in our example shows that four of the cubes, p^7, p^8, p^9 and p^{11}, are candidates for transference to array E (each requires a 3-input AND gate for realization). We could choose any one of these arbitrarily, but our Pascal procedure *momin* has been programmed to select the last cube found to have minimum cost. We will follow this rule here; thus we select the cube $p^{11} = 010x\ 0x0$ and add it to the E array. p^{11} is deleted from the PI array and sharped away from the ON array. The three arrays now have the form

$$
PI = \left\{ \begin{array}{l} 2: 0100\ xx0 \\ 5: 1101\ xx0 \\ 7: x100\ x00 \\ 8: x101\ 0x0 \\ 9: 110x\ x00 \end{array} \right\} \quad
ON = \left\{ \begin{array}{l} 1101\ 010 \\ 0100\ 100 \\ 1101\ 100 \end{array} \right\} \quad
E = \left\{ \begin{array}{l} 1100\ x0x \\ 00x1\ 00x \\ 101x\ xxx \\ x010\ x0x \\ 010x\ 0x0 \end{array} \right\}
$$

We are now once again in a position to apply the procedure of Section 3.8.3 and search the PI array for non-contributing cubes. This procedure identifies p^2 = 0100 xx0 to be less than p^7 = x100 x00, because both p^2 and p^7 cover one and the same outstanding vertex (0100 100) and p^7 costs less than p^2.

Having deleted the less-than cube p^2 from the PI array, we recommence the search for essential prime implicants. On this occasion just one cube, p^7 = x100 x00, is found to be essential; p^7 is added to the array E, deleted from the PI array and sharped away from the ON array. This gives

$$PI = \begin{Bmatrix} 5: 1101\ xx0 \\ 8: x101\ 0x0 \\ 9: 110x\ x00 \end{Bmatrix} \quad ON = \begin{Bmatrix} 1101\ 010 \\ 1101\ 100 \end{Bmatrix} \quad E = \begin{Bmatrix} 1100\ x0x \\ 00x1\ 00x \\ 101x\ xxx \\ x010\ x0x \\ 010x\ 0x0 \\ x100\ x00 \end{Bmatrix} \quad (3.17)$$

At this point, we again search the PI array for less-than cubes. On this occasion, no such cubes can be found. The reason is basically the same as that which led to a similar situation earlier in this example, but in this case it is rather easier to see: p^5 covers both outstanding vertices, but is more expensive to realize than either p^8 or p^9, each of which covers only one outstanding vertex.

As before, our procedure chooses the last of the minimum-cost cubes in the PI array (in this case p^9 = 110x x00) and places it in the E array; p^9 is deleted from the PI array and sharped away from the ON array. The various arrays are now as below:

$$PI = \begin{Bmatrix} 5: 1101\ xx0 \\ 8: x101\ 0x0 \end{Bmatrix} \quad ON = \{1101\ 010\} \quad E = \begin{Bmatrix} 1100\ x0x \\ 00x1\ 00x \\ 101x\ xxx \\ x010\ x0x \\ 010x\ 0x0 \\ x100\ x00 \\ 110x\ x00 \end{Bmatrix}$$

We now search the PI array for less-than cubes; p^5 is found to be less than

p^8, and so p^5 is deleted from the *PI* array. This leaves p^8 as the sole cover for the remaining outstanding cube 1101 010; p^8 is therefore added to the E array to give the final solution:

$$
E = \left\{
\begin{array}{l}
1100\ \ x0x \\
00x1\ \ 00x \\
101x\ \ xxx \\
x010\ \ x0x \\
010x\ \ 0x0 \\
x100\ \ x00 \\
110x\ \ x00 \\
x101\ \ 0x0
\end{array}
\right\}
\qquad (3.18)
$$

This example has brought out the fact that our procedure does not necessarily lead to the absolute minimum cover. If we look back at Equations (3.17), we can see that the two outstanding cubes in the *ON* array are both covered by the prime implicant $p^5 = 1101\ xx0$. Our procedure fails to recognize this and chooses to cover the outstanding cubes with p^8 and p^9 thereby providing a solution requiring one more AND gate than is strictly necessary. This has occurred because our procedure employs an extremely simple rule for selecting a prime implicant when cyclic or similar structures are encountered. More complex rules and procedures are available [1] that guarantee a minimum or near-minimum cover, but in this text we prefer the simpler rule which, in any case, always leads to a solution close to the minimum.

3.8.6. Connection Minimization

The purposes of this section are twofold. First, we point out that the procedure we have developed for multiple-output systems frequently leads to realizations in which some of the connections between gates are redundant. Second, we develop a simple procedure for locating and eliminating redundant connections. Let us commence by examining the solution to the example in the previous section.

The array E in Equation (3.18) gives us a realization of the *ON* array in Equation (3.16). For convenience, the two arrays (with the entries in E reordered) are displayed here.

$$E = \left\{ \begin{array}{l} ABCD \\ x\,100 \;\; x\,00 \\ 110x \;\; x\,00 \\ 101x \;\; xxx \\ 010x \;\; 0x0 \\ x\,101 \;\; 0x0 \\ 1100 \;\; x\,0x \\ x\,010 \;\; x\,0x \\ 00x\,1 \;\; 00x \end{array} \right\} \quad ON = \left\{ \begin{array}{l} ABCD \\ 0001\;\; 001 \\ x\,01x\;\; 001 \\ 1100\;\; 001 \\ 010x\;\; 010 \\ 101x\;\; 010 \\ 1101\;\; 010 \\ 0010\;\; 100 \\ 0100\;\; 100 \\ 101x\;\; 100 \\ 110x\;\; 100 \end{array} \right\} \qquad (3.19)$$

To obtain an AND/OR realization from E, we note that the x's in the last three columns of E indicate the outputs to which each cube applies. In Equation (3.19) we have labelled the four inputs A, B, C, and D; the AND/OR realization implied by array E is shown in Figure 3.13.

In order to simplify the following discussion we will refer to the OR gate whose output is z_j as "the OR gate of z_j". We will refer to the AND gates in a similar fashion; thus the AND gate whose input is $B\overline{C}\overline{D}$ will be referred to as "the AND gate of $B\overline{C}\overline{D}$".

In Figure 3.13, the OR gate of z_1 is connected to 5 AND gates; a close examination indicates that one of these connections is unnecessary. The connection between the AND gate of $A\overline{B}C\overline{D}$ and the OR gate of z_1 is made so that output z_1 takes on the value "1" whenever the input 1100 occurs. However, the AND gate of $B\overline{C}\overline{D}$ ensures that $z_1 = 1$ whenever the input $x\,100$ occurs (i.e., when either 0100 *or* 1100 occurs). Thus, we can delete the connection between the AND gate of $A\overline{B}C\overline{D}$ and the OR gate of z_1 and still maintain the required input/output behaviour.

Having demonstrated that our procedure may lead to redundant connections, we now wish to develop a systematic procedure for locating such redundancies.

Let E_i be the array of inputs (taken from the minimum cover array E) for which the output z_i takes on the value 1. Thus, for the array E in Equation (3.19) we have

$$E_1 = \left\{ \begin{array}{l} x\,100 \\ 110x \\ 101x \\ 1100 \\ x\,010 \end{array} \right\} \quad E_2 = \left\{ \begin{array}{l} 101x \\ 010x \\ x\,101 \end{array} \right\} \quad E_3 = \left\{ \begin{array}{l} 101x \\ 1100 \\ x\,010 \\ 00x\,1 \end{array} \right\} \qquad (3.20)$$

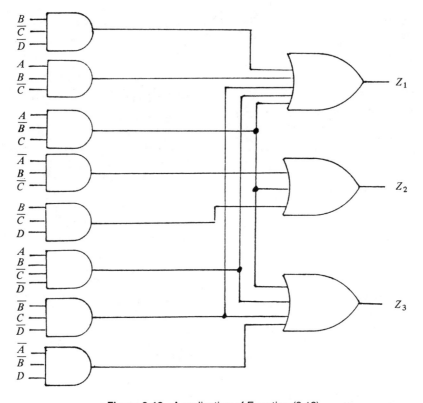

Figure 3.13. A realization of Equation (3.12).

Similarly, let ON_i be the array of inputs (taken from the ON array) for which output z_i is required to taken on the value 1. For the ON array in Equation (3.19) we have

$$ON_1 = \begin{cases} 0010 \\ 0100 \\ 101x \\ 110x \end{cases} \quad ON_2 = \begin{cases} 010x \\ 101x \\ 1101 \end{cases} \quad ON_3 = \begin{cases} 0001 \\ x01x \\ 1100 \end{cases} \quad (3.21)$$

Now, noting that array E provides a complete cover for the ON array, we see that each E_i must completely cover each ON_i. A redundant connection occurs when an entry in one of the E_i does not provide a unique cover for any 0-cube in ON_i (i.e., the cubes in ON_i which are covered by such an entry are also covered by other entries in E_i). Our procedure for detecting such entries is as below.

First of all, let the jth entry in E_i be written e^j_i. Then, for each j we form the intersection

$$e^j_i \cap ON_i$$

This intersection gives us those cubes in ON_i which are covered by e^j_i. If we additionally apply the sharp operation

$$(e^j_i \cap ON_i) \# (E_i - e^j_i) \qquad \qquad (3.22)$$

we will be left with those cubes in ON_i which are uniquely covered by e^j_i. If the outcome of Equation (3.22) is empty, then e^j_i does not provide a unique cover for any cube in ON_i and can be deleted from E_i. Such a deletion is equivalent to the removal of a connection in the realization of the minimum cover array E. As a simple example, we already know that entry 1100 in array E_1 of Equation (3.20) is unnecessary. We can check this by using the arrays in Equation (3.20) and Equation (3.21) to form

$$e^4_1 \cap ON_1 = 1100 \cap ON_1 = 1100$$

$$(e^4_1 \cap ON_1) \# (E_1 - e^4_1) = 1100 \# \begin{Bmatrix} x\,100 \\ 110x \\ 101x \\ x010 \end{Bmatrix} = \phi$$

indicating that $e^4_1 = 1100$ is, indeed, unnecessary.

In Figure 3.13, e^4_1 corresponds to the redundant connection between the AND gate of $\overline{ABCD}$ and the OR gate of z_1. Application of the above procedure to all the other entries in the arrays of Equation (3.20) and Equation (3.21) fails to reveal any further redundant connections.

The procedure of this section constitutes the final act in the determination of a multiple-output combinational logic design. It is listed at the end of this chapter as procedure *conmin*.

REFERENCES

[1] D. L. Dietmeyer, *Logic design of digital systems*, 2nd Edition, Allyn and Bacon, 1978.

Exercises

3.1. Show that

$$PI(f) = U_n \# \left(U_n \# (ON(f) \cup DC(f)) \right)$$

3.2. Use the above result to obtain the *PI* array for

$$ON = \begin{Bmatrix} 100 \\ 101 \end{Bmatrix}; DC = \begin{Bmatrix} 110 \\ 111 \\ 000 \end{Bmatrix}$$

3.3. How many 0-cubes, 1-cubes, etc., do each of the following cover?

(a) 0000

(b) $0x10$

(c) $x1x1$

(d) $xx0x$

(e) $0xxx1$

3.4. (a) A switching function of four variables consists of the whole of the unit 4-cube except for the 1-cube $11x1$. Describe the sum-of-products expression of this function as a set of cubes.

(b) Perform the computation $A = xxxx \# 11x1$. Compare your answer to that of (a).

3.5. (a) Delete subsuming terms from the following arrays:

$$A = \begin{Bmatrix} 0010 \\ xx00 \\ x1x1 \\ x0x0 \\ x111 \end{Bmatrix} B = \begin{Bmatrix} 0x0x \\ 01xx \\ 0x01 \\ 01x0 \end{Bmatrix}$$

(b) Form $A \cap B$, $A \cup B$, and $A \# B$.

3.6. If $A = \{a_1, a_2, \cdots\}$ and $B = \{b_1, b_2, \cdots\}$ are sets of cubes of the same number of variables, then there are two ways of calculating the sharp product $A \# B$:

(i) $A \# B = \{\cdots \{\{A \# b_1\} \# b_2\} \cdots\}$

(ii) $A \# B = \{\{a_1 \# B\} \cup \{a_2 \# B\} \cdots\}$

Examine these two methods, test them on example arrays, and attempt to determine which is in general the more efficient method of computing $A \# B$.

3.7. Show that the essential prime implicants of the switching function

$$F = \Sigma m(0, 2, 4, 6, 7, 8, 10, 12, 13, 14)$$

are $xxx0$, $011x$, and $110x$.

3.8. Use generalized consensus to show that the prime implicants for the switching function

$$f = \Sigma m(0, 1, 2, 3, 4, 6, 8, 9, 12) + d(11, 13)$$

are

$$\left\{\begin{array}{c} 00xx \\ 0xx0 \\ xx00 \\ x00x \\ x0x1 \\ 1x0x \end{array}\right\}$$

3.9. Show that the prime implicants for the function array F below are as in the PI array below.

$$F = \left\{\begin{array}{c} 0001\ 001 \\ 0010\ 101 \\ 0011\ 001 \\ 0100\ 110 \\ 0101\ 010 \\ 1010\ 111 \\ 1011\ 111 \\ 1100\ 101 \\ 1101\ 110 \end{array}\right\} \qquad PI = \left\{\begin{array}{cc} 00x1 & 00x \\ 0100 & xx0 \\ 101x & xxx \\ 1100 & x0x \\ 1101 & xx0 \\ x010 & x0x \\ x100 & x00 \\ x101 & 0xC \\ 110x & x00 \\ x01x & 00x \\ 010x & 0x0 \end{array}\right\}$$

3.10. Use the procedure of Section 3.8.2 to determine the essential prime implicants in the PI array obtained in Exercise 3.9 (for the given function array F). Show that the application of the procedure produces the three arrays below:

$$PI = \left\{\begin{array}{cc} 0100 & xx0 \\ 1101 & xx0 \\ x100 & x00 \\ x101 & 0x0 \\ 110x & x00 \\ 010x & 0x0 \end{array}\right\} \quad ON = \left\{\begin{array}{cc} 010x & 010 \\ 1101 & 010 \\ 0100 & 100 \\ 1101 & 100 \end{array}\right\} \quad E = \left\{\begin{array}{cc} 1100 & x0x \\ 00x1 & 00x \\ 101x & xxx \\ x010 & x0x \end{array}\right\}$$

3.11. A completely specified Boolean function is given by the array

$$\left\{\begin{array}{c} 0000 \\ 0010 \\ 0100 \\ 0101 \\ 0111 \\ 1000 \\ 1010 \\ 1101 \\ 1111 \end{array}\right\}$$

Find the prime implicants by each of the following algorithms:

(a) Quine-McCluskey algorithm.

(b) Sharp algorithm (from Exercise 3.1).

(c) Iterative consensus algorithm.

(d) Generalized consensus algorithm.

In each case carefully count all the cube comparisons you make. Compare the counts and determine which method is more efficient in terms of cube comparisons.

Appendix 3A

DESCRIPTION OF THE PASCAL PROCEDURES FOR COMBINATIONAL LOGIC DESIGN

3A.1. INTRODUCTION

All of the logic array manipulation operators discussed in the body of this chapter are implemented in the package of procedures which follows in Appendix B. In this appendix we give a brief description of the procedures; subsequent appendices will illustrate their use.

Some knowledge of the internal storage of cubes and arrays is necessary in the practical application of these procedures. No dynamic storage of arrays is used. Upper bounds are specified on cube size and on array size in a **const** declaration by assigning values to the variables "cubemax" and "arraymax" respectively.

The reader will understand that for problems involving many variables, the values assigned to "arraymax" would have to be very large. In our program listing we have assigned a value that has proved satisfactory for problems and examples considered in this book. For problems with up to 4 inputs, arraymax should only rarely need to exceed 100. For problems with more variables, some experimentation may occasionally be necessary to avoid either array overflow or memory overflow.

Each element of a cube is encoded using the **set of** construct of Pascal according to the following listing:

Cube Element	Pascal Encoding
0	[0]
1	[1]
x	[0, 1]
null	[ ]

where [ ] indicates the null or empty set.

The following sections provide details of each of the routines which appear in Appendix B.

3A.2. SYSTEM PROCEDURES

procedure error(a: errtype);

This procedure is called whenever other procedures encounter an error; "a" is used to select an error message to be printed and causes the program to stop execution. The non-standard Pascal procedure *halt* is called to cause rapid termination of the program; other versions of Pascal contain some similar procedures to cause this effect; if not, then the user will have to modify the code to make use of a non-local **goto** statement. This is the only non-standard Pascal feature that exists in the complete package.

procedure initcube(**var** p: cubep);

The cube *p* is initialized to contain all don't-care entries (*x*).

procedure initarray(**var** a: larray; ncubes: arraysize; ninputs, noutputs; cubesize);

The header information of each array is initialized by this procedure. The number of cubes in the array *a* (*NoCubes*) is set to *ncubes*, the number of inputs (*NoInputs*) is set to *ninputs*, and the number of outputs (*NoOutputs*) is set to *noutputs*.

procedure readarray(**var** a: larray);

This procedure reads the number of cubes and the number of inputs and outputs from the standard input, one number per line, and stores this information in the header of the array *a*. Only 0, 1, X, or x are valid input characters. Arrays are specified with one cube per line. Any extra characters on a line are ignored.

Error Message: *READARRAY: c is not a valid character*

where *c* is the offending character. This error causes the program to terminate.

procedure writecube(a: cubep; ni, no: integer);

The cube *a* is written to *output* with *ni* inputs and *no* outputs.

procedure writearray(**var** a: larray);

This procedure prints the array contained in *a* on the *output*.

Error message: *PRINTARRAY: Empty array*

This occurs if the array *a* is empty, i.e., if the number of cubes in the array is 0.

3A.3. UTILITY PROCEDURES

procedure deletecube(**var** a: larray; n: arraysize);

Cube *n* is deleted from array *a* only if cube *n* exists.

Error message: *DELETECUBE: nonexistent cube*

The message is printed if n refers to a cube n not present in the array.

procedure movecube(**var** a, b: larray; n: arraysize);

Array a is initialized to be an array containing a single cube. Cube n is then deleted from array b and placed in array a.

Error message: *MOVECUBE: nonexistent cube*

The message is printed if array b does not contain a cube n.

procedure appendcube(**var** a: larray; b: cube);

Cube b is appended to array a.

Error message: *APPENDCUBE: array overflow*

This message occurs if appending cube b to array a would result in array a having more than *arraymax* cubes.

function subsume(a, b: cube; n: cubesize): **boolean**;

subsume returns **true** if cube a is subsumed by cube b, otherwise it returns **false.**

procedure combine(**var** a, b: larray);

Array b is appended to array a. Subsuming terms are not deleted.

Error Message: *COMBINE: unequal number of variables*

This message is printed if the total number of inputs and outputs of arrays a and b are not identical.

Error Message: *COMBINE: array overflow*

This message occurs if appending array b to array a would result in array a having more than *arraymax* cubes.

procedure changecolumn(**var** a: larray; columno: cubesize; changed: small-details);

Column *columno* of array a is altered in the manner prescribed by *changed*; *changed* is a 3-character string of characters in the set [0, 1, x, X]. If *changed* is the string $c_1 c_2 c_3$, then the 0's in column *columno* are replaced by c_1, the 1's are replaced by c_2, and the x's are replaced by c_3. If array a is empty, no change is made.

Error message: *CHANGECOLUMN: column out of range*

This message is printed if an attempt is made to access a column greater than the total number of inputs and outputs.

Error message: *CHANGECOLUMN: unknown character c interpreted as an x*

character *c* is an illegal character that has been specified in variable *changed*.

function cubecost(a: cube; n: cubesize);

This function returns the count of 1's and 0's in the first *n* elements of *cube*.

3A.4. LOGIC OPERATORS

procedure absorb(**var** a: larray);

Subsuming terms are deleted from array a.

procedure intersection(**var** a, b, c: larray);

The intersection of arrays *b* and *c* is placed in array *a*. Array *a* must not be either of arrays *b* or *c*. *Absorb* is used to keep the size of the array *a* to a minimum.
Error messages: *INTERSECTION: array overflow*

Array *a* has exceeded *arraymax* cubes.

Error message: *INTERSECTION: unequal number of variables*

Arrays *b* and *c* have differing totals of inputs and outputs.

procedure sharp(**var** c: larray; a: larray; **var** b: larray);

The result of the sharp of arrays *a* and *b* is placed in array *c*. Arrays *a* and *c* may occupy the same memory locations.

Error message: *SHARP: unequal number of variables*

Arrays *a* and *b* have differing totals of inputs and outputs.

procedure splitarray(**var** b, a: larray; mask: cube);

All cubes of array *a* that subsume the cube *mask* are removed from array *a* and placed in array *b*.

procedure consensus(**var** a: larray);

The cubes of array *a* are converted into prime implicants using the generalized consensus algorithm. It is assumed that all the 1's in the output columns have already been encoded as x's. Cubes with all-0 output parts are not generated.

Error Message: *CONSENSUS: array overflow*

Array *a* has exceeded *arraymax* variables.

Appendix 3B

PASCAL PROCEDURES FOR COMBINATIONAL LOGIC DESIGN

program logic(input, output);   *logic*

{   *Combinational Logic Minimization Package.* }

const
       arraymax = 40;   { *Maximum number of cubes* }
       cubemax = 11;   { *Maximum number of inputs and outputs* }

type
       arraysize = 0..arraymax;
       cubesize = 0..cubemax;
       bool = 0..1;
       logic = **set of** bool;
       cube = **array** [1..cubemax] **of** logic;
       larray =
          record
              NoInputs: cubesize;
              NoOutputs: cubesize;
              NoCubes: arraysize;
              cubes: **array** [1..arraymax] **of** cube
          end;
       smalldetails = **array** [1..3] **of** char;
       errtype = (INITTMV, COMBUNV, COMBAOV, CHNGCOR, DELCUNC,
           APCUAOV, SHRPUNV, INTXAOV, INTXUNV, CONSAOV);

procedure error(errno: errtype);   *error*

begin { *error* }
      case errno **of**
         INITTMV:
             writeln(output, 'INITARRAY: too many variables');
         COMBUNV:
             writeln(output, 'COMBINE: unequal number of variables');
         COMBAOV:
             writeln(output, 'COMBINE: array overflow');
         CHNGCOR:
             writeln(output, 'CHANGECOLUMN: Column out of range');
         DELCUNC:
             writeln(output, 'DELETECUBE: nonexistent cube');
         APCUAOV:
             writeln(output, 'APPENDCUBE: array overflow');

```
        SHRPUNV:
            writeln(output, 'SHARPS: unequal number of variables');
        INTXAOV:
            writeln(output, 'INTERSECTION: array overflow');
        INTXUNV:
            writeln(output, 'INTERSECTION: unequal number of variables');
        CONSAOV:
            writeln(output, 'CONSENSUS: array overflow')
        end;
    halt
end; { error }
```

procedure initcube(**var** a: cube);   *initcube*

```
var
    i: cubesize;

begin { initcube }
    for i := 1 to cubemax do
        a[i] := [0, 1]
end; { initcube }
```

procedure initarray(**var** a: larray; ncubes: arraysize; ninputs, noutputs: cubesize);   *initarray*

```
var
    i: arraysize;

begin { initarray }
    if ninputs + noutputs > cubemax then
        error(INITTMV);
    with a do begin
        NoOutputs := noutputs;
        NoInputs := ninputs;
        NoCubes := ncubes;
        for i := 1 to ncubes do
            initcube(a.cubes[i])
    end
end; { initarray }
```

procedure readarray(**var** a: larray);   *readarray*

```
var
    i: arraysize;
    j: cubesize;
    c: char;
    err: boolean;
    ncubes: arraysize;
    ninputs, noutputs: cubesize;

begin { readarray }
    readln(ncubes);
    readln(ninputs);
    readln(noutputs);
    initarray(a, ncubes, ninputs, noutputs);
    for i := 1 to ncubes do
        repeat
            err := false;
            for j := 1 to ninputs + noutputs do begin
                if not err then begin
                    read(c);
```

```
            while c = ' ' do
                read(c);
            if not (c in ['0', '1', 'x', 'X']) then begin
                writeln(c, ' is not a valid character');
                    halt
                end else
                    with a do
                        if c = '0' then
                            cubes[i][j] := [0]
                        else if c = '1' then
                            cubes[i][j] := [1]
                        else
                            cubes[i][j] := [0, 1]
            end
        end;
        if not err then
            while not eoln(input) do
                read(c)
    until not err
end; { readarray }

procedure writecube(var c: cube; ni, no: cubesize);                    writecube

var
    j, n: cubesize;

begin { writecube }
    n := ni + no;
    for j := 1 to n do begin
        if j = ni + 1 then
            write(' ');
        if c[j] = [0] then
            write('0')
        else if c[j] = [1] then
            write('1')
        else if j > ni then
            write('-')
        else
            write('x')
    end
end; { writecube }

procedure writearray(var a: larray);                                   writearray

var
    i: arraysize;

begin { writearray }
    with a do
        if NoCubes = 0 then
            writeln('PRINTARRAY: Empty array')
        else
            for i := 1 to NoCubes do begin
                writecube(cubes[i], NoInputs, NoOutputs);
                writeln
            end
end; { writearray }

procedure combine(var a, b: larray);                                   combine

var
    i: arraysize;
```

```
begin { combine }
    with a do begin
        if NoInputs + NoOutputs <> b.NoInputs + b.NoOutputs then
            error(COMBUNV)
        else if NoCubes + b.NoCubes > arraymax then
            error(COMBAOV)
        else begin
            for i := 1 to b.NoCubes do
                cubes[i + NoCubes] := b.cubes[i];
            NoCubes := NoCubes + b.NoCubes
        end
    end
end; { combine }
```

procedure changecolumn(var a: larray; column: cubesize; changed: smalldetails),   *changecolumn*

```
var
    i: arraysize;
    c: cube;

begin { changecolumn }
    with a do
        if column > NoInputs + NoOutputs then
            error(CHNGCOR)
        else if NoCubes > 0 then begin
            for i := 1 to 3 do
                if changed[i] = '0' then
                    c[i] := [0]
                else if changed[i] = '1' then
                    c[i] := [1]
                else if changed[i] in ['x', 'X', 'd', 'D'] then
                    c[i] := [0, 1]
                else begin
                    writeln('CHANGECOLUMN: unknown character: ',
                        changed[i],  interpreted as an X');
                    c[i] := [0, 1]
                end;
            for i := 1 to NoCubes do
                if cubes[i][column] = [0] then
                    cubes[i][column] := c[1]
                else if cubes[i][column] = [1] then
                    cubes[i][column] := c[2]
                else
                    cubes[i][column] := c[3]
        end
end; { changecolumn }
```

procedure deletecube(var a: larray; n: arraysize);   *deletecube*

```
    var
        i: arraysize;

    begin { deletecube }
        with a do
            if (n > a.NoCubes) or (n = 0) then
                error(DELCUNC)
            else begin
                for i := n to NoCubes − 1 do
                    cubes[i] := cubes[i + 1];
                NoCubes := NoCubes − 1
            end
    end; { deletecube }
```

function cubecost(a: cube; n: cubesize): cubesize;   *cubecost*

```
var
    i, count: cubesize;

begin { cubecost }
    count := 0;
    for i := 1 to n do
        if a[i] <> [0, 1] then
            count := count + 1;
    cubecost := count
end; { cubecost }

procedure movecube(var a, b: larray; cubeno: arraysize);        movecube

begin { movecube }
    initarray(a, 1, b.NoInputs, b.NoOutputs);
    a.cubes[1] := b.cubes[cubeno];
    deletecube(b, cubeno)
end; { movecube }

procedure appendcube(var a: larray; b: cube);                   appendcube

begin { appendcube }
    with a do
        if NoCubes + 1 < arraymax then begin
            NoCubes := NoCubes + 1;
            cubes[NoCubes] := b
        end else
            error(APCUAOV)
end; { appendcube }

function subsume(a, b: cube; n: cubesize): boolean;             subsume

var
    i: cubesize;
    break: boolean;

begin { subsume }
    break := false;
    i := 1;
    while not break and (i <= n) do
        if a[i] − b[i] <> [] then
            break := true
        else
            i := i + 1;
    subsume := not break
end; { subsume }

function cubex(var a: cube; b, c: cube; n: cubesize): boolean;  cubex

label
    1;

var
    i: cubesize;

begin { cubex }
    cubex := true;
    for i := 1 to n do begin
        a[i] := b[i] * c[i];
        if a[i] = [] then begin
            cubex := false;
            goto 1
        end
```

```
            end;
    1:
            null
    end; { cubex }
```

```
    procedure absorb(var a: larray);
```
absorb

```
    label
            1;

    var
            i, j: arraysize;
            nvars: cubesize;

    begin { absorb }
            with a do
                    if NoCubes > 0 then begin
                            i := 1;
                            nvars := NoInputs + NoOutputs;
                            while i <= NoCubes - 1 do begin
    1:

                                    j := i + 1;
                                    while j <= NoCubes do begin
                                            if subsume(cubes[i], cubes[j], nvars) then begin
                                                    deletecube(a, i);
                                                    goto 1
                                            end else if subsume(cubes[j], cubes[i], nvars) then
                                                    deletecube(a, j)
                                            else
                                                    j := j + 1
                                    end;
                                    i := i + 1
                            end
                    end
    end; { absorb }
```

```
    procedure sharp(var c: larray; a: larray; var b: larray);
```
sharp

```
    var
            nvars, j, k: arraysize;
            t: larray;

    procedure cubesharp(var x: larray; a, b: cube; n: cubesize);
```
cubesharp

```
    var
            i: cubesize;
            y: logic;
            c: cube;

    begin { cubesharp }
            with x do
                    if not cubex(c, b, a, n) then begin
                            NoCubes := 1;
                            cubes[1] := a
                    end else begin
                            NoCubes := 0;
                            for i := 1 to n do begin
                                    y := a[i] - c[i];
                                    if y <> [] then begin
                                            NoCubes := NoCubes + 1;
                                            cubes[NoCubes] := a;
                                            cubes[NoCubes][i] := y
                                    end
```

```
                        end
                    end
            end; { cubesharp }

    begin { sharp }
            nvars := a.NoInputs + a.NoOutputs;
            if nvars <> b.NoInputs + b.NoOutputs then
                    error(SHRPUNV)
            else begin
                    t := a;
                    c := a;
                    for j := 1 to b.NoCubes do begin
                            c.NoCubes := 0;
                            for k := 1 to a.NoCubes do begin
                                    cubesharp(t, a.cubes[k], b.cubes[j], nvars);
                                    combine(c, t);
                                    if c.NoCubes > arraymax div 2 then
                                            { reduce chance of verflow }
                                            absorb(c)
                            end;
                            a := c
                    end;
                    absorb(c)
            end
    end; { sharp }

    procedure splitarray(var b, a: larray; mask: cube);          splitarray

    var
            j: arraysize;
            nvars: cubesize;

    begin { splitarray }
            with a do begin
                    initarray(b, 0, NoInputs, NoOutputs);
                    nvars := NoInputs + NoOutputs;
                    if NoCubes > 0 then begin
                            j := 1;
                            while (j <= NoCubes) and (NoCubes > 0) do begin
                                    if subsume(cubes[j], mask, nvars) then begin
                                            appendcube(b, cubes[j]);
                                            deletecube(a, j)
                                    end else
                                            j := j + 1
                            end
                    end
            end
    end; { splitarray }

    procedure intersection(var a, b, c: larray);                intersection

    var
            i, j: arraysize;
            nv: cubesize;

    begin { intersection }
            with b do begin
                    initarray(a, 0, NoInputs, NoOutputs);
                    if NoInputs + NoOutputs = c.NoInputs + c.NoOutputs then begin
                            nv := NoInputs + NoOutputs;
                            for i := 1 to NoCubes do
                                    for j := 1 to c.NoCubes do
                                            with a do begin
```

```
                              if NoCubes + 1 > arraymax then
                                    error(INTXAOV)
                              else if cubex(cubes[NoCubes + 1], b.cubes[i], c.cubes[j], nv) then
                                    NoCubes := NoCubes + 1;
                              if NoCubes + 1 > arraymax div 2 then
                                    absorb(a)
                        end;
                  absorb(a)
            end else
                  error(INTXUNV)
      end

end; { intersection }

procedure consensus(var a: larray);                                    consensus

var
      nv, i, j: integer;
      b, c, d: larray;
      mask, all0mask: cube;

begin { consensus }
      with a do begin
            nv := NoInputs + NoOutputs;
            for j := NoInputs + 1 to nv do
                  changecolumn(a, j, '0~x')
      end;
      initcube(mask);
      if a.NoOutputs > 0 then begin
            initcube(all0mask);
            for j := a.NoInputs + 1 to nv do
                  all0mask[j] := [0]
      end;
      for i := 1 to a.NoInputs do begin
            mask[i] := [1];
            splitarray(b, a, mask);
            mask[i] := [0];
            splitarray(c, a, mask);
            combine(a, b);
            combine(a, c);
            if (b.NoCubes > 0) and (c.NoCubes > 0) then begin
                  changecolumn(b, i, 'xxx');
                  changecolumn(c, i, 'xxx');
                  intersection(d, b, c);
                  initcube(mask);
                  { delete cubes with all-0 outputs }
                  if (a.NoOutputs > 0) and (d.NoCubes > 0) then
                        splitarray(b, d, all0mask);
                  absorb(a);
                  if a.NoCubes + d.NoCubes > arraymax then
                        error(CONSAOV);
                  combine(a, d);
                  absorb(a)
            end;
            mask[i] := [0, 1]
      end
end; { consensus }

#include "domain.i"

begin
      domain
end.
```

Appendix 3C

MULTIPLE-OUTPUT MINIMIZATION PROCEDURE

```
procedure momin(var cover:larray; PI, ON: larray);                          momin

var
     loop: boolean;
     i, npi: arraysize;

     procedure epi(var e, f, ON: larray);                                   epi

     var
          a, b, d1: larray;
          npi, i: arraysize;

     begin { epi }
          i := 1;
          npi := f.NoCubes;
          while (i <= npi) and (ON.NoCubes > 0) do begin
               movecube(d1, f, 1);
               intersection(a, ON, d1);
               { if a.NoCubes = 0 then cube d1 need not be returned to f }
               { since it does not cover any of the ON 0-cubes.        }
               if a.NoCubes > 0 then begin
                    sharp(b, a, f);
                    if b.NoCubes = 0 then
                         combine(f, d1)
                    else begin
                         combine(e, d1);
                         sharp(a, ON, d1);
                         ON := a
                    end
               end;
               i := i + 1
          end
     end; { epi }

     procedure lessthan(var PI: larray);                                    lessthan

     var
          i, j, npi: arraysize;
          a, b, d1, d2: larray;
          delcube, break: boolean;
          costi: cubesize;
```

```
begin { lessthan }
        npi := PI.NoCubes;
        initarray(d2, 1, PI.NoInputs, PI.NoOutputs);
        break := false;
        i := 1;
        while (i <= npi) and not break do begin
                delcube := false;
                movecube(d1, PI, 1);
                intersection(a, ON, d1);
                if a.NoCubes = 0 then
                        delcube := true
                else begin
                    costi := cubecost(d1.cubes[1], PI.NoInputs);
                    j := 1;
                    while (j <= PI.NoCubes) and not break do begin
                            if costi >= cubecost(PI.cubes[j], PI.NoInputs) then begin
                                    d2.cubes[1] := PI.cubes[j];
                                    sharp(b, a, d2);
                                    if b.NoCubes = 0 then begin
                                            delcube := true;
                                            break := true
                                    end
                            end;
                            j := j + 1
                    end
                end;
                if not delcube then
                        combine(PI, d1);
                i := i + 1
        end
end; { lessthan }

procedure pickcube(var cover, PI, ON: larray);                              pickcube

var
        mincost, cost: cubesize;
        i, j: arraysize;
        a, b: larray;

begin { pickcube }
        mincost := PI.NoInputs;
        for i := 1 to PI.NoCubes do begin
                cost := cubecost(PI.cubes[i], PI.NoInputs);
                if cost < mincost then begin
                        mincost := cost;
                        j := i
                end
        end;
        movecube(a, PI, j);
        { Extraction picked cube PI[j] }
        combine(cover, a);
        sharp(b, ON, a);
        ON := b
end; { pickcube }

begin { momin }
    initarray(cover, 0, ON.NoInputs, ON.NoOutputs);
    loop := true;
    repeat
        epi(cover, PI, ON);
        if ON.NoCubes > 0 then begin
                npi := PI.NoCubes;
```

```
                    lessthan(PI);
                    if npi = PI.NoCubes then begin
                        pickcube(cover, PI, ON);
                        if ON.NoCubes = 0 then
                                    loop := false
                    end
                    end else
                            loop := false
          until not loop;

          { Convert x's to 1's in output columns }
          with cover do
                for i := NoInputs + 1 to NoInputs + NoOutputs do
                    changecolumn(cover, i, '011')
    end; { momin }
```

Appendix 3D

CONNECTION MINIMIZATION PROCEDURE

```
procedure conmin(var E: larray; ON: larray);                              conmin

var
      ni, nvars, i, j, EINcubes: integer;
      Mask, eij: cube;
      Ei, EINi, Etemp, ONi, d: larray;

begin { conmin }
      if (E.NoCubes > 0) and (ON.NoCubes > 0) then begin
            ni := E.NoInputs;
            nvars := ni + E.NoOutputs;
            initcube(Mask);
            for i := ni + 1 to nvars do begin
                  Mask[i] := [1];
                  changecolumn(E, i, '011');
                  splitarray(Ei, E, Mask);
                  if Ei.NoCubes > 0 then begin
                        EINi := Ei;
                        EINcubes := Ei.NoCubes;
                        EINi.NoOutputs := 0; {Delete all the output columns }
                        splitarray(ONi, CN, Mask);
                        combine(ON, ONi);
                        ONi.NoOutputs := 0; {Delete all output columns}
                        for j := 1 to EINcubes do begin
                              eij := Ei.cubes[1];
                              deletecube(Ei, 1);
                              movecube(Etemp, EINi, 1);
                              intersection(d, Etemp, ONi);
                              sharp(d, d, EINi);
                              if d.NoCubes > 0 then begin
                                    appendcube(EINi, Etemp.cubes[1]);
                                    appendcube(Ei, eij)
                              end else begin
                                    eij[i] := [0];
                                    appendcube(E, eij)
                              end
                        end;
                        combine(E, Ei)
                  end;
                  Mask[i] := [0, 1]
            end;
            { Remove cubes with all 0 output terms }
            for i := ni + 1 to nvars do
                  Mask[i] := [0];
            splitarray(Ei, E, Mask)
      end
end; { conmin }
```

163

Appendix 3E

GATE-REPORTING PROCEDURE

This is a simple-minded procedure which derives a wiring description for a two-level NAND-gate realization of a network. The input to the procedure is a minimized function array, with all outputs having a value of 0 or 1 (there can be no don't-care entries). The procedure gives a list of the inputs to each gate, along with the fan-in and fan-out counts for each gate. As an added feature, it also gives a report on the number of 2-, 3-, 4- and 8-input NAND gates that are required to realize the function.

```
procedure publish(f: larray);                                          publish

type
      gatetype =
          record
                inputs: integer;
                count: integer
          end;

var
      nvars, i, k, fanin, fanout: integer;
      outfanin: array [cubesize] of integer;
      gate: array [1..5] of gatetype;

      procedure pgate(g: char; gateno: arraysize; x: logic);           pgate

      begin { pgate }
          write(' ');
          if x = [0] then
                write('-')
          else
                write(' ');
          write(g);
          if gateno > 9 then begin
                write(gateno div 10: 1);
                gateno := gateno mod 10
          end else
                write('0');
          write(gateno: 1)
      end; { pgate }

      procedure updategate(incount: integer);                          updategate
      { update the fanin count for a gate type }
```

164

```
begin { updategate }
    if incount > 8 then
        incount := 9;
    case incount of
        1, 2:
                { use 2-input gates for inverters}
                gate[1].count := gate[1].count + 1;
            3:
                gate[2].count := gate[2].count + 1;
            4:
                gate[3].count := gate[3].count + 1;
        5, 6, 7, 8:
                gate[4].count := gate[4].count + 1;
            9:
                gate[5].count := gate[5].count + 1
    end
end; { updategate }


procedure writedigit(k: integer);                                   writedigit

begin { writedigit }
    if k < 10 then
        write(' ')
    else
        write(chr(k div 10 + ord('0')))
end; { writedigit }


procedure statistics(nc, nout: integer);                            statistics
{ form gate and ic pack statistics }

var
    i, k, packcount: integer;

    procedure ICcount(i: integer);                                  ICcount
    { write out the number of ICs needed of a particular type }

    var
        k: integer;

    begin { ICcount }
        with gate[i] do
            case i of
                1:      { 2-input: 4 gates per pack }
                        k := (count+3) div 4;
                2:      { 3-input: 3 gates per pack }
                        k := (count+2) div 3;
                3:      { 4-input: 2 gates per pack }
                        k := (count+1) div 2;
                4, 5:   { >=8-input: 1 gate per pack }
                        k := 1
            end;
        packcount := packcount + k;
        writeln(k: 7, ' IC packs')
    end; { ICcount }

    procedure writegate(i:integer);                                 writegate
    { write out the number of inputs for a given gate type }

    begin { writegate }
        write(' ': 10, gate[i].count: 4);
        if i < 5 then
            write(gate[i].inputs: 4, '-input NAND gates ')
```

```
                else
                        write(' ': 4, 'special NAND gates')
        end; { writegate }

begin { statistics }
        gate[1].inputs := 2;
        gate[2].inputs := 3;
        gate[3].inputs := 4;
        gate[4].inputs := 8;
        writeln;
        writeln;
        packcount := 0;

        for i := 1 to 5 do
                if gate[i].count > 0 then begin
                        writegate(i);
                        ICcount(i)
                end;

        { IC totals }
        writeln(' ': 10, '——', ' ': 25, '——');
        i := nc + nout;
        write(' ': 10, i: 5, ' NAND gates');
        writeln(' ': 12, packcount: 5, ' IC packs')
end; { statistics }

begin { publish }
        for i := 1 to 5 do
                gate[i].count := 0;
        with f do begin
                { print out the connection array first }
                nvars := NoInputs + NoOutputs;
                for k := 1 to NoInputs do
                        write('X');
                write(' ');
                for k := 1 to NoOutputs do
                        write('Z');
                writeln;
                if (NoInputs > 9) or (NoOutputs > 9) then begin
                        for k := 1 to NoInputs do
                                writedigit(k);
                        write(' ');
                        for k := 1 to NoOutputs do
                                writedigit(k);
                        writeln
                end;
                for k := 1 to NoInputs do
                        write(chr(k div 10 + ord('0')));
                write(' ');
                for k := 1 to NoOutputs do
                        write(chr(k div 10 + ord('0')));
                writeln;
                writeln;
                writearray(f);
                writeln;
                writeln;
                writeln(' ': 25, 'NAND Gate Realization');
                writeln;
                writeln;
                writeln(' Gate  Fan   Fan    Driving Signals');
                writeln(' No  –in  –out');
                writeln;
```

```
for i := 1 to NoCubes do
     if cubecost(cubes[i], NoInputs) > 1 then begin
          { derive each gate input term }
          pgate('G', i, [1]);
          fanout := 0;
          for k := NoInputs + 1 to nvars do
               if cubes[i][k] = [1] then
                    fanout := fanout + 1;
          fanin := cubecost(cubes[i], NoInputs);
          write(fanin: 4, fanout: 6, ' ': 4);
          updategate(fanin);
          { derive driving signals }
          for k := 1 to NoInputs do
               if cubes[i][k] <> [0, 1] then
                    pgate('X', k, cubes[i][k]);
          writeln
     end;
     { derive each output gate term }
     for k := 1 to NoOutputs do
          outfanin[k] := 0;
     for i := 1 to NoCubes do
          for k := NoInputs + 1 to nvars do
               if cubes[i][k] = [1] then
                    outfanin[k - NoInputs] := outfanin[k - NoInputs] + 1;
     for k := NoInputs + 1 to nvars do begin
          pgate('Z', k - NoInputs, [1]);
          write(outfanin[k - NoInputs]: 4, '1': 6, ' ': 4);
          updategate(outfanin[k - NoInputs]);

          { derive driving signals }
          for i := 1 to NoCubes do
               if cubecost(cubes[i], NoInputs) = 1 then begin
                    if cubes[i][k] = [1] then
                         pgate('X', i, [1])
                    end else if cubes[i][k] = [1] then
                         pgate('G', i, [1]);
          writeln
     end;
     statistics(NoCubes, NoOutputs)
end;
end; { publish }
```

Appendix 3F

A WORKED EXAMPLE

This appendix shows how the procedures defined in this chapter may be applied to the solution of a fairly typical problem. We have taken the problem examined in Section 3.8.5 and shown how to solve it using the Pascal routines.

In order to reduce the duplication of Pascal code that has appeared in the previous appendices, we have utilized a non-standard Pascal construction. You will observe that the code which appears below has lines beginning with

#include ". . .";

where we have some text string enclosed in the double quote (") symbols. This string refers to the name of a file on our computer system where the Pascal code for a particular procedure can be found. The Pascal code from the file is then inserted directly into the current file while the compiler is running. This approach gives us the advantage of not having to edit the code of Appendix 3-B for every different application. If a similar feature does not exist in your Pascal compiler, then you will have to resort to replacing the "#include" line with the appropriate code.

For example, the procedure *domain* (pronounced "do main") is always included in the code given in Appendix 3-B. The procedure *domain* requires the procedures *momin*, *conmin* and *publish*, which are defined in Appendices 3-C through 3-E. On our computer system, these procedures are kept in files called "momin.i", "conmin.i" and "publish.i" respectively. To comply with the rules of Pascal which state that a routine must be defined before it can be used, we use the "#include" statement to have the Pascal compiler read the procedure declarations before they are used in the body of the procedure *domain*. Thus, this facility reduces the amount of editing and simplifies the software maintenance procedures.

With more advanced Pascal compilers, there is often a mechanism for compiling procedures individually and saving them in a special format which enables us to automatically load only those routines we need, without having to first explicitly declare the procedures. This mechanism very often depends on the type of Pascal compiler you have, and the operating system under which the compiler is running. We have not made use of this feature here because of the strong dependence of this method upon particular computer systems.

3F.1. THE PASCAL PROGRAM

```
procedure domain;                                                    domain

var
            nin, nout, i, j: cubesize;
            a, f, ON: larray;
            mask: cube;

#include "momin.i"
#include "conmin.i"
#include "publish.i"

begin { domain }
            { Read the function array and print it out as a check }
            readarray(f);
            writeln('Array f');
            writearray(f);
            writeln;

            { form the ON array }

            nin := f.NoInputs;
            nout := f.NoOutputs;
            initcube(mask);
            initarray(ON, 0, nin, nout);
            for i := nin + 1 to nin + nout do begin
                      mask[i] := [1];
                      splitarray(a, f, mask);
                      combine(f, a);
                      for j := nin + 1 to nin + nout do
                                if i <> j then
                                          changecolumn(a, j, '000');
                      combine(ON, a);
                      mask[i] := [0, 1]
            end;
            consensus(f);                   { Determine the PIs for f }
            momin(a, f, ON);                { determine the minimum cover for f }
            conmin(a, ON);                  { remove redundancies from the connect array }
            publish(a)                      { publish the results using NAND gates }
end; { domain }
```

3F.2. DATA-INPUT FORMAT

Following is the input data used for the problem in Section 3.8.5. The first number (9) specifies the number of cubes in the array to be read; the second number (4) specifies the number of inputs; and the third number (3) specifies the number of outputs. The remaining nine lines specify the cubes of the array, with the inputs separated from the outputs by a single-space (i.e., blank) character.

```
9
4
3
0001 001
0010 101
0011 001
0100 110
0101 010
1010 111
1011 111
1100 101
1101 110
```

3F.3. RESULTING OUTPUT

What now follows is the printout of the output produced by the program. The first array is the input-function array. The second array is the minimized-function array, with redundant connections deleted. Following this is the NAND-gate realization of the second array.

```
Array f

0001 001
0010 101
0011 001
0100 110
0101 010
1010 111
1011 111
1100 101
1101 110

XXXX ZZZ
1234 123

110x 100
x100 100
x101 010
010x 010
00x1 001
1100 001
x010 101
101x 111
```

NAND Gate Realization

Gate No	Fan -in	Fan -out	Driving Signals			
G01	3	1	X01	X02	-X03	
G02	3	1	X02	-X03	-X04	
G03	3	1	X02	-X03	X04	
G04	3	1	-X01	X02	-X03	
G05	3	1	-X01	-X02	X04	
G06	4	1	X01	X02	-X03	-X04
G07	3	2	-X02	X03	-X04	
G08	3	3	X01	-X02	X03	
Z01	4	1	G01	G02	G07	G08
Z02	3	1	G03	G04	G08	
Z03	4	1	G05	G06	G07	G08

```
        8   3-input NAND gates      3 IC packs
        3   4-input NAND gates      2 IC packs
        ----                        ----
       11 NAND gates                5 IC packs
```

In the above output, the gates numbered G01 through G08 are NAND gates to which the input signals X01 through X04 are connected. The remaining NAND gates (Z01 through Z03) provide the circuit outputs. The actual connections are detailed on the right-hand side. Thus, gate G01 is fed by inputs X01, X02 and by the complement of X03. Similarly, gate Z01 is fed by the ouputs of gates G01, G02, G07 and G08.

4

SEQUENTIAL CIRCUITS

4.1 INTRODUCTION

The previous two chapters were concerned with the design of combinational circuits. If we ignore the effect of gate delays, the output of a combinational circuit at any given time is simply a function of the inputs at that time; previous values of the inputs have no effect whatever upon the output. Because of this, we say that combinational circuits have no *memory*. Circuits without memory are incapable of carrying out one of the fundamental operations of computer systems, namely storage of data.†

Logic circuits that *do* possess memory are referred to as *sequential circuits*, this term arising from the fact that the output of a sequential circuit at any given time depends not only upon the current input but also upon the *sequence* of inputs that has been applied to the circuit up to that time.

Our discussion of sequential circuits commences with a description of the simple, but very widely used, memory devices known as *flip-flops*.

4.2. FLIP-FLOPS

4.2.1. The SR Flip-Flop

The SR (set-reset) flip-flop is a 2-input, 2-output device which is represented by the symbol shown in Figure 4.1. The two inputs are labelled S and R and the two outputs are complements of one another, one being labelled Q and the other $\overline{Q}$. (It is usual practice to provide complementary outputs to flip-flops in this way because in the design of logic systems the complement of a variable is very often required.)

The basic operation of the SR flip-flop is quite simple. A positive pulse (i.e., a "1") applied to the S input causes the output Q to go to the 1 level; the flip-

---

†This statement ignores the fact that the structure of a combinational circuit is sometimes interpreted as a form of memory. See, for instance, the discussion of read-only memories in Chapter 6.

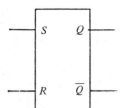

Figure 4.1. Block diagram of SR flip-flop.

flop is then said to be "set". A positive pulse applied to the R input causes the flip-flop to "reset", i.e., the output Q goes to the 0 level.

The SR flip-flop can be realized using two NOR gates with feedback, as shown in Figure 4.2. That this circuit gives the required behavior can be explained as follows.

First note that one possible input/output combination is $S = 0$, $R = 0$, $Q = 0$, $\overline{Q} = 1$. To see this, observe that $Q = 0$ and $S = 0$ ensures that the upper NOR gate in Figure 4.2 has output $\overline{Q} = 1$. In addition, the fact that $\overline{Q} = 1$ ensures that the lower NOR gate has the output $Q = 0$. We will use this particular input/output combination as a starting point for our explanation of the behavior of the circuit in Figure 4.2.

Thus, we commence with the assumption that the circuit is in a steady-state condition with $S = 0$, $R = 0$, $Q = 0$, $\overline{Q} = 1$. First consider the following sequence of events in which the input R is held at 0. If input S goes to 1, the output of the upper NOR gate, $\overline{Q}$, will go to 0 driving the output of the lower NOR gate, Q, to 1. Note that with R held at 0, S can now return to 0 and Q will remain on 1 with $\overline{Q} = 0$. In other words, the flip-flop can be *set* by the application of a positive pulse (a change from level 0 to level 1 and back again to 0) at input S.

Now consider what happens when the flip-flop is in the set state ($Q = 1$, $\overline{Q} = 0$) and a positive pulse is applied to input R with input S held at 0. In this case, when R goes to 1, the output of the lower NOR gate, Q, goes to 0 and in doing so drives the output of the upper NOR gate to 1. With S held at 0, the return of R to 0 leaves the flip-flop in the *reset* state ($Q = 0$, $\overline{Q} = 1$).

Thus, the circuit of Figure 4.2 does indeed perform the operations of an SR

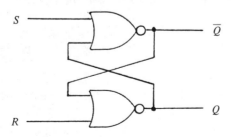

Figure 4.2. Realization of SR flip-flop using NOR gates.

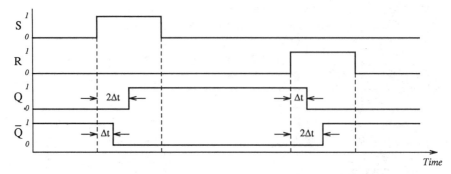

Figure 4.3. Timing diagram indicating behavior of SR flip-flop.

flip-flop. A positive pulse arriving at the S input sets the flip-flop and a positive pulse arriving at the R input resets it.

The sequence of operations involved in setting and then resetting the flip-flop from the initial state in which $S = 0$, $R = 0$, $Q = 0$, $\overline{Q} = 1$ is indicated in the timing diagram shown in Figure 4.3. This diagram emphasizes that the flip-flop does not change state instantaneously upon arrival of pulses at the S or R terminals. Each logic gate takes a finite time to respond to a change of input and we have assumed for simplicity here that the propagation delays† of the two NOR gates are the same and equal to Δt. Thus, when the S input of the circuit in Figure 4.2 goes from 0 to 1, the output $\overline{Q}$ responds after a delay of Δt, by going from 1 to 0. When $\overline{Q}$ goes from 1 to 0, the lower NOR gate responds, after a further delay of Δt, by going from 0 to 1. Thus, as indicated in Figure 4.3, there is a delay of $2\Delta t$ between the S input going from 0 to 1 and the output Q going from 0 to 1. Clearly the S input must remain at the 1 level for a time longer than $2\Delta t$ in order to ensure that when S returns to 0, the flip-flop remains set. For similar reasons, the duration of the reset pulse should also be greater than $2\Delta t$.

Note that the SR flip-flop is not intended for use when it can be exposed to the input condition $S = 1$, $R = 1$. As an indication of this, observe that if the circuit of Figure 4.2 were subjected to this input condition, the two NOR gates would respond by producing the output condition $Q = 0$, $\overline{Q} = 0$, which is logically contradictory.

The logical behavior of the SR flip-flop can be summarized in tabular form as shown in Table 4.1(a). This table shows the effect of all possible pairs of input values R and S (applied at time t) upon the output Q. The effect of changing inputs is only observable after a short delay (for the circuit of Figure 4.2 this delay is equal to $2\Delta t$) and in Table 4.1(a) this delay is represented by τ.

---

† The "propagation delay" of a gate is the time taken for a signal at the input of the gate to cause a change of state at the output. More discussion of this can be found in the Appendix at the end of the book.

Table 4.1 Logical behavior of SR flip-flop: (a) Detailed representation; (b) abbreviated representation.

Input at time t		Output at time t	Output at time $t + \tau$
$S(t)$	$R(t)$	$Q(t)$	$Q(t+\tau)$
0	0	0	0
0	0	1	1
0	1	0	0
0	1	1	0
1	0	0	1
1	0	1	1
1	1	0	undefined
1	1	1	undefined

(a)

Inputs		Next value of output, Q^+
S	R	
0	0	Q
0	1	0
1	0	1
1	1	undefined

(b)

This tabular representation is usually abbreviated as shown in Table 4.1(b), where the fact that the input values $S = 0$, $R = 0$ leave the output unchanged is indicated in the obvious way.

4.2.2. System Clocks and the Clocked SR Flip-Flop

That the output of the SR flip-flop is undefined for the input condition $S = 1$, $R = 1$ implies that considerable care must be exercised in the design and implementation of circuits containing SR flip-flips. If an SR flip-flop is located within a complex switching network, the signals arriving at the S and R inputs may come from quite different sources and in such a case are unlikely to arrive at precisely the same time. As an example of the difficulty this fact can create, consider the case in which the input condition $S = 1$, $R = 0$ is required to change to $S = 0$, $R = 1$. Since the inputs are very likely to change values at slightly different times, there is a good chance that input R will change from 0 to 1 before input S has changed from 1 to 0. In such circumstances, the flip-flop would have the input conditions $S = 1$, $R = 1$ for a short time and the effects on overall circuit behavior could be serious.

In most sequential circuits, problems of this kind can easily arise. One way of avoiding a good many of these problems is through the use of a *system clock*.

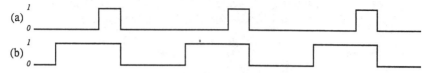

Figure 4.4. Clock signals.

The system clock provides a periodic train of *clock pulses* which is used by each flip-flop in the circuit as a means of synchronizing the times of arrival of its input signals. The clock pulses may be generated in the form of rectangular pulses or a square wave, as depicted in Figure 4.4. The arrival of inputs to a given flip-flop can be synchronized by "ANDing" each input signal with the clock pulses. In the case of the SR flip-flop, the resulting circuit is as shown in Figure 4.5(a). In this arrangement, the clock input is designed to go to level 1 some time after the arrival of signals at the S and R inputs. In this way, any slight variation in the arrival times of the signals at the S and R inputs is of no consequence because the AND gates prevent their transfer to the flip-flop until the clock input goes to level 1. (When the clock input goes to level 1, it is said to *enable* the flip-flop.) Once the S and R signals have been transferred to the flip-flop, the clock input can return to zero; this causes the outputs of the AND gates to go to zero but has no effect on the new state of the flip-flop outputs (if in doubt about this, refer to Table 4.1(b)).

Sequential circuits that employ a system clock to synchronize operations in this way are known as *synchronous* sequential circuits. Sequential circuits that do not employ a system clock in this way are called *asynchronous* circuits. Most digital systems are synchronous and most of the remainder of this book is concerned with synchronous systems. Because of the regularity that the system

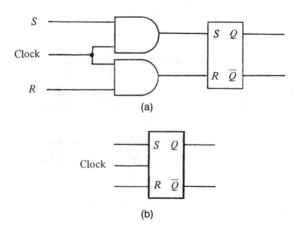

Figure 4.5. Clocked SR flip-flop: (a) explicit representation; (b) symbolic representation.

Table 4.2. Logical behavior of clocked SR flip-flop.

\multicolumn{2}{Inputs}		Output
S^n	R^n	Q^{n+1}
0	0	Q^n
0	1	0
1	0	1
1	1	undefined

clock imposes, synchronous systems are much easier to design (and trouble-shoot) than asynchronous systems.

Note that with the arrangement of Figure 4.5(a), it is important that the inputs S and R do not change while a clock pulse is present. If there is any possibility of this restriction being violated, then additional circuitry is required in order to ensure that the restriction be enforced.

The clocked SR flip-flop is usually represented symbolically as shown in Figure 4.5(b), where the AND gate arrangement of Figure 4.5(a) is assumed to be incorporated within the flip-flop. The clocking scheme allows us to give a more precise tabular description of the SR flip-flop than the one given in Table 4.1(b). If the clock pulses are numbered $1, 2, \ldots, n, n + 1, \ldots$, then at the time of arrival of clock pulse n, the flip-flop will have input values S^n and R^n and an output value Q^n. Clock pulse n enables the flip-flop and produces a new output value Q^{n+1} which, for the various possible input conditions S^n, R^n, is given by Table 4.2.

The SR flip-flop we have looked at here is enabled when the clock pulse goes to level 1. For some applications it can be useful to have flip-flops that are enabled when the clock signal goes to level 0 and are disabled when the clock goes to level 1 (and some flip-flops of this type *are* manufactured). However, for the remainder of this chapter we will assume that all the flip-flops considered are enabled when the clock signal goes to level 1. To avoid repetition, we will express the enabling of the flip-flop in various ways. Thus, instead of saying 'the clock goes to level 1'', we will sometimes say ''a clock pulse arrives'' or ''the clock becomes active''. Similarly, instead of saying ''the clock is at level 1'' we may say ''a clock pulse is present'' or ''the clock is active''.

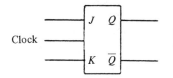

Clock

Figure 4.6. Symbolic representation of clocked JK flip-flop.

Table 4.3. Logical behavior of clocked JK flip-flop.

Inputs		Output
J^n	K^n	Q^{n+1}
0	0	Q^n
0	1	0
1	0	1
1	1	$\overline{Q}^n$

4.2.3. The JK Flip-Flop

The clocked SR flip-flop is rarely used in practice; a modified form, known as the clocked JK flip-flop is usually preferred. The JK flip-flop, depicted in Figure 4.6, is a 2-input device (plus clock input) which behaves exactly like the SR flip-flop except when its two inputs are at level 1. If, at clock pulse n, the inputs are $J^n = 1$, $K^n = 1$, then, at the next clock pulse, the output has a value equal to the complement of its previous value, i.e., $Q^{n+1} = \overline{Q}^n$. The behavior of the clocked JK flip-flop is summarized in Table 4.3, which should be compared with Table 4.2.

A JK flip-flop may be realized by modifying an SR flip-flop as shown in Figure 4.7. To verify this, note that in this circuit we can express the inputs to the SR flip-flop as functions of the J and K inputs as follows:

$$S^n = J^n \overline{Q}^n; \; R^n = K^n Q^n$$

Thus, when $J^n = K^n = 0$, we will have $S^n = R^n = 0$ and hence, from Table 4.2, $Q^{n+1} = Q^n$. This verifies the first row of Table 4.3.

When $J^n = 0$ and $K^n = 1$, we have $S^n = 0$ and $R^n = Q^n$. Hence, if $Q^n = 0$, $R^n = 0$ and, from Table 4.2, $Q^{n+1} = 0$; if $Q^n = 1$, $R^n = 1$ and, from Table 4.2 we again find $Q^{n+1} = 0$. Thus, we have shown that $J^n = 0$, $K^n = 1$ gives $Q^{n+1} = 0$, in agreement with the second row of Table 4.3.

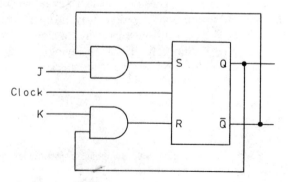

Figure 4.7. JK flip-flop constructed from *SR* flip-flop.

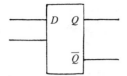

Figure 4.8. Symbolic representation of D flip-flop.

Similar arguments for the other two combinations of J^n and K^n confirm that the circuit behaves according to Table 4.3.

The arguments used in verifying that the circuit in Figure 4.7 behaves as a JK flip-flop are, in fact, only valid so long as the clock is active for a very short time. To see this, suppose a clock pulse arrives when $J = K = Q = 1$. According to Table 4.3, this will cause Q to change from 1 to 0. This change will immediately be fed back to the K input and, if the clock is still active, output Q will be driven back to 1 again. Depending on how much longer the clock input remains active, the output might oscillate several times between 0 and 1. This is a most undesirable form of behavior that can be avoided in the circuit of Figure 4.7 only by making sure that the clock pulse duration is less than the propagation delay of the flip-flop. The propagation delay of a flip-flop is typically of the order of nanoseconds, so that a requirement that clock pulse duration be less than propagation delay would be very restrictive for most applications. Consequently, the circuit of Figure 4.7 is not used in practice.

The undesirable behavior of the circuit of Figure 4.7 is known as a *race condition*, presumably because signals propagate through the device and back to the input before the clock pulse ceases (i.e., rather as if they were winning a race). Two standard techniques for avoiding race conditions are described in Section 4.2.6, but before discussing these we introduce two other flip-flop types that find frequent application in sequential logic design.

4.2.4. The D Flip-Flop

The D flip-flop provides a means of delaying signals within a digital network. It has a single input, as shown in Figure 4.8, and, upon arrival of a clock pulse, the value of the input is transferred to the output. In this way, the flip-flop can be used to delay the passage of a signal by one clock pulse, as is indicated in Table 4.4.

Table 4.4. Logical behavior of D flip-flop.

Input D^n	Output Q^{n+1}
0	0
1	1

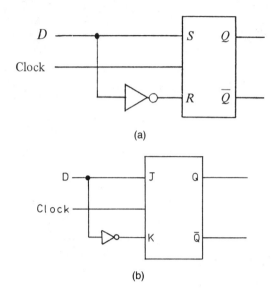

(a)

(b)

Figure 4.9. Realization of D flip-flop: (a) using SR flip-flop; (b) using JK flip-flop.

The D flip-flop can be realized using flip-flops of the SR or JK types by simply adding an inverter as shown in Figure 4.9.

4.2.5. The T Flip-Flop

The T flip-flop is usually referred to as the "toggle" flip-flop. It has a single input, as shown in Figure 4.10, and its behavior is very simple. If the T input is held at the value 1, the output changes state ("toggles") every time a clock pulse arrives. If T is held at the value 0, then clock pulses have no effect on the output of the flip-flop. This behavior is summarized in Table 4.5.

The T flip-flop is not directly available as an IC but is very easily constructed from a JK flip-flop (which *is* available as an IC—see Section 4.2.7). A T flip-flop realized from a JK flip-flop is shown in Figure 4.11; the fact that this is indeed a T flip-flop is easily seen by reference to Table 4.3.

In later sections of this book we will, for convenience, represent a T flip-flop as a single-input device in the form shown in Figure 4.10.

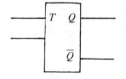

Figure 4.10. Symbolic representation of T flip-flop.

Table 4.5. Logical behavior of T flip-flop.

Input T^n	Output Q^{n+1}
0	Q^n
1	$\bar{Q}^n$

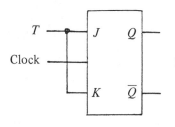

Figure 4.11. Realization of T flip-flop.

4.2.6. Methods of Clocking Flip-Flops

In Section 4.2.3 we saw how the circuit in Figure 4.7 operates as a JK flip-flop if the duration of the clock pulse is shorter than the signal propagation delay from input to output. If this condition is not met, the output may oscillate between 0 and 1 several times before the clock signal returns to the 0-level. This problem can be avoided if the output of the flip-flop is prevented from changing before the clock signal returns to the 0-level. One way of achieving this is by means of the *master-slave principle*, which is discussed below. Another approach, that has certain advantages over the master-slave method, is known as *edge-triggering*. A positive edge-triggered flip-flop changes state according to the values of its inputs at the time that the clock signal changes from level 0 to level 1 (i.e. at the time of the positive edge of the clock). Once the clock signal has risen to level 1, any change of signal at the input has no effect. In normal operation, the rise time of the clock pulse is much shorter than the propagation delay of the flip-flop so that any signal fed back to the input following a change of state has no effect. Edge-triggering schemes are also discussed below.

The Master-Slave Flip-Flop. The master-slave idea was developed in the early days of integrated circuit technology and the basic principle involved can be explained in terms of the JK flip-flop depicted in Figure 4.12. There are two SR flip-flops in this figure, one called the master and the other called the slave. Note that the system outputs are fed back to the input AND gates in exactly the same way as in the circuit in Figure 4.7. The "slave" flip-flop has been inserted in the circuit in order to prevent the changes in the outputs of the master from being fed back to the input while the clock is active. This is achieved by feeding the slave with the complement of the clock waveform, ensuring that when the

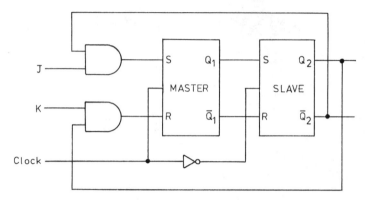

Figure 4.12. Master-slave *JK* flip-flop.

master is enabled, the slave is disabled. Hence, while the clock is at level 1, the master behaves like a JK flip-flop but the slave remains unchanged. Thus there is no chance of the system output Q changing and affecting the input while the clock is at level 1. When the clock goes to level 0, the master is disabled and the slave is enabled. In this state the outputs of the master (Q_1 and $\overline{Q}_1$) are transferred to the outputs of the slave. To check this, note that the S and R inputs of the slave receive complementary values (Q_1 and $\overline{Q}_1$) and, according to Table 4.2, under these circumstances, the Q output takes on the value of S and $\overline{Q}$ takes on the value of R. Any changes in the output of the master-slave flip-flop therefore take place following the trailing edge of the clock pulse.

The master-slave flip-flop clearly avoids the problem of an oscillating output that occurs if the clock pulse has duration longer than the signal propagation delay. In an ideal environment, the master-slave flip-flop would be a very satisfactory device but, unfortunately, practical circuits do not provide an ideal environment. For various reasons (see Section 4.5) noise pulses (or "glitches") can appear on lines connecting logic devices and such pulses can cause the master-slave flip-flop to behave incorrectly. For instance, suppose that, just prior to the clock going from 0 to 1, the inputs J and K in Figure 4.12 are both held at 0 and the output Q is also at 0. According to Table 4.3, when the clock has gone from 0 to 1 and back again, the output Q should remain unchanged on 0. However, if, while the clock is at level 1, a noise pulse arrives that causes input J to go briefly high, this will set the master flip-flop and, when the clock returns to 0, the output Q will take on the erroneous value 1. This undesirable behavior is termed "one's-catching" and can be avoided by using the edge-triggering approach which we describe next.

Edge-Triggering. We will explain the basic principles involved in the construction of edge-triggered flip-flops in terms of the D flip-flop, because this flip-flop type appears to allow the simplest explanation. We will commence with a basic D flip-flop of the type already met and then we will modify it to

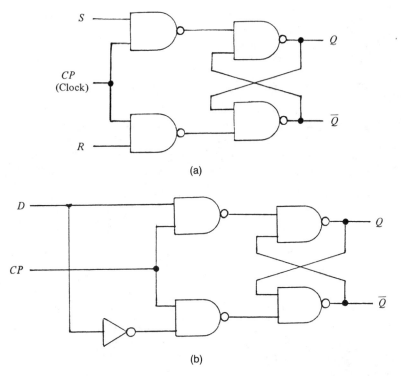

Figure 4.13. (a) *SR* flip-flop; (b) *D* flip-flop constructed using SR flip-flop.

allow edge-triggering. Our basic D flip-flop will be constructed by simply add-ing an inverter to an SR flip-flop in the manner shown in Figure 4.9(a). The SR flip-flop we will use is constructed from NAND gates and is shown in Figure 4.13(a). (Demonstrating that this circuit is indeed an SR flip-flop is given as Exercise 4.1.) From Figure 4.9(a) our basic D flip-flop has the form shown in Figure 4.13(b).

Let us look a little more closely at the SR flip-flop in Figure 4.13(a). When the CP input goes high, this "enables" the two NAND gates to which the *S* and *R* inputs are connected. In this condition, these two NAND gates simply invert the *S* and *R* signals and feed them to the inputs of the two cross-connected NAND gates. This implies that the two cross-connected NAND gates (depicted separately in Figure 4.14(a)) provide behavior complementary to the SR flip-flop. This behavior is summarized in Figure 4.14(b). The fact that the cross-coupled NAND gates provide behavior complementary to that of the SR flip-flop can be seen by comparing the state table in Figure 4.14(b) with Table 4.2. In manufacturers' data books, the circuit in Figure 4.14(a) is often called an *SR latch* or *RS latch* but, considering that its behavior is complementary to that of the SR flip-flop, this can be a source of confusion. We will refer to the circuit as a *NAND latch*.

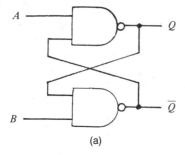

A

Q

B

$\overline{Q}$

(a)

Figure 4.14. (a) Cross-coupled NAND gates (NAND latch); (b) logical behavior of NAND latch.

A^n	B^n	Q^{n+1}
0	0	-
0	1	1
1	0	0
1	1	Q^n

(b)

The basic idea underlying edge-triggering circuits is to use latches of this type to store the input values as soon as the clock pulse arrives. Once these values have been stored, the inputs can change (due to noise, or whatever) without affecting the behavior of the system, even if the clock pulse is still present.

In the case of the D flip-flop, the method used to store the input values as soon as the clock pulse arrives consists of little more than replacing the NAND gates at the inputs of the circuit in Figure 4.13(b) by NAND latches. The circuit is shown in Figure 4.15. Comparison of this circuit with the one in Figure 4.13(b) shows two additional differences, over and above the replacement of the input NAND gates by NAND latches. The inverter in Figure 4.13(b) has been dispensed with, and an extra connection, between the output of NAND gate 2 and the input of NAND gate 3, has been inserted. This latter connection is necessary to avoid the possibility of the output NAND latch (made up of gates 5 and 6) being fed logic 0 to both of its inputs simultaneously (see Exercise 4.5).

In order to simplify the description of the operation of this D flip-flop, the outputs of NAND gates 1, 2, 3 and 4 in Figure 4.15 have been labelled j, k, l and m, respectively. The behavior of the circuit in response to a sequence of inputs can then be detailed as in Table 4.6. For simplicity in this description, we have assumed that the propagation delay for each NAND gate is exactly the same; this allows us to represent time by a sequence of integers, each integer representing one gate delay.

In Table 4.6, the input sequence commences, at time $T = 0$, with $CP = 0$ and $D = 0$. Noting that if any input to a NAND gate is 0 its output is 1, we

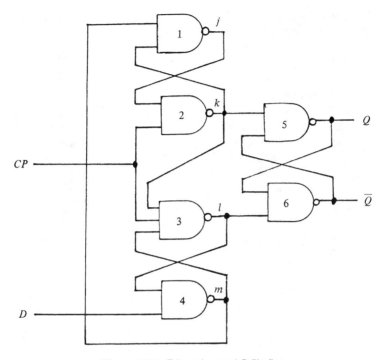

Figure 4.15. Edge-triggered *D* flip-flop.

see that these inputs ensure that outputs k, l and m take on the value 1 and the
fact that $k = m = 1$ causes j to take on the value 0. The output NAND latch
has a valid† pair of inputs ($k = l = 1$) and Q will have some value depending
on the previous input sequence. We will assume $Q = 1$ at time $T = 0$. The
state of the circuit at time $T = 0$ is summarized in the first row of Table 4.6.

Table 4.6.   Internal behavior of edge-triggered D flip-flop.

Time, T	CP	D	j	k	l	m	Q	$\bar{Q}$
0	0	0	0	1	1	1	1	0
1	1	0	0	1	1	1	1	0
2	1	0	0	1	0	1	1	0
3	1	0	0	1	0	1	1	1
4	1	0	0	1	0	1	0	1
...								
n	0	0	0	1	1	1	0	1
$n+1$	0	1	0	1	1	1	0	1
$n+2$	0	1	0	1	1	0	0	1
$n+3$	0	1	1	1	1	0	0	1

†Recall from Figure 4.14(b) that the inputs $k = l = 0$ are invalid.

If CP goes to level 1 at time $T = 1$, this will not affect any of the other variables until one gate delay has elapsed. Thus, at time $T = 2$, variable l changes its value to 0. The output NAND latch now has inputs $k = 1$ and $l = 0$; after one further gate delay $\overline{Q}$ goes to 1 and this causes Q to take on the value 0 at time $T = 4$. Thus, the value of D at the time of arrival of the clock pulse ($T = 1$) has been transferred to the output after three gate delays.

Now note the major significance of this edge-triggering circuit. The clock pulse arrives at $T = 1$ and variable l goes to 0 at $T = 2$. As soon as l has gone to 0 the input D can change without affecting the behavior of the flip-flop. This is because with $l = 0$ we have $m = 1$ regardless of the value of D. Hence, the fact that $D = 0$ at the time of arrival of the clock pulse will be registered by the flip-flop so long as the value of D does not change in the time required for variable l to change from 1 to 0. In other words, when the clock pulse arrives, the input variable D has to be held at level 0 for one gate delay for the flip-flop to function correctly. We say that the *hold time* of the flip-flop is one gate delay. (A proper definition of hold time is given below). The significance of this is that a noise glitch can only cause an incorrect value to be stored if it arrives at the D input within one gate delay of the time of arrival of the clock pulse. Compare this with the master-slave flip-flop in which the inputs have to be held unchanging (i.e. free of glitches) for half a clock cycle.

Returning to Table 4.6, suppose that at time n the clock has returned to level 0 and that the D input is still 0. If D goes to 1 at time $n + 1$, it is not until time $n + 3$ that the internal variables (i.e. the variables j, k, l, m) have settled down to constant values. If the new value of D is to be stored successfully the clock signal should not be allowed to go active until the internal variables have settled down. Thus, any change to the value of D should occur at least three gate delays before the clock signal goes active. This minimum time between a change in input and the arrival of a clock pulse is known as the *set-up time*.

We now take this opportunity to define more generally the terms set-up time and hold time.

Definitions of Set-Up Time and Hold Time

The set-up time, t_{SU}, *for a flip-flop is defined as the time required for input data to settle into the flip-flop before the arrival of the triggering edge of the clock.*

The hold time, t_H, *is defined as the time for which the input data must remain stable after the arrival of the triggering edge of the clock.*

Set-up and hold times are specified by IC manufacturers. If a designer fails to make sure that these timing requirements are met, unexpected circuit behavior may occur.

Note that the definition of set-up time implies that for a master-slave flip-flop the set-up time is equal to the duration of the clock pulse. This is because the flip-flop is triggered by the trailing edge of the clock pulse and the input data to the master flip-flop must be maintained at a constant value while the clock pulse is active.

4.2.7. Integrated Circuit Packages

The SR flip-flop was introduced in Section 4.2.1 as a pair of cross-coupled NOR gates. This structure is not available in the 74 series, chiefly because the basic TTL gate is a NAND. Instead, the NAND latch (depicted in Figure 4.14), which provides behavior complementary to that of the SR flip-flop, is available. Manufacturers insist on referring to this device as an *RS latch* and so the 74279, which contains four NAND latches, is listed in data books as a *quad RS latch*.

Another form of latch, which finds frequent application, is a development of one of the D flip-flop structures shown in Figure 4.9. The basic structure of this latch, which is often called a *follow/hold latch*, is depicted in Figure 4.16. The circuit shown here differs from that in Figure 4.9(a) through the addition of two AND gates that allow an ''enable'' input to be provided. When the enable input is low, the input A has no effect on the output because $S = R = 0$. When the enable is high, Q takes on the value of A. If A changes its value while the enable is high, the value of Q changes also; in other words, Q *follows* the input. When the enable goes low, Q *holds* whatever value the input has at that time; hence the name follow/hold latch. The 7475 package contains four of these latches.

Of the clocked flip-flops, almost all are now edge-triggered. Flip-flops of the master-slave variety have been gradually superceded and the only ones that remain in the 74 series are of JK type (e.g. the 7473 and 7476) but even in these cases, the LS variety† is edge-triggered. Some master-slave flip-flops have been modified to eliminate the need to hold the inputs stable while the clock is active. An example is the 74110, but it does not offer any advantages over edge-

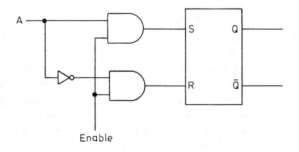

Figure 4.16. Follow-hold latch.

---

†The different varieties of devices in the 74 series are detailed in the Appendix at the end of the book.

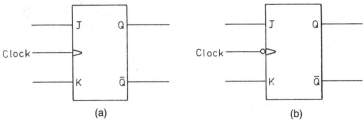

Figure 4.17. Edge-triggered JK flip-flops. (a) positive edge-triggering; (b) negative edge-triggering.

triggered devices. As a general rule, edge-triggered flip-flops should be employed in new designs.

In circuit diagrams, edge-triggered flip-flops are distinguished by a small triangle drawn adjacent to the clock input as shown in Fig. 4.17. The symbol in Fig. 4.17(a) indicates that the flip-flop is triggered on the rising edge of the clock (ie the device is positive-edge triggered). Some flip-flops (about 50% of the available range) are negative-edge triggered. Negative-edge triggering is indicated by the addition of a small circle at the clock input, as indicated in Fig. 4.17(b).

It should also be mentioned that clocked flip-flops of the SR and T variety are not available in IC packages. The clocked SR flip-flop is of little value because the JK flip-flop can exhibit identical behavior and does not suffer from the restriction that its inputs are not allowed to take on the value 1 simultaneously. The T flip-flop is so easily constructed from the JK flip-flop (see Figure 4.11) that there really is no need for T flip-flops to be manufactured separately. Thus, the clocked flip-flops listed in manufacturers' catalogues are all of the JK and D variety. They usually come in dual packages, i.e. two to a pack.

4.3. REGISTERS AND COUNTERS

Two important applications of flip-flops are in the construction of registers and counters. The basic property of a *register* is its ability *to store data*; the basic property of a *counter* is its ability *to count through a sequence of numbers*.

A common form of register is known as a *shift register*. The chief application of shift registers is in the storage of data which arrives, or must be sent, in the form of a sequence of digits. A shift-register circuit which employs JK flip-flops is shown in Figure 4.18. The manner in which this circuit operates can be seen by noting that each flip-flop is connected so as to operate like a D flip-flop (refer back to Figure 4.9). Thus, on arrival of a clock pulse, the input of each flip-flop is transferred to its output. At the time of arrival of clock pulse $n + 1$ there will be some data value at the input to the register. This data value can be assumed to have arrived at the register input following clock pulse n and so we will call it X^n. Then, when clock pulse $n + 1$ arrives, the data value X^n is transferred to the output of FF_1, i.e., $Q^{n+1} = X^n$. Similarly the output of FF_2

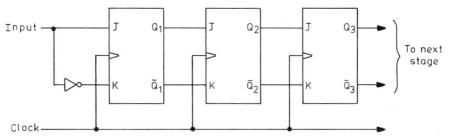

Figure 4.18. Shift register.

Table 4.7.   Behavior of shift register.

Time, n	Input	Q_1^{n+1}	Q_2^{n+1}	Q_3^{n+1}	Q_4^{n+1}	Q_5^{n+1}
1	1	1	0	0	0	0
2	1	1	1	0	0	0
3	0	0	1	1	0	0
4	0	0	0	1	1	0
5	1	1	0	0	1	1

takes on the value of its input at the time of arrival of the clock pulse, i.e., $Q_2^{n+1} = Q_1^n$. And so it goes on: $Q_3^{n+1} = Q_2^n$, $Q_4^{n+1} = Q_3^n$, etc. In this way, an input-data sequence is gradually accommodated into the register by shifting the digits in the sequence along the series of flip-flops (from left to right in Figure 4.18).

As an example, consider a shift register made up of five flip-flops each with its output initially set to 0. The effect of the input sequence 11001 upon the outputs of the flip-flops is illustrated in Table 4.7.

The shift register presented here is a very simple form of sequential circuit, consisting merely of a group of flip-flops and an inverter gate. In most sequential circuits, a good deal of combinational logic circuitry is required; as introductory examples we will consider two forms of counter.

4.3.1. Modulo-8 Counter

A modulo-8 counter is one which counts pulses (usually clock pulses) from 0 up to 7 and then returns to 0 and starts again. The behavior of such a counter can be described by means of a *state diagram*. The state diagram for a modulo-8 counter which counts in binary is shown in Figure 4.19(a). The diagram shows that if the counter is in state 000, the arrival of a pulse causes the counter to make a transition to state 001. Further pulses cause transitions to states 010, 011 and so on up to 111 from which state a further pulse causes a transition to state 000 and the whole process can repeat indefinitely.

Figure 4.19(b) depicts a modulo-8 counter which has been constructed using

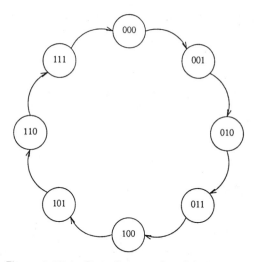

Figure 4.19(a). State diagram of modulo-8 counter.

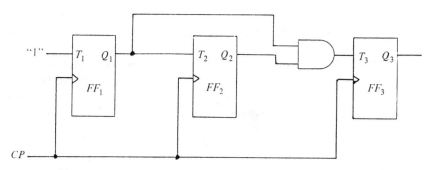

Figure 4.19(b). Realization of modulo-8 counter using T flip-flops.

T flip-flops of the edge-triggered variety. The fact that the circuit in Figure 4.19(b) behaves according to the state diagram of Figure 4.19(a) can be seen by first assuming that the three outputs Q_1, Q_2, Q_3 are initially all equal to 0. The initial state of the counter is written $Q_3 Q_2 Q_1 = 000$. When the active edge of the first clock pulse arrives, FF_1 is the only flip-flop to change state because the inputs to the other flip-flops are at level 0. Thus, after the first clock pulse has been and gone the state of the counter is $Q_3 Q_2 Q_1 = 001$. With Q_1 now equal to 1, the arrival of the next pulse causes both FF_1 and FF_2 to change state, and the resulting state of the counter is $Q_3 Q_2 Q_1 = 010$. It can be easily verified that the counter continues to count the arriving pulses (in binary) until it reaches the state $Q_3 Q_2 Q_1 = 111$; arrival of the next pulse then restores the counter to the state $Q_3 Q_2 Q_1 = 000$.

In the counter of Figure 4.19(b), we have used T flip-flops. A modulo-8

Table 4.8. State table for modulo-8 counter.

Present state $Q_3^n Q_2^n Q_1^n$	Next state $Q_3^{n+1} Q_2^{n+1} Q_1^{n+1}$	Flip-flop inputs $T_3^n T_2^n T_1^n$
000	001	001
001	010	011
010	011	001
011	100	111
100	101	001
101	110	011
110	111	001
111	000	111

counter can also be constructed using SR, JK, or D flip-flops, but for each flip-flop type, the required counting property can only be obtained by using a different combinational logic arrangement. In each case, the required combinational logic can be determined using the techniques of the previous two chapters. For a simple problem like the one in hand, K-maps can be used as follows.

We commence by drawing up a *state table* for the counter (Table 4.8). This table indicates the manner in which the counter is required to change state each time a clock pulse arrives. In Table 4.8 we have assumed that T flip-flops are to be employed and have included a column which lists the inputs that are required at each flip-flop in order to provide each change of state. This column is derived from the other two by noting that whenever the output of a flip-flop is required to change state, the T input to that flip-flop must be at level 1. For instance, the second row of the table is concerned with the change of state from 001 to 010; in order for this change to be effected, the output of FF_1 must change from 1 to 0, and the output of FF_2 must change from 0 to 1 and the output of FF_3 should remain on 0. The required change of state is achieved by providing a 1 input at FF_1 and FF_2 and a 0 input at FF_3.

From Table 4.8 we see that T_1, the input to FF_1, is required to be 1 each time a clock pulse arrives; this can be achieved by connecting T_1 directly to the voltage-supply rail.† The inputs required at the other two flip-flops depend upon the state of the counter (i.e. the "present state" in Table 4.8). These requirements can be represented on K-maps as shown in Figure 4.20. The map in Figure 4.20(a) indicates that we require $T_2^n = Q_1^n$ and the map in Figure 4.20(b) indicates the requirement $T_3^n = Q_1^n Q_2^n$. These expressions hold for all n (i.e. for every clock pulse) so that whenever a clock pulse arrives, we require $T_2 = Q_1$ and $T_3 = Q_1 Q_2$. These facts, along with the additional fact that clock pulses

---

†The reader might think that this could also be achieved by connecting T_1 to the source of clock pulses. Certainly this would ensure that $T_1 = 1$ each time a clock pulse arrives, but it would fail to satisfy the set-up time requirement for FF_1.

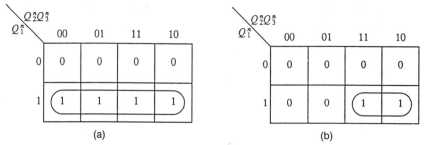

Figure 4.20. K-maps for modulo-8 counter: (a) $T_2^n = Q_1^n$; (b) $T_3^n = Q_1^n Q_2^n$.

are required to trigger the flip-flops provide us directly with the circuit in Figure 4.19(b).

The reader should now have no difficulty in designing a similar counter using D flip-flops (see Exercise 4.9). The design of a modulo-8 counter using JK flip-flops is also set as an exercise at the end of this chapter, but the solution of this exercise does not follow quite so directly from the T flip-flop example, chiefly because the JK flip-flop is a 2-input device. In order to assist the reader, we will now give an example in which the JK flip-flop is employed.

4.3.2. More General Counters

In some applications a device is required which, upon the arrival of a sequence of clock pulses, makes transitions from state to state, where the sequence of states is in some order other than the standard binary order. As an example, consider the state diagram of Figure 4.21. This state diagram differs from the state diagram for the modulo-8 counter in two ways; first of all the ordering of the states is different and secondly, there are only six states on this diagram. None the less, the state diagram in Figure 4.21 is quite similar to that of the modulo-8 counter (in Figure 4.19(a)) and devices whose behavior can be represented by state diagrams of this type (i.e. with a circular topology) are generally known as counters. The device represented by Figure 4.21 "counts" through a sequence of states that is not in the standard binary order.

Our problem now is to obtain a circuit that behaves according to the state diagram in Figure 4.21; in other words, we wish to realize the state diagram in Figure 4.21. In order to achieve this objective, we can follow a procedure similar to that employed in the realization of the modulo-8 counter. However, recall that for this problem we have decided to use JK flip-flops and because of this, some preliminary discussion is necessary.

The JK flip-flop is a 2-input device and, in order to determine the inputs necessary to give the required flip-flop transitions, we must look again at the general behavior of such flip-flops. This behavior is summarized in Table 4.3 which, for convenience, is repeated as Table 4.9.

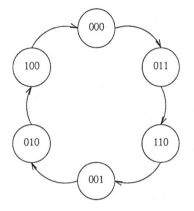

Figure 4.21. State diagram of more general counter.

There are four types of transitions that we will generally require of the outputs of the flip-flops. If the output is 0 at some particular time, then, upon the arrival of the next pulse, we will require either that the output changes to 1 (denote this transition $0 \rightarrow 1$) or that the output stays on 0 (denote this "transition" $0 \rightarrow 0$). Similarly, if the output is 1 we will require either the transition $1 \rightarrow 0$ or the transition $1 \rightarrow 1$.

Table 4.9 tells us that if the output is 0 at time n, then in order for the output to become 1 at the arrival of the next clock pulse we must have either the condition $J^n = 1$, $K^n = 0$ or the condition $J^n = 1$, $K^n = 1$. In other words, if the output is 0 at time n, it will become 1 at time $n + 1$ so long as $J^n = 1$; the value of K^n does not matter—it is a don't-care. The inputs required for the four possible transitions are listed in Table 4.10 where, as usual, x denotes a don't-care condition.

Now we can proceed with the realization of the state diagram of Figure 4.21. As in the case of the modulo-8 counter, three flip-flops will be needed and we commence with the drawing up of a state table. This is shown in Table 4.11 where the input pairs required to ensure that each flip-flop makes the necessary change of state have been listed. Note that no "next state" is specified for "present states" 101 and 111 (these states do not appear on the state diagram of Figure 4.21) so that don't-cares can be assigned to all inputs for these "present states".

Table 4.9. Logical behaviour of JK flip-flop.

Inputs		Output
J^n	K^n	Q^{n+1}
0	0	Q^n
0	1	0
1	0	1
1	1	$\bar{Q}^n$

Table 4.10. Transition table for JK flip-flop.

Transition	J	K
$0 \rightarrow 1$	1	x
$0 \rightarrow 0$	0	x
$1 \rightarrow 0$	x	1
$1 \rightarrow 1$	x	0

To determine the combinational logic necessary to provide the various flip-flop inputs listed in Table 4.11, we now draw up a K-map for each input, as shown in Figure 4.22. The expressions derived from these K-maps indicate the required relationships between the inputs and the outputs of the three flip-flops. These relationships hold for all n, so that the superscript n is rather superfluous. Using these relationships, a circuit which realizes the state diagram of Figure 4.21 can be drawn. The circuit is shown in Figure 4.23. Note that two of the inputs must be held at level 1 throughout the operation of the device.

4.3.3. Hang-Up States

Before we move on to consider more general problems in sequential circuit design, we will consider one important practical aspect of design that can be explained in terms of the counter circuit we have just realized. This aspect arises out of the fact that the counter circuit has two don't-care states. If the circuit is always started in state 000 and if there is no noise in the system, then the circuit should behave exactly as planned. However, when power is first switched on, the state of a sequential system is normally indeterminate. It is not very difficult to ensure that a circuit such as the one shown in Fig. 4.23 commences in the required starting state; almost all clocked flip-flops have asynchronous inputs

Table 4.11. State table for more general counter.

Present state	Next state	Flip-flop inputs					
$Q_3^n Q_2^n Q_1^n$	$Q_3^{n+1} Q_2^{n+1} Q_1^{n+1}$	J_3^n	K_3^n	J_2^n	K_2^n	J_1^n	K_1^n
000	011	0	x	1	x	1	x
001	010	0	x	1	x	x	1
010	100	1	x	x	1	0	x
011	110	1	x	x	0	x	1
100	000	x	1	0	x	0	x
101	---	x	x	x	x	x	x
110	001	x	1	x	1	1	x
111	---	x	x	x	x	x	x

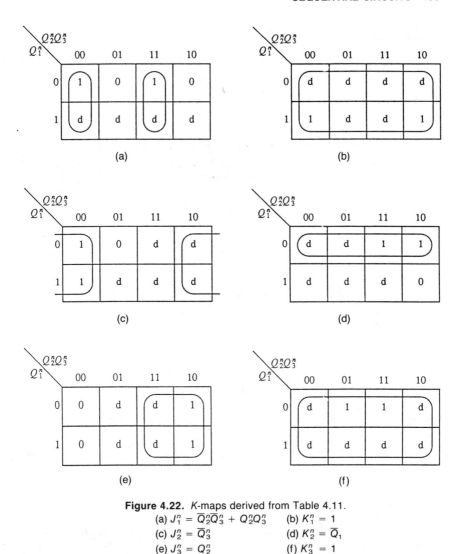

Figure 4.22. K-maps derived from Table 4.11.

(a) $J_1^n = \overline{Q_2^n}\overline{Q_3^n} + Q_2^n Q_3^n$ (b) $K_1^n = 1$

(c) $J_2^n = \overline{Q_3^n}$ (d) $K_2^n = \overline{Q}_1$

(e) $J_3^n = Q_2^n$ (f) $K_3^n = 1$

for the operations of "preset" and "clear" and these can be used for this purpose.

Another problem, however, concerns the effects of noise on the system. It is possible that a noise disturbance will cause the flip-flop outputs to take on values corresponding to a don't-care state. Note that in Table 4.11, we have not specified a next state for states 101 and 111. It is very important that we check how the circuit will behave if, due to some noise disturbance, the flip-flop outputs take on values corresponding to one of these states. It is quite conceivable that,

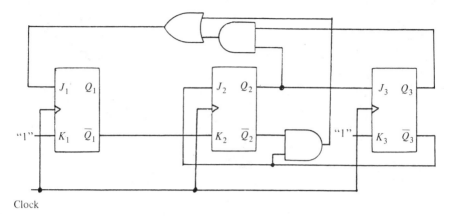

Figure 4.23. Final realization of counter.

with the design we have constructed, if the system gets into one of the don't-care states, the next clock pulse will take it into the other don't-care state and the following clock pulse will take it back to the first don't-care state. If this were to happen, the system would simply oscillate between the don't-care states and never move back into the counting cycle. In such a circumstance the system would "hang up" and never return to the task for which it was designed; the don't-care states that cause such a situation to arise are called *hang-up states*.

It is not very difficult to check for hang-up states. In the case of the counter circuit we are considering here, the input expressions derived from K-maps in Figure 4.22 can be used to determine the state transitions that would occur if the system were ever to enter a don't-care state.

For instance, if the system entered state 101, the state that the system would enter next is given by setting $Q_3^n = 1$, $Q_2^n = 0$, $Q_1^n = 1$ in the input expressions of Figure 4.22. This gives (i) $J_1^n = 0$, $K_1^n = 1$, implying $Q_1^{n+1} = 0$; (ii) $J_2^n = 0$, $K_2^n = 0$, implying $Q_2^{n+1} = 0$; and (iii) $J_3^n = 0$, $K_3^n = 1$, implying $Q_3^{n+1} = 0$. Thus, if the system were to enter don't-care state 101, the arrival of the next clock pulse would drive the system into state 000. Similarly, it can be easily determined that if the system ever got into state 111, the next clock pulse would drive it into state 010.

In this way we have established that the circuit in Figure 4.23 has no hang-up states. From state 101 the system does directly to the starting state, but from state 111 the system goes to the intermediate state 010. For many applications it would be preferable for the system to enter the starting state after being driven into a don't-care state. This can easily be arranged by specifying the transition explicitly in the state table. (In Table 4.11, the next states for 101 and 111 would be specified as 000). For other applications, more elaborate precautions might have to be taken to cope with the possibility of entering don't-care states, but these are beyond the scope of this book. The approach adopted for the remainder of this text is to take full advantage of the existence of don't-care states in order to minimize the combinational logic requirement. Adoption of this approach, of course, requires that hang-up states be checked for whenever a system with don't-care states is designed.

4.4. DESIGN TECHNIQUES FOR SYNCHRONOUS CIRCUITS

The previous section presented a brief treatment of shift registers and counters and this allowed an introduction to some of the basic concepts involved in the design of more general sequential circuits. In this section we will show how these concepts can be developed to provide systematic techniques for the design of general synchronous sequential circuits.

4.4.1. The Problem of Converting a Specification into a State Table

The procedure employed for the design of the two counters in the previous section commenced with the drawing up of a state table to represent required behavior. In the design of more complex sequential systems a similar approach is normally used, but for such systems the drawing up of the state table usually requires considerably more effort than was necessary for the two counters. As an illustration of this fact, consider the following example.

Example 4.1. A clocked sequential circuit is to be designed which receives a sequence of data bits at its input and which is required to recognize, within the sequence, each occurrence of the four-bit pattern 1101. The incoming bit stream is synchronized with the source of clock pulses and, whenever the pattern 1101 occurs, the circuit is required to output a 1 at the clock time coinciding with the final 1 in the pattern. At all other times the output of the circuit is required to be 0. Draw up a state table that describes the required circuit behavior.

Solution. This problem can be interpreted in two different ways, depending upon whether or not possible overlapping of the bit pattern is to be taken into account. This fact is illustrated in Figure 4.24 where output y_1 indicates circuit behavior in the case where overlapping is ignored and output y_2 indicates behavior where overlapping is taken into account. We will consider only the case where overlapping is ignored.

The procedure we follow in attempting to draw up a state table for this problem commences with the construction of a state diagram to represent required circuit behavior. The state diagrams we draw for this and future examples differ somewhat from those employed to represent the behavior of the two counters in the previous section. The main difference lies in the fact that alongside each of the arrows denoting transitions between states we indicate the value of the

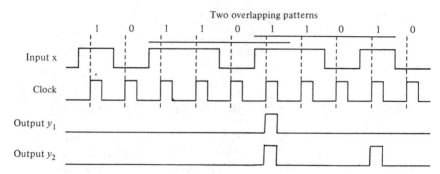

Figure 4.24. Illustration of two possible interpretations of Example 4.1.

input x which causes the transition and we also indicate the resulting value of the output y; these two values are written in the form x/y.

To construct the state diagram we assume that the circuit commences in some initial state A. If the first input bit is a 1, this could be the start of the required bit pattern and the circuit should move to a new state (designated B in Figure 4.25) in order to "remember" that a 1 has been received. Alongside the arrow showing the transition from state A to state B we write $1/0$ to indicate that this

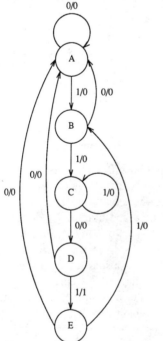

Figure 4.25. State diagram for Example 4.1.

transition is brought about by the input of a 1 and that the output resulting from this input should be 0. Figure 4.25 also shows that if the circuit is in state A and a 0 is received, the circuit should remain in state A (and output a 0) and wait for a 1; when a 1 eventually arrives the circuit goes to state B.

When in state B, if a 0 is received (indicating reception of the sequence 10) it is clear that the current sequence is not part of the bit pattern sought and the circuit should return to state A. If, on the other hand, a 1 is received when the circuit is in state B, the circuit should move to a new state (designated C) in order to remember that the sequence 11 has been received.

Following similar arguments, the remainder of the state diagram can be constructed; it should be obvious that the diagram in Figure 4.25 fully describes the required circuit behavior. Note that only in the transition between states D and E (following reception of the bit pattern 1101) is an output of 1 obtained.

The state table for the circuit can now be constructed directly from Figure 4.25. In order to provide a basis for design, the table must give a complete description of circuit behavior and so it must display, for each possible input, both the outputs and the changes of state. The state table corresponding to Figure 4.25 is shown in Table 4.12. □

This example has illustrated the use of a state diagram as an intermediate step in the construction of a state table. It should be clear to the reader that the state diagram and state table provide equivalent representations of sequential circuit behavior. However, as we saw in relation to the two counters considered in the previous section, the state table takes us closer to the final design. Thus, in general, the state diagram should be considered simply as a useful pictorial tool for the construction of state tables.

The following example illustrates a problem that often arises in the construction of state tables.

Example 4.2. In this example, we wish to design a sequential circuit which, after receiving a sequence of four binary digits, generates a 1 at its output if the sequence contains exactly two 1's and which generates a 0 at its output otherwise. Construct a state table that describes the required circuit behavior.

Table 4.12. State table for Example 4.1.

Current state	Next state		Outputs	
	$x=0$	$x=1$	$x=0$	$x=1$
A	A	B	0	0
B	A	C	0	0
C	D	C	0	0
D	A	E	0	1
E	A	B	0	0

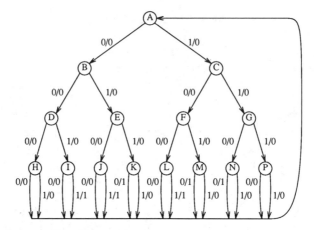

Figure 4.26. State diagram for Example 4.2.

Solution. A state diagram for this problem has been constructed in Figure 4.26. In drawing this diagram, we have assumed that the circuit output remains on 0 until all four digits have been received; when all four digits have been received the circuit outputs a 1 or 0 as required and then returns to the initial state to await the next sequence.

The state diagram in Figure 4.26 was constructed in a quite systematic way, with all possible sequences of inputs being separately treated. A state table is readily constructed from this diagram and is shown in Table 4.13. A glance at this table indicates that the systematic approach employed in the drawing of Figure 4.26 can lead to the creation of a number of redundant states. For in-

Table 4.13.   State table for Example 4.2.

Current state	Next state		Outputs	
	$x=0$	$x=1$	$x=0$	$x=1$
A	B	C	0	0
B	D	E	0	0
C	F	G	0	0
D	H	I	0	0
E	J	K	0	0
F	L	M	0	0
G	N	P	0	0
H	A	A	0	0
I	A	A	0	1
J	A	A	0	1
K	A	A	1	0
L	A	A	0	1
M	A	A	1	0
N	A	A	1	0
P	A	A	0	0

stance, when the system is in state H, it behaves in exactly the same way as when it is in state P; when the system is in either of these states, it will, upon arrival of the next digit, go to state A, and output a 0. It follows that when the system is in state P, its future behavior will be exactly the same as if it were in state H. Thus, in Table 4.13, we can replace P by H in the row corresponding to current state G and the system behavior described by the table will be unchanged. When this has been done, the table no longer allows state P to be reached and row P of the table can be deleted. This method of eliminating redundant state P is indicated in Table 4.14, where other redundant states (which we shall come to shortly) have also been eliminated.

States H and P in this example are said to be *equivalent states*, and we write $H \equiv P$.

Definition 4.1
Two states of a sequential system are said to be equivalent if, for any sequence of inputs, the system produces the same output sequence when started in either state.

In Table 4.13, the rows corresponding to "current" states H and P are identical. We say that states H and P have an identical pattern of next states and an identical output pattern. It should be clear that any other pair of states with identical patterns of next states and identical patterns of outputs will also be equivalent. Thus, the states I, J and L are all equivalent, as are states K, M and N. As a consequence, in Table 4.14, states J, L, M and N have all been eliminated.

Examination of Table 4.14 shows that the process of elimination of redundant

Table 4.14.   Elimination of redundant states.

Current	Next state		Outputs	
state	$x=0$	$x=1$	$x=0$	$x=1$
A	B	C	0	0
B	D	E	0	0
C	F	G	0	0
D	H	I	0	0
E	~~J~~I	K	0	0
F	~~L~~I	~~M~~K	0	0
G	~~N~~K	~~P~~H	0	0
H	A	A	0	0
I	A	A	0	1
~~J~~	~~A~~	~~A~~	~~0~~	~~1~~
K	A	A	1	0
~~L~~	~~A~~	~~A~~	~~0~~	~~1~~
~~M~~	~~A~~	~~A~~	~~1~~	~~0~~
~~N~~	~~A~~	~~A~~	~~1~~	~~0~~
~~P~~	~~A~~	~~A~~	~~0~~	~~0~~

Table 4.15. Final reduced table.

Current state	Next state		Outputs	
	$x=0$	$x=1$	$x=0$	$x=1$
A	B	C	0	0
B	D	E	0	0
C	E	G	0	0
D	H	I	0	0
E	I	K	0	0
G	K	H	0	0
H	A	A	0	0
I	A	A	0	1
K	A	A	1	0

states has revealed a pair of equivalent states which were not obviously equivalent in Table 4.13. These are states E and F.

The final reduced form of the state table is shown in Table 4.15. □

Reducing the state table in this way has advantages other than simply eliminating unnecessary detail from the description of system behavior. Most importantly, reducing the number of system states leads to a reduction in the amount of hardware required to realize the system. Reducing the number of states almost always leads to a reduction in the amount of combinational logic required and often leads to a reduction in the required number of flip-flops (note that a system with between $2^M + 1$ and 2^{M+1} states requires $M + 1$ flip-flops for its realization).

If the reader turns back a few pages and reads again the discussion surrounding the development of the state diagram for Example 4.1 (Figure 4.25) it can be seen that some effort was made to avoid generation of redundant states. However, a glance at the state table obtained from this state diagram (Table 4.12) indicates immediately that states A and E are equivalent. This points to the fact that in general, and especially in relation to large and complex systems, it is quite difficult to avoid introducing redundant states into a system description. Thus, a method of eliminating redundant states is important. The method given above is not really suitable for direct computer implementation and an algorithmic technique, due to Paull and Unger [1] is described in the next section.

4.4.2. The Paull-Unger Method of State Minimization

The Paull-Unger method is simply a systematized version of the state reduction technique employed in the previous section. We will now apply the method to Example 4.2.

The method commences with the construction of a chart (Table 4.16(a)) which contains a square for each possible pair of states. The top left-hand square cor-

Table 4.16.   Paull-Unger charts for Example 4.2; (a) initial chart.

	A	B	C	D	E	F	G	H	I	J	K	L	M	N
B	BD CE													
C	BF CG	DF EG												
D	BH CI	DH EI	FH GI											
E	BJ CK	DJ EK	FJ GK	HJ IK										
F	BL CM	DL EM	FL GM	HL IM	JL KM									
G	BN CP	DN EP	FN GP	HN IP	JN KP	LN MP								
H	BA CA	DA EA	FA GA	HA IA	JA KA	LA MA	NA PA							
I	X	X	X	X	X	X	X	X						
J	X	X	X	X	X	X	✓	X	X					
K	X	X	X	X	X	X	X	X	X	X				
L	X	X	X	X	X	X	✓	✓	X	X	X			
M	X	X	X	X	X	X	X	X	X	X	✓	X		
N	X	X	X	X	X	X	X	X	X	X	✓	X	✓	
P	BA CA	DA EA	FA GA	HA IA	JA KA	LA MA	NA PA	✓	X	X	X	X	X	X

responds to the pair of states A and B (it is located in row B and column A) and will be referred to as the B-A square. In this square, information is recorded regarding the possible equivalence of states A and B. Note that the state table (Table 4.13) indicates that states A and B have identical output patterns, but will only have identical patterns of next states if B is equivalent to D and if C is equivalent to E. Thus A and B can only be equivalent if $B \equiv D$ and $C \equiv E$; this is the meaning of the entry in the B-A square of Table 4.16(a).

Proceeding down column A of the chart, the requirements for state equivalence are entered in the same way until row I is reached. In the I-A square a cross is entered to indicate that it is impossible for states A and I to be equivalent, the reason being that the output patterns (in Table 4.13) for the two states differ. States A and I are known as *incompatibles*.

The remainder of column A is then filled out in the obvious way, as are

Table 4.16. (b) chart after one pass;

	A	B	C	D	E	F	G	H	I	J	K	L	M	N
B	BD CE													
C	BF CG	DF EG												
D	~~BH CI~~	~~DH EI~~	~~FH GI~~											
E	~~BJ CK~~	~~DJ EK~~	~~FJ GK~~	~~HJ IK~~										
F	~~BL CM~~	~~DL EM~~	~~FL GM~~	~~HL IM~~	JL KM									
G	~~BN CP~~	~~DN EP~~	~~FN GP~~	~~HN IP~~	~~JN KP~~	~~LN MP~~								
H	BA CA	DA EA	FA GA	~~HA IA~~	~~JA KA~~	~~LA MA~~	~~NA PA~~							
I	⊗	⊗	⊗	⊗	⊗	⊗	⊗	⊗						
J	⊗	⊗	⊗	⊗	⊗	⊗	⊗	⊗	✓					
K	⊗	⊗	⊗	⊗	⊗	⊗	⊗	⊗	⊗	⊗				
L	⊗	⊗	⊗	⊗	⊗	⊗	⊗	⊗	✓	✓	⊗			
M	⊗	⊗	⊗	⊗	⊗	⊗	⊗	⊗	⊗	⊗	✓	⊗		
N	⊗	⊗	⊗	⊗	⊗	⊗	⊗	⊗	⊗	⊗	✓	⊗	✓	
P	BA CA	DA EA	FA GA	~~HA IA~~	~~JA KA~~	~~LA MA~~	~~NA PA~~	✓	⊗	⊗	⊗	⊗	⊗	⊗
	A	B	C	D	E	F	G	H	I	J	K	L	M	N

columns B, C, D, E, F and G. When we come to column H, we find a pair of states which can, directly from the state table, be declared as equivalent (namely states H and P). This is indicated in the chart by placing a check mark in the P-H square. The remaining entries in the chart should be self-explanatory.

The chart in Table 4.16(a) is referred to as an *implication chart*. The reason for this terminology can be seen by considering the B-A square; here the entries indicate that if $B \equiv D$ and $C \equiv E$ then *by implication*, $B \equiv A$.

When the chart has been completed as in Table 4.16(a), it is examined, starting at the extreme right-hand column, for squares containing a cross. The P-N square contains a cross and this indicates that states P and N are incompatible (i.e. $P \not\equiv N$). We now examine all other squares to see if equivalence of any other pair of states depends upon the equivalence of P and N. If any such pair of states is found, we know that that pair cannot be equivalent and the entries

Table 4.16. (c) final chart.

	A	B	C	D	E	F	G	H	I	J	K	L	M	N
B	BD/CB ⊗													
C	BF/CG ⊗	DF/EG ⊗												
D	BH/CI ⊗	DH/EI ⊗	FH/GI ⊗											
E	BJ/CK ⊗	DJ/EK ⊗	FJ/GK ⊗	HJ/IK ⊗										
F	BJ/CM ⊗	DJ/EM ⊗	FJ/GM ⊗	HJ/IM ⊗	JL KM									
G	BN/CP ⊗	DN/EP ⊗	FN/GP ⊗	HN/IP ⊗	JN/KP ⊗	LN/MP ⊗								
H	BA/CA ⊗	DA/EA ⊗	FA/GA ⊗	HA/IA ⊗	JA/KA ⊗	LA/MA ⊗	NA/PA ⊗							
I	⊗	⊗	⊗	⊗	⊗	⊗	⊗	⊗						
J	⊗	⊗	⊗	⊗	⊗	⊗	⊗	⊗	✓					
K	⊗	⊗	⊗	⊗	⊗	⊗	⊗	⊗	⊗	⊗				
L	⊗	⊗	⊗	⊗	⊗	⊗	⊗	⊗	✓	✓	⊗			
M	⊗	⊗	⊗	⊗	⊗	⊗	⊗	⊗	⊗	⊗	✓	⊗		
N	⊗	⊗	⊗	⊗	⊗	⊗	⊗	⊗	⊗	⊗	✓	⊗	✓	
P	BA/CA ⊗	DA/EA ⊗	FA/GA ⊗	HA/IA ⊗	JA/KA ⊗	LA/MA ⊗	NA/PA ⊗	✓	⊗	⊗	⊗	⊗	⊗	⊗
	A	**B**	**C**	**D**	**E**	**F**	**G**	**H**	**I**	**J**	**K**	**L**	**M**	**N**

in the corresponding square are crossed out. In this particular case, no pair of states depends upon the equivalence of states, P and N. At the conclusion of the search a circle is drawn around the cross in the P-N square.

We now move left to column M and look for a square containing a cross. A cross is located in the P-M square and we now search the other squares to see if any pair of states depends upon the equivalence of states P and M. One such pair is found, namely G and F, the G-F square containing the entry MP. Thus, the pair G and F cannot be equivalent and the entries in the G-F square are crossed out. No other pair depends upon the equivalence of P and M and at the completion of the search a circle is drawn around the cross in the P-M square.

The process is continued until the situation depicted in Table 4.16(b) is reached. At this point all the crosses in Table 4.16(a) have been circled and we say that the "first pass" has been completed. In going from Table 4.16(a) to

Table 4.16(b) we have discovered several more incompatible pairs (indicated by those squares whose entries have been crossed out). We must now search the chart for any pairs of states whose equivalence depends upon the newly discovered incompatibles. The search proceeds exactly as before, starting with the pair P, G. Following completion of the second pass, it is found that two further passes (the last one involving a single square) are required before the final chart, shown in Table 4.16(c) is obtained. (Note that in practice, only one chart is actually used.)

The final step in the process is to determine the equivalent states. These are given in Table 4.16(c) by those squares that have not been crossed out. Hence we have

$$F \equiv E, J \equiv I, L \equiv I, L \equiv J, M \equiv K, N \equiv K, N \equiv M, P \equiv H$$

Thus, Table 4.16(c) gives the equivalent states of the system in pairs. We can group these pairs into sets of equivalent states to obtain the four sets below:

$$(E, F), (I, J, L), (K, M, N), (H, P).$$

Several states in the system are not equivalent to any other state; these are A, B, C, D and G. Listing these with the above groupings gives the minimum number of states required to describe system behavior; the list is:

$$A, B, C, D, G, (E, F), (I, J, L), (K, M, N), (H, P).$$

This list agrees with the reduced state table obtained earlier (Table 4.15). To check this, note that in Table 4.15, each of the equivalent sets of states obtained above is represented by its first member (i.e. the set (E, F) is represented by state E; the set (I, J, L) is represented by state I, etc.).

4.4.3. The Incompletely Specified Case

In the realm of sequential circuits, it is quite common to have systems in which certain inputs can never occur and, in such situations, don't-care conditions arise which can be used to advantage in design. An example is readily forthcoming if we consider again Example 4.2 under the assumption that the incoming sequences of four binary digits are BCD representations of the decimal numbers 0–9. For this case, the input sequences 1010, 1011, 1100, 1101, 1110 and 1111 can never occur. The state diagram for this modified example is shown in Figure 4.27 where it has been assumed that the least significant digit is read in first. This diagram should be compared with the state diagram of the original example (Figure 4.26).

From the state diagram, a state table can be drawn and this is shown in Table

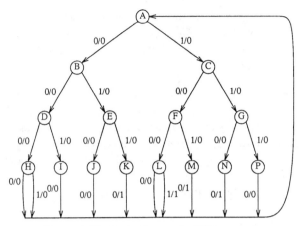

Figure 4.27. State diagram for BCD example.

4.17. This table is very similar to the table drawn up for the original example (Table 4.13); the only difference is that some of the entries in Table 4.13 have been replaced by x's in Table 4.17. The x's correspond to situations which should never occur. Thus, in the row corresponding to state I, x's have been placed in the columns corresponding to input x = 1 because we know that when the system is in state I it can only receive the input $x = 0$. (Input $x = 0$ corresponds to the input sequence 0100 which *can* occur, and input $x = 1$ corresponds to the input sequence 1100 which *cannot* occur.)

Table 4.17. State table for BCD example.

Current state	Next State		Outputs	
	$x=0$	$x=1$	$x=0$	$x=1$
A	B	C	0	0
B	D	E	0	0
C	F	G	0	0
D	H	I	0	0
E	J	K	0	0
F	L	M	0	0
G	N	P	0	0
H	A	A	0	0
I	A	x	0	x
J	A	x	0	x
K	A	x	1	x
L	A	A	0	1
M	A	x	1	x
N	A	x	1	x
P	A	x	0	x

Examination of Table 4.17 indicates how we might attempt to take advantage of the presence of don't-cares. Consider again the row corresponding to state *I*: we see that state *I* could be made equivalent to state *H* if the x in the next state column were replaced by *A* and the x in the output column were replaced by 0. Similarly, we see that state *I* could be made equivalent to state *L* if the x in the next state column were replaced by *A* and the x in the output column were replaced by 1. Now clearly state *I* cannot be equivalent to both state *H* *and* state *L* because states *H* and *L* are not themselves equivalent (they have different output patterns). In situations like this, we use the term *compatibility* of states. In this case the pair of states *H* and *I* is said to be compatible, as is the pair *I* and *L*.

In order to economize on terminology (in the incompletely specified case) *equivalent* states are also referred to as *compatible* states—they do, after all, constitute a special case of compatibility. With this in mind, compatible states can be defined as follows:

Definition 4.2
Two states of an incompletely specified sequential system are said to be compatible if, when the system is started in either state, the output sequence produced (for any input sequence) is the same at every instant where both are specified.

This definition should be compared with Definition 4.1.

States which are not compatible are said to be *incompatible*. Thus, states *H* and *L* in Table 4.17 are incompatible.

In the presence of don't-care conditions, the state-reduction process is essentially a process of grouping compatible states. Don't-care conditions allow some states to be included in more than one group (though for this to occur, at least one don't-care must take on a different value in each group).

The Paull-Unger technique provides a systematic method for taking full advantage of the presence of don't-cares. The implication chart is drawn up much as before, but in this case, the entries in the squares indicate the conditions under which pairs of states are compatible (rather than equivalent as in the fully-specified case).

The chart representing Table 4.17 is shown in Table 4.18(a). The squares marked with a check indicate those pairs of states that are immediately identifiable as compatible and the squares which have been crossed out indicate those pairs of states that are immediately identifiable as incompatible. The remaining squares indicate the conditions that must be satisfied if further compatibilities are to exist. For instance, the pair of states *A* and *B* can only be compatible if *B* and *D* are compatible and if, in addition, *C* and *E* are compatible.

Compatible pairs are determined from the implication chart of Table 4.18(a) in exactly the same way that equivalent pairs were determined from Table 4.16(a). The final form of the chart is shown in Table 4.18(b).

Table 4.18. Paull-Unger charts for BCD example: (a) initial chart.

	A	B	C	D	E	F	G	H	I	J	K	L	M	N
B	BD CE													
C	BF CG	DF EG												
D	BH CI	DH EI	FH GI											
E	BJ CK	DJ EK	FJ GK	HJ IK										
F	BL CM	DL EM	FL GM	HL IM	JL KM									
G	BN CP	DN EP	FN GP	HN IP	JN KP	LN MP								
H	BA CA	DA EA	FA GA	HA IA	JA KA	LA MA	NA PA							
I	BA	DA	FA	HA	JA	LA	NA	✓						
J	BA	DA	FA	HA	JA	LA	NA	✓	✓					
K	✕	✕	✕	✕	✕	✕	✕	✕	✕	✕				
L	✕	✕	✕	✕	✕	✕	✕	✕	✓	✓	✕			
M	✕	✕	✕	✕	✕	✕	✕	✕	✕	✕	✓	✕		
N	✕	✕	✕	✕	✕	✕	✕	✕	✕	✕	✓	✕	✓	
P	BA	DA	FA	HA	JA	LA	NA	✓	✓	✓	✕	✓	✕	✕

The next step in the process is to identify groups of compatible states. This can be done in a systematic way (suitable for computer implementation) as follows. Start at the right-hand column of Table 4.18(b) and look for a compatible pair. In this case, no such pair exists so we move left to column M. In this column, the compatible pair (N, M) is evident and this can be recorded, as shown in Table 4.19. Moving to column L we note the compatible pair (P, L) and record it as shown. When we move to column K, two further compatible pairs $(N, K$ and $M, K)$ are noted. Compatibility of the pairs (N, K), (M, K) and (N, M) implies compatibility of the triple (N, M, K) and this is entered in the table as shown.

Note that compatibility of the triple is only guaranteed by compatibility of all three pairs. This is in contrast to the fully specified case where equivalence of two pairs, say (N, K) and (M, K), would imply equivalence of the pair (N, M) and hence of the triple (N, M, K). This difference arises because, in the

Table 4.18. (b) final chart.

	A	B	C	D	E	F	G	H	I	J	K	L	M	N
B	BD/CB ✗													
C	BF/CG ✗	DF/EG ✗												
D	BF/CI ✗	DF/EI ✗	FH/GI ✗											
E	BI/CK ✗	DI/EK ✗	FI/GK ✗	HI/IK ✗										
F	BI/CM ✗	DI/EM ✗	FI/GM ✗	HI/IM ✗	JL KM									
G	BN/CP ✗	DN/EP ✗	FN/GP ✗	HN/IP ✗	IN/KP ✗	LN/MP ✗								
H	BA/CA ✗	DA/EA ✗	FA/GA ✗	HA/IA ✗	IA/KA ✗	LA/MA ✗	NA/PA ✗							
I	✗	✗	✗	✗	✗	✗	✗	✓						
J	✗	✗	✗	✗	✗	✗	✗	✓	✓					
K	✗	✗	✗	✗	✗	✗	✗	✗	✗	✗				
L	✗	✗	✗	✗	✗	✗	✗	✗	✓	✓	✗			
M	✗	✗	✗	✗	✗	✗	✗	✗	✗	✗	✓	✗		
N	✗	✗	✗	✗	✗	✗	✗	✗	✗	✗	✓	✗	✓	
P	✗	✗	✗	✗	✗	✗	✗	✓	✓	✓	✗	✓	✗	✗

incompletely specified case, compatibility of two pairs often depends upon a don't-care entry taking on one value in one pair and a different value in the other pair. As an example of this, refer again to Table 4.17 and observe the compatibility of the pairs (H, I) and (L, I) and the incompatibility of the pair (H, L).

The remainder of Table 4.19 is filled out in a fairly obvious way. We simply draw the reader's attention to two further points:

(i) When the procedure reaches column I, compatibility of state I with states J, L and P implies compatibility of all four states because compatibility of the triple (P, L, J) has already been established.

(ii) In column H, compatibility of state H with states I, J and P implies compatibility of all four states because compatibility of states I, J and P

Table 4.19. Compatibility table.

Column	Compatibles
N	
M	(N,M)
L	(P,L),(N,M)
K	(N,M,K),(P,L)
J	(N,M,K),(P,L,J)
I	(N,M,K),(P,L,J,I)
H	(P,J,I,H),(N,M,K),(P,L,J,I)
G	(P,J,I,H),(N,M,K),(P,L,J,I)
F	(P,J,I,H),(N,M,K),(P,L,J,I)
E	(E,F),(P,J,I,H),(N,M,K),(P,L,J,I)
D	(E,F),(P,J,I,H),(N,M,K),(P,L,J,I)
C	(E,F),(P,J,I,H),(N,M,K),(P,L,J,I)
B	(E,F),(P,J,I,H),(N,M,K),(P,L,J,I)
A	(E,F),(P,J,I,H),(N,M,K),(P,L,J,I)
Final	A,B,C,D,G,(E,F),(P,J,I,H),(N,M,K),(P,J,L,I)

has already been established. Note, however, that state H is not compatible with state L and so we have to distinguish between the two groups of compatibles (P, J, I, H) and (P, L, J, I).

In the final row of Table 4.19, the groups of compatible states that have been identified are entered along with the individual states A, B, C, D and G, each of which is incompatible with all other states. For convenience we will refer to these latter entries as ''groups'' of states (each of which has a single member) so that the final row of Table 4.19 can be said to contain nine separate groups of compatible states. Each of these groups contains *all* of the states that belong to a particular compatibility type. For this reason, these groups are termed *maximal compatibles*. For this problem, then, there are nine maximal compatibles.

In general, the set of maximal compatibles provides an *upper bound* on the number of states necessary to describe the behavior of a sequential circuit. Thus, in general, the procedure described here is not guaranteed to produce the *minimum* number of states required for system description. Consequently a procedure is required to select, from the set of maximal compatibles, a set of groupings which is *sufficient* to describe system behavior. In carrying out such a selection, it should be obvious that every state in the original state table must be included in at least one grouping of the selection (otherwise, a complete description of system behavior would not be possible). This immediately shows us that in this particular example the set of maximal compatibles constitutes the minimum set of groupings of states necessary for describing system behavior. This is so because it is impossible to delete any one maximal compatible from the set without deleting at least one state (from the original state table) from the set.

Thus, for this example, nine states are required for a complete system description. Recall that in Example 4.2, where the problem was completely specified, the minimum number of states required was also nine. In this particular case, then, the presence of don't-cares has not led to any reduction in the minimum number of states, but in general, the presence of don't-cares can lead to a reduction (one such example is given as Exercise 4.18). Thus, when a problem is incompletely specified, a procedure designed specifically for the incompletely specified case should be followed.

The problem of finding a *minimum* set of states in the incompletely specified case is, in general, quite a complex one. We will postpone further discussion of this problem until the next chapter where superior, though more complex, techniques, along with program listings, are presented.

4.4.4. State Assignment

The previous section has detailed methods for minimizing the number of states required to represent the behavior of a given system. State minimization ensures that any such system is realized using the minimum possible number of flip-flops. The final step in the design involves the determination of the manner in which the flip-flops are to be connected. We have seen earlier (Figures 4.19(b) and 4.23) that the interconnections between flip-flops usually contain some elements of combinational logic. It turns out that there are usually many ways in which these interconnections can be made, some requiring significantly less combinational hardware than others. It is the purpose of this section to investigate the problem of determining the best interconnection scheme.

To illustrate the problem we will consider the completion of the design of the system whose state minimization is set as Exercise 4.18 at the end of this chapter. For this system, the state table prior to minimization is shown in Table E4.18 and, following minimization, the set of maximal compatibles obtained is A, B, C, D, G, (E, F), (I, J, L), (H, K, M, N, P). Thus, the system can be described by eight states, implying that it can be realized using three flip-flops. Suppose that we wish to realize the system using T flip-flops. Let these flip-flops have inputs T_1, T_2 and T_3 with corresponding outputs Q_1, Q_2 and Q_3. We can then define the state of the system at any given time, in the same way as we did previously (see Figure 4.19 and associated discussion), by the values of the outputs at that time. That is, we will represent the state of the system by the values of the outputs arranged in the sequence $Q_3 Q_2 Q_1$; the outputs Q_3, Q_2 and Q_1 are, in this context, called the *state variables*.

To realize this system, each of the eight system states must be identified with one of the eight possible values (i.e., bit combinations) of $Q_3 Q_2 Q_1$. In other words, each of the states must be assigned one of the eight possible bit combinations. Three such assignments are shown in Table 4.20. Obviously, many more such assignments could be made and, since the circuit will be required to make predefined transitions from state to state (on receipt of a stream of input

Table 4.20. Three possible state assignments.

System state	Assignment 1 $Q_3Q_2Q_1$	Assignment 2 $Q_3Q_2Q_1$	Assignment 3 $Q_3Q_2Q_1$
A	000	010	100
B	001	011	101
C	010	000	000
D	011	001	001
G	100	110	110
(E,F)	101	111	111
(I,J,L)	110	100	010
(H,K,M,N,P)	111	101	011

bits), it should be clear that many of these assignments will lead to substantially different circuit realizations. Some of these realizations are likely to require significantly less combinational logic than others and so it is important that we study in some detail the problem of assigning bit combinations to system states. This problem is usually referred to as the *state-assignment problem*.

It is not very hard to see that some of the possible assignments are virtually equivalent. For instance, assignment 2 in Table 4.20 can be obtained from assignment 1 by simply complementing output Q_2. Consequently, the only difference that will exist between circuit realizations obtained from these two assignments will be that connections made to the outputs Q_2 and $\overline{Q}_2$ in one circuit will be made to $\overline{Q}_2$ and Q_2, respectively, in the other; apart from this, the combinational logic for the two circuits will be identical. As a second example, assignment 3 in Table 4.20 can be obtained from assignment 2 by simply interchanging Q_3 and Q_2. This implies that circuit realizations obtained from these two assignments will differ only in the fact that the functions of flip-flops 2 and 3 will be interchanged; again, the combinational logic requirements will be identical.

Obviously there are many state assignments that exhibit these minor differences and which lead to circuits whose combinational hardware requirement is exactly the same. Recall that our interest is in finding a circuit whose combinational hardware requirement is a minimum. Thus, we have no interest whatever in state assignments which differ in the trivial ways explained above.

It has been shown by McCluskey and Unger [2] that for a system with n state variables and r states, the number of state assignments which differ in nontrivial ways (i.e. those that can be expected to lead to significantly different circuit realizations) is given by the expression†

$$\frac{(2^n - 1)!}{(2^n - r)!\, n!}$$

---

† It is shown in [3] that although this expression holds for all four flip-flop types (SR, JK, T, and D), the case of the D flip-flop has to be carefully argued.

Table 4.21. Minimized state table from Exercise 4.18.

Current state		Next state		Outputs	
Old label	New label	$x=0$	$x=1$	$x=0$	$x=1$
A	a	b	c	0	0
B	b	d	f	0	0
C	c	f	e	0	0
D	d	h	g	0	0
G	e	h	h	0	0
(E,F)	f	g	h	0	0
(I,J,L)	g	a	a	1	0
(H,K,M,N,P)	h	a	a	0	1

This implies that for the problem in hand, in which $n = 3$ and $r = 8$, the number of state assignments which differ in non-trivial ways is 840‡. Some of these assignments will undoubtedly lead to circuits requiring less combinational hardware than others. A systematic method exists (for synchronous sequential systems) which allows determination of an assignment that leads to a circuit requiring minimum combinational hardware. This method is detailed in the next chapter, and a Pascal listing for the method is provided. In this chapter we will do no more than introduce a few rules and guidelines which have been found to be of assistance in reducing the combinational hardware requirement. In order to see where these rules and guidelines originate, we will consider the completion of the design of the system specified in Exercise 4.18.

The state minimization required in Exercise 4.18 leads to a state table having the form shown in Table 4.21. Here, for convenience we have introduced a new set of labels for the system states. Suppose that we wish to realize this system using T flip-flops and suppose also that we choose to assign bit combinations to states according to assignment 1 in Table 4.20. Since assignment 1 follows the standard ordering of the binary numbers, it is sometimes referred to as "binary assignment". With this binary assignment the state table can be redrawn as in Table 4.22. In this table we have added the flip-flop inputs that will be required to cause the changes of state indicated in the columns headed "next state".

Combinational logic circuitry is required to provide the inputs to the three flip-flops and to provide the system output. This circuitry has available for its own inputs the system input x^n and the outputs of the three flip-flops Q_1^n, Q_2^n and Q_3^n. We can obtain suitable circuitry by using Table 4.22 to draw up the four K-maps shown in Figure 4.28.

The switching functions obtained from the maps in Figure 4.28 are as fol-

---

‡The number of distinct assignments for a range of values of n and r is given in Table 5.11.

Table 4.22. State table with binary assignment.

Current state	Next state		Output Z^n		Flip-flop inputs	
	$x^n=0$	$x^n=1$			$x^n=0$	$x^n=1$
			$x^n=0$	$x^n=1$		
$Q_3^n Q_2^n Q_1^n$	$Q_3^{n+1} Q_2^{n+1} Q_1^{n+1}$	$Q_3^{n+1} Q_2^{n+1} Q_1^{n+1}$			$T_3^n T_2^n T_1^n$	$T_3^n T_2^n T_1^n$
000	001	010	0	0	001	010
001	011	101	0	0	010	100
010	101	100	0	0	111	110
011	111	110	0	0	100	101
100	111	111	0	0	011	011
101	110	111	0	0	011	010
110	000	000	1	0	110	110
111	000	000	0	1	111	111

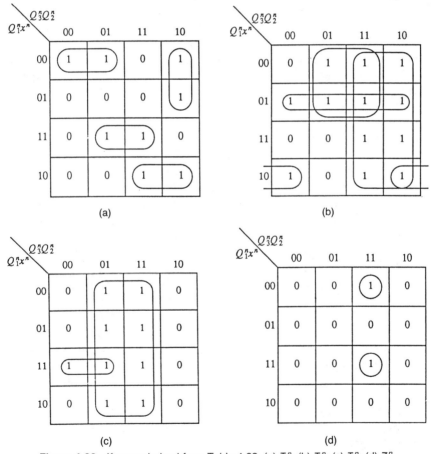

Figure 4.28. K-maps derived from Table 4.22: (a) T_1^n; (b) T_2^n; (c) T_3^n; (d) Z^n.

lows:

$$T_1^n = \overline{Q}_3^n\overline{Q}_1^n\overline{x}^n + Q_3^n\overline{Q}_2^n\overline{Q}_1^n + Q_2^nQ_1^nx^n + Q_3^nQ_1^n\overline{x}^n$$

$$T_2^n = Q_2^n\overline{Q}_1^n + \overline{Q}_1^nx^n + \overline{Q}_2^nQ_1^n\overline{x}^n + Q_3^n \qquad (4.1)$$

$$T_3^n = Q_2^n + \overline{Q}_3^nQ_1^nx^n$$

$$Z^n = Q_3^nQ_2^n\overline{Q}_1^n\overline{x}^n + Q_3^nQ_2^nQ_1^nx^n$$

Realization of these switching functions would require 4 OR gates and 10 AND gates. This set of switching functions was obtained from one (rather arbitrarily chosen) state assignment out of the 840 possible assignments that are available. Obviously, it is very unlikely that the chosen assignment leads to a circuit which requires the minimum possible amount of combinational logic. How can we set about the problem of obtaining a better realization without laboriously working through all 840 possibilities?

One possible approach is to observe the manner in which the above realization was obtained and to note in particular the way in which function simplifications came about. Note that in Figure 4.28 the K-maps for both T_2^n and T_3^n each contain a group of eight 1-entries that have been looped. Each such group provides a major simplification of the corresponding switching function and it is worthwhile investigating how these groups arise out of the chosen state assignment.

As an aid to this investigation, we draw up the two maps shown in Figure 4.29. The map in Figure 4.29(a) is simply a representation of the chosen state assignment; for instance, when $Q_3 = Q_2 = Q_1 = 0$, the system is in state a (regardless of whether the input x is equal to 0 or 1) and this is indicated by the presence of the letter a in the top two squares of the left-hand column. The other entries in Figure 4.29(a) arise in a similar fashion.

Figure 4.29(b) shows the way in which the system state will change, at the arrival of a clock pulse, for each of the combinations of system state and input value marked in Figure 4.29(a). Thus, if the system is in state a and the input $x = 0$, the arrival of a clock pulse will cause the system to move to state b (see Table 4.21). This is indicated by the fact that the top left-hand square in Figure 4.29(a) contains an a and the top left-hand square in Figure 4.29(b) contains a b. All other state transitions are similarly represented, and this can be checked by comparing Figure 4.29 with Table 4.21. The map in Figure 4.29(a) is termed the *present-state map* and the map in Figure 4.29(b) is termed the *next-state map*.

Return again now to the maps for T_2^n and T_3^n in Figure 4.28. Note that in each of these maps the third column (corresponding to $Q_3 = 1$, $Q_2 = 1$) is a column of 1's. This column obviously contributes substantially to the simplifications available for the switching functions representing T_2^n and T_3^n. The map of next states in Figure 4.29(b) allows us to see how these simplifications come about.

Q_1x \ Q_3Q_2	00	01	11	10
00	a	c	g	e
01	a	c	g	e
11	b	d	h	f
10	b	d	h	f

(a)

Q_1x \ Q_3Q_2	00	01	11	10
00	b	f	a	h
01	c	e	a	h
11	f	g	a	h
10	d	h	a	g

(b)

Figure 4.29. (a) Present state map; (b) next state map.

Figure 4.29 shows that the system will go to state *a* from either state *g* or state *h* regardless of the value of the input *x*. State *g* has been assigned the bit pattern 110 (i.e., $Q_3 = 1$, $Q_2 = 1$, $Q_1 = 0$), state *h* has been assigned the bit pattern 111 and state *a* the bit pattern 000. Thus, in moving from state *g* (which implies moving to state *a*) the outputs Q_3 and Q_2 are required to change value, implying that the inputs T_3 and T_2 are required to take on the value 1. Similarly, in moving from state *h* to state *a*, all three outputs are required to change, implying that all three flip-flop inputs should take on the value 1. This explains why the third column in each of the K-maps for T_3^n and T_2^n (in Figure 4.28) is a column of 1's.

The column of 1's has been obtained because states *g* and *h*, which have the same "next state" (state *a*), have been assigned bit patterns that cause them to lie in the same column of the present-state map. States *g* and *h* are said to have adjacent assignments because their bit patterns differ in only one position (g is assigned 110 and h is assigned 111).

Out of reasoning such as this, two general rules have been produced for state assignment. These rules are usually helpful in reducing the combinational logic requirement in sequential circuit design and they are applicable to realizations using any type of flip-flop. They can be stated as follows:

Rule 1

If two or more states have the same next states, they should be given adjacent assignments.

Rule 2

If two or more states are the next states of a particular state, they should be given adjacent assignments.

The reductions obtained by implementing Rule 1 are generally more extensive than those obtainable through implementation of Rule 2. Thus, the course of action which should be followed in applying these rules is to apply Rule 1 first and then use Rule 2 where possible without conflicting with assignments suggested by Rule 1. In other words, Rule 1 should take precedence over Rule 2.

Example 4.3. Let us now apply these rules in the assignment of states for the system described by Table 4.21. Assignment 1 in Table 4.20 has already been applied to this problem and led to the switching functions in Equation 4.1. We would now like to see in what way (if any) implementation of the two rules above will lead to simplified switching functions.

We can identify those states that have the same next states by using the maps in Figure 4.29 to draw up Table 4.23 which, for each next state, lists the present states from which transitions can occur. For instance, if the present state is

Table 4.23. Identification of states with same next states.

Next state	Present state
a	g,h
b	a
c	a
d	b
e	c
f	b,c
g	d,f
h	d,e,f

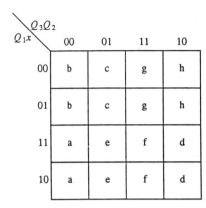

Figure 4.30. State assignment based upon Rules 1 and 2.

either g or h, the next state is a. Using Rule 1, this implies that states g and h should be given adjacent assignments. Similarly, Rule 1 implies that the pairs of states (b, c) and (d, f) should be given adjacent assignments along with the triple (d, e, f).

In order to apply Rule 2 we refer to the state table (Table 4.21) which indicates that the pairs of states (b, c), (d, f), (f, e) and (h, g) should be given adjacent assignments. None of these is in conflict with Rule 1; in fact the adjacencies recommended by Rule 2 are virtually a repeat of those recommended by Rule 1. A suitable assignment based upon these recommendations is shown in Figure 4.30.

A state table based upon the assignment in Figure 4.30 is shown in Table 4.24. The fact that it represents the required behavior can be seen by comparison with Table 4.21.

The switching functions for the combinational logic circuitry required to drive the flip-flop inputs, and provide the system output, are obtained from the K-

Table 4.24. State table with assignment based upon Rules 1 and 2.

	Current state	Next state		Output Z^n		Flip-flop inputs	
		$x^n=0$	$x^n=1$	$x^n=0$	$x^n=1$	$x^n=0$	$x^n=1$
	$Q_3^n Q_2^n Q_1^n$	$Q_3^{n+1} Q_2^{n+1} Q_1^{n+1}$	$Q_3^{n+1} Q_2^{n+1} Q_1^{n+1}$			$T_3^n T_2^n T_1^n$	$T_3^n T_2^n T_1^n$
a	001	000	010	0	0	001	011
b	000	101	111	0	0	101	111
c	010	111	011	0	0	101	001
d	101	100	110	0	0	001	011
e	011	100	100	0	0	111	111
f	111	110	100	0	0	001	011
g	110	001	001	1	0	111	111
h	100	001	001	0	1	101	101

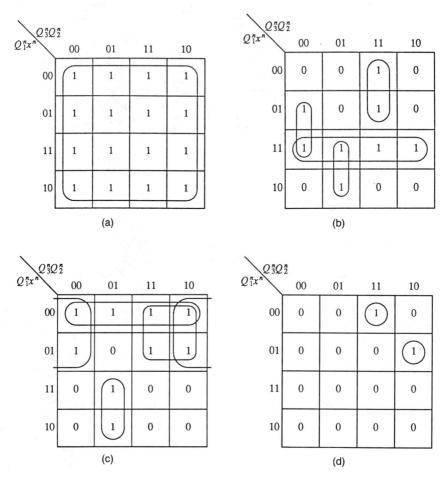

Figure 4.31. K-maps derived from Table 4.24. (a) T_1^n; (b) T_2^n; (c) T_3^n; (d) Z^n.

maps in Figure 4.31. They are as follows:

$$T_1^n = 1$$
$$T_2^n = Q_1^n x^n + \overline{Q}_3^n \overline{Q}_2^n x^n + Q_3^n Q_2^n \overline{Q}_1^n + \overline{Q}_3^n Q_2^n Q_1^n$$
$$T_3^n = \overline{Q}_1^n \overline{x}^n + \overline{Q}_2^n \overline{Q}_1^n + Q_3^n \overline{Q}_1^n + \overline{Q}_3^n Q_2^n Q_1^n$$
$$Z^n = Q_3^n Q_2^n \overline{Q}_1^n \overline{x}^n + Q_3^n \overline{Q}_2^n \overline{Q}_1^n x^n$$

$$(4.2)$$

Realization of these switching functions will require 3 OR gates and 10 AND gates, representing a reduction of only 1 gate from the realization obtained using the earlier (binary) state assignment. However, we should bear in mind that

Table 4.25. State table derived from Exercise 4.20.

Current state	Next state x=0	Next state x=1	Output x=0	Output x=1
a	b	c	0	0
b	d	e	0	0
c	e	d	0	0
d	g	f	0	0
e	f	g	0	0
f	a	a	1	0
g	a	a	0	1

binary assignment led to some quite substantial simplifications. In practice, we would not normally expect to be so fortunate with an arbitrary state assignment. The fact that implementation of Rules 1 and 2 above has led to a further reduction in the combinational logic requirement is certainly indicative of the value of these rules. □

As a further illustration, let us now consider an example in which D flip-flops are used.

Example 4.4. Exercise 4.20 leads to a state table having the form displayed in Table 4.25. A list of present states for each next state is shown in Table 4.26 and a suitable state assignment, based upon Rules 1 and 2 is indicated in Figure 4.32. This assignment leads to the state table shown in Table 4.27 where the required inputs for a D flip-flop realization have been included. Note that because the system has only seven states, one bit combination (arbitrarily chosen in Figure 4.32 as 101) is not assigned to any system state and leads to don't-cares for all flip-flop inputs.

The switching functions for the combinational logic circuitry required to drive the flip-flop inputs, and provide the system output, are obtained from the K-

Table 4.26. Table of states with same next state.

Next state	Present state
a	f,g
b	a
c	a
d	b,c
e	b,c
f	d,e
g	d,e

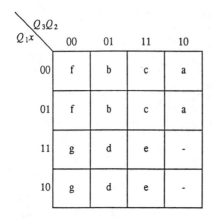

Figure 4.32. State assignment for Example 4.4.

maps shown in Figure 4.33. These functions are as follows:

$$D_3^n = \overline{Q}_3^n \overline{Q}_2^n + \overline{Q}_3^n \overline{Q}_1^n x^n + \overline{Q}_2^n x^n + Q_3^n Q_2^n \overline{Q}_1^n \overline{x}^n$$

$$D_2^n = Q_2^n \overline{Q}_1^n + Q_3^n \overline{Q}_1^n$$

$$D_1^n = Q_2^n \overline{Q}_1^n + \overline{Q}_3^n Q_2^n \overline{x}^n + Q_3^n Q_2^n x^n$$

$$Z^n = \overline{Q}_3^n \overline{Q}_2^n \overline{Q}_1^n \overline{x}^n + \overline{Q}_3^n \overline{Q}_2^n Q_1^n x^n$$

Note that we have avoided taking advantage of the don't-cares in determining the switching function for Z^n. This avoids having the circuit give a spurious 1 output if it is ever driven into the don't-care state 101 (either on start-up or due to noise). We should, of course, check that state 101 is not a hang-up state—it is just conceivable that the switching functions above will cause the system to stay permanently in state 101 if it ever enters that state. However, substitution of the values $Q_3^n = 1$, $Q_2^n = 0$, $Q_1^n = 1$ into the switching functions gives D_3^n

Table 4.27. State table for Example 4.4.

	Current state	Next state		Output Z^n		Flip-flop inputs	
		$x^n=0$	$x^n=1$	$x^n=0$	$x^n=1$	$x^n=0$	$x^n=1$
	$Q_3^n\ Q_2^n\ Q_1^n$	$Q_3^{n+1}\ Q_2^{n+1}\ Q_1^{n+1}$	$Q_3^{n+1}\ Q_2^{n+1}\ Q_1^{n+1}$			$D_3^n\ D_2^n\ D_1^n$	$D_3^n\ D_2^n\ D_1^n$
a	1 0 0	0 1 0	1 1 0	0	0	0 1 0	1 1 0
b	0 1 0	0 1 1	1 1 1	0	0	0 1 1	1 1 1
c	1 1 0	1 1 1	0 1 1	0	0	1 1 1	0 1 1
d	0 1 1	0 0 1	0 0 0	0	0	0 0 1	0 0 0
e	1 1 1	0 0 0	0 0 1	0	0	0 0 0	0 0 1
f	0 0 0	1 0 0	1 0 0	1	0	1 0 0	1 0 0
g	0 0 1	1 0 0	1 0 0	0	1	1 0 0	1 0 0
h	1 0 1	—	—	—	—	x x x	x x x

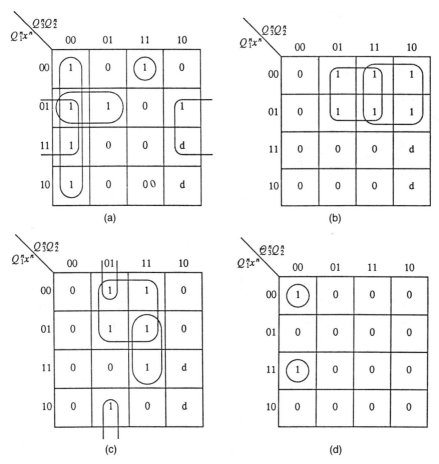

Figure 4.33. K-maps derived from Table 4.27. (a) D_3^n; (b) D_2^n; (c) D_1^n; (d) Z^n.

$= x^n$; $D_2^n = D_1^n = 0$ indicating that after entry into the don't-care state, the system would return to the required sequence upon arrival of the next clock pulse.

A circuit realization of the switching functions would require 4 OR gates and 10 AND gates. □

4.5. SOME PRACTICAL CONSIDERATIONS

In our description of the development of the JK flip-flop from the SR flip-flop (Section 4.2.3) we observed how a timing problem called a race condition can arise. This particular problem can be overcome in the case of the JK flip-flop either by using the master–slave idea or by using edge-triggering. In this section we will look briefly at one or two other timing, and related, problems that can arise in practice.

4.5.1. Hazards and Glitches

The Boolean algebra that we have employed as a basis for combinational logic design takes no account of the fact that a finite amount of time is required for signals to propagate from the input to the output of each gate in a combinational circuit. This fact can lead to circumstances in which spurious (and brief) outputs, not predicted by the Boolean algebra underlying the design of a circuit, can occur. The circumstances that lead to these spurious outputs are called *hazards*; the spurious outputs are called *glitches*. Various kinds of hazards exist in combinational circuits, but we will examine only one type in detail here.

   Consider the circuit shown in Figure 4.34(a). This circuit is a realization of the combinational logic function $Z = \overline{A}C + A\overline{B}$. The presence of a hazard in this circuit becomes clearer when one notes that the signal A and its complement are both required as inputs. If we indicate explicitly the inverters required for this realization, the circuit takes on the appearance of Figure 4.34(b). Now note that with $B = 0$ and $C = 1$, the output of the circuit should be $Z = 1$, regardless of the value of A. Thus, if we hold input B at logic 0 and input C at logic 1, a change in the value of A should make no difference to Z. Now observe what

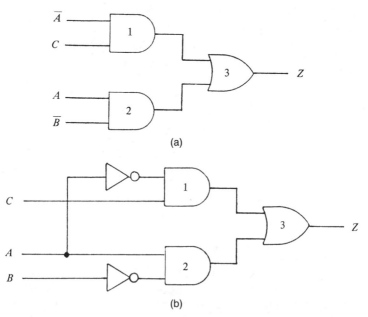

(a)

(b)

Figure 4.34. (a) Realization of $Z = \overline{A}C + A\overline{B}$; (b) realization with inverters shown explicitly.

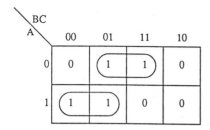

Figure 4.35. K-map showing potential hazard.

actually happens when we hold B at 0 and C at 1 and change A from 1 to 0. The instant that A changes, the inputs to gate 2 become $A = 0$, $\overline{B} = 1$ and, because of the time taken for the changed value of A to propagate through the upper inverter, the inputs to gate 1 remain (briefly) at $\overline{A} = 0$, $C = 1$. Thus, until the changed value of A propagates through the upper inverter, both AND gates have a 0 input and this causes Z to go briefly to zero. Once the changed value of A propagates through the inverter, gate 1 has inputs $\overline{A} = 1$, $C = 1$, causing Z to return to 1. The brief excursion to logic 0 at the output Z is a glitch, typically (with TTL) of just a few nanoseconds duration.

That a potential hazard exists for this particular circuit can be observed on a K-map. The circuit has been realized from the grouping shown in Figure 4.35. The hazard exists when B is held at logic 0 and C is held at logic 1. Then when A is at logic 1, the lower grouping in the map (representing $A\overline{B}$) is asserted. When A changes to 0, the other grouping (representing $\overline{A}C$) is asserted. The glitch occurs as the transition is made from the assertion of one grouping to the assertion of the other. The problem can be avoided by adding the third grouping shown in Figure 4.36 (representing $\overline{B}C$) so that Z remains 1 when $B = 0$ and $C = 1$ regardless of any transitions in the value of A. Thus, the circuit in Figure 4.37 is hazard-free.

This example illustrates the fact that a K-map which has adjacent 1's that have been looped into different groupings indicates the existence of a potential hazard. The hazard can be "covered" by adding an extra loop to group these adjacent 1's. This, of course, means that the resulting hazard-free realization will be non-minimal.

The type of hazard described here is known as a *static hazard* because it leads to a glitch on an output that should be unchanging. Another type, called

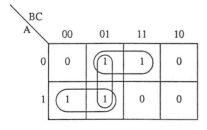

Figure 4.36. Grouping of terms of produce hazard-free realization.

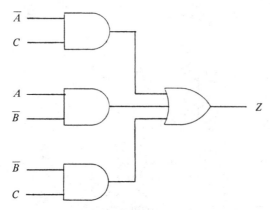

Figure 4.37. Hazard-free realization.

a *dynamic hazard*, leads to glitches or brief oscillations in outputs when the outputs change value. We will not go into further details on hazards here because, in synchronous sequential circuits where edge-triggered flip-flops are used, glitches do not normally cause problems. Care should be taken, of course, in situations where combinational circuitry forms the output of a device where good "clean" waveforms are required (for instance where the output feeds to a pulse counter). In such circumstances it is necessary to cover all hazards. In simple cases, this can be done using K-maps in the manner indicated above. For more complicated cases, the problem of eliminating hazards is quite complex and will not be pursued further here. Some details of more general techniques for hazard-free design are given in [4].

Before leaving this topic we point out one further item of practical significance. Almost all clocked flip-flops have asynchronous inputs for the operations of "preset" and "clear". Any combinational logic attached to these inputs should be hazard-free for reasons that should be obvious.

4.5.2. Race Conditions

A race condition was encountered in Section 4.2.3 when the SR flip-flop was modified to produce the JK type. The possibility of this kind of race condition occurring led to the development of flip-flops of the master–slave and edge-triggered varieties. These days most flip-flops are edge-triggered.

When using edge-triggered flip-flops in a synchronous circuit, the only way that race conditions can arise is where, following an active clock edge, the output of a flip-flop changes and this leads to a change in the input at another (possibly the same) flip-flop in a time interval shorter than the hold time of the second flip-flop. For any given logic family (say 74Sxxx or 74LSxxx), the propagation delay through a flip-flop is specified in data sheets as being greater than the flip-flop hold time so that, when flip-flops of the same family are used, race conditions should not occur. If, however, flip-flops from more than one family are employed in the same circuit, race conditions can occur if the hold times of one family are greater than the propagation delays of another. Thus, if the output of a flip-flop with propagation delay τ is connected directly to the input of a flip-flop with hold time greater than τ, a race condition exists. The condition can be avoided by interposing a gate (say a two-input AND gate with one input held "high") between the two flip-flops in order to delay the passage of changes in the output of the first flip-flop to the input of the second.

4.5.3. Clock Skew

In the design of a sequential circuit, the assumption is usually made that the active edge of the clock arrives at each flip-flop in the circuit at precisely the same time. In practice, due to inevitable delays imposed on signals being carried in circuit wiring†, the active clock edge arrives at different flip-flops at different times. In most circuits, the differences in arrival times are negligible, but there *are* circumstances in which these differences can be significant. For instance, if a clock line is required to drive many flip-flops, a designer might choose to insert some gating to increase the fan-out of the line. This, of course, introduces delays and may mean that some flip-flops receive the active edge of the clock at significantly later times than others. This is the phenomenon of *clock skew*. In very-high-speed circuits, such as those based upon the logic family ECL, delays in wiring can be sufficient to cause substantial clock skew.

If clock skew is sufficiently great, a sequential circuit will not operate properly. For instance, consider the case in which the output of one flip-flop (say FF_1) is connected directly to the input of another (say FF_2). Suppose that when the active edge of clock pulse number i arrives, the input to FF_1 has a value that will cause the output of FF_1 to change. The changed output of FF_1 will arrive at the input to FF_2 at some time τ after the arrival of the active edge of clock pulse i. Now, if the flip-flops are of the same family, we can assume that τ is greater than the hold time of FF_2. Hence, under normal operation (i.e., with all flip-flops properly synchronized) the changed value of the output of FF_1 will arrive at the input of FF_2 too late to have any influence on the behavior of FF_2 until the arrival of clock pulse $i + 1$. If clock skew is present, we could have clock pulses arriving at FF_2 substantially later than they arrive at FF_1. Suppose the time difference in clock pulse arrivals at FF_1 and FF_2 is greater than τ. In such a case, a change in the output of FF_1 following clock pulse i would arrive at the input to FF_2 before FF_2 received clock pulse i. As a consequence, FF_2 would respond to the change in the output of FF_1 at the time of arrival of clock pulse i instead of at the time of arrival of clock pulse $i + 1$.

---

† Signal delays in wiring amount to 1.5–2 ns per foot of wire.

Thus, because of the possibility of creating problems of this sort, it is essential that a designer who inserts delays into clock lines or who is working with high-speed logic takes steps to ensure that the delay times from the source of clock pulses to each flip-flop are approximately the same.

4.5.4. Maximum Clock Rate

Examination of data sheets for flip-flops indicates that a maximum clock rate is usually specified for each flip-flop type. It is important to realize that a sequential circuit employing a particular type of flip-flop cannot normally be driven at the rate specified for that type. The reason for this is that most sequential systems are constructed using both flip-flops and combinational circuitry so that, when the maximum clock rate for a system is being worked out, allowance has to be made for the time taken for signals to propagate not only through the flip-flops, but also through the combinational part of the circuit.

As an example, consider again the modulo-8 counter circuit realized using T flip-flops in Figure 4.19(b). A practical implementation of this circuit is shown in Figure 4.38. The T flip-flops have been implemented using JK flip-flops of the type 74LS109A, and the AND gate is 74LS08. The data sheets on these devices give us the following information that we will need to evaluate the maximum clock rate for this system.

74LS109A

$$\textit{Set-up time: } t_{SU} = \begin{cases} \textit{high-level data 35 ns} \\ \textit{low-level data 25 ns} \end{cases}$$

$$\textit{Propagation delay: } \begin{cases} t_{PLH}(\textit{max}) = 25 \textit{ ns} \\ t_{PHL}(\textit{max}) = 40 \textit{ ns} \end{cases}$$

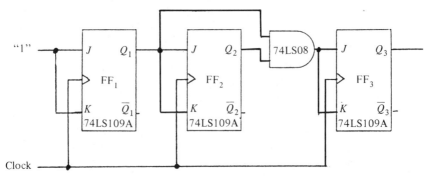

Figure 4.38. Module-8 counter.

74LS08

$$Propagation\ delay: \begin{cases} t_{PLH}(max) = 15\ ns \\ t_{PHL}(max) = 20\ ns \end{cases}$$

In order to determine the maximum allowable clock rate we must identify the path between flip-flops that imposes the longest signal delay. In this case, the longest signal delay is experienced by signals that have to pass through the AND gate. The outputs of FF_1 and FF_2 both have to pass through the AND gate and both will experience the same delay (ignoring delays due to wire lengths and other minor variations). We can therefore establish the maximum clock rate by determining the time taken for signals to propagate from FF_1 or from FF_2; let us consider FF_1.

When the active edge of the clock arrives at FF_1, the inputs $J = 1$, $K = 1$ will cause output Q_1 to change value after some propagation delay (which we will call the flip-flop delay). The change in Q_1 can cause the output of the AND gate to change, but only after a further delay (call it the AND-gate delay). Any change in the output of the AND gate must take place before the next clock pulse, and must do so by an amount of time equal to at least the flip-flop set-up time. Thus, the minimum allowable clock period for proper system operation is given by

minimum clock period = flip-flop delay + AND-gate delay

+ flip-flop set-up time.

From the data on the 74LS109A, we see that the propagation delay for a low-to-high transition at the output is specified as being no greater than 25 ns and, for a high-to-low transition, the propagation delay is specified as being no greater than 40 ns. Since both types of transitions will occur in FF_1, we must select the worst case value in order to determine the minimum clock period. That is, we set *flip-flop delay* = 40 ns. For the other two items, we also select worst-case values; that is, we set *AND-gate delay* = 20 ns and *flip-flop set-up time* = 35 ns. Hence, we find

minimum clock period = 95 ns

giving

maximum clock frequency = 10.53 MHz.

In general, the maximum clock rate is given by the reciprocal of the minimum clock period, where

$$minimum\ clock\ period\ =\ flip\text{-}flop\ delay\ +\ combinational\ logic\ delay$$
$$+\ set\text{-}up\ time$$

where the parameters on the right-hand side represent the worst-case signal path (from the input of one flip-flop to the input of another) in the system.

REFERENCES

[1] M. C. Paull and S. H. Unger, *Minimizing the number of states in incompletely specified switching functions*, IRE Trans. Electron. Comp., EC-8, pp. 356–367, 1959.
[2] E. J. McCluskey and S. H. Unger, *A note on the number of internal variable assignments for sequential switching circuits*, IRE Trans. Electon. Comp., EC-8, pp. 439–440, 1959.
[3] V. T. Rhyne and P. S. Noe, *On the number of distinct state assignments for a sequential machine*, IEEE Trans. Comp., C-26, pp. 73–75, 1977.
[4] W. I. Fletcher, *An Engineering Approach to Digital Design*, Prentice-Hall, 1980.

Exercises

4.1. Verify, by applying a suitable sequence of inputs, that the circuit shown in Figure 4.13(a) behaves as an SR flip-flop.

4.2. Suppose the waveforms in Figure E4.2 are applied to the Set and Reset inputs of an unclocked SR flip-flop. Draw the resulting waveform for the Q output assuming that Q is initially at logic 0. Assume also that propagation delays within the flip-flop are negligible.

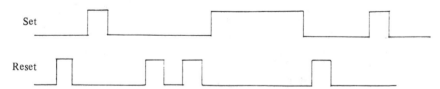

Figure E4.2. Set/reset waveforms.

4.3. The waveforms in Figure E4.3 are applied to a positive edge-triggered JK flip-flop. Draw the resulting waveform for the Q output assuming Q is initially at logic 0. Assume also that the propagation delays within the flip-flop are negligible.

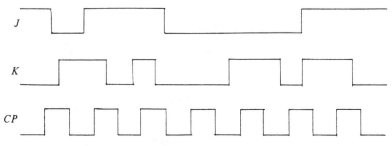

Figure E4.3. Waveforms for edge-triggered *JK* flip-flop.

4.4. Repeat Exercise 4.3 for the case in which the JK flip-flop is of the negative edge-triggered variety (see Figure E4.3).

4.5. Draw the circuit for the edge-triggered D flip-flop (Figure 4.15) with the link between the output of gate 2 and the input of gate 3 removed. Check that the application of the input sequence in Table 4.6 to this modified circuit leads to behavior identical to that of the "true" edge-triggered D flip-flop. Then take the input sequence further by allowing CP to return to 1 and, after the internal variables have settled down, allow D to go to 0. Observe that the circuit settles with $Q = \overline{Q} = 1$. Check that the true edge-triggered D flip-flop does not exhibit this undesirable behavior.

4.6. The circuit shown in Figure E4.6 is a form of toggle flip-flop. Determine the manner in which the behavior of this toggle flip-flop differs from that of the one given in the text.

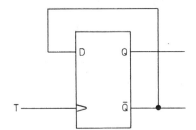

Figure E4.6. A form of toggle flip-flop.

4.7. Two variations of the SR flip-flop exist which are known as the *set-dominant flip-flop* and the *reset-dominant flip-flop*. Each of these variations has S and R inputs and their behavior differs from that of the ordinary SR flip-flop only for the inputs $S = R = 1$. In the case of the set-dominant flip-flop the inputs $S = R = 1$ result in the flip-flop being set and in the case of the reset-dominant flip-flop $S = R = 1$ causes the flip-flop to reset. Show how each of these variations can be constructed by adding one or more gates to a standard SR flip-flop.

4.8. For the modulo-8 counter in Figure 4.19(b), draw a diagram indicating the behavior of the outputs of each of the three flip-flops when the clock pulse waveform indicated in Figure E4.8 is applied to the system. Hence observe how this counter can be used to reduce the frequency of a clock pulse waveform by a factor of 2 and by a factor of 4.

Figure E4.8. Clock waveform.

4.9. Design a modulo-8 counter using

(a) D flip-flops.

(b) JK flip-flops.

4.10. Design a counter that counts through the repetitive sequence 000, 010, 011, 001, 101, 100, 000, · · · . Use T flip-flops.

4.11. Design a counter that counts through the sequence of numbers 0 through 9 in binary-coded decimal and then repeats the sequence. Use D flip-flops.

4.12. Figure E4.12(a) illustrates the phenomenon of contact bounce which occurs when mechanical or electromechanical switches are opened or closed. This phenomenon occurs because when mechanical switches are in the process of making or breaking contact, several separate contacts are made before the process is complete. In some applications this can have undesirable effects and some means of eliminating the phenomenon is required; in other words, a *switch debouncer* is needed. Figure E4.12(b) shows a mechanical switch whose terminals have been connected to a NAND latch. Use Figure 4.14(b) to establish that the NAND latch

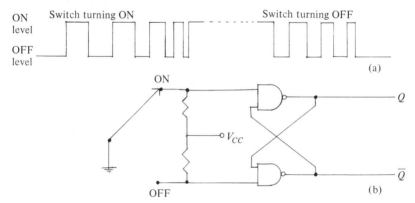

Figure E4.12. Switch debouncing: (a) switching waveform when debouncer not present; (b) debouncing circuit.

acts as a switch debouncer; i.e., establish that when the mechanical switch moves to the ON position (and makes several contacts in the process), the Q output makes a "clean" transition to logic 1 and similarly when the mechanical switch moves to the OFF position, the Q output makes a clean transition to logic 0.

4.13. Design a switch debouncer with two (clocked) JK flip-flops using the state table shown in Table E4.13, which lists the circuit requirements. Use an arbitrary state assignment.

Table E4.13. State table for switch debouncer.

Present	Next State		Output
State	$x^n = 0$	$x^n = 1$	z^n
OFF	OFF	Turning ON	0
Turning ON	OFF	ON	0
ON	Turning OFF	ON	1
Turning OFF	OFF	ON	1

4.14. By inspection (i.e., without using the Paull-Unger method), reduce the number of states in Table E4.14 and tabulate the reduced state table.

Table E4.14.   State table for Exercise 4.14.

Present	Next State		Output	
State	$x = 0$	$x = 1$	$x = 0$	$x = 1$
A	C	B	0	0
B	D	F	0	0
C	C	B	1	1
D	H	A	1	0
E	D	F	0	0
F	C	E	0	0
G	H	A	1	0
H	H	G	0	1

4.15. For the state table in Table E4.15, observe that minimizing the number of states by inspection would be quite difficult. Then carry out the minimization using the Paull-Unger method.

Table E4.15.   State table for Exercise 4.15.

Present	Next State		Output	
State	$x = 0$	$x = 1$	$x = 0$	$x = 1$
A	×	B	×	×
B	G	A	0	0
C	E	D	0	×
D	D	×	0	1
E	×	F	0	×
F	G	E	×	0
G	B	H	1	1
H	A	C	0	×

4.16 Use the Paull-Unger method to reduce the number of states in the system description given in Table 4.12 in the text. Then realize the system using T flip-flops.

4.17. A single-output sequential circuit is required which, after receiving a sequence of four binary digits, generates a 1 at its output if the sequence contains exactly one 1 and generates a 0 at its output otherwise. Assume that all possible sequences of 4 bits can be received and that, after receipt of a 4-bit sequence, the circuit is to return to its starting state, ready to receive a new sequence. Follow the procedure employed in Example 4.2 in the text to draw up a state diagram which represents the behavior required of the circuit. From this, draw up a state table and hence show that the minimum number of states required to represent the system is nine.

4.18. Consider the design of a sequential system whose specification is identical to that in Exercise 4.17 except that the 4-bit sequences received at the input are restricted to BCD. Assume that the least significant bit is received first and follow the procedure at the beginning of Section 4.4.3 to draw up a state transition diagram to represent the required system behavior. From this, show that the state table for the system is as shown in Table E4.18. Use the Paull-Unger method to show that the minimum number of states required to describe this system is eight and that the maximal compatibles are A, B, C, D, G, (E, F), (I, J, L) and (H, K, M, N, P).

Table E4.18. State table for Exercise 4.18.

Current state	Next state		Outputs	
	$x=0$	$x=1$	$x=0$	$x=1$
A	B	C	0	0
B	D	E	0	0
C	F	G	0	0
D	H	I	0	0
E	J	K	0	0
F	L	M	0	0
G	N	P	0	0
H	A	A	0	1
I	A	x	1	x
J	A	x	1	x
K	A	x	0	x
L	A	A	1	0
M	A	x	0	x
N	A	x	0	x
P	A	x	0	x

4.19. Realize the system specified in Exercise 4.18 using

(a) JK flip-flops.

(b) D flip-flops.

(c) SR flip-flops.

Use the state assignment rules given in Section 4.4.4.

4.20. A sequential circuit is required which will generate a parity bit whenever it receives a sequence of four binary digits. The parity bit should equal 1 when the number of 1's in the 4-bit word is odd and it should equal 0 otherwise. Assume that the 4-bit sequences received at the input to the circuit are restricted to BCD and that in each case the least-significant bit is received first. Draw up a state-transition diagram to represent required system behavior and from this draw up a state table. Hence show that the minimum number of states required to describe this system is 7 and that the required state table has the form shown in Table 4.25 in the text.

4.21. Realize the system specified in Exercise 4.20 using

(a) JK flip-flops.

(b) T flip-flops.

Use the state assignment rules given in Section 4.4.4.

4.22. The circuit shown in Figure E4.22 has a static hazard. Use a K-map to determine how to cover the hazard and then draw a new circuit which realizes the same function and which is free of hazards.

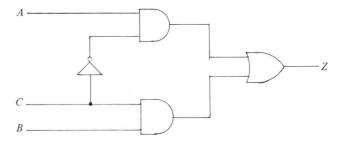

Figure E4.22. AND/OR circuit with static hazard.

4.23. The circuit shown in Figure E4.23 has a static hazard. Use a K-map to determine how to cover the hazard and then draw a new circuit which realizes the same function and which is free of hazards.

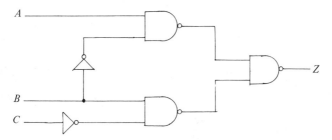

Figure E4.23. NAND circuit with static hazard.

4.24. Determine the maximum clock rate for the circuit in Figure 4.23. Assume that the JK flip-flops are 74LS109A, the AND gates are 74LS08 and the OR gate is a 74LS32. The relevant characteristics of the JK flip-flops and AND gates are given in Section 4.5.4. For the OR gate, the relevant characteristics are:

$$t_{PLH}(max) = t_{PHL}(max) = 22 \ ns$$

4.25. *(Courtesy of L. V. Skattebol)* In the remote Ruritian kingdom of Erewhon, the citizens are much addicted to puzzles. The ruler of that land, King Jimmy XXVIII has decided to encourage his subjects by marketing a puzzle, and passing a law that every citizen must buy at least one unit.

The puzzle is the well known one of the farmer, fox, hen and bag of grain. The farmer must ensure that the fox does not eat the hen, nor that the hen is allowed to eat the grain. The farmer is traveling and comes to a river, on which there is a ferryboat. The boat is small, and can only take the farmer, who must row, and one of his charges at a time. The farmer's problem is how to carry the fox, hen and grain across the river, without loosing the hen or the grain.

King Jimmy has given the exclusive franchise to manufacture the puzzle to a local company: James Rex and Co. Pty. Ltd. He has assured his people that the accident of names does not imply that he has a majority shareholding. King Jimmy has decreed that the puzzle is to be made entirely from NAND gates. He has also issued an assurance that this decree has nothing to do with the fact that several years ago a traveling salesman sold him 3,786,592 assorted NAND gates at a flat rate of $1 per gate.

You are to suppose that you are fortunate enough to be employed as chief designer at James Rex and Co. It is up to you to design a logic circuit to be implemented and sold as the puzzle. The only small cloud on your horizon is that King Jimmy has further decreed that the maximum number of puzzles must be made from the stock of gates, and that unless this is done, the chief designer will lose his head.

Note: You can set about the problem in any way you like, but we point out that one approach would employ push-button switches to represent the presence or absence of farmer, fox, etc. in the boat and a two-way switch to represent the direction in which the boat is crossing the river. The output could be a pair of lights, one green and one red to indicate good or bad moves. Note also that NAND gates can be used to construct flip-flops.

4.26. *(Courtesy of L. V. Skattebol)* In the great temple of Benares, beneath the dome which marks the center of the world, is a brass plate in which are fixed, at the corners of an equilateral triangle, three diamond needles, each a cubit high and as thick as the body of a bee. On one of these needles God placed at the Creation sixty-four disks of pure gold, the largest disk resting on the brass plate. This is the Tower of Brahma. Day and Night unceasingly the priests transfer the disks from one diamond needle to another according to the fixed and immutable laws of Brahma, which require that the priests on duty must not move more than one disk at a time, and that no disk may be placed on a needle which holds a smaller disk. When the 64 disks shall have been thus transferred from the needle on which at the Creation God placed them to one of the other needles, then towers, temple, and priests alike will crumble into dust, and with a thunderclap the world will vanish.

The High Priest of the temple is seriously disturbed; for the younger priests are not as careful as those in the past, and many mistakes are made. Often when a large disk is placed upon a smaller one the error is unnoticed and many more steps are made before the mistake is noted. When this happens the process must be reversed until the error is reached and corrected.

This has happened so often lately, that the end of the world is falling seriously behind schedule. The High Priest has consulted the engineering firm by which you are employed, and you have been assigned to design an indicating machine to tell the priests which disk to move at any time. The rule for moving disks is relatively simple. Suppose the disks are numbered in powers of 2, such that:

the smallest is number 1,
the next smallest is number 2,
the next smallest is number 4,
the next smallest is number 8, and so on.

Suppose also that the moves are numbered from the first in binary notation, i.e., move

$1 = 00001$
$2 = 00010$
$3 = 00011$
$4 = 00100$
$5 = 00101$
. . .

then the rules for moving disks are as follows:

(a) The proper disk to move is given by the power of two of the rightmost 1 in the binary move number; and

(b) Disks with (i) an ODD power of two, i.e., an odd numbered column in the binary numbers always move LEFT and (ii) an EVEN power of two always move RIGHT.

Thus in move

$1 = 0000\mathbf{1}$: disk 1 $= 2^0$ moves right
$2 = 000\mathbf{1}0$: disk 2 $= 2^1$ moves left
$3 = 0001\mathbf{1}$: disk 1 $= 2^0$ moves right
$4 = 00\mathbf{1}00$: disk 4 $= 2^2$ moves right
$5 = 0010\mathbf{1}$: disk 1 $= 2^0$ moves right and so on

where the move signifying digit is in **bold** in the foregoing example.

Design a circuit which would indicate how to proceed on the first 32 moves. Asume that the priests will press a button on your circuit after each move in order to determine how to move next.

How many moves are required before the end of the world will occur?

Can you see how your circuit should be extended to indicate to the priests the full set of necessary moves?

5

COMPUTER TECHNIQUES FOR SEQUENTIAL LOGIC DESIGN

5.1. INTRODUCTION

In the previous chapter, the basic problems of sequential logic design were introduced and some elementary techniques for their solution, suitable for hand-calculation, were described. The two major problems addressed in Chapter 4 were those of state minimization and state assignment. The reader will recall that for the incompletely specified case, the question of finding a minimum set of states was only partially addressed with further discussion being reserved for this chapter. For the state-assignment problem, two rules of thumb were introduced in Chapter 4, but implementation of these rules does not guarantee the selection of an optimum or near-optimum assignment.

In this chapter methods of state minimization and state assignment, suitable for computer implementation, are described and a set of Pascal procedures are provided. The method of state minimization is based upon the techniques described in [1–3] and employs several heuristics to ensure that a near-minimal solution is obtained (a tractable technique for determining the true minimum solution has not yet been found). The method of state assignment is based upon the technique described in [4] and this method guarantees the optimum assignment though for solutions involving more than three flip-flops, computation time can be quite long and it may be necessary to terminate the procedure prematurely. Such action in general leads to a sub-optimal solution, though the solution obtained is usually at least as good as any solution obtained by techniques based upon heuristics, and is often equal to the optimum solution.

5.2. AN ALGORITHM FOR STATE-TABLE REDUCTION

We have used the term state-table *reduction* in the title of this section because the algorithm we shall describe is not guaranteed, in the incompletely specified case, to produce a system description requiring the minimum possible number

Table 5.1. State table for Example 5.1.

Present State	Next State				Output			
	00	01	10	11	00	01	10	11
A	x	x	F	I	x	1	x	x
B	G	x	x	x	1	x	0	x
C	x	x	x	B	x	0	x	1
D	x	D	I	x	x	x	x	x
E	H	A	x	x	1	0	0	x
F	x	A	x	C	x	x	x	1
G	C	C	x	I	x	x	0	x
H	x	E	x	D	x	x	x	0
I	G	I	D	x	0	x	1	x

of states. It will be seen that in the completely specified case the algorithm always finds a minimum solution.

The algorithm will be most easily described by means of an example.

Example 5.1. We will reduce the state table shown in Table 5.1. The following three subsections outline the steps involved.

5.2.1. Determination of Incompatible Pairs

The algorithm commences with the determination of all incompatible pairs of states. This determination involves the following steps:

Step 1:
For each row of the state table in turn (from the first to the last) search the lower rows for states with incompatible outputs.

In Table 5.1, we commence with state A and note that the outputs of state A are incompatible with those of states C and E. This fact is recorded in a table of *backwards incompatibles* as shown in Table 5.2. The term *backwards in-*

Table 5.2. First step in formation of table of backwards incompatibles.

State	Backwards Incompatibles
A	
B	
C	A
D	
E	A
F	
G	
H	
I	

compatibles is used to indicate the fact that against each state in the table, only those incompatible states from higher up in the table are recorded. This method of recording incompatible states ensures that each incompatible pair is entered only once in the table.

After recording those states whose outputs are incompatible with the outputs of state A, a search is made through the states below *B* in the state table to locate any states whose outputs are incompatible with those of state *B*. In this case, we can see that the outputs of state *I* are incompatible with those of state *B*. This is recorded in the table of backwards incompatibles by entering *B* in row *I*. The method proceeds in the obvious fashion until all pairs of states with incompatible outputs have been recorded. The resulting table of backwards incompatibles is shown in Table 5.3. This completes Step 1 in the determination of incompatible pairs of states.

Step 2 of the process uses the information obtained in Step 1 to identify further incompatible pairs, this time from the *next-state* portion of the state table. For instance, the table of backwards incompatibles indicates that states *A* and *C* are incompatible. The state table (Table 5.1) indicates that with input 01, if the system is in state *E* it will go to state *A* and if in state *G* it will go to state *C*. It follows immediately that states *E* and *G* are incompatible. For similar reasons, states *F* and *G* are also incompatible. The next step in the process of determining incompatible pairs is therefore as follows:

Step 2:
Search the "next state" columns of the state table for the presence of states for which backwards incompatibles have been recorded. On finding any such state, search the input column in which it was found for the presence of any of the backwards incompatibles recorded against that state. If any such incompatible is found, this indicates the existence of an incompatible pair; if this pair has not already been recorded, it is added to the table of backwards incompatibles.

Table 5.3.   Table of backwards incompatibles after recording all pairs of states with incompatible outputs.

State	Backwards Incompatibles
A	
B	
C	A
D	
E	A
F	
G	
H	CF
I	BEG

Table 5.4. Table of backwards incompatibles after completion of Step 2.

State	Backwards Incompatibles
A	
B	
C	A
D	
E	A
F	
G	CEF
H	CEF
I	BEGH

Thus, in terms of our example, Step 2 would commence by noting that state C has backwards incompatible state A recorded against it. State C occurs in three of the input columns, but only in the 01 input column does state A also occur. The occurrences of state A in this column indicate the incompatible pairs E, G and F, G.

Application of Step 2 in our example leads to the table of backwards incompatibles shown in Table 5.4. Comparison of Table 5.4 with Table 5.3 shows that Step 2 located several further incompatible pairs. It should be clear that we must now repeat Step 2 in order to check whether these new incompatible pairs will reveal further incompatibilities.

Thus, the final step in the process of determining incompatible pairs may be stated as follows:

Step 3:
Repeat Step 2 until no new incompatibilities are revealed.

On completion of Step 3, the table of backwards incompatibles is as shown in Table 5.5.

Table 5.5. Final table of backwards incompatibles.

State	Backwards Incompatibles
A	
B	
C	A
D	
E	A
F	
G	BCEF
H	CEF
I	BEGH

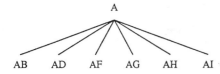

Figure 5.1. Compatibility tree for pairs of states including state A.

This completes the process of determination of incompatible pairs; the next stage in the algorithm requires the setting-up of *compatibility trees*.

5.2.2. Construction of Compatibility Trees

The construction of compatibility trees allows automated determination of the set of maximal compatibles. Each tree is constructed by commencing with a single state, which forms the root of the tree, and then growing branches which link pairs of compatible states. In our example we commence with state A and, by reference to Table 5.5, we note that state A is compatible with states B, D, F, G, H, I so that, with state A as the root, a compatibility tree can be drawn which has the six branches shown in Figure 5.1. Note that the *leaves* of the tree in the figure represent compatible pairs of states.

The process can now be taken further by extending the tree to include compatible triples. For instance, Table 5.5 indicates compatibility of the pair AB with states D, F, and H and three branches can be *grown* from *leaf AB* to represent this, as shown in Figure 5.2. Table 5.5 also indicates compatibility of the pair AD with states B, F, G, H and I. Note, however, that the compatible triple ADB has already been "recorded" by a branch grown from leaf AB. Thus, to avoid duplication for each compatible pair, we search for compatible triples only in those rows of Table 5.5 corresponding to states below the last named state in the pair. For the pair AD, then, we search for compatible triples by scanning rows E through I in Table 5.5. This gives the compatible triples ADF, ADG, ADH and ADI, as shown in Figure 5.2.

The manner in which the remaining branches of Figure 5.2 are obtained should now be obvious. The tree is completed by growing further branches, where possible, to form larger sets of compatible states. Duplication is avoided

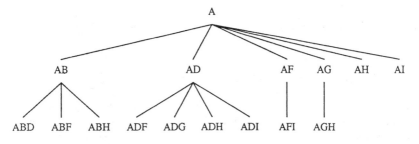

Figure 5.2. Compatibility tree for triples including state A.

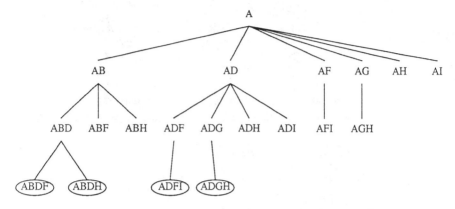

Figure 5.3. Completed compatibility tree for state A.

in the same way as before. The final form of the compatibility tree is shown in Figure 5.3.

The process of generating the compatibility tree in Figure 5.3 has generated four maximal compatibles (MCs), which have been circled in the figure. The remaining leaves of the tree do not represent MCs because each represents a set of states that is a subset of one of the circled (maximal) sets. All the MCs generated by the tree necessarily contain state *A* because *A* is at the root of the tree. The procedure now continues with a search for other MCs.

The next logical step is to search for MCs containing state *B*, but in carrying out the search we must bear in mind that some have already been generated by means of the tree in Figure 5.3. In order to avoid generating these MCs again, the tree with root *B* is constructed using only those states located below state *B* in Table 5.5. The resulting tree is shown in Figure 5.4(a). Note that only one MC has been generated by this tree. All other sets of compatibles are either subsets of *BCDEF* or subsets of an MC generated by the tree in Figure 5.3.

The process continues by constructing compatibility trees for the remaining states. For each tree, only those states located below the root state (in Table 5.5) are considered; as explained above, this avoids duplication of MCs. The resulting compatibility trees are shown in Figure 5.4(b)–(h).

We see that, in total, six MCs exist for this problem. Note that it is essential that the full set of compatibility trees be generated in order to ensure that no MCs are missed.

5.2.3. Determination of a Minimum Cover

The next stage of the algorithm involves a problem very similar to one already met in relation to combinational logic. Recall that our objective is to obtain a state table which describes a system whose behavior (to the outside observer) is indistinguishable from the behavior of the system described in Table 5.1 but

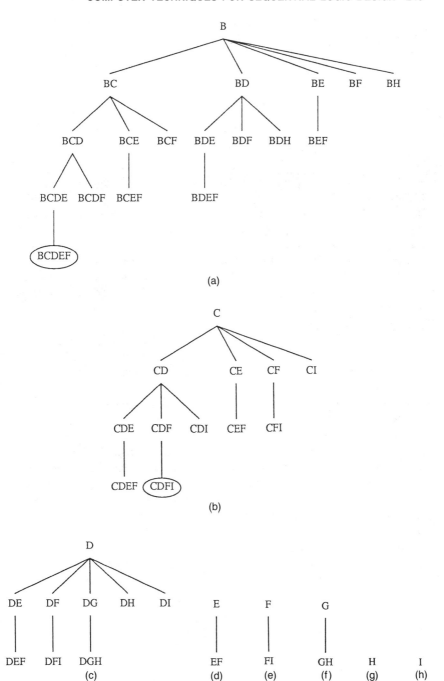

Figure 5.4. Completed compatibility trees for remaining states: (a) State B; (b) State C; (c) State D; (d) State E; (e) State F; (f) State G; (g) State H; (h) State I.

Table 5.6. Labeling of maximal compatibles.

Maximal Compatible	Label
ABDF	C1
ABDH	C2
ADFI	C3
ADGH	C4
BCDEF	C5
CDFI	C6

which also requires a smaller number of states than those employed in Table 5.1. The compatibility trees in Figures 5.3 and 5.4 have given us a set of MCs, each of which represents a group of compatible states. As we shall see below, it is not necessary to use all of these MCs in order to provide a complete description of required system behavior. In other words, the set of MCs provides a redundant cover for the states in Table 5.1. We will seek a minimum cover.

We commence by labeling the MCs. Any labeling will do and in this example we have arbitrarily assigned labels as shown in Table 5.6. The important features of the process of determination of a minimum cover should become clear in the following preamble.

Preamble. The process commences with a search for essential maximum compatibles (EMC's) and, if any are found, they must be included in the final cover.

In this example there are two EMCs, viz $C4$, which provides the only cover for state G, and $C5$, which provides the only cover for state E. Thus, these two MCs must be included in the final cover.

Now note that each of the EMCs is made up of a group of states and that, according to the state table (Table 5.1), each state has four next states (some of which may be don't-cares), with each next state corresponding to a particular input. One of the conditions for a group of states to be compatible is that the next state of each state in the group, for a given input, should also be compatible.

The EMC $C4$ has the next states shown in Table 5.7 (these next states are taken directly from the state table). The table indicates that if the group of states

Table 5.7. The next states for EMC C4.

Present State	Next State			
	00	01	10	11
A	x	x	F	I
D	x	D	I	x
G	C	C	x	I
H	x	E	x	D

ADGH is compatible, then the groups *DCE*, *FI*, and *ID* must also be groups of compatible states.

Our objective is to obtain a minimum state description of the system using MCs as states. We have seen that MC *C*4 has to be included in the state description (it provides the only cover for state *G*) but we now see from Table 5.7 that the final cover must allow the system to move from state *C*4 to states with other compatibility properties. There are three such states and they are as follows:

(i) a state compatible with states *C*, *D*, E.
(ii) a state compatible with states *F*, *I*.
(iii) a state compatible with states *D*, *I*.

From Table 5.6 we see that MC *C*5 constitutes the only state compatible with the three states *C*, *D*, *E*. This implies that *C*5 should be included in the final cover, and of course, we have already decided to include it because it is an EMC.

There are two MCs that include states *F*, *I*, viz *C*3 and *C*6. In addition, *C*3 and *C*6 include the pair *D*, *I* so that inclusion of one of these MCs in the final cover (along with *C*5) will allow satisfaction of the next-state requirements of *C*4.

How do we decide whether to select *C*3 or *C*6 for the final cover? In the general case, this kind of selection problem can be quite important because, very often, the selection of one MC rather than another will lead to a better solution (i.e., one with fewer states). We are not aware of any selection procedure that guarantees a minimum-state solution and the procedure we adopt is based upon heuristic rules. The two basic rules that we employ are as follows:

Rule 1:
Pick the MC that covers the largest number of states.

Rule 2:
If there is more than one candidate for selection under Rule 1, then select from these candidates the MC that has the smallest closure function. †

We actually apply these rules from the very beginning, i.e., in the selection of the EMCs, because it turns out that the order in which EMCs are selected can influence the number of MC's in the final cover.

The Procedure. For the example we are considering, in which there are two EMCs, Rule 1 tells us that we should select *C*5 first. Having selected *C*5, we

---

† See below for an explanation of the term *closure function.*

Table 5.8.   The next states for EMC C5.

Present	Next State			
State	00	01	10	11
B	G	x	x	x
C	x	x	x	B
D	x	D	I	x
E	H	A	x	x
F	x	A	x	C

then check the state table (Table 5.1) to determine the next-state conditions implied by C5. These conditions are displayed in Table 5.8, where we see that selection of C5 requires that the final cover contains a state in which G and H are compatible, a state in which D and A are compatible and a state in which B and C are compatible.

The first of these requirements is satisfied if we select C4 (*ADGH*) for the final cover. The second requirement (a state in which D and A are compatible) can be satisfied by selection of any one of the MCs C1, C2, C3 or C4. The final requirement will be satisfied by selection of C5 itself.

Thus, following selection of C5, we have now established that we must also select C4 *and* either C1 or C2 or C3 or C4. This can be written as a Boolean expression:

$$C5 \Rightarrow C4.(C1 + C2 + C3 + C4)$$

which should be read "selection of C5 implies selection of C4 and either C1 or C2 or C3 or C4." The right-hand side is called the *closure function* for C5— the reason for the term *closure* will become clear later. In this case, by the elementary rule of Boolean algebra that $X.(X + Y) = X$, the closure function reduces to a single MC:

$$C5 \Rightarrow C4$$

so we see that selection of C5 implies that C4 must also be selected.

We already knew that C4 had to be selected (it is an EMC), but in general, the closure function indicates that other MCs, not previously considered, should also be added to the cover. In this case, the closure function tells us that C4 should be added to the cover next and, whenever an MC is added to the cover, we must draw up its closure function to see if it requires the addition of further MC's to the cover.

We have already investigated the next-state requirements of C4 (in the preamble to the solution of this problem) and from our investigations we know that the closure function for C4 can be written

$$C4 \Rightarrow C5.(C3 + C6)$$

Since C5 has already been selected, we now have to decide whether to add either $C3$ or $C6$ to the final cover. Rule 1 does not assist us in our selection because both $C3$ and $C6$ cover the same number of states. Therefore, we apply Rule 2 and draw up the closure function for each of the MCs. For $C3$, the next state requirements imply the need for states in which ADI, DFI, and CI form compatible groups. Thus, the closure function for $C3$ is

$$C3 \Rightarrow C3.(C3 + C6).C6 = C3.C6$$

and since we are looking for the next-state requirements following selection of $C3$, the closure function requirement can be written

$$C3 \Rightarrow C6$$

Similarly, for $C6$, the closure function is

$$C6 \Rightarrow C3.(C3 + C6).C5 = C3.C5$$

and since $C5$ has already been selected, the closure function requirement is

$$C6 \Rightarrow C3$$

Thus, we have found that if we select $C3$ we will also have to select $C6$, and if we select $C6$ we will also have to select $C3$. Hence both $C3$ and $C6$ are selected for the cover.

The cover now contains the MCs $C3$, $C4$, $C5$, and $C6$. $C4$ and $C5$ are both EMCs and, to satisfy their next-state requirements, the MCs $C3$ and $C6$ had to be included in the cover. Addition of $C3$ and $C6$ to the cover does not generate any next-state requirements that cannot be satisfied by the four MCs $C3$, $C4$, $C5$ and $C6$ and, as a consequence, these four MCs are said to form a *closed* group. This is the origin of the term *closure function*.

Having selected a closed group of MCs for the cover, we now check to see if any states remain to be covered. In this case, the MCs $C3$, $C4$, $C5$, and $C6$ provide a complete cover and the procedure terminates.

When a closed group of MCs has been determined and the group does *not* provide a complete cover, the procedure continues with a search for a minimum cover of the remaining states. It can happen that one or more of the EMCs has not yet been included in the cover and the procedure would recommence with a consideration of these. In other cases there may be quasi-essential MCs (i.e., MCs that provide a unique cover for one of the remaining states) and the procedure would recommence with these. The third possibility is that there are neither essential nor quasi-essential MCs remaining and the procedure would then recommence by implementing Rules 1 and 2.

Table 5.9.   Reduced state table for Example 5.1.

Present State	Next State				Output			
	00	01	10	11	00	01	10	11
C3 (ADFI)	G	ADI	DFI	CI	0	1	1	1
C4 (ADGH)	C	CDE	FI	DI	x	1	0	0
C5 (BCDEF)	GH	AD	I	BC	1	0	0	1
C6 (CDFI)	G	ADI	DI	BC	0	0	1	1

To complete our example, we must now redraw the state table. We have established that the MC's $C3$, $C4$, $C5$ and $C6$ provide a complete and closed cover for the states of the system. Each row of the new state table represents a group of compatible states and the entries in a given row are obtained by merging the corresponding entries from the original state table. For instance, $C3$ represents the group of states $ADFI$ and so, in the new state table, the row corresponding to $C3$ is drawn up by merging the entries in rows A, D, F and I of the original state table. The new state table is shown in Table 5.9.

The final step is to relabel the new states. Note that some of the next state entries can be identified with more than one MC (e.g., DFI can be identified with either $C3$ or $C6$). In such a case, it does not matter which choice is made.† Thus, there is not, in general, a unique relabelling scheme. One relabelling of Table 5.9 is shown in Table 5.10.

The basic steps of the procedure are thus as follows:

1. Select an EMC, using Rule 1 or 2 if necessary. If there is no EMC, use Rule 1 or 2 to select an initial MC.
2. Generate the closure function for the selected MC.
3. Satisfy the closure function by adding the minimum possible number of MCs to the cover; use Rule 1 or 2 where necessary.
4. For each MC added to the cover, return to step 2.
5. Once a closed group of MCs has been found, check to see if all states are covered by the group and any groups previously added to the cover. If they are, go to 9.
6. Check for any remaining EMCs. If any are found, go to 1.
7. Check for any quasi-essential MCs. If there are any, select one, using Rule 1 or 2 and go to 2.
8. Select an MC using Rule 1 or 2; go to 2.
9. Merge and relabel the state table.

A Pascal program based upon the above procedure is listed at the end of the chapter. □

---

†In general, for a given input sequence, different choices of MCs will lead to different output sequences but any differences in outputs will correspond to don't-care entries in the output columns of Table 5.1.

Table 5.10. Relabeled state table.

Present	Next State				Output			
State	00	01	10	11	00	01	10	11
a	b	a	a	d	0	1	1	1
b	c	c	a	a	x	1	0	0
c	b	a	a	c	1	0	0	1
d	b	a	a	c	0	0	1	1

5.3. OPTIMUM-STATE ASSIGNMENT BY THE SHR METHOD

As we saw in Section 4.4.4, the number of non-equivalent state assignments is generally so large that it is not possible to try them all in order to find the minimum-cost realization. The SHR method (due to Story, Harrison and Reinhard [4]) leads to a radical reduction in the number of state assignments which must be tried in order to find the optimal solution.

Refer to Table 4.20 in which three possible assignments for an eight-state system are displayed. Each assignment consists of eight *rows* of three binary digits or, viewed another way, each assignment consists of three *columns* of eight binary digits. It has been pointed out in [4] that by viewing state assignment as a process of selection of sets of columns of binary digits, a systematic algorithm can be developed which guarantees the optimum (i.e., minimum cost) solution. Thus, the SHR method is a technique for finding the set (or sets) of *columns* of binary digits which provide the optimum-state assignment.

To get some idea of the tractability of the technique, consider Table 5.11 which lists, for problems requiring up to four flip-flops, the number of distinct state-assignment columns which have to be considered and compares this with the overall number of distinct state assignments. As is explained in the next section, the SHR method requires that an initial, and fairly simple, calculation be applied to each of the possible state-assignment columns; essentially this

Table 5.11. Numbers of possible assignments.

Number of states	Number of distinct state assignments	Number of distinct assignment columns
2	1	1
3	3	3
4	3	3
5	140	15
6	420	25
7	840	35
8	840	35
9	10,810,800	255
	...	...
16	5.449×10^{10}	6435

calculation identifies those columns most likely to appear in the optimum assignment and ranks them according to likely cost. The second stage of the procedure then involves carrying out a series of realizations to determine the actual cost. This stage commences with a realization based upon the combination of columns identified in the initial stage as being most likely to provide the minimum cost solution. The procedure continues with a realization based upon the combination of columns identified as having the second best chance of providing the minimum cost solution. And so the procedure continues, until a stopping criterion is reached. The minimum-cost realization obtained prior to reaching the stopping criterion is the optimal solution. With this held in mind, Table 5.11 indicates that the SHR method could possibly be used in hand calculations for problems involving up to eight states, but experience shows that such calculations can become quite tedious. The Pascal procedures implementing the SHR method which are listed at the end of this chapter offer a far less taxing alternative for most practical problems.

5.3.1. The Basic SHR Technique

We will introduce the SHR technique by considering again the system described by the state table listed in Table 4.21. As in Section 4.4.4, we will realize the system using T flip-flops. The system has 8 states so that, from Table 5.11, a total of 35 distinct assignment columns will have to be considered. The first problem we must solve is that of determining the 35 distinct columns.

Note that a valid assignment for this problem requires that each system state be assigned a unique 3-bit code. It is common practice to assign to the first state (state a in Table 4.21) the code 000; no generality is lost in so doing and we shall adopt this practice here. Suppose we now fill out the first column arbitrarily as shown in Table 5.12 and commence filling out the second column. Once we arrive at state e in the second column, it becomes clear that a valid assignment is not possible. Only four 3-bit codes commence with 0 (viz, 000, 001, 010, and 011) and if the assignments to states a, b, c and d are to be used,

Table 5.12. An invalid assignment.

System	Assignment		
state	Q_3	Q_2	Q_1
a	0	0	
b	0	1	
c	0	0	
d	0	1	
e	0	?	
f	1		
g	1		
h	1		

then they must each be allocated one of these four codes. Thus, it is not possible to allocate unique 3-bit codes to the *five* states a, b, c, d, e in Table 5.12.

This fact implies that each assignment column must have no more than four zeros if a valid assignment is to be obtained. For similar reasons, each. column must have no more than four ones. Since eight binary digits are required in each column in this example, it is clear that each column must have exactly four zeros and four ones (fewer than four zeros implies more than four ones, and vice versa).

The above imposes a helpful restriction on the set of distinct assignment columns. A further restriction is imposed by the fact that the top entry in each column is chosen as zero (the first state is assigned code 000). Thus, to generate the full set of distinct assignment columns, we simply have to generate the set of all columns containing four zeros and four ones whose top entry is zero. The full set of 35 columns is shown in Table 5.13 where each column is labelled C_n, where n is the decimal equivalent of the binary digits making up the column.

A still further restriction on column assignments can be seen directly from Table 5.13. The first three columns C_{15}, C_{23}, and C_{27} cannot be used together because this would lead to the top three states, a, b, and c, each being assigned the identical code 000 and the bottom two states, g and h, each being assigned the code 111. Other combinations of columns which cannot provide a valid assignment can be readily seen and so it is clear that only a restricted number of combinations of columns can be used. This fact has to be taken into account at a later stage in the procedure.

5.3.2. Determining a Lower Bound on Column-Assignment Costs

Once the full set of distinct assignment columns has been generated, the next step is to identify those columns most likely to appear in the optimum assignment. This is done by computing a lower bound on the cost of each column assignment, where cost is measured in terms of the combinational logic requirement.

The computation commences with the drawing up of a partial state table in which one of the state variables, say Q_1^n, has been assigned one of the columns in Table 5.13, with the other two state variables remaining unassigned. For the purposes of illustration we will choose column C_{85} for our first assignment to Q_1^n, the reason being that this column was assigned to Q_1^n in Table 4.22 and so comparisons can be easily drawn.

Table 4.22 defines the effects of this column assignment on Q_1^{n+1} and hence the required inputs T_1^n can be determined. The resulting partial state table is shown in Table 5.14 where S_a, S_b, etc., represent the unassigned portions of states a, b, etc., respectively. The reader may now find it helpful to compare Table 5.14 with Table 4.22 which contains a "complete" state table with col-

Table 5.13. The set of column assignments for an 8-state problem.

C_{15}	C_{23}	C_{27}	C_{29}	C_{30}	C_{39}	C_{43}	C_{45}	C_{46}
0	0	0	0	0	0	0	0	0
0	0	0	0	0	0	0	0	0
0	0	0	0	0	1	1	1	1
0	1	1	1	1	0	0	0	0
1	0	1	1	1	0	1	1	1
1	1	0	1	1	1	0	1	1
1	1	1	0	1	1	1	0	1
1	1	1	1	0	1	1	1	0

C_{51}	C_{53}	C_{54}	C_{57}	C_{58}	C_{60}	C_{71}	C_{75}	C_{77}
0	0	0	0	0	0	0	0	0
0	0	0	0	0	0	1	1	1
1	1	1	1	1	1	0	0	0
1	1	1	1	1	1	0	0	0
0	0	0	1	1	1	0	1	1
0	1	1	0	0	1	1	0	1
1	0	1	0	1	0	1	1	0
1	1	0	1	0	0	1	1	1

C_{78}	C_{83}	C_{85}	C_{86}	C_{89}	C_{90}	C_{92}	C_{99}	C_{101}
0	0	0	0	0	0	0	0	0
1	1	1	1	1	1	1	1	1
0	0	0	0	0	0	0	1	1
0	1	1	1	1	1	1	0	0
1	0	0	0	1	1	1	0	0
1	0	1	1	0	0	1	0	1
1	1	0	1	0	1	0	1	0
0	1	1	0	1	0	0	1	1

C_{102}	C_{105}	C_{106}	C_{108}	C_{113}	C_{114}	C_{116}	C_{120}
0	0	0	0	0	0	0	0
1	1	1	1	1	1	1	1
1	1	1	1	1	1	1	1
0	0	0	0	1	1	1	1
0	1	1	1	0	0	0	1
1	0	0	1	0	0	1	0
1	0	1	0	0	1	0	0
0	1	0	0	1	0	0	0

umn C_{85} assigned to state variable Q_1^n. Note that our partial state table does not include columns for the output variable Z^n. The SHR procedure does not take output equations into consideration.

Recall now that the combinational logic requirement for the system described by Table 4.22 was determined by drawing up K-maps for T_1^n, T_2^n and T_3^n (see Figure 4.28). As mentioned above, in Table 4.22 state variable Q_1^n was assigned column C_{85}. The other two state variables, Q_2^n and Q_3^n, were assigned, in Table 4.22, the columns C_{51} and C_{15} respectively. The K-map drawn for T_1^n using Table 4.22 is reproduced in Figure 5.5(a).

Table 5.14.   Partial state table for column C_{85}.

Current state		Next partial state		Flip-flop input	
		$x^n = 0$	$x^n = 1$	$x^n = 0$	$x^n = 1$
$Q_3^n Q_2^n$	Q_1^n	Q_1^{n+1}	Q_1^{n+1}	T_1^n	T_1^n
S_a	0	1	0	1	0
S_b	1	1	1	0	0
S_c	0	1	0	1	0
S_d	1	1	0	0	1
S_e	0	1	1	1	1
S_f	1	0	1	1	0
S_g	0	0	0	0	0
S_h	1	0	0	1	1

Comparing Table 5.14 with Table 4.22, we see that the state assignment used in Table 4.22 corresponds to $S_a = S_b = 00$, $S_c = S_d = 01$, $S_e = S_f = 10$ and $S_g = S_h = 11$. With this particular assignment, then, the K-map for T_1^n can be redrawn as shown in Figure 5.5(b). A double line has been drawn across the center of this map to emphasize that each of the S_a, S_b, etc. correspond to only two squares in the map. For instance, S_a corresponds only to the squares in the left-hand column in which $Q_1^n = 0$, $x^n = 0$ and $Q_1^n = 0$, $x^n = 1$; the remainder of the left-hand column relates to S_b.

Now let us observe what happens if we maintain the column assignment C_{85} for Q_1^n, but change some of the bit codes associated with S_a, S_b, etc. For instance, let us swap the codes associated with S_e and S_g, i.e., set $S_e = 11$ and $S_g = 10$. The partial state table for this modified assignment remains unchanged, but the K-map now has the form shown in Figure 5.6(a). The cost of the modified assignment is obviously slightly less than that of the first assignment considered. More precisely, the cost of the combinational logic requirement indicated by Figure 5.6(a) is 15 gate inputs† while the cost indicated by Figure 5.5 is 16 gate inputs.

Observe that the effect on the K-map of swapping the codes associated with S_e and S_g is simply a swap in the K-map squares associated with the two "partial" states S_e and S_g. Clearly we can search for further simplifications by making further changes to the codes assigned to the S_a, S_b, etc. Our freedom of choice in making such changes is, however, restricted by the fact that the partial states S_a, S_c, S_e and S_g are confined to the upper half of the K-map and the remaining partial states are confined to the lower half.

With this restriction, we find that the greatest simplifications are achieved by

---

† For convenience, in this section we follow [4] and measure cost in terms of the required number of gate inputs rather than the number of individual gates required.

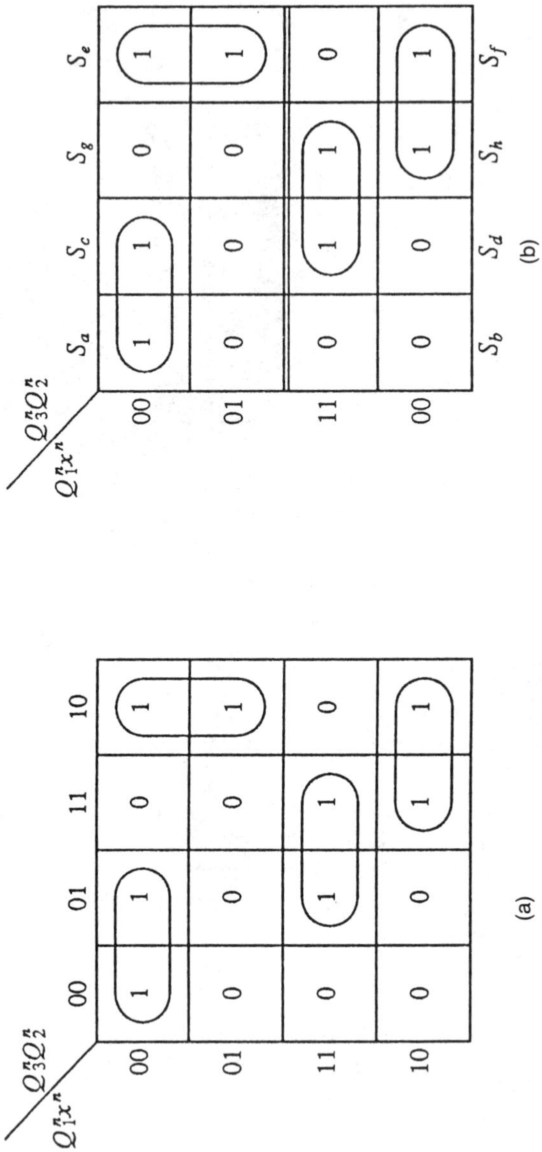

Figure 5.5. K-maps for C_{85}: (a) Standard notation; (b) new notation.

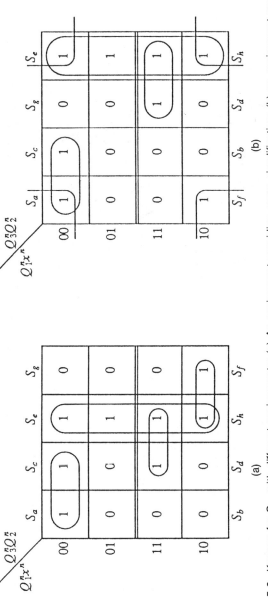

Figure 5.6. K-maps for C_{85} with different assignments: (a) An assignment providing some simplification; (b) an assignment providing maximum simplification.

the partial state assignment $S_a = S_f = 00$, $S_c = S_b = 01$, $S_g = S_d = 11$, $S_e = S_h = 10$. The K-map resulting from this assignment is shown in Figure 5.6(b). The cost of the combinational logic requirement indicated by this figure is 14 gate inputs. Thus, we have established that the minimum possible cost in combinational circuitry which could be incurred by assigning column C_{85} to the state variable Q_1^n is 14 gate inputs.

Recall that interchanging columns in a state assignment has no effect on the combinational hardware requirement (this was explained in terms of assignments 2 and 3 in Table 4.20). This implies that if column C_{85} is assigned to any one of the state variables Q_1^n, Q_2^n or Q_3^n, the minimum possible combinational hardware requirement is 14 gate inputs. In other words, we have established that a lower bound on the cost of column assignment C_{85} is 14 gate inputs.

Before listing the lower bounds for each assignment column, we will consider one further example. For column C_{54} the partial state table is as shown in Table 5.15 (assuming as before that C_{54} is assigned to state variable Q_1^n). Note that S_a, S_b, S_e and S_h correspond to states in which $Q_1^n = 0$ and hence these quantities relate to the upper half of the K-map representation; make the straightforward assignment $S_a = 00$, $S_b = 01$, $S_e = 11$, $S_h = 10$. Similarly, the states S_c, S_d, S_f and S_g correspond to states in which $Q_1^n = 1$ and hence relate to the lower half of the K-map representation; make the assignment $S_c = 00$, $S_d = 01$, $S_f = 11$, $S_g = 10$.

With this assignment the K-map has the form shown in Figure 5.7(a). The cost of this assignment is clearly 20 gate inputs. By rearrangement of the upper and lower halves of the map, a minimum-cost arrangement can be obtained. One such arrangement is shown in Figure 5.7(b); the cost of this arrangement is 14 gate inputs.

Table 5.15. Partial state table for column C_{54}.

Current state		Next partial state		Flip-flop input	
		$x^n = 0$	$x^n = 1$	$x^n = 0$	$x^n = 1$
$Q_3^n Q_2^n$	Q_1^n	Q_1^{n+1}	Q_1^{n+1}	T_1^n	T_1^n
S_a	0	0	1	0	1
S_b	0	1	1	1	1
S_c	1	1	0	0	1
S_d	1	0	1	1	0
S_e	0	0	0	0	0
S_f	1	1	0	0	1
S_g	1	0	0	1	1
S_h	0	0	0	0	0

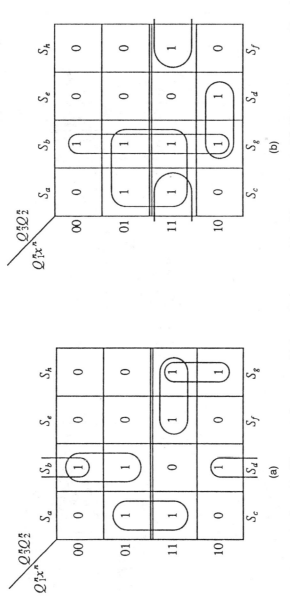

Figure 5.7. K-maps for C_{54} with different assignments: (a) An assignment requiring 20 gate inputs; (b) an assignment requiring 14 gate inputs.

Table 5.16. The full set of lower bounds on cost.

Assignment column	C_{15}	C_{23}	C_{27}	C_{29}	C_{30}	C_{39}	C_{43}	C_{45}	C_{46}
Lower bound on cost	4	4	10	10	9	7	7	12	9
Assignment column	C_{51}	C_{53}	C_{54}	C_{57}	C_{58}	C_{60}	C_{71}	C_{75}	C_{77}
Lower bound on cost	11	13	14	11	14	10	7	8	6
Assignment column	C_{78}	C_{83}	C_{85}	C_{86}	C_{89}	C_{90}	C_{92}	C_{99}	C_{101}
Lower bound on cost	13	9	14	7	11	14	9	0	13
Assignment column	C_{102}	C_{105}	C_{106}	C_{108}	C_{113}	C_{114}	C_{116}	C_{120}	
Lower bound on cost	14	9	12	10	7	13	10	14	

Note that any initial assignment can be made to the S_a, S_b, $\cdots$, so long as the correct partial states are assigned to the upper and lower halves of the K-map. The minimum cost arrangement is then easily found.

Lower bounds on cost for each assignment are computed in this way. The full set of lower bounds is given in Table 5.16.

The next stage of the technique commences with a search for a *valid* set of columns which has the minimum lower bound on cost. In Table 5.16 it is clear that the minimum lower bound on cost is given by columns C_{15}, C_{23}, and C_{99}, but as the reader should check, these three columns do not provide a valid state assignment. The valid set which has minimum lower bound on cost is the set C_{23}, C_{77} and C_{99}; this set has a lower-bound cost of 10. We now proceed to determine the actual cost of realization with this choice of column assignments. The actual cost is determined by drawing up a state table and setting about the realization in the usual way. The state table is shown in Table 5.17 and the cost of realization is determined from the K-maps (Figure 5.8) which indicate the

Table 5.17. State table with assignments $C_{23}C_{77}C_{99}$.

Current State			Next State						Flip-flop Inputs					
			$x^n = 0$			$x^n = 1$			$x^n = 0$			$x^n = 1$		
Q_3^n	Q_2^n	Q_1^n	Q_3^n	Q_2^n	Q_1^n	Q_3^n	Q_2^n	Q_1^n	T_3^n	T_2^n	T_1^n	T_3^n	T_2^n	T_1^n
0	0	0	0	1	1	0	0	1	0	1	1	0	0	1
0	1	1	1	0	0	1	1	0	1	1	1	1	0	1
0	0	1	1	1	0	0	1	0	1	1	1	0	1	1
1	0	0	1	1	1	1	0	1	0	1	1	0	0	1
0	1	0	1	1	1	1	1	1	1	0	1	1	0	1
1	1	0	1	0	1	1	1	1	0	1	1	0	0	1
1	0	1	0	0	0	0	0	0	1	0	1	1	0	1
1	1	1	0	0	0	0	0	0	1	1	1	1	1	1

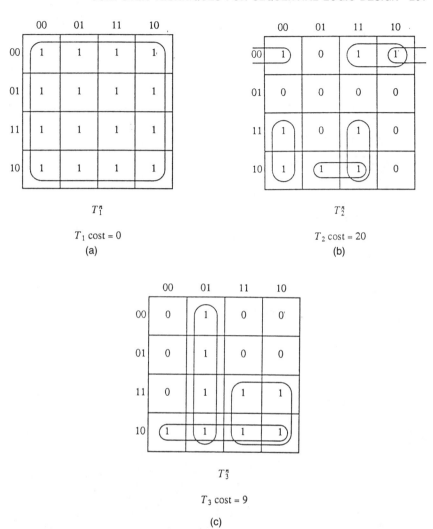

Figure 5.8. K-maps determining cost of assignment $C_{23}C_{77}C_{99}$. (a) T^n; cost $= 0$; (b) T_2^n; cost $= 20$; (c) T_3^n; cost $= 9$.

combinational requirement for each flip-flop input. Thus we see that the cost of combinational logic with state assignment $C_{23} C_{77} C_{99}$ is 29.

Having obtained a realization whose combinational logic cost is 29 allows us to eliminate from consideration all combinations of columns whose overall lower bound on cost is 29 or greater. For instance, the valid combination $C_{71} C_{92} C_{114}$, whose lower bound on cost is 29, can be eliminated from consideration because it cannot provide a realization whose cost is less than that of the realization just obtained. As is explained below, it is this kind of argument which provides a stopping rule for the technique.

We now find the valid combination of columns which has the next lowest lower bound on cost; this combination turns out to be $C_{15} C_{86} C_{99}$ and a realization using this combination as the state assignment gives an actual cost of 29. Thus this combination offers no improvement in cost.

The method proceeds by finding the combination with the next lowest lower bound in cost, determination of actual cost, and so on.

The combination $C_{23} C_{90} C_{99}$, whose lower bound on cost is 18, is found to lead to an actual cost of 19. The procedure terminates soon after because only those untried combinations with a lower bound of 18 need be considered (combinations with a lower bound of 19 or more cannot improve on the realization obtained with $C_{23} C_{90} C_{99}$).

It is found that the combination $C_{23} C_{90} C_{99}$ does, in fact, provide the minimum-cost solution and it is perhaps of some interest to compare the minimum cost of 19 with the cost of 28 obtained by applying the assignment rules in Chapter 4 (see Equations 4.2).

The Question of Lower Bounds. Before presenting a tabular method for determining lower bounds, we discuss briefly the question of why the costs computed for individual columns provide *lower bounds* on the actual cost that will be incurred when a given set of columns is used in a state assignment.

The first example we gave of determining a lower bound on cost involved column C_{85}, and we found that the lower bound of 14 gate inputs was achieved by the partial state assignments $S_a = S_f = 00$, $S_c = S_b = 01$, $S_g = S_d = 11$, $S_e = S_h = 10$. This partial state assignment implies the use of columns C_{27} and C_{114} along with C_{85} in the "full" assignment. (To see this, simply arrange the partial state assignment in a column, in the order S_a, S_b, etc., and compare with Table 5.13). A realization using this assignment leads to a total combinational logic cost of 47 gate inputs. The combinational logic requirement associated with each column is as follows: $C_{85} = 14$, $C_{27} = 15$, $C_{114} = 18$. Comparing this with Table 5.16, we see that with this assignment C_{85} attains its lower bound, but the other two columns do not. The lower bounds for C_{27} and C_{114} occur when these two columns are used in other assignments; specifically, the lower bound on C_{27} occurs when the assignment $C_{27} C_{39} C_{85}$ is employed, and the lower bound on C_{114} occurs when the assignment $C_{114} C_{105} C_{85}$ is employed.

In general, each column (say, C_i) attains its lower bound on cost when associated with a particular pair of other columns† (say, C_j, C_k) to give the assignment $C_i C_j C_k$. The columns C_j and C_k do not normally attain their lower bounds on cost when this assignment is used, so that addition of the lower bounds on cost for columns C_i, C_j, and C_k really does give a lower bound on cost of a realization using the assignment $C_i C_j C_k$.

----

† The pair need not be unique.

Table 5.18. State table for parity bit generator.

Current state	Next state x=0	Next state x=1	Output x=0	Output x=1
a	b	c	0	0
b	d	e	0	0
c	e	d	0	0
d	g	f	0	0
e	f	g	0	0
f	a	a	1	0
g	a	a	0	1

5.3.3. Tabular Method for the Determination of Lower Bounds

The K-map method is unsuitable for automation and a tabular method, based upon the Quine-McCluskey technique, has been developed for the determination of lower bounds on cost. The method is a refinement of one presented by Story in his thesis [5]. We do not use the consensus approach here for reasons that will be clear later.

The tabular approach is best described by means of an example. Consider again the parity bit generator realized by D flip-flops in Example 4.4. and described by the state table Table 4.25, repeated here for convenience as Table 5.18. The system has seven states and Table 5.11 tells us that for a 7-state system there are 35 distinct column assignments; these column assignments are precisely those listed in Table 5.13. As before, we will be required to set up a partial-state table for each of the column assignments dictated by Table 5.13. For the first column in Table 5.13, the corresponding partial state table is shown in Table 5.19.

We must now compute a lower bound on the combinational logic needed to

Table 5.19. Partial state table for column C_{15}.

Current state $Q_3^n Q_2^n$	Q_1^n	Next partial state $x^n = 0$ Q_1^{n+1}	Next partial state $x^n = 1$ Q_1^{n+1}	Flip-flop inputs $x^n = 0$ D_1^n	Flip-flop inputs $x^n = 1$ D_1^n
S_a	0	0	0	0	0
S_b	0	0	1	0	1
S_c	0	1	0	1	0
S_d	0	1	1	1	1
S_e	1	1	1	1	1
S_f	1	0	0	0	0
S_g	1	0	0	0	0
S_h	1	-	-	x	x

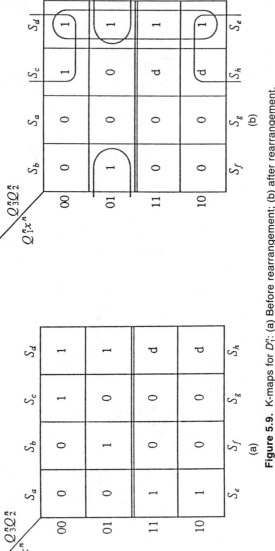

Figure 5.9. K-maps for D_1^n: (a) Before rearrangement; (b) after rearrangement.

provide D_1^n. As a basis for illustration of the tabular method, we will first compute the lower bound using a K-map. The K-map for D_1^n is shown in Figure 5.9(a); the lower bound on cost is obtained after some rearrangement of the columns in both the upper and lower halves of the map, as indicated in Figure 5.9(b), which indicates a lower bound on cost for D_1^n of 10 (gate inputs).

Note again that upper and lower halves of the map are "segregated" in the K-map approach; columns in the upper half may be freely interchanged as may those in the lower half, but columns in the upper half must not change places with columns in the lower half. (If this is allowed, and it *was* allowed in the original presentation of the SHR method [5], the bounds obtained on cost are lower than they need be and the whole procedure takes considerably longer to implement.) In order to take this into account in the tabular approach, we commence with a table (similar to that employed in the Quine-McCluskey method) that is divided into upper and lower parts—see Figure 5.10(a).

The procedure we follow is basically the same as the Quine-McCluskey procedure so that the initial table in Figure 5.10(a) includes don't-care entries in the usual way. Each 0-cube in Figure 5.10(a) is represented by a letter and two digits. The meaning of this representation is probably most easily understood by referring to the K-map in Figure 5.9(a). The first 0-cube in Figure 5.10(a) is denoted $b01$ and corresponds to the 1 entry in column S_b in the upper half of the K-map; this entry represents the case $Q_1^n = 0$, $x^n = 1$—hence the designation $b01$. The other 0-cubes are described by a letter and two digits in the same way. Note that each 0-cube has also been assigned a number in Figure 5.10(a); these numbers will allow us to keep track of the 0-cubes covered as higher-order cubes are formed.

We commence by looking for 1-cubes that can be formed from pairs of 0-cubes contained in the upper portion of Figure 5.10(a). We note that $b01$ and $d01$ can be combined to form a 1-cube (compare with Figure 5.9(b)); we designate the resulting 1-cube $bd01$ and enter it in the table of 1-cubes (Figure 5.10(b)). There are two other pairs of 0-cubes that combine in the upper portion of Figure 5.10(a). The first pair is $c00$ and $d00$ which gives the 1-cube $cd00$. The other pair is $d00$ and $d01$ and we denote the resulting 1-cube by $d0x$. We then turn to the lower portion of the table and identify all pairs of 0-cubes that combine; this gives the set of four 1-cubes listed in the portion of Figure 5.10(b) marked "lower".

Note, from Figure 5.9(b), that a cube from the lower half of the K-map can combine with a cube from the upper half; thus, we now search for pairs of 0-cubes, one from each portion of Figure 5.10(a), that combine to form 1-cubes. The list of resulting 1-cubes is contained in the portion of Figure 5.10(b) marked "mixed".

Observe that the rules for combining 0-cubes are quite simple. Pairs of 0-cubes from within the upper and lower portions of the table combine if either (i) they have identical digits or (ii) they have the same letter. Combination of a 0-cube from the upper portion and a 0-cube from the lower portion of the table is possible for all pairs of 0-cubes that differ in a single digit. The reader

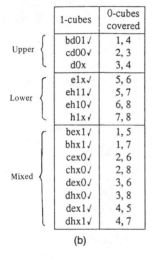

	0-cubes	No.
Upper	b01✓	1
	c00✓	2
	d00✓	3
	d01✓	4
Lower	e11✓	5
	e10✓	6
	h11✓	7
	h10✓	8

(a)

	1-cubes	0-cubes covered
Upper	bd01 ✓	1, 4
	cd00✓	2, 3
	d0x	3, 4
Lower	e1x✓	5, 6
	eh11✓	5, 7
	eh10✓	6, 8
	h1x✓	7, 8
Mixed	bex1✓	1, 5
	bhx1✓	1, 7
	cex0✓	2, 6
	chx0✓	2, 8
	dex0✓	3, 6
	dhx0✓	3, 8
	dex1✓	4, 5
	dhx1✓	4, 7

(b)

Figure 5.10. Quine-McCluskey tables. (a) 0-cubes; (b) 1-cubes; (c) 2-cubes.

	2-cubes	1-cubes covered
Lower	eh1x	5, 6, 7, 8
Mixed	bdehx1	1, 4, 5, 7
	cdehx0	2, 3, 6, 8

(c)

should be able to see that by allowing 0-cubes to combine in this way, we implicitly incorporate the effect of interchange of columns within the upper (or lower) half of the K-map.

Before we proceed further, we must introduce one extra item of terminology. Notice that in Figure 5.10(b), some of the 1-cubes contain two letters in their representation (e.g., *bd*01) while others contain only one letter (e.g., *d*0*x*). We shall soon see that 2-cubes may contain up to four letters in their representation. For any given cube, the letters contained in its representation will be termed the *letter set* for that cube.

With this in mind, the procedure for forming higher-order cubes can be described as follows. Higher-order cubes are formed from pairs of lower-order cubes located *within* any of the three portions of the table (i.e., upper, lower or mixed portions). The lower-order cubes can be combined if either

(i) they have identical digits (i.e., 1's, 0's or x's) and their letter sets do not have any letters in common; or
(ii) they have identical letter sets and their digits differ in one place.

The procedure is best illustrated by reference to the example in hand. In Figure 5.10(b), none of the 1-cubes in the portion marked "upper" can be combined. In the portion marked "lower", the pair $e1x$ and $h1x$ satisfy condition (i) above and combine to give $eh1x$; also, the pair $eh11$ and $eh10$ satisfy condition (ii) and combine to give the same 2-cube $eh1x$. The 2-cubes obtained from the "lower" and "mixed" portions are listed in Figure 5.10(c). (Note that the 2-cubes formed from the "mixed" portion of Figure 5.10(b) each cover one of the 1-cubes in the "upper" portion and these 1-cubes have been checked).

A little thought should convince the reader that after the first step (i.e., the combination of 0-cubes) there is no need to consider combinations of cubes chosen from different portions of the table. All possible higher-order cubes of the "mixed" type can be formed from within the mixed portion of the table.

The process of forming higher-order cubes terminates with Figure 5.10(c) because it is not possible to form any 3-cubes. The reader should compare with Figure 5.9(a) to check that all possible combinations of cubes have been formed by this procedure. (Bear in mind, of course, that columns in the upper and lower halves of the K-map can be interchanged freely.)

Now recall that our objective in this example is to find a lower bound on the cost of combinational logic for the input to D_1^n. We can find such a bound by setting up a prime implicant table in the usual way. According to Figure 5.10, the prime implicants consist of three 2-cubes and one 1-cube; the prime implicant table is shown in Table 5.20. (Note that 0-cubes representing don't-cares are omitted from the table because they need not be covered.)

Following the Quine-McCluskey procedure described earlier, we mark with an asterisk (*) those prime implicants that provide the sole cover for one or more 0-cubes. Table 5.20 then appears to be saying that there are two essential

Table 5.20. Prime implicant table.

Prime Implicants	0-cubes					
	$b01$ 1	$c00$ 2	$d00$ 3	$d01$ 4	$e11$ 5	$e10$ 6
$d0x$			✓	✓		
$eh1x$					✓	✓
$bdehx1$ *	✓			✓	✓	
$cdehx0$ *		✓	✓			✓

prime implicants† and that these EPIs provide a full cover for the required function. This implies that a lower bound on cost is given by the cost of realizing two 2-cubes (which, for a 4-variable problem, implies 6 gate inputs). Thus, the bound indicated by Table 5.20 is lower than the bound obtained using the K-maps in Figure 5.9.

How can this be? The answer is quite simple. A close examination of the two EPIs indicates that it is impossible for both to be realized simultaneously. This is most easily explained in terms of K-maps. The EPI *cedhx*0 requires that columns *c* and *d* be adjacent in the upper half of the K-map and that they be directly above columns *e* and *h*. Similarly, the EPI *bedhx*1 requires that columns *b* and *d* be adjacent in the upper half of the K-map and that they be directly above columns *e* and *h*. Clearly it is not possible for both EPIs to occur simultaneously.

Obviously, Table 5.20 gives us a lower bound on cost, but it is clear that by taking account of the juxtaposition of columns, a tighter lower bound can be obtained. It is important, from the point of view of computational efficiency, that the bounds obtained be as tight as possible. The actual juxtaposition of columns in each EPI is available from its letter set so that impossible pairs of EPIs of the type encountered here are readily identified.

A heuristic method of eliminating impossible pairs is readily devised. From any impossible pair, select the EPI that provides the greatest cover of 0-cubes of the function in hand and delete the other EPI. Deletion of an EPI will lead to the requirement that one or more lower-order cubes be included in the cover. This is best explained in terms of the example in hand.

From Table 5.20, we arbitrarily delete *cdehx*0. This then requires us to find a lower-order cube (from Figure 5.10(b)) that covers 0-cube number 2. In Figure 5.10(b), we see that there are available three 1-cubes covering 0-cube number 2. Two of these, *cex*0 and *chx*0, are impossible to pair with the retained EPI, *bdehx*1, but the other one, *cd*00, can be used. The new prime implicant table is shown in Table 5.21.

Table 5.21. Modified prime implicant table.

Prime Implicants	0-cubes					
	b01 1	c00 2	d00 3	d01 4	e11 5	e10 6
d0x .			✓	✓		
eh1x *					✓	✓
bdehx1 *	✓			✓	✓	
cd00 *		✓	✓			

---

† Note that these are not really EPIs in this case because we are here searching for a lower bound on cost, not the actual cost. However, the presentation is simplified if we employ the term here.

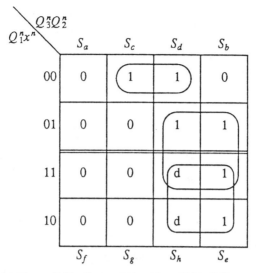

Figure 5.11. *K*-map derived from Table 5.21.

There are three EPIs in Table 5.21 and they provide a full cover for D_1^n. These EPIs (representing two 2-cubes and one 1-cube) indicate a lower bound of 10 gate inputs, as was also indicated by the K-map in Figure 5.9(b). It is worth noting that the Quine-McCluskey procedure employed here has produced a solution that corresponds to a different arrangement of the K-map; the K-map corresponding to Table 5.21 is shown in Figure 5.11.

Note that the procedure outlined in this section is directly applicable to single-input problems with more than four variables. This is so because, regardless of the number of variables involved, only the input and one flip-flop output are assigned values in the search for lower bounds.

REFERENCES

[1] J. Kella, *State minimization of incompletely specified sequential machines*, IEEE Trans. on Computers, Vol. C-19, No. 4, April 1970, pp. 342–348.

[2] R. G. Bennetts, *An improved method of prime C-class derivation in the state reduction of sequential networks*, IEEE Trans. on Computers, Vol. C-20, 1971, pp. 229–231.

[3] R. G. Bennetts, J. L. Washington, D. W. Lewin, *A computer algorithm for state table reduction*, The Radio and Electronic Engineer, Vol. 42, No. 11, November 1972, pp. 513–520.

[4] J. R. Story, H. J. Harrison, and E. A. Reinhard, *Optimum state assignment for synchronous sequential circuits*, IEEE Trans. on Computers, Vol. C-21, No. 12, December 1972, pp. 1365–1373.

[5] J. R. Story, *State assignment optimization for synchronous sequential systems*, Ph.D. dissertation, Univ. Alabama, Tuscaloosa, May 1971.

Exercises

5.1. **(a)** Minimize the following state table using the method given in Section 5.2. (The dashes in this table represent don't cares).

Present State	Next State							Output						
a	a	-	d	e	b	a	-	0	-	0	1	0	-	-
b	b	d	a	-	a	a	-	0	1	-	-	-	1	-
c	b	d	a	-	-	-	g	0	1	1	-	-	-	0
d	-	e	-	b	b	-	a	-	-	-	-	0	-	-
e	b	e	a	-	b	e	a	-	-	-	-	-	-	1
f	b	c	-	h	f	g	-	0	-	1	1	1	0	-
g	-	c	-	e	-	g	f	-	1	-	1	-	0	0
h	a	e	d	b	b	e	a	1	0	1	0	-	-	1

(b) For the above state table, prepare a data file suitable for use with the state minimization program in Appendix 5-B. Run the program and compare the result with that of part (a) above.

5.2. Write a Pascal program which reads a file containing a state table expressed in the input data format specified in Section 5-A.1 and prints the state table in a form similar to that shown in Exercise 5.1(a). Use the program to print the minimized state table obtained in Exercise 5.1(b).

5.3. Use the program in Appendix 5-D to perform state assignment for the minimized state table produced in Exercise 5.1(b). The following flip-flop types are to be used:

(a) JK flip-flops

(b) T flip-flops

(c) D flip-flops

5.4. Take the outputs from Exercise 5.3 and feed them into the Pascal program given in Appendix 3F.1 and the logic minimization package given in Appendix 3B. Compare the number of gates and the number of ICs used for the realization with each flip-flop type. Which type of flip-flop realization uses

(i) The least number of gates;

(ii) The greatest number of gates;

(iii) The least number of IC's;

(iv) The greatest number of IC's?

5.5. *Project.* Extend the Pascal program of Appendix 5-D for state assignment so as to produce circuit realizations in order to determine the best solution. Compare the costs of assignments produced by the new program with those produced by the program of Appendix 5-D. Compare the size of the programs. Compare the execution times of the two programs. From these figures comment on the usefulness of the two programs.

Appendix 5A

DESCRIPTION OF THE PASCAL PROCEDURES FOR STATE MINIMIZATION

5A.1. INPUT DATA FORMAT

The format of the data in the input file is as follows:

> CAD flag DEMO flag
> Number of inputs
> Number of states
> Next-state list for state *a*
> . . .
> Number of outputs
> Output list for state *a*
> . . .
> Number of bits in input code
> Input code number 1
> . . .
> Flip-flop type to be used in realization (JK, SR, D. T)

The first line contains the CAD and DEMO flags, which take the values T (TRUE) or F (FALSE). These two flags must appear in columns 1 and 2, respectively, of the line. If the CAD flag is set to T, then the output of the state minimization program is presented in a form suitable for input to the state assignment program. If the DEMO flag is set to T, then some of the internal steps of the state minimization will be printed on the output file. If the CAD flag is set to T, then the DEMO flag is set automatically to F. If both flags are set to F, then a "human-readable" output is produced.

In the input data file format detailed above, the items commencing "Number of bits in input code" through the end of the file are concerned with state assignment. If one wishes to carry out a state minimization without going on to state assignment, these items can be omitted. The state assignment procedures are described in Appendix 5-C.

A typical example of both the input and output data is given in Appendix 5-E.

5A.2. INPUT-OUTPUT PROCEDURES

procedure readtable;

readtable reads a state table from *input* and stores the table in the array *nextstate*. The format of the input data is as follows:

a single line containing the number of input columns in the state table;

a single line containing the number of states (rows) in the state table;

the rows of the state table (one row per line corresponding to each present state) containing the next state entries in the state table (note that the state variables must be entered as single alphabetic characters—both upper or lower case are treated as the same state, i.e., "a" and "A" are treated as the same state). The rows MUST be entered in alphabetic order of the present states, i.e., present state "a" first, present state "b" second, etc. Don't-care entries for states are specified as "-".

A single line containing the number of output columns in the state table;

The rows of the output table (one row per line corresponding to each present state) containing the output for each input. Only one output is allowed in this implementation and is represented by the binary digit "0", "1", or "x".

If the variable DEMO is set to **true** then the state table is printed on the output file. This is useful for checking the correctness of the input data.

function readstate(c: char): integer;

readstate is called by *readtable* to convert ASCII characters in the range "a" to "z" or "A" to "Z" into numbers in the range 1 to 26. Don't-care entries for states are stored as number zero.

procedure writetable;

writetable writes the state table stored in the array *nextstate* to the file *output*, converting from the internal representation to lower case alphabetic characters in the range "a" to "z". Don't-care entries are printed as the character "-".

If the variable DEMO is set to **true,** then the numbers of inputs, outputs, and states in the table are also printed.

procedure writestate(s: integer);

> *writestate* converts the integer *s* to a lower-case ASCII character in the range "a" to "z".

procedure writeclass(x: mctype);

> *writeclass* prints each of the states covered by the maximal compatible *x*. It calls *writestate* to print the names of the states.

procedure writecset(x: mctype);

> *writecset* prints a closure term *x*.

5A.3. MEMORY MANAGEMENT

procedure freeitem(**var** y: cptr; p: cptr);

> *freeitem* returns an item *p* of type *citem* (i.e., a maximal compatible or a cover term) to the free list (*y*). There are two free lists maintained, one for maximal compatibles (*freecomp*) and one for closure terms (*freescomp*).

procedure freelists(**var** y: cptr; **var** p: cptr);

> *freelist* removes all the items in the list *p* and updates the list *y*.

procedure additem(**var** y: cptr; p: cptr);

> *additem* adds item *p* to the end of list *y*.

function newitem(x: ctype; y: mctype): cptr;

> The function *newitem* allocates a new item of type *x* (either *scomp* or *compclass*) from the free list of the appropriate type. If the free list is empty, a new record is dynamically allocated using the Pascal procedure *new*.

5A.4. STATE MINIMIZATION PROCEDURES

procedure issm;

> This is the main procedure for minimizing the state table. If the variable DEMO is set to **true,** then information about the internal operation of the procedure can be viewed on *output* by the user.

procedure maxcompatibles;

> *maxcompatibles* uses the technique explained in Section 5.2 to generate the maximal compatibles. The maximal compatibles are stored in a linked list pointed to by the variable *compats*; the number of maximal compatibles is stored in *ncompats*. The linked list representation is used because of the variability in the number of maximal compatibles which may occur.

Maximal compatibles are identified by a unique number (stored in field *index*). Associated with each maximal compatible is the set of states which it covers (stored in field *class*) and the number of states which it covers (stored in field *size*).

If the variable DEMO is set to **true,** then the maximal compatibles will be listed, along with the states covered by each maximal compatible.

If the number of maximal compatibles reduces to one (1), then the problem under consideration is really a combinational logic program. In this case, the user is warned of the fact, and the program execution is terminated immediately.

procedure formincompatibles;

formincompatibles is called by *maxcompatibles* to determine the incompatible sets of states, storing the results in the array *incompats*.

function sameoutput(i, j: integer): boolean;

sameoutput is called by *formincompatibles* to determine if two states (*i* and *j*) have compatible outputs. If the outputs of the two states are compatible, then **true** is returned.

procedure maxclasses(cc: mctype; init: integer);

maxclasses is a recursive procedure used to generate the compatibility trees discussed in Section 5.2. If a unique maximal compatible is determined, it is stored in the linked list pointed to by *compats* (see *maxcompatibles* above).

Later procedures make use of sets of maximal compatibles. This fact is utilized in the Pascal code by finding a type which is the set of all maximal compatibles. Pascal requires that the range of a set be defined at compile time. Consequently, the code is constrained to have no more than *MAXPAIRS* of maximal compatibles. If, during the execution of *maxclasses*, it is found that this bound has been exceeded, an error message is printed and program execution is terminated immediately. The only remedy to this problem is to edit the file and increase the value of *MAXPAIRS* (defined to be 90 in this implementation).

procedure formcoverlist;

formcoverlist examines the list of maximal compatibles, and determines for each state the number of maximal compatibles which cover it. The count of covering maximal compatibles for each state is stored in the array *coverlist*. This information is used to select essential maximal compatibles.

procedure choosecover;

choosecover selects a minimum cover from the list of maximal compatibles, using the procedures *findessential* and *closeon*. If the variable DEMO is set to **true,** the user is notified of each essential maximal compatible as it is located, and of the states which it covers.

function findessential: cptr;

findessential returns a state with the minimum number of covering maximal compatibles. Any state which has only one covering maximal compatible is returned immediately as an essential maximal compatible; otherwise the maximal compatible with the smallest closure term (using the function *selectbestfit*) is returned.

procedure closeon(p: cptr);

closeon is a recursive function which uses the heuristics of Section 5.2 to determine the closure function for the given maximal compatible *p*. It first calls the procedure *formcf* to form the closure function for the maximal compatible *p*. It then calls the function *selectbestfit* to determine the maximal compatible with the smallest number of branches to follow, and then calls itself to form the closure function of the selected maximal compatible.

function selectbestfit(p: cptr): cptr;

The function *selectbestfit* examines a list of closure terms and returns the one which has the least number of uncovered maximal compatibles.

procedure formcf(p: cptr; sieve: mctype);

formcf takes the maximal compatible *p* and a list of maximal compatibles already covered (stored in the power set *sieve*) and selects the implied maximal compatibles. It uses the procedures *genimp* (to determine the implied maximal compatibles not yet covered) and *disjunct* to form the disjunctive normalized closure function. The procedure *addterm* is used to add disjunctive terms to the closure function.

procedure genimp(x: mctype; **var** nss: cptr);

genimp takes the maximal compatible *x* and returns the list of (as yet) uncovered implied maximal compatibles through the pointer *nss*.

procedure disjunct(**var** c: cptr; s: cptr; result: mctype);

disjunct takes the closure function pointed to by *s* and produces a new closure function in disjunctive normal form (i.e., sum of products form). As new maximal compatibles are covered they are recorded in the power set *result*. The closure function is returned via the pointer *c*. It calls the procedure *addterm* to add closure terms to the closure function.

procedure addterm(**var** c: cptr; x: mctype);

addterm adds a closure term to the closure list if it does not already appear in the list. If it subsumes an existing term in the closure function, then the subsumed term is also deleted from the list of closure terms. It calls the procedures *additem* (to add a closure term to the list) and *freelist* to remove a subsumed closure term.

function findmc(x: integer): cptr;

The function *findmc* scans the list of maximal compatibles (*compats*) and returns a pointer to the maximal compatible number x.

procedure prbasic;

prbasic scans the list of maximal compatibles and, for each maximal compatible in turn, prints both an (internally generated) number of the maximal compatible and the states which the maximal compatible covers. It calls *writeclass* to print the set of states covered.

function covered(x: mctype; y: cptr): boolean;

The function *covered* scans the list y of powersets (maximal compatibles or closure terms) to determine if x is already covered by one of the entries. It returns **true** if x is already covered.

procedure newstatetable;

newstatetable produces a new state table given the minimal cover of maximal compatibles (stored in the power set *used*). It merges the outputs of compatible states and produces a reduced output table as well. States are labelled with names in the range "a" to "z" (not to be confused with the original labelling).

function power(x: integer): integer;

The function *power* returns the number of flip-flops needed to handle a state table with x states.

Appendix 5B

PASCAL PROGRAM FOR STATE MINIMIZATION

```pascal
program statereduce(input, output);
```
statereduce

```pascal
const
        MAXINPUTS = 8;
        MAXOUTPUTS = 8;
        MAXSTATES = 16;

type
        statearray = array [1..MAXINPUTS, 1..MAXSTATES] of 0..MAXSTATES;
        outarray = array [1..MAXOUTPUTS, 1..MAXSTATES] of 0..2;

var
        ninputs, noutputs, nstates: integer;
        nextstate: statearray;
        outputs: outarray;
        cad, demo: boolean;

        procedure writestate(s: integer);
        { write state as an alphabetic character }
```
writestate

```pascal
        begin { writestate }
            write(' ', chr(ord('a') + s - 1))
        end; { writestate }

        procedure writetable;
```
writetable

```pascal
        var
            i, j: integer;
            c: char;

            procedure writebool(x: boolean);
```
writebool

```pascal
            begin { writebool }
                if x then
                        write('T')
                else
                        write('F')
            end; { writebool }
```

```
begin { writetable }
    if demo then begin
        writeln(ninputs, ' Inputs');
        writeln(noutputs, ' Outputs');
        writeln(nstates, ' States')
    end;
    if not cad then
        for j := 1 to nstates do begin
            for i := 1 to ninputs do
                if nextstate[i, j] = 0 then
                    write(' -')
                else
                    writestate(nextstate[i, j]);
            write(' ': 4);
            for i := 1 to noutputs do
                if outputs[i, j] in [1, 2] then
                    write(outputs[i, j] - 1: 2)
                else
                    write(' -');
            writeln
        end
    else begin
        writebool(cad);
        writebool(demo);
        writeln;
        writeln(ninputs);
        writeln(nstates);
        for j := 1 to nstates do begin
            for i := 1 to ninputs do
                if nextstate[i, j] = 0 then
                    write(' -')
                else
                    writestate(nextstate[i, j]);
            writeln;
        end;
        writeln(noutputs);
        for j := 1 to nstates do begin
            for i := 1 to ninputs do
                if outputs[i, j] in [1, 2] then
                    write(outputs[i, j] - 1: 2)
                else
                    write(' -');
            writeln
        end;
        while not eof(input) do begin
            while not eoln(input) do begin
                read(c);
                write(c)
            end;
            readln;
            writeln
        end
    end
end; { writetable }


function readstate(c: char): integer;                              readstate
```

```
begin { readstate }
    if c in ['a'..'z'] then
        readstate := ord(c) - ord('a') + 1
    else if c in ['A'..'Z'] then
        readstate := ord(c) - ord('A') + 1
    else begin
        writeln(' *** Illegal character in state table (', c, ')');
        halt
    end
end; { readstate }


procedure readtable;                                        readtable

var
    i, j: integer;
    c: char;


begin { readtable }
    read(c);          { get CAD output-compatible flag }
    cad := c = 'T';
    readln(c);        { demo-stration flag }
    if cad then
        demo := false
    else
        demo := c = 'T';
    readln(ninputs);
    if ninputs > MAXINPUTS then begin
        message(' Too many inputs specified (max =', MAXINPUTS: 3, ')');
        halt
    end;
    readln(nstates);
    if nstates > MAXSTATES then begin
        message(' Too many states specified (max =', MAXSTATES: 3, ')');
        halt
    end;
    for j := 1 to nstates do begin
        for i := 1 to ninputs do begin
            read(c);
            while c = ' ' do
                read(c);
            if c = '-' then
                nextstate[i, j] := 0
            else
                nextstate[i, j] := readstate(c)
        end;
        readln
    end;
    readln(noutputs);
    if noutputs > MAXOUTPUTS then begin
        message(' Too many outputs specified (max =', MAXOUTPUTS: 3, ')');
        halt
    end;
    for j := 1 to nstates do begin
        for i := 1 to noutputs do begin
            read(c);
```

```
                    while c = ´´ do
                        read(c);
                    if c = ´0´ then
                        outputs[i, j] := 1
                    else if c = ´1´ then
                        outputs[i, j] := 2
                    else
                        outputs[i, j] := 0
            end;
            readln
        end;
        if demo then
            writetable
end; { readtable }

procedure issm;                                                    issm

const
    MAXPAIRS = 90;
    MAXINT = maxint;

type
    mctype = set of 0..MAXPAIRS;
    ctype = (compclass, scomp);
    cptr = ^ citem;
    citem =
        record
            next, last: cptr;
            class: mctype;
            case typ: ctype of
                scomp: (
                        closfun: cptr;
                        index: integer;
                        size: integer;
                        cfdone: boolean
                    );
                compclass: (
                    )
        end;

var
    oldnstates: integer;
    freecomp, freescomp: cptr;
    compats: cptr;
    ncompats: integer;
    coverlist: array [1..MAXSTATES] of integer;
    used: mctype;


function power(x: integer): integer;                               power

var
    i: integer;

begin { power }
    i := 0;
    x := x - 1;
```

```
      while x > 0 do begin
          i := i + 1;
          x := x div 2
      end;
      power := i
end; { power }
```

procedure freeitem(var y: cptr; p: cptr);   *freeitem*

{ remove item p from list y and place on appropriate free list }

```
begin { freeitem }
    if p <> nil then
        with p^ do begin
            if last = nil then begin
                y := next;
                if y <> nil then
                        y^.last := nil
            end else if next = nil then
                    last^.next := nil
            else begin
                    last^.next := next;
                    next^.last := last
            end;
            if typ = compclass then begin
                    next := freecomp;
                    freecomp := p
            end else begin
                    next := freescomp;
                    freescomp := p
            end
        end
end; { freeitem }
```

procedure freelist(var y: cptr; var p: cptr);   *freelist*
{ return item (and any list) to free list }

```
var
    q: cptr;

begin { freelist }
    if p <> nil then
        with p^ do begin
            q := next;
            if typ = scomp then begin
                while closfun <> nil do
                        freeitem(closfun, closfun)
            end;
            freeitem(y, p);
            p := q
        end
end; { freelist }
```

procedure additem(var y: cptr; p: cptr);   *additem*
{ add item to tail of list }

```
var
    q: cptr;
```

```
begin { additem }
     if y = nil then
         y := p
     else begin
         q := y;
         while q^.next <> nil do
             q := q^.next;
         q^.next := p;
         p^.last := q
     end;
     p^.next := nil
end; { additem }
```

```
function newitem(x: ctype; y: mctype): cptr;                         newitem
{ get an item from free list or create a new one }

var
     p: cptr;

begin { newitem }
     if x = scomp then begin
         if freescomp = nil then
             new(p, scomp)
         else begin
             p := freescomp;
             freescomp := p^.next
         end;
         p^.cfdone := false;
         p^.closfun := nil
     end else if freecomp = nil then
         new(p, compclass)
     else begin
         p := freecomp;
         freecomp := p^.next
     end;
     with p^ do begin
         typ := x;
         next := nil;
         last := nil;
         class := y
     end;
     newitem := p
end; { newitem }
```

```
function covered(x: mctype; y: cptr): boolean;                       covered
{ checks to see if class 'x' is already covered by classes in array y }

begin { covered }
     covered := false;
     while y <> nil do
         if x <= y^.class then begin
             y := nil;
             covered := true
         end else
             y := y^.next
end; { covered }
```

```
procedure writeclass(x: mctype);                                     writeclass
```

```
var
     i: integer;

begin { writeclass }
     write(' ');
     i := 1;
     while (i <= nstates) and (x <> []) do begin
          if i in x then begin
               writestate(i);
               x := x − [i]
          end;
          if x <> [] then
               i := i + 1
     end
end; { writeclass }

procedure prbasic;                                              prbasic

var
     p, q: cptr;

begin { prbasic }
     writeln;
     writeln(' Maximum Compatibles');
     writeln(' ******************');
     writeln;
     p := compats;
     while p <> nil do
          with p^ do begin
               { print the result }
               write(index: 3);
               writeclass(class);
               if cfdone then begin
                    write(' => ');
                    if closfun = nil then
                         write(' −')
                    else begin
                         q := closfun;
                         while q <> nil do begin
                              writeclass(q^.class);
                              q := q^.next
                         end
                    end
               end;
               p := next;
               writeln
          end
end; { prbasic }

function findmc(x: integer): cptr;                             findmc

var
     p: cptr;
     break: boolean;

begin { findmc }
     p := compats;
     break := false;
     while (p <> nil) and not break do
```

```
                    if p^.index = x then
                            break := true
                    else
                            p := p^.next;
              findmc := p
         end; { findmc }
```

```
procedure maxcompatibles;
```
maxcompatibles

```
var
         i: integer;
         incompats: array [1..MAXSTATES] of mctype;
         used: mctype;
```

```
         procedure formincompatibles;
```
formincompatibles

```
         var
                    i, j, k, m, n: integer;
                    changed: boolean;
```

```
                    function sameoutput(i, j: integer): boolean;
```
sameoutput

```
                    var
                            k: integer;
                            same: boolean;

                    begin { sameoutput }
                            same := true;
                            k := 1;
                            while (k <= noutputs) and same do begin
                                    if (outputs[k, i] <> 0) and (outputs[k, j] <> 0) then
                                            if outputs[k, i] <> outputs[k, j] then
                                                    same := false;
                                    k := k + 1
                            end;
                            sameoutput := same
                    end; { sameoutput }
```

```
                    procedure continue;
```
continue

```
                    { This is here purely for formatting purposes – it }
                    { really should be inline code. }

                    begin { continue }
                            if nextstate[k, m] in incompats[i] then
                                    if (n < m) and not (n in incompats[m]) then begin
                                            changed := true;
                                            incompats[m] := incompats[m] + [n]
                                    end else if (n > m) and not (m in incompats[n]) then begin
                                            changed := true;
                                            incompats[n] := incompats[n] + [m]
                                    end
                    end; { continue }
```

```
         begin { formincompatibles }
                    for i := 1 to nstates do
                            incompats[i] := [];
```

```
{ find those incompatibles caused by different outputs alone }
for i := 1 to nstates − 1 do
        for j := i + 1 to nstates do
                if not sameoutput(i, j) then
                        incompats[j] := incompats[j] + [i];
        { now form the incompatibles implied by these ones }
        repeat
                changed := false;
                for i := 1 to nstates do
                        if incompats[i] <> [] then   { check if i has any incompatibles }
                                for k := 1 to ninputs do
                                        for n := 1 to nstates do   { then check col. k for state i }
                                                if i = nextstate[k, n] then
                                                        for m := 1 to nstates do
                                                                continue;
        until not changed
end; { formincompatibles }


procedure maxclasses(cc: mctype; init: integer);                    maxclasses

var
        i, cnt: integer;
        p: cptr;

begin { maxclasses }
        cnt := ncompats;
        for i := init + 1 to nstates do
                if cc * incompats[i] = [] then   { cc is compatible with i }
                        maxclasses(cc + [i], i);
        if cnt = ncompats then
                if not (cc <= used) then
                        if not covered(cc, compats) then begin
                                ncompats := ncompats + 1;
                                if ncompats > MAXPAIRS then begin
                                        write(' Too many compatibles generated ');
                                        writeln('(max. =', MAXPAIRS: 3, ')');
                                        halt
                                end;
                                cnt := ncompats;
                                p := newitem(scomp, cc);
                                p^.size := card(cc);
                                p^.index := ncompats;
                                additem(compats, p)
                        end
end; { maxclasses }
begin { maxcompatibles }
        formincompatibles;
        ncompats := 0;
        compats := nil;
        for i := 1 to nstates do begin
                used := [];
                maxclasses([i], i)
        end;
        if ncompats = 1 then begin
                writeln(' Problem reduces to a single state');
                halt
        end;
```

```
            if demo then
                prbasic
    end; { maxcompatibles }
```

```
    procedure writecset(x: mctype);                                     writecset

    var
        i: integer;

    begin { writecset }
        write(' [');
        i := 0;
        while (i <= MAXPAIRS) and (x <> []) do begin
            if i in x then begin
                if i < 10 then
                    write(i: 2)
                else
                    write(i: 3);
                x := x - [i]
            end;
            if x <> [] then
                i := i + 1
        end;
        write(']')
    end; { writecset }
```

```
    procedure formcoverlist;                                        formcoverlist

    var
        p: cptr;
        i: integer;

    begin { formcoverlist }
        for i := 1 to nstates do begin
            coverlist[i] := 0;
            p := compats;
            while p <> nil do begin
                if i in p^.class then
                    coverlist[i] := coverlist[i] + 1;
                p := p^.next
            end
        end
    end; { formcoverlist }
```

```
    procedure choosecover;                                           choosecover
    { Use heuristics to find a reasonable cover }

    var
        uncovered, yet2use: mctype;
        i: integer;
        p: cptr;
        break: boolean;


        procedure formcf(p: cptr; sieve: mctype);                       formcf
        { form the closure function - index on maximum compatible }
```

```
var
     q, r, sets: cptr;
     x: mctype;
     break: boolean;
     procedure genimp(x: mctype; var nss: cptr);            genimp
     { generate the classes implied by class 'x'. }
     { returns implied pairs in 'nss' }

var
     i, j, m: integer;
                                                   procedure continue;
     { This is here for the same reason as the previous continue procedure }

var
     tclass: mctype;

begin { continue }
     if m in x then
          if nextstate[i, j] <> nextstate[i, m] then
               if nextstate[i, m] <> 0 then begin
                    tclass := [nextstate[i, j]] + [nextstate[i, m]];
                    if not (tclass <= x) then
                         if not covered(tclass, nss) then
                              additem(nss, newitem(compclass, tclass))
          end

     end; { continue }


begin { genimp }
     nss := nil;
     if card(x) > 1 then
          for i := 1 to ninputs do
               for j := 1 to nstates − 1 do
                    if (j in x) and (nextstate[i, j] <> 0) then
                         for m := j + 1 to nstates do
                              continue;
     end; { genimp }


procedure addterm(var c: cptr; x: mctype);              addterm
     { add disjunctive term to the list }

var
     p: cptr;
     quit: boolean;

begin { addterm }
     p := c;
     quit := false;
     while (p <> nil) and not quit do
          if p^.class <= x then{ dont add subsumed set }
               quit := true
          else if x <= p^.class then{ delete subsumed set }
               freelist(c, p)
          else
               p := p^.next;
```

```
                    if not quit and (x <> []) then
                            additem(c, newitem(compclass, x))
              end; { addterm }


              procedure disjunct(var c: cptr; s: cptr; result: mctype);          disjunct
              { perform disjunctive normalization }

              var
                    i: integer;

              begin { disjunct }
                    if s <> nil then begin
                          for i := 1 to ncompats do
                                if (i in s^.class) and not (i in sieve) then
                                      disjunct(c, s^.next, result + [i])
                    end else
                          addterm(c, result)
              end; { disjunct }

        begin {formcf}
              if p <> nil then
                    with p^ do begin
                          genimp(class, closfun);
                          sets := nil;
                          if closfun <> nil then begin
                                q := closfun;
                                while q <> nil do begin
                                      x := [];
                                      r := compats;
                                      break := false;
                                      while (r <> nil) and not break do begin
                                            if q^.class <= r^.class then
                                                  if r^.index in sieve then
                                                        break := true
                                                  else
                                                        x := x + [r^.index];
                                            r := r^.next
                                      end;
                                      if not break then
                                            addterm(sets, x);
                                      q := q^.next
                                end;
                                while closfun <> nil do
                                      freelist(closfun, closfun);
                                if sets <> nil then begin
                                      disjunct(closfun, sets, []);
                                      while sets <> nil do
                                            freelist(sets, sets)
                                end
                          end;
                          cfdone := true
                    end
        end; { formcf }

  function selectbestfit(p: cptr): cptr;                                      selectbestfit

  var
        break: boolean;
        bestfit: integer;
```

```
begin { selectbestfit }
     selectbestfit := nil;
     if p <> nil then begin
          bestfit := MAXINT;
          break := false;
          while (p <> nil) and not break do
               with p^ do begin
                    if card(class − (used + yet2use)) < bestfit then begin
                         { pick one with smallest number of branches left to follow }
                         selectbestfit := p;
                         bestfit := card(class − (used + yet2use));
                         break := bestfit = 0
                    end;
                    if not break then
                         p := next
               end
     end
end; { selectbestfit }
```

function findessential: cptr;   *findessential*
{ *Find a state with a minimum number of covering MCSs. It is* }
{ *essential if there is only one, otherwise it is quasi−essential* }

```
var
     i, min, bigsize, small: integer;
     p, q: cptr;
     biggest, essentstates: mctype;

begin { findessential }
     { Find (quasi−)essential MCSs }
     min := MAXINT;
     for i := 1 to nstates do
          if i in uncovered then
               if coverlist[i] < min then begin
                    min := coverlist[i];
                    essentstates := [i]
               end else if coverlist[i] = min then
                    essentstates := essentstates + [i];
     { Find unique MCS covering largest no. of states }
     bigsize := 0;
     p := compats;
     while p <> nil do
          with p^ do begin
               if essentstates * class <> [] then
                    if size > bigsize then begin
                         biggest := [index];
                         q := p;
                         bigsize := size
                    end else if size = bigsize then
                         biggest := biggest + [index];
               p := next
          end;
     if card(biggest) = 1 then
          { found unique MCS }
          findessential := q
     else begin
          small := MAXINT;
```

```
                    p := compats;
                    break := false;
                    while (p <> nil) and not break do begin
                        if p^.index in biggest then begin
                            if not p^.cfdone then
                                    formcf(p, used);
                            { More than one; pick one with smallest closure term }
                            q := selectbestfit(p);
                            break := q = nil;
                            if q = nil then
                                    findessential := p
                            else begin
                                    i := card(q^.class − (used + yet2use));
                                    if i < small then begin
                                        small := i;
                                        findessential := p;
                                        break := small = 0
                                    end
                            end
                        end;
                        if not break then
                            p := p^.next
                    end
                end
end; { findessential }


procedure closeon(p: cptr);                                              closeon
{ The closure list of MCS p may have more than one entry }
{ The best entry is chosen from the list following the    }
{ application of the following two heuristics:            }
{   1: if one entry is covered by the selection of        }
{       previous MCSs then no futher closure is reqd.     }
{   2: the entry selected has the smallest number         }
{       of MCSs yet to be covered.                        }

var
        i: integer;
        q: cptr;

begin { closeon }
        used := used + [p^.index];
        yet2use := yet2use − [p^.index];
        uncovered := uncovered − p^.class;
        if not p^.cfdone then
                formcf(p, used + yet2use);
        if demo then begin
                write(´ ==> ´);
                q := p^.closfun;
                while q <> nil do begin
                        writecset(q^.class);
                        q := q^.next
                end;
                writeln
        end;
        p := selectbestfit(p^.closfun);
        if p <> nil then begin
                yet2use := yet2use + p^.class − used;
                for i := 1 to ncompats do
```

```
                        if i in p^.class then
                            if not (i in used) then begin
                                if demo then
                                    write('Closing on', i: 3);
                                closeon(findmc(i))
                            end
            end
        end; { closeon }

begin { choosecover }
    uncovered := [];
    used := [];
    yet2use := [];
    for i := 1 to nstates do
        uncovered := uncovered + [i];
    while uncovered <> [] do begin
        p := findessential;
        if demo then
            write('Essential MC is:', p^.index: 3);
        closeon(p)
    end;
    if demo then begin
        write('Closed cover is');
        writecset(used);
        writeln
    end
end; { choosecover }


procedure newstatetable;
```
newstatetable

```
var
    i, j, k, count, nnewstates: integer;
    a: mctype;
    ns: statearray;
    w: outarray;
    cover: array [1..MAXSTATES] of mctype;
    p: cptr;

begin { newstatetable }
    if demo then begin
        writeln;
        writeln(' New State Table');
        writeln(' **************');
        writeln
    end;
    ns := nextstate;
    w := outputs;
    { form a list of the newstates showing the    }
    { old states that are covered by each new state }
    nnewstates := 0;
    for i := 1 to ncompats do
        if i in used then begin
            nnewstates := nnewstates + 1;
            p := findmc(i);
            cover[nnewstates] := p^.class
        end;
    for i := 1 to nnewstates do begin
        for j := 1 to noutputs do begin
```

```
                    outputs[j, i] := 0;
                    { merge outputs }
                    for k := 1 to nstates do
                            if k in cover[i] then
                                    if w[j, k] <> 0 then
                                            outputs[j, i] := w[j, k]
            end;
            for j := 1 to ninputs do begin
                    a := [];
                    for k := 1 to nstates do
                            if k in cover[i] then
                                    if ns[j, k] <> 0 then
                                            a := a + [ns[j, k]];
                    { set up new states }
                    count := 0;
                    nextstate[j, i] := 0;
                    for k := 1 to nnewstates do
                            if (a <= cover[k]) and (a <> []) then begin
                                    count := count + 1;
                                    if count = 1 then    { pick first match }
                                                    nextstate[j, i] := k
                                    end;
                            if count = nnewstates then
                                    nextstate[j, i] := 0
                            end
                    end;
                    nstates := nnewstates
            end; { newstatetable }

begin { issm }
        freecomp := nil;
        freescomp := nil;
        readtable;
        maxcompatibles;
        formcoverlist;
        choosecover;
        oldnstates := nstates;
        if card(used) >= nstates then
                message('No state reduction achieved. Continuing...')
        else begin
                oldnstates := nstates;
                newstatetable
        end;
        writetable;
        if not cad then begin
                writeln;
                writeln('Original number of memory elements: ', power(oldnstates): 3);
                if card(used) < oldnstates then
                        writeln('New number of memory elements: ', power(card(used)): 8)
        end
end; { issm }

begin { main }
        issm
end.
```

Appendix 5C

DESCRIPTION OF THE PASCAL PROCEDURES
FOR STATE ASSIGNMENT

5C.1. INTRODUCTION

The Pascal procedures listed here are based upon the state assignment technique detailed in Section 5.3. They do not, however, constitute a full implementation of the SHR algorithm because a set of listings for the complete technique would take up far too many pages. The procedures we list here provide the state assignment which is given by the (valid) set of columns which has minimum lower-bound cost. Thus, the procedures listed here do not go on to produce circuit realizations in order to determine the actual minimum-cost assignment. The interested reader may wish to write his or her own procedures in order to implement the complete technique.

5C.2. INPUT DATA FORMAT

In Appendix 5-A, a description is given of the input data file required for carrying out a state minimization followed by a state assignment. Sometimes a designer may not require the state minimization step to be carried out and if so, the input data are fed directly to the state assignment procedures. In such a case, the input data file has exactly the same format as is given in Appendix 5-A. That is:

CAD flag *DEMO* flag (T or F)
Number of inputs
Number of states
Next-state list for state *a*

. . .

Number of outputs
Output list for state *a*

. . .

Number of bits in input code

Input code number 1

. . .

Flip-flop type to be used in realization (JK, SR, D, T)

The meaning of the data items up to "Number of bits in input code" is the same as is explained in Appendix 5-A. For the state assignment to be carried out correctly, the input code information must be added.

An example showing the input data format is given in Appendix 5-E.

5C.3. INPUT-OUTPUT PROCEDURES

procedure writestate(s: integer);

  writestate converts the integer s (in the range $1 . . .$ MAXSTATES) into an alphabetic character in the range $a . . . z$.

procedure writetable;

  writetable writes the state table and the output table to *output*. It also prints the number of inputs, outputs and states. This is primarily used as a check of the input data.

function readstate(c: char): integer;

  readstate converts the ASCII character c (in the range $a . . . z$ or $A . . . Z$) into an integer in the range $1 . . .$ MAXSTATES.

procedure readtable;

  readtable reads only the state table data from *input*.

procedure readincoding;

  readincoding reads the encoding of the input variables from *input*. The data takes the form of the number of bits per input code, followed on successive lines by the input coding (left-justified on the line). Input code bits must be in the range "0", "1", "x", "-". No blanks may appear in the bit coding.

procedure readrealization;

  readrealization reads a one line entry from *input* to determine the type of flip-flop with which to realize the circuit. The type of flip-flop must be specified as one of the following: D, T, SR, or JK. This information is stored in the array *realize*, along with the number of inputs to the flip-flop stored in *nffinputs*.

procedure results;

  results prints both the state assignment found and the function array. Setting the variable CAD to **true** will cause output to be produced in a form suitable for direct input to the Pascal program in Appendix 3F.1.

procedure writecoding(code: integer);

writecoding writes the state assignment for the state given by *code* to *output*.

procedure writeinputs(inputnumber: integer);

writeinputs writes the input code bits for input *inputnumber* to the file *output*.

procedure writerealization;

writerealization writes the flip-flop type used in the realization to the file *output*.

procedure writenextstate(cs, ns: integer);

writenextstate writes the flip-flop input(s) necessary to cause a state transition from state *cs* to state *ns* to the file *output*.

5C.4. UTILITY PROCEDURES

function power(n: integer): integer;

power returns the smallest integer k that satisfies the relation $n \le 2^k$.

function exp(n: integer): integer;

exp returns the value of 2^n.

procedure decode(codeno, code: integer);

decode converts *code* into a series of binary bits, which are stored in the array *s[codeno].bits*.

procedure codes;

codes determines all the possible column assignments. It uses the function *isunique* to determine that an assignment is unique (i.e., has not been generated previously) and the function *nbits* to establish that it has the same number of 1's and 0's.

function isunique(codeno: integer): boolean;

isunique returns **true** if the column coding stored in *s[codeno].coding* (and as a string of binary digits in *s[codeno].bits*) is unique. *codeno* points to the next free location in the array *s*.

function nbits(codepattern: integer): integer;
THIS IS A MACHINE-DEPENDENT ROUTINE—IT DEPENDS UPON THE VARIANT RECORDS MAPPING TO THE SAME MEMORY LOCATION AND UPON AN INTEGER OCCUPYING 32 BITS. *nbits* returns the number of 1s in the binary representation of the integer *codepattern*. It uses the NONSTANDARD function *card* to determine the cardinality of a

(power)set. This will need recoding if this feature is not available on your computer. *card* is used for speed in this implementation; it can reduce the execution time by up to 12 percent.

5C.5. MEMORY MANAGEMENT

The variation on the Q-M method used in this chapter employs a table to store intermediate results. In this program, we have represented the tables as linked lists of data items. This allows arbitrary-length tables to be constructed, without requiring editing and recompilation of the program (the power sets must still be specified at compile time, but this is a less stringent requirement).

function newshrentry: shrptr;

procedure addshrentry(**var** x, p: shrptr);

procedure rmshrentry(**var** l, p: shrptr);

procedure addlist(**var** l, q: shrptr);

function uniquentry(l, p: shrptr): boolean;

These five procedures and functions are used to manipulate the entries of the tabular SHR method. *newshrentry* is used either to allocate a new table entry from the list of currently unused entries (pointed to by *freelist*), or if none are available, to allocate a new entry from the heap (using the inbuilt function *new*). *addshrentry* adds item *p* to the head of the list *x*. *rmshrentry* removes the item *p* from anywhere within the list *l*. *addlist* appends the list *q* to the list *l*. This procedure is also used to return a list to the free list. *uniquentry* returns **true** if item *p* does not appear in the list *l*.

5C.6. SHR PROCEDURES

procedure lowerbounds;

lowerbounds determines the lower bounds on the cost of each column encoding using the tabular method of SHR. Upon completion of this procedure, the lower bounds on the cost are set, for each column encoding, in the entry *s[codenumber].cost*. The procedure *costit* is called for each column coding in turn. The maximum number of '0-cubes' is set by the constant MAXIDENTRY (= MAXSTATES * MAXINPUTS). This value should be changed if MAXSTATES or MAXINPUTS is ever changed.

procedure costit(codeno: integer; typ: fftype);

costit returns the cost of column encoding number *codeno* (where the encoding is given in the array entry *s[codeno].bits*) using flip-flop input type *typ*.

typ is one of the types T, D, J, K, S, or R. For JK and SR flip-flops, the cost is given by the cost of realizing the logic for both flip-flop inputs.

procedure flipflop(cs, ip: integer; typ: fftype; **var** t: logic);

Given the transition from the state *cs* to the nextstate for input *ip* for a flip-flop input of type *typ*, *flipflop* returns the input excitation required (in the variable *t*).

function listcost(l: shrptr): integer;

function cubecost(p: shrptr): integer;

cubecost returns the number of inputs required by the cube *p*. *listcost* returns the cost (i.e., the number of inputs) to realize the function given by the list of cubes pointed to by *l*. The realization is a simple two-level AND/OR realization.

procedure shrmethod(codeno: integer; typ: fftype);

shrmethod implements the tabular SHR method outlined in Section 5.3. It determines all the prime implicants, locates the essential prime implicants, and generates a cover for the state table. The resulting cover is pointed to by the variable *epi*.

procedure shrsetup(typ: fftype);

shrsetup generates the 0-cubes in the upper and lower halves of the table, for flip-flop input type *typ*.

function combinecube(**var** e: shrptr; c1, c2: shrptr; ismixed: boolean): boolean;

function compare(x, y: cubepattern; **var** n: integer): boolean;

combinecube returns **true** if two cubes *c1* and *c2* can be combined, placing a pointer to the resulting cube in *e*. Two cubes can be combined if

(i) they have identical bit entries AND they have no common entries in their lettersets; OR
(ii) They have identical lettersets AND the cubes differ in only one bit position; OR
(iii) if a mixed cube is being generated (i.e., *ismixed* = **true**) they have no common entries in their lettersets AND the cubes differ in only one bit position.

compare returns **true** and sets $n < 0$ if the cubes match identically, or returns **true** and sets $n >= 0$ if the cubes match in all but one bit position; otherwise compare returns **false**. *n* is the bit position where the difference is detected.

procedure onegenerate(**var** list1: shrptr; p, list2: shrptr; ismixed: boolean);

onegenerate generates combinations of cube *p* with each cube in the list pointed to by *list2*, placing new (unique) cubes in the list *list1*.

procedure selfgenerate(**var** list1, list2: shrptr);

selfgenerate generates all unique combinations of cubes in the list *list2* and places the new cubes in the list *list1*.

procedure mixedgenerate(**var** list1, list2, list3: shrptr);

mixedgenerate generates all the (unique) cubes from combinations of cubes from *list2* with cubes from *list3*, placing the results in the list *list1*. This is used to generate the cubes in the 'mixed' area of the tabular method.

procedure markused;

procedure markall(l: shrptr);

procedure freeused(**var** l: shrptr);

markused marks all those cubes in the 'upper' portion and the 'lower' portion of the table which are covered by cubes in the newly generated 'mixed' portion of the table. *markall* marks all those cubes of list *l* which are covered by cubes in the list *newmixed*. *freeused* removes all cubes from the list *l* which are marked as 'used', i.e., the *used* field is set to **true.** Cubes deleted are added to the freelist for use again.

procedure pickessential;

When the tabular method terminates, all prime implicants are held in the list *finalcubes. pickessential* scans this list looking for essential prime implicants, returning those selected to the list *epi*. Cubes which are covered are listed in the power set *cubescovered*.

procedure findcover;

If all cubes are not covered, *findcover* scans the cubes remaining in the list *finalcubes* and selects those cubes which cover the largest number of uncovered 0-cubes; if there is more than one to choose from, then the first one found is transferred to the list *epi*.

procedure sortcosts;

sortcosts sorts the column encodings array into ascending order of column costs. This is done to reduce the time to scan for valid column combinations of low cost.

procedure validcombinations;

procedure initselect(**var** s: selarray; range, upperbound: integer);

function select(**var** s: selarray): boolean;

function isvalid(c: combination): boolean;

> *validcombinations* uses *select* to generate all possible combinations of columns, and then calls the function *isvalid* to determine if the combination is valid (i.e., two states are not assigned the same state encoding). *initselect* is used to set up the first selection. In order to keep the code in this package to a minimum, we keep a copy of the lowest cost combination found and realize ONLY this circuit. It is left as an exercise to the reader to add the code which completes the search for the optimum assignment. The combination selected is returned in the variable *combarray*.

procedure init;

> *init* initializes the array *convert* to convert from the integer values 0, 1, and 2 to the internal set representation. It also initializes the excitation tables for the flip-flops.

Appendix 5D

PASCAL PROGRAM FOR STATE ASSIGNMENT

```
program assign(input, output);

const
  MAXCOLS = 255;
  MAXBITS = 16;
  MAXSTATES = 9;
  MAXVARS = 4;
  MAXROWS = 16;
  MAXINPUTS = 8;
  MAXINCODES = 16;
  MAXOUTPUTS = 8;

type
  partial = array [0..MAXBITS] of integer;
  statearray = array [1..MAXINPUTS, 1..MAXROWS] of 0..MAXROWS;
  outarray = array [1..MAXOUTPUTS, 1..MAXROWS] of 0..2;
  logic = set of 0..1;
  cubepattern = array [0..MAXINCODES] of logic;
  transarray = array [0..1, 0..1] of logic;
  fftype = (J, K, S, R, T, D);
  makearray = array [1..2] of fftype;
  costentry =
    record
      coding: integer;
      bits: partial;
      cost: integer
    end;
  combination = array [1..MAXVARS] of integer;

var
  cad: boolean;
  convert: array [0..2] of logic;
  Jtransition: transarray;  { JK flip–flop transition array }
  Ktransition: transarray;
  Stransition: transarray;  { SR flip–flop transition array }
  Rtransition: transarray;
  Ttransition: transarray;  { T flip–flop transition array }
  Dtransition: transarray;  { D flip–flop transition array }
  realize: makearray;      { type of realization }
```

```
nffinputs: integer;       { number of inputs to a flip–flop (1..2) }
s: array [1..MAXCOLS] of costentry;
ncols: integer;
maxrows: integer;         { number of rows to encode over }
nvars: integer;           { number of state variables }
ninbits: integer;         { number of bits in input code }
ninputs, noutputs, nstates: integer;
nextstate: statearray;
outputs: outarray;
incodes: array [1..MAXINPUTS] of cubepattern;
i: integer;
mincombination: combination;
mincost: integer;

function power(n: integer): integer;                                power
{ find the integral power of two such that n = 2**power }

var
  i: integer;

begin { power }
  n := n – 1;
  i := 0;
  while n > 0 do begin
   i := i + 1;
   n := n div 2
  end;
  power := i
end; { power }

function exp(n: integer): integer;                                  exp
{ calculate 2**n }

var
  i: integer;
  result: integer;

begin { exp }
  if n = 0 then
   exp := 1
  else begin
   result := 1;
   for i := 1 to n do
      result := result * 2;
   exp := result
  end
end; { exp }

procedure decode(codeno, code: integer);                          decode
{ convert ´code´ into a binary bit pattern and }
{ store it in the ´bits´ field of ´s[codeno]´. }

var
  i: integer;

begin { decode }
  for i := maxrows – 1 downto 0 do begin
```

```
    if odd(code) then
       s[codeno].bits[i] := 1
    else
       s[codeno].bits[i] := 0;
    code := code div 2
  end
end; { decode }


procedure codes;                                        codes
{ produce the coding for each column }


var
  i: integer;
  codeno: integer;
  nones: integer;
  startcode, endcode: integer;


  function isunique(codeno: integer): boolean;          isunique
  { check that a coding is unique over the necessary number of bits }


  var
    i: integer;
    break: boolean;


  begin { isunique }
    break := false;
    i := 1;
    while not break and (i < codeno) do begin
      break := s[i].coding = s[codeno].coding;
       i := i + 1
    end;
    isunique := not break
  end; { isunique }


  function nbits(codepattern: integer): integer;        nbits
  { count the number of 1s in the 'codepattern'. }


  type
    unpack =
      record
       case boolean of
         true: (
          si: integer
         );
         false: (
          sb: set of 0..31
         )              { 31 IS IMPLEMENTATION DEPENDENT }
       end;


  var
    bitcount: unpack;


  begin { nbits }
    bitcount.si := codepattern;
    nbits := card(bitcount.sb)
  end; { nbits }
```

```
begin { codes }
  nones := maxrows div 2;
  { determine the starting code pattern }
  { pattern: 000...0011...11        }
  startcode := 1;
  for i := 1 to nones − 1 do
    startcode := startcode * 2 + 1;
  { determine the end code pattern }
  { pattern: 011...1100...00      }
  endcode := startcode;
  for i := 1 to nones − 1 do
    endcode := endcode * 2;
  { check each pattern for even numbers of 1s and 0s }
  codeno := 1;
  for i := startcode to endcode do
    if nbits(i) = nones then begin
      decode(codeno, i);
      { check that pattern is unique over the given }
      { number of states.                          }
      if isunique(codeno) then begin
        s[codeno].coding := i;
        codeno := codeno + 1
      end
    end
end; { codes }
```

procedure writestate(s: integer);   *writestate*
{ write state as an alphabetic character }

```
begin { writestate }
  write(' ', chr(ord('a') + s − 1))
end; { writestate }
```

procedure writetable;   *writetable*

```
var
  i, j: integer;

begin { writetable }
  writeln('STATE TABLE');
  writeln;
  writeln(ninputs: 3, ' Inputs');
  writeln(noutputs: 3, ' Outputs');
  writeln(nstates: 3, ' States');
  for j := 1 to nstates do begin
    for i := 1 to ninputs do
      if nextstate[i, j] = 0 then
        write(' −')
      else
        writestate(nextstate[i, j]);
    write(' ': 4);
    for i := 1 to noutputs do
      if outputs[i, j] in [1, 2] then
        write(outputs[i, j] − 1: 2)
      else
        write(' −');
    writeln
  end
end; { writetable }
```

```
function readstate(c: char): integer;                                    readstate

begin { readstate }
 if c in ['a'..'z'] then
  readstate := ord(c) − ord('a') + 1
 else if c in ['A'..'Z'] then
  readstate := ord(c) − ord('A') + 1
 else begin
  writeln(' *** Illegal character in state table (', c, ')');
  halt ⁻
 end
end; { readstate }


procedure readtable;                                                    readtable

var
 i, j: integer;
 c: char;

begin { readtable }
 readln(c); { read output option − CAD form or human form }
 cad := c = 'T';
 readln(ninputs);
 if ninputs > MAXINPUTS then begin
  message(' Too many inputs specified (max =', MAXINPUTS: 3, ')');
  halt
 end;
 readln(nstates);
 if nstates > MAXSTATES then begin
  message(' Too many states specified (max =', MAXSTATES: 3, ')');
  halt
 end;
 for j := 1 to nstates do begin
  for i := 1 to ninputs do begin
     read(c);
     while c = ' ' do
       read(c);
     if c = '−' then
       nextstate[i, j] := 0
     else
       nextstate[i, j] := readstate(c)
  end;
  readln
 end;
 readln(noutputs);
 if noutputs > MAXOUTPUTS then begin
  message(' Too many outputs specified (max =', MAXOUTPUTS: 3, ')');
  halt
 end;
 for j := 1 to nstates do begin
  for i := 1 to noutputs do begin
     read(c);
     while c = ' ' do
       read(c);
     if c = '0' then
       outputs[i, j] := 1
     else if c = '1' then
```

```
      outputs[i, j] := 2
      else
      outputs[i, j] := 0
    end;
    readln
  end
end; { readtable }
```

procedure readincoding;   *readincoding*
{ read in the encoding of the input columns }

```
var
  i, j, k: integer;
  c: char;

begin { readincoding }
  readln(ninbits);
  if ninbits > MAXINCODES then begin
    writeln(' *** ERROR: too many bits in input coding(max:', MAXINCODES: 3, ')');
    halt
  end;
  for i := 1 to ninputs do begin
    for j := 1 to ninbits do begin
      read(c);
      if not (c in ['0', '1', 'x', '-']) then begin
        writeln(' *** ERROR: incorrect input code');
        halt
      end else if c = '0' then
        k := 0
      else if c = '1' then
        k := 1
      else
        k := 2;
        incodes[i][j] := convert[k]
    end;
    readln
  end
end; { readincoding }
```

procedure readrealization;   *readrealization*
{ determine the type of flip–flop to be used for realization }

```
var
  c: char;

begin { readrealization }
  read(c);
  if c = 'T' then begin
    nffinputs := 1;
    realize[1] := T
  end else if c = 'D' then begin
    nffinputs := 1;
    realize[1] := D
  end else if c = 'S' then begin
    nffinputs := 2;
    realize[1] := S;
    realize[2] := R
  end else if c = 'J' then begin
```

```
      nffinputs := 2;
      realize[1] := J;
      realize[2] := K
    end else begin
      writeln(´ *** ERROR – unknown flip–flop type´);
      halt
    end
  end; { readrealization }
```

```
  procedure lowerbounds;
  { Use the tabular method of SHR to determine the lower bounds on }
  { each column encoding we derive.                               }
```

lowerbounds

```
  const
    MAXIDENTRY = 72;{ MAXSTATES * MAXINPUTS }
    { This may cause problems on some versions of PASCAL }
```

```
  type
    powerset = set of 0..MAXSTATES;
    idset = set of 1..MAXIDENTRY;
    shrptr = ˆ shrentry;
    shrentry =
      record
        letterset: powerset;
        cube: cubepattern;
        cubeid: idset;
        used: boolean;
        next, last: shrptr
      end;
```

```
  var
    i, j: integer;
    maxcost: integer;
    freelist: shrptr;        { list of available entries }
```

```
    procedure costit(codeno: integer; typ: fftype);
```

costit

```
    var
      upper, lower, mixed: shrptr;
      newupper, newlower, newmixed, finalcubes, epi: shrptr;
```

```
      function newshrentry: shrptr;
      { create a new (empty) entry record }
```

newshrentry

```
      var
        p: shrptr;
        i: integer;
```

```
      begin { newshrentry }
        if freelist <> nil then begin
          p := freelist;
          freelist := pˆ.next
        end else
          new(p);
        with pˆ do begin
          letterset := [];
          for i := 0 to ninbits do
            cube[i] := [];
```

```
        cubeid := [];
        used := false;
        next := nil;
        last := nil
      end;
    newshrentry := p
  end; { newshrentry }


procedure addshrentry(var x, p: shrptr);
{ add the entry 'p' to the head of list 'x'. }


begin { addshrentry }
  if p <> nil then begin
    with p^ do begin
      next := x;
      last := nil;
      if x <> nil then
        x^.last := p
    end;
    x := p
  end else begin
    writeln(' *** ERROR: attempt to add NIL to a list');
    halt
  end
end; { addshrentry }


procedure rmshrentry(var l, p: shrptr);
{ remove 'p' from list 'l'. }


begin { rmshrentry }
  if p <> nil then begin
    if l = p then begin
      { if its the first item in the list }
      l := p^.next;
      if l <> nil then
        l^.last := nil
    end else if p^.next = nil then begin
      { if its the last item in the list }
      if p^.last = nil then
        { it is the only item in the list }
        l := nil
      else
        p^.last^.next := nil
    end else begin
      { it must be in the middle of the list }
      p^.next^.last := p^.last;
      p^.last^.next := p^.next
    end
  end
end; { rmshrentry }


procedure addlist(var l, q: shrptr);
{ append list 'q' to list 'l' }


var
  p: shrptr;
```

addshrentry

rmshrentry

addlist

```
begin { addlist }
  if q <> nil then begin
    if l <> nil then begin
    p := l;
    while p^.next <> nil do
      p := p^.next;
    p^.next := q;
    q^.last := p
    end else
    l := q;
    q := nil
  end
end; { addlist }
```

```
procedure flipflop(cs, ip: integer; typ: fftype; var t: logic);
{ convert current state(cs) to next state(ns) transition (t) }
{ for respective JKSRTD entry (typ) and input (ip).  }
```
flipflop

```
var
  cscode, nscode, ns: integer;
```

```
begin { flipflop }
  ns := nextstate[ip, cs + 1];
  if (cs > nstates − 1) or (ns = 0) then
    t := [0, 1]
  else begin
    cscode := s[codeno].bits[cs];
    nscode := s[codeno].bits[ns − 1];
    case typ of
    J:
      t := Jtransition[cscode, nscode];
    K:
      t := Ktransition[cscode, nscode];
    S:
      t := Stransition[cscode, nscode];
    R:
      t := Rtransition[cscode, nscode];
    T:
      t := Ttransition[cscode, nscode];
    D:
      t := Dtransition[cscode, nscode]
    end
  end
end; { flipflop }
```

```
procedure freeused(var l: shrptr);
{ remove an entry from list 'l' if it is marked as used }
```
freeused

```
var
  p, save: shrptr;
```

```
begin { freeused }
  save := nil;
  while l <> nil do begin
    p := l^.next;
    if l^.used then begin
      addshrentry(freelist, l)
```

```
    end else
      addshrentry(save, l);
    l := p
    end;
    l := save
end; { freeused }
```

```
function listcost(l: shrptr): integer;                                    listcost
{ find cost of a list of cubes in list 'l'. }

var
  orcost: integer;
  andcost: integer;

    function cubecost(p: shrptr): integer;                                cubecost
    { find the cost of a cube − letterset plus cubepattern. }

    begin { cubecost }
      { # 0−cubes = 2 ** ( (nvars − 1) + (ninbits + 1) ) }
      cubecost := maxcost − power(card(p^.cubeid))
    end; { cubecost }

begin { listcost }
  orcost := 0;
  andcost := 0;
  while l <> nil do begin
    andcost := andcost + cubecost(l);
    orcost := orcost + 1;
    l := l^.next
  end;
  if orcost > 1 then
    listcost := andcost + orcost
  else
    listcost := andcost
end; { listcost }
```

```
procedure shrmethod(codeno: integer; typ: fftype);                        shrmethod
{ perform the SHR tabular method to derive the cost of lower bound }

var
  break: boolean;
  firsttime: boolean;
  allcarecubes, cubescovered: idset;

    procedure shrsetup(typ: fftype);                                      shrsetup
    { set up the initial 'upper' and 'lower' arrays }

    var
      i, j: integer;
      cnt: integer;
      transition: logic;
      p: shrptr;

    begin { shrsetup }
      upper := nil;
      lower := nil;
      mixed := nil;
```

```
finalcubes := nil;
cnt := 1;
allcarecubes := [];
for j := 1 to ninputs do
  for i := 0 to maxrows − 1 do begin
    flipflop(i, j, typ, transition);
    if 1 in transition then begin
      cnt := cnt + 1;
      p := newshrentry;
      p^.letterset := [i];
      p^.cubeid := [cnt];
      p^.cube := incodes[j];
      p^.cube[0] := convert[s[codeno].bits[i]];
      if s[codeno].bits[i] = 0 then
        addshrentry(upper, p)
      else if s[codeno].bits[i] = 1 then
        addshrentry(lower, p);
      if transition = [1] then
        allcarecubes := allcarecubes + [cnt]
    end
  end;
end; { shrsetup }


function combinecube(var e: shrptr; c1, c2: shrptr; ismixed: boolean): boolean;   combinecube
{ Two cubes can be combined if:                                   }
{                    (i)   they have identical cube entries       }
{                          AND                                    }
{                          they have no common entries in their lettersets; }
{          OR                                                     }
{ (ii)                     they have identical letter sets        }
{                          AND                                    }
{                          the cube entries differ in only one position.   }
{          OR if generating MIXED cubes ('ismixed = TRUE)         }
{ (ii)                     they have no common entries in their lettersets; }
{                          AND                                    }
{                          the cube entries differ in only one position.   }


var
  bitno: integer;
  result: boolean;
  docombine: boolean;


  function compare(x, y: cubepattern; var n: integer): boolean;              compare
  {-returns TRUE and n < 0 if the cubes match identically }
  { returns TRUE and n >= 0 if cubes match in all but one }
  {                 bit position                          }
  { returns FALSE otherwise                               }


  var
    i: integer;
    break: boolean;


  begin { compare }
    i := 0;
    n := −1;
    break := false;
```

```
  while not break and (i <= ninbits) do
  if x[i] = y[i] then
     i := i + 1
  else if n >= 0 then
     break := true
  else begin
     n := i;
     i := i + 1
  end;
  compare := not break
end; { compare }


begin { combinecube }
  docombine := false;
  result := compare(c1^.cube, c2^.cube, bitno);
  if c1^.letterset = c2^.letterset then begin
    if result and (bitno >= 0) then begin
      docombine := true;
      e := newshrentry;
      with e^ do begin
        cube := c1^.cube;
        cube[bitno] := [0, 1]
      end
    end
  end else if result and (bitno < 0) then begin
    if c1^.letterset * c2^.letterset = [] then begin
      docombine := true;
      e := newshrentry;
      e^.cube := c1^.cube
    end
  end else if ismixed then
    if result and (bitno >= 0) then
      if c1^.letterset * c2^.letterset = [] then begin
        docombine := true;
        e := newshrentry;
        with e^ do begin
          cube := c1^.cube;
          cube[bitno] := [0, 1]
        end
      end;
  combinecube := docombine;
  if docombine then begin
    with e^ do begin
      letterset := c1^.letterset + c2^.letterset;
      cubeid := c1^.cubeid + c2^.cubeid
    end;
    c1^.used := true;
    c2^.used := true
  end
end; { combinecube }


function uniquentry(l, p: shrptr): boolean;
{ returns TRUE is entry 'p' does not already exist in list 'l'. }


var
  break: boolean;
```

uniquentry

```
begin { uniquentry }
 break := false;
 while not break and (l <> nil) do begin
  break := l^.cubeid = p^.cubeid;
  l := l^.next
 end;
 uniquentry := not break
end; { uniquentry }

procedure onegenerate(var list1: shrptr; p, list2: shrptr; ismixed: boolean);
{ generate combinations of cube 'p' with each cube in 'list2', }
{ and place successful (unique) candidates in 'list1'.   }

var
 q, r: shrptr;

begin { onegenerate }
 if p <> nil then begin
  q := list2;
  while q <> nil do begin
   if combinecube(r, p, q, ismixed) then
    if uniquentry(list1, r) then
     addshrentry(list1, r)
    else                    { return 'r' to the pool }
     addshrentry(freelist, r);
   q := q^.next
  end
 end
end; { onegenerate }

procedure selfgenerate(var list1, list2: shrptr);

var
 p: shrptr;

begin { selfgenerate }
 list1 := nil;
 if list2 <> nil then begin
  p := list2;
  while p <> nil do begin
   onegenerate(list1, p, p^.next, false);
   p := p^.next
  end
 end
end; { selfgenerate }

procedure markused;
{ mark those cubes in 'upper' and 'lower' which are }
{ covered by cubes in 'newmixed'.          }

procedure markall(l: shrptr);
{ mark cubes in 'l' which are covered by cubes 'newmixed'. }

var
 p: shrptr;
```

onegenerate

selfgenerate

markused

markall

```
begin { markall }
  while l <> nil do begin
    p := newmixed;
    while p <> nil do begin
      if l^.cubeid - p^.cubeid = [] then
        l^.used := true;
      p := p^.next
    end;
    l := l^.next
  end
end; { markall }

begin { markused }
  markall(upper);
  markall(lower)
end; { markused }
```

```
procedure mixedgenerate(var list1, list2, list3: shrptr);
```
mixedgenerate

```
var
  p: shrptr;

begin { mixedgenerate }
  if list2 <> nil then begin
    p := list2;
    while p <> nil do begin
      onegenerate(list1, p, list3, true);
      p := p^.next
    end
  end
end; { mixedgenerate }
```

```
procedure pickessential;
{ select the EPIs from the list of 'finalcubes' }
```
pickessential

```
var
  q, e: shrptr;
  break: boolean;
  i: integer;
  cares: idset;

begin { pickessential }
  cubescovered := [];
  epi := nil;
  i := 1;
  cares := allcarecubes;
  while (cares <> []) and (i <= nstates * ninputs) do begin
    if i in cares then begin
      cares := cares - [i];
      e := nil;
      break := false;
      q := finalcubes;
      while not break and (q <> nil) do begin
        if i in q^.cubeid then
          if e = nil then
            e := q
```

```
        else
          break := true;
        q := q^.next
      end;
      if not break and (e <> nil) then
        { unique entry 'e' is added to list of EPIs(epi). }
        if uniquentry(epi, e) then begin
          rmshrentry(finalcubes, e);
          addshrentry(epi, e);
          cares := cares - e^.cubeid; { remove other cares now covered }
          cubescovered := cubescovered + e^.cubeid
        end
      end;
      i := i + 1
    end;
  end; { pickessential }


procedure findcover;                                              findcover
  { now find a cover for the function. }


var
  p: shrptr;
  uncovered: idset;
  i: integer;
  resultp: shrptr;
  sizeofresult: integer;

begin { findcover }
  uncovered := allcarecubes - cubescovered;
  if uncovered <> [] then begin
    { select the cube which covers the largest number }
    { of uncovered 0-cubes.                           }
    i := 1;
    while (uncovered <> []) and (i <= nstates * ninputs) do begin
      resultp := nil;
      sizeofresult := 0;
      if i in uncovered then begin
        p := finalcubes;
        while p <> nil do begin
          if i in p^.cubeid then
            if card(uncovered * p^.cubeid) > sizeofresult then begin
              sizeofresult := card(uncovered * p^.cubeid);
              resultp := p
            end;
          p := p^.next
        end;
        if resultp = nil then begin
          writeln(' *** ERROR: uncovered 0-cube detected (', i: 2, ')');
          halt
        end else begin
          rmshrentry(finalcubes, resultp);
          addshrentry(epi, resultp);
          cubescovered := cubescovered + resultp^.cubeid;
          uncovered := uncovered - resultp^.cubeid
        end
      end;
      i := i + 1
```

```
      end
    end;
  end; {findcover}

begin { shrmethod }
  shrsetup(typ);
  break := false;
  firsttime := true;
  while not break do begin
    newupper := nil;
    newlower := nil;
    newmixed := nil;
    selfgenerate(newupper, upper);
    selfgenerate(newlower, lower);
    if firsttime then begin
      firsttime := false;
      mixedgenerate(newmixed, upper, lower)
    end else begin
      selfgenerate(newmixed, mixed);
      markused
    end;
    break := (newupper = nil) and (newlower = nil) and (newmixed = nil);
    if not break then begin
      freeused(upper);
      addlist(finalcubes, upper);
      freeused(lower);
      addlist(finalcubes, lower);
      freeused(mixed);
      addlist(finalcubes, mixed);
      upper := newupper;
      lower := newlower;
      mixed := newmixed
    end else begin
      addlist(finalcubes, upper);
      addlist(finalcubes, lower);
      addlist(finalcubes, mixed)
    end
  end;
  pickessential;
  findcover
end; { shrmethod }

begin { costit }
  shrmethod(codeno, typ);
  s[codeno].cost := s[codeno].cost + listcost(epi);
  addlist(freelist, epi);
  addlist(freelist, finalcubes)
end; { costit }

begin { lowerbounds }
  freelist := nil;
  maxcost := nvars + ninbits;
  for i := 1 to ncols do begin
    s[i].cost := 0;
    for j := 1 to nffinputs do
      costit(i, realize[j])
  end
end; { lowerbounds }
```

```
procedure sortcosts;                                        sortcosts
{ sort costs in 's' into ascending order }

var
  i, j, earliest: integer;
  temp: costentry;
  move: boolean;

begin { sortcosts}
  for i := 1 to ncols − 1 do begin
    earliest := i;          { save ith posn }
    temp := s[i];           { save ith entry }
    move := false;
    for j := i + 1 to ncols do
      if s[j].cost < temp.cost then begin
        move := true;
        earliest := j;        { save posn }
        temp := s[j]          { save value }
      end;
    if move then begin
      s[earliest] := s[i];   { exchange palces }
      s[i] := temp
    end
  end
end; { sortcosts }


procedure validcombinations;                          validcombinations
{ Determine valid combinations of column codes }

const
  MAXSELECT = 15;

type
  selarray =
    record
      upperbound: integer;
      range: integer;
      state: (startup, running, done);
      v: array [1..MAXSELECT] of integer
    end;

var
  i: integer;
  sel: selarray;
  combarray: combination;
  thiscost: integer;

  procedure initselect(var s: selarray; range, upperbound: integer);    initselect

  var
    i: integer;

  begin { initselect }
    s.upperbound := upperbound;
    s.range := range;
    s.state := startup;
```

```
  if range > upperbound then begin
    writeln(' SELECT: range(', range: 2, ') > upperbound(', upperbound: 2, ')');
    halt
  end;
  for i := 1 to range do
    s.v[i] := i
end; { initselect }
```

```
function select(var s: selarray): boolean;                                    select

label
  1;

var
  i, j: integer;

begin { select }
  select := true;
  if s.state = startup then
    s.state := running
  else if s.state = done then begin
    writeln(' SELECT: all selections exhausted');
    halt
  end else begin
    i := s.range;
    j := s.upperbound;
1:
    if s.v[i] < j then begin
      s.v[i] := s.v[i] + 1;
      while i < s.range do begin
        i := i + 1;
        s.v[i] := s.v[i - 1] + 1
      end
    end else begin
      j := j - 1;
      i := i - 1;
      if i > 0 then
        goto 1;
      s.state := done;
      select := false
    end
  end
end; { select }
```

```
function isvalid(c: combination): boolean;                                    isvalid
{ check if this code assignment is a valid one }

var
  i, j: integer;
  val: integer;
  sarray: array [1..MAXROWS] of integer;
  break: boolean;

begin { isvalid }
  { First – determine the value of each state (base 10) }
  for i := 0 to maxrows - 1 do begin
    val := 0;
```

```
        for j := 1 to nvars do
          val := val * 2 + s[c[j]].bits[i];
          sarray[i + 1] := val
      end;
      { Second – check for the "uniqueness" of each state coding }
      i := 1;
      break := false;
      while not break and (i < maxrows) do begin
        j := i + 1;
        while not break and (j <= maxrows) do
          if sarray[i] = sarray[j] then
            break := true
          else
            j := j + 1;
          i := i + 1
      end;
      isvalid := not break
    end; { isvalid }

begin { validcombinations }
  initselect(sel, nvars, ncols);
  mincost := maxint;
  while select(sel) do begin
    for i := 1 to sel.range do
      combarray[i] := sel.v[i];
    if isvalid(combarray) then begin
      thiscost := 0;
      for i := 1 to sel.range do
        thiscost := thiscost + s[sel.v[i]].cost;
      if thiscost < mincost then begin
        mincost := thiscost;
        mincombination := combarray
      end;
    end
  end
end; { validcombinations }

procedure init;
{ overall initialization }

begin { init }
  { specify number to logic repn. conversion }
  convert[0] := [0];
  convert[1] := [1];
  convert[2] := [0, 1];
  Jtransition[0, 0] := [0];
  Jtransition[0, 1] := [1];
  Jtransition[1, 0] := [0, 1];
  Jtransition[1, 1] := [0, 1];
  Ktransition[0, 0] := [0, 1];
  Ktransition[0, 1] := [0, 1];
  Ktransition[1, 0] := [1];
  Ktransition[1, 1] := [0];
  Stransition[0, 0] := [0];
  Stransition[0, 1] := [1];
  Stransition[1, 0] := [0];
  Stransition[1, 1] := [0, 1];
  Rtransition[0, 0] := [0, 1];
```

init

```
    Rtransition[0, 1] := [0];
    Rtransition[1, 0] := [1];
    Rtransition[1, 1] := [0];
    Ttransition[0, 0] := [0];
    Ttransition[0, 1] := [1];
    Ttransition[1, 0] := [1];
    Ttransition[1, 1] := [0];
    Dtransition[0, 0] := [0];
    Dtransition[0, 1] := [1];
    Dtransition[1, 0] := [0];
    Dtransition[1, 1] := [1]
end; { init }

procedure results;                                              results
var
 j: integer;
 statecodes: array [1..MAXROWS, 1..MAXVARS] of 0..1;

  procedure writecoding(code: integer);                        writecoding

  var
   i: integer;

  begin { writecoding }
   for i := 1 to nvars do
     write(statecodes[code, i]: 1)
  end; { writecoding }

  procedure writeinputs(inputnumber: integer);                 writeinputs

  var
   i: integer;

  begin { writeinputs }
   for i := 1 to ninbits do
     if incodes[inputnumber][i] = [0, 1] then
       write('x')
     else if incodes[inputnumber][i] = [0] then
       write('0')
     else
       write('1')
  end; { writeinputs }

  procedure writerealization;                                  writerealization

  var
   i: integer;

  begin { writerealization }
   writeln;
   write(' Realized using ');
   for i := 1 to nffinputs do
     case realize[i] of
      T:
       write('T');
      D:
       write('D');
```

```
      S:
        write('S');
      R:
        write('R');
      J:
        write('J');
      K:
        write('K')
      end;
    writeln(' flip–flops');
    writeln
  end; { writerealization }


  procedure writenextstate(cs, ns: integer);                              writenextstate


  var
    i, j: integer;
    t: logic;

  begin { writenextstate }
    for j := 1 to nvars do
      for i := 1 to nffinputs do begin
        case realize[i] of
        J:
          t := Jtransition[statecodes[cs, j], statecodes[ns, j]];
        K:
          t := Ktransition[statecodes[cs, j], statecodes[ns, j]];
        S:
          t := Stransition[statecodes[cs, j], statecodes[ns, j]];
        R:
          t := Rtransition[statecodes[cs, j], statecodes[ns, j]];
        T:
          t := Ttransition[statecodes[cs, j], statecodes[ns, j]];
        D:
          t := Dtransition[statecodes[cs, j], statecodes[ns, j]]
        end;
        if t = [0, 1] then
          write('x')
        else if t = [1] then
          write('1')
        else
          write('0')
      end
  end; { writenextstate }


  begin { results }
    if not cad then begin
      writeln;
      writeln('State encoding')
    end;
    for j := 0 to maxrows − 1 do begin
      if not cad then begin
        writestate(j + 1);
        write(' ')
      end;
      for i := 1 to nvars do begin
        if not cad then
```

```
        write(s[mincombination[i]].bits[j]: 1);
        statecodes[j + 1, i] := s[mincombination[i]].bits[j]
  end;
  if not cad then
    writeln
  end;
  if not cad then
    writerealization
  else begin
    writeln(maxrows*ninputs { number of cubes }
    writeln(ninbits + nvars { number of inputs }
    writeln(nffinputs * nvars + { number of outputs }
  end;
  for j := 1 to ninputs do begin
    for i := 1 to maxrows do begin
      writeinputs(j);
      writecoding(i);
      write(' ');
      if i > nstates then
        writenextstate(i, 1)
      else if nextstate[j, i] = 0 then
        writenextstate(i, 1)
      else
        writenextstate(i, nextstate[j, i]);
      if i > nstates then
        write('0')
      else if ninputs = noutputs then
        if outputs[j, i] in [1, 2] then
          write(outputs[j, i] - 1: 1)
        else
          write('x')
      else if noutputs = 1 then
        if outputs[1, i] in [1, 2] then
          write(outputs[1, i] - 1: 1)
        else
          write('x');
      writeln
    end
  end
end; { results }

begin { main }
  init;
  readtable;
  readincoding;
  readrealization;
  if nstates = 2 then
    ncols := 1
  else if (nstates = 3) or (nstates = 4) then
    ncols := 3
  else if nstates = 5 then
    ncols := 15
  else if nstates = 6 then
    ncols := 25
  else if (nstates = 7) or (nstates = 8) then
    ncols := 35
  else if nstates = 9 then
    ncols := 255
```

```
    writeln('*** ERROR: too many states ***');
    halt
  end;
  nvars := power(nstates);
  maxrows := exp(nvars);
  if not cad then
    writetable;
  { determine the column codings }
  codes;
  lowerbounds;
  sortcosts;
  validcombinations;
  results
end. { main }
```

Appendix 5E

A WORKED EXAMPLE

This appendix shows how the procedures defined in Chapter 5 may be applied to the solution of a fairly typical sequential design problem. We have taken Example 5.1 and shown how to use the Pascal program of Appendix 5B to minimize the state table; we then show how to use the Pascal program of Appendix 5D to carry out the state assignment. We use the output from this step as the input to the Pascal program of Appendix 3F to determine the input connections to the flip-flops.

5E.1. DATA INPUT FORMAT

The following data is a copy of the input data used for Example 5.1. The first line shows the *CAD* option flag set to T (TRUE), indicating that we require the output data to be in a form suitable for other Pascal programs to read. The *DEMO* flag is set to F (FALSE) since we do not want the tracing information presented to the following programs. The first number (4) specifies the number of input columns; the second number (9) specifies the number of states. This is followed by nine lines of next state information (compare with Table 5.1), starting with state a and continuing down through state i. The four (4) on line 12 specifies that there are 4 output columns (i.e., one output per each input). This is followed by nine lines of output information for states a through i. The information which follows in the remainder of the data file is relevant only to the state assignment problem. The two (2) on line 22 specifies that the input code for each of the four inputs is a two bit code and the next four lines contain the input codes used (in the order in which they appear in the state table). The final line indicates that JK flip-flops are to be used.

```
TF
4
9
- - f i
g - - -
- - - b
- d i -
```

```
h a - -
- a - c
c c - i
- e - d
g i d -
4
- 1 - -
1 - 0 -
- 0 - 1
- - - -
1 0 0 -
- - - 1
- - 0 -
- - - 0
0 - 1 -
2
00
01
10
11
JK
```

5E.2. OUTPUT FROM STATE MINIMIZATION PROGRAM

5E.2.1. Detailed Output

If the option flags in the first line of the data had been set to FT (i.e., DO NOT produce output for a following program, and DO show the internal steps of the minimization process), then the following output would be produced:

```
        4   Inputs
        4   Outputs
        9   States
- - f i      - 1 - -
g - - -      1 - 0 -
- - - b      - 0 - 1
- d i -      - - - -
h a - -      1 0 0 -
- a - c      - - - 1
c c - i      - - 0 -
- e - d      - - - 0
g i d -      0 - 1 -


Maximum Compatibles
*******************

   1   a b d f
   2   a b d h
   3   a d f i
   4   a d g h
   5   b c d e f
   6   c d f i
```

```
Essential MC is:  5   ==>   [ 4]
Closing on  4  ==>   [ 3] [ 6]
Closing on  3  ==>   [ 6]
Closing on  6  ==>
Closed cover is [ 3 4 5 6]
```

```
New State Table
***************

          4   Inputs
          4   Outputs
          4   States
b a a d       0 1 1 1
c c a a       - 1 0 0
b a a c       1 0 0 1
b a a c       0 0 1 1

Original number of memory elements:   4
New number of memory elements:        2
```

5E.2.2. Abbreviated Output

With the option flags in the first line of the data set to FF (i.e., DO NOT
produce output for a following program, and DO NOT show the internal steps
of the minimization process), the following output is produced:

```
b a a d      0 1 1 1
c c a a      - 1 0 0
b a a c      1 0 0 1
b a a c      0 0 1 1

Original number of memory elements:   4
New number of memory elements:        2
```

5E.2.3. Reusable Output

If the option flags in the first line of the data are set to TF (i.e., DO produce
output for a following program, and DO NOT show the internal steps of the
minimization process), then the following output is produced:

```
TF
          4
          4
b a a d
c c a a
b a a c
b a a c
          4
0 1 1 1
- 1 0 0
```

```
1 0 0 1
0 0 1 1
2
00
01
11
10
JK
```

5E.3. STATE ASSIGNMENT

If we now take the output from Section 5E.2.3 and feed it into the state assignment program, but set the option flags differently, we can examine the state assignment process.

5E.3.1. Detailed Output

If the option flags in the first line of the data are set to FT (i.e., DO NOT produce output for a following program, and DO show the internal steps of the state assignment process), then the details of the state assignment can be examined. For this example, such action results in over 80 pages of printout and is not shown here. (Note that the amount of print out increases with the number of column assignments that have to be considered).

5E.3.2. Abbreviated Output

If the option flags in the first line of the data are set to FF (i.e., DO NOT produce output for a following program, and DO NOT show the internal steps of the state assignment process), then the following output is produced:

```
STATE TABLE

   4  Inputs
   4  Outputs
   4  States
 b a a d     0 1 1 1
 c c a a     - 1 0 0
 b a a c     1 0 0 1
 b a a c     0 0 1 1

State encoding
 a 00
 b 01
 c 10
 d 11


 Realized using JK flip-flops

0000 0x1x0
0001 1xx1x
```

```
0010 x11x1
0011 x1x00
0100 0x0x1
0101 1xx11
0110 x10x0
0111 x1x10
1000 0x0x1
1001 0xx10
1010 x10x0
1011 x1x11
1100 1x1x1
1101 0xx10
1110 x00x1
1111 x0x11
```

Note that the program has chosen to assign bit patterns to the states a, b, c, d in binary order.

The output following the statement "Realized using JK flip-flops" is a representation of the final-state table. In each row the first two entries contain values of input 1 and input 2 (i.e., x_1^n and x_2^n in our earlier notation); the second two entries contain values Q_1^n and Q_2^n; the next four entries contain the required values of J_1^n, K_1^n, J_2^n and K_2^n (in that order) and the final entry is the system output Z^n.

5E.3.3. Reusable Output

If the option flags in the first line of the data are set to TF (i.e., DO produce output for a following program, and DO NOT show the internal steps of the minimization process), then the following output is produced:

```
      16
       4
       5
0000 0x1x0
0001 1xx1x
0010 x11x1
0011 x1x00
0100 0x0x1
0101 1xx11
0110 x10x0
0111 x1x10
1000 0x0x1
1001 0xx10
1010 x10x0
1011 x1x11
1100 1x1x1
1101 0xx10
1110 x00x1
1111 x0x11
```

5E.4. COMBINATIONAL LOGIC MINIMIZATION

If we take the output from Section 5E.3.3 and feed it into the logic minimization package given in Appendix 3F, we obtain the following, which describes the combinational logic for the inputs of the (JK) flip-flops:

```
Array f
0000 0-1-0
0001 1--1-
0010 -11-1
0011 -1-00
0100 0-0-1
0101 1--11
0110 -10-0
0111 -1-10
1000 0-0-1
1001 0--10
1010 -10-0
1011 -1-11
1100 1-1-1
1101 0--10
1110 -00-1
1111 -0-11

XXXX ZZZZZ
1234 12345

0xxx 01000
x0xx 01000
0xx1 10000
00xx 00100
110x 00100
x1xx 00010
xx0x 00010
11x0 10001
1x00 00001
010x 00001
0010 00001
1x11 00011
```

NAND Gate Realization

Gate No	Fan-in	Fan-out	Driving Signals		
G03	2	1	-X01	X04	
G04	2	1	-X01	-X02	
G05	3	1	X01	X02	-X03
G08	3	2	X01	X02	-X04

```
G09    3    1      X01 -X03 -X04
G10    3    1     -X01  X02 -X03
G11    4    1     -X01 -X02  X03 -X04
G12    3    2      X01  X03  X04
Z01    2    1      G03  G08
Z02    2    1      X01  X02
Z03    2    1      G04  G05
Z04    3    1      X06  X07  G12
Z05    5    1      G08  G09  G10  G11  G12
```

```
        5    2-input NAND gates        2 IC packs
        6    3-input NAND gates        2 IC packs
        1    4-input NAND gates        1 IC packs
        1    8-input NAND gates        1 IC packs
       ----                           ----
       13 NAND gates                   6 IC packs
```

The first array is the input function array. The second array is the minimized function array, with redundant connections deleted. The third section gives the NAND-gate realization of the second array. A more detailed explanation of this type of output is given at the end of Appendix 3F.

6

DESIGNING WITH MSI/LSI DEVICES

6.1. DEVICE TYPES

6.1.1. Multiplexers

Multiplexing is a term which arose in telecommunications to express the idea of transmitting information from several different sources over a single communications channel. In digital systems the multiplexer is employed as a means of selecting data from one out of several input lines and feeding it to a single output line. For obvious reasons, multiplexers are sometimes referred to as *data selectors*.

Commercially available multiplexers (MUXs) have 2^n data-input lines (where n is an integer), a single output line and n further lines that are used in the process of selecting the input which is to be connected through to the output. A 4-to-1 line MUX is shown in Figure 6.1(a) and a block diagram representation for the device appears in Figure 6.1(b).

In the circuit of Figure 6.1(a), the input EN provides a measure of control in that the device is operative only if EN is low (EN is known as the *enable* input). When EN is high, it imposes a zero input on each of the four AND gates thereby ensuring that each AND gate has a zero output regardless of the values of the four MUX inputs.

When the MUX is enabled, the line connected through to the output is determined by the bit pattern appearing at the select inputs. For instance, if $S_1 = 0$ and $S_0 = 0$, the upper AND gate has three of its inputs equal to 1 (due to the select and enable inputs) and the other three AND gates have at least one input equal to 0. Thus, the output of the OR gate is effectively "connected" to MUX input I_0; when $I_0 = 0$, the MUX output is 0 and when $I_0 = 1$ the MUX output is 1. The other MUX inputs are connected through to the output in a similar way. For instance, if $S_1 = 0$ and $S_0 = 1$, input I_1 is connected.

As one would expect, the main application of multiplexers in digital systems is in data selection, i.e., in selecting data from one of several available sources. The device can, however, also be used to generate combinational logic functions, and we will look at this application first.

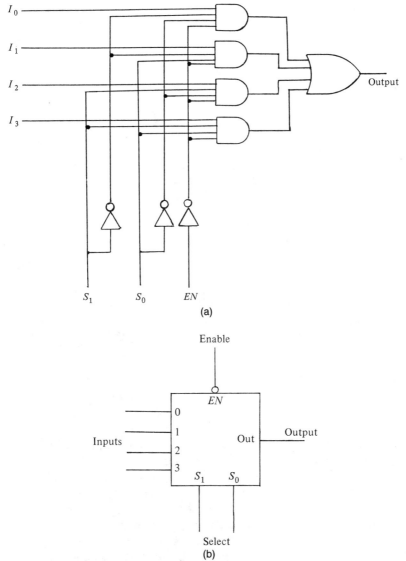

I_0

I_1

I_2

I_3

S_1 S_0 EN

(a)

Enable

EN

Inputs

0

1

2

3

S_1 S_0

Out

Output

Select

(b)

Figure 6.1. 4-to-1 line MUX: (a) AND/OR implementation; (b) block diagram representation.

Realization of Combinational Logic Functions.

The multiplexer can be used to implement a combinational logic function directly from its truth table. An example is shown in Figure 6.2.

The truth table shown in Figure 6.2(a) can be realized using a 4-to-1 MUX as shown in Figure 6.2(b). The variables A and B are connected to the select inputs of the MUX and, when $A = B = 0$, the upper MUX input (which is set

A	B	F
0	0	0
0	1	1
1	0	1
1	1	0

(a)

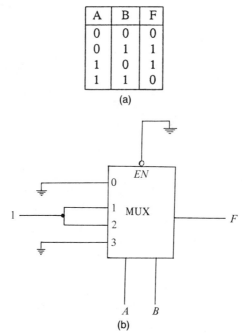

(b)

Figure 6.2. (a) Truth table of 2-variable logic function; (b) Realization using 4-to-1 line MUX.

to logic zero by earthing) is selected and connected through to the output thus setting $F = 0$ as required. The reader should be able to see that the other entries in the truth table are similarly realized by this MUX arrangement.

It should be clear from the example in Figure 6.2 that a 4-to-1 MUX can be used to realize any 2-variable logic function. It is less obvious that a 4-to-1 MUX can be used to realize any 3-variable logic function. However, consider the truth table shown in Figure 6.3(a). The first two rows of the table indicate that when $A = B = 0$, F is required to take on the same values as the variable C. This can be arranged as shown in Figure 6.3(b): when $A = B = 0$, the upper MUX input is selected and this is connected to variable C. The other MUX inputs are similarly obtained from the truth table.

It is, in fact, a general property that a MUX with n select inputs can be used to realize any logic function with up to $n + 1$ variables. The most straightforward procedure for achieving this is simply a generalization of the procedure indicated in Figure 6.3. The first n columns of the truth table in a $n + 1$ variable problem should be chosen as the select inputs. This leaves one outstanding variable; let it be variable X. For each bit combination of the chosen select inputs, the required logic function can then be identified from the truth table as being equal to one of the four quantities: X, $\overline{X}$, 1 and 0. This immediately gives the required MUX inputs. A further illustrative example involving a 4-variable problem, is shown in Figure 6.4.

A	B	C	F
0	0	0	0
0	0	1	1
0	1	0	1
0	1	1	0
1	0	0	1
1	0	1	1
1	1	0	0
1	1	1	0

$\left.\begin{array}{l}\\\\\end{array}\right\}$ $F = C$

$\left.\begin{array}{l}\\\\\end{array}\right\}$ $F = \overline{C}$

$\left.\begin{array}{l}\\\\\end{array}\right\}$ $F = 1$

$\left.\begin{array}{l}\\\\\end{array}\right\}$ $F = 0$

(a)

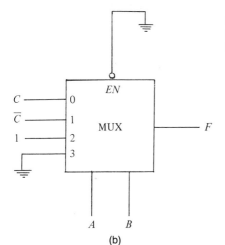

(b)

Figure 6.3. (a) Truth table of 3-variable logic function; (b) Realization using 4-to-1 line MUX.

The above examples show that realization of combinational logic functions by means of multiplexers is very simple. In particular, simplification of a given logic function by means of K-maps and the like is not necessary. One might ask at this point, then, whether or not a MUX realization is always preferable to a realization using discrete gates. The answer to this question is definitely "no." For one thing, multiplexer ICs are significantly more expensive than discrete gate ICs. And for another, because of limitations on the number of pins that can be attached to an IC package, the largest commercially available MUX is 16-to-1; this implies that single MUXs can only be used for realizing combinational logic functions with up to 5 variables. We shall see below how MUXs can be connected together to produce larger MUXs but, by and large, the main application of MUX realizations is in situations where the number of IC packages required to realize a system is critical. For instance, a K-map reduction of the function F in the truth table of Figure 6.4(a) gives

$$F = B\overline{C}\,\overline{D} + AB\overline{D} + A\overline{B}\,\overline{C} + \overline{B}CD \qquad (6.1)$$

A	B	C	D	F	
0	0	0	0	0	0
0	0	0	1	0	
0	0	1	0	0	D
0	0	1	1	1	
0	1	0	0	1	$\overline{D}$
0	1	0	1	0	
0	1	1	0	0	0
0	1	1	1	0	
1	0	0	0	1	1
1	0	0	1	1	
1	0	1	0	0	D
1	0	1	1	1	
1	1	0	0	1	$\overline{D}$
1	1	0	1	0	
1	1	1	0	1	$\overline{D}$
1	1	1	1	0	

(a)

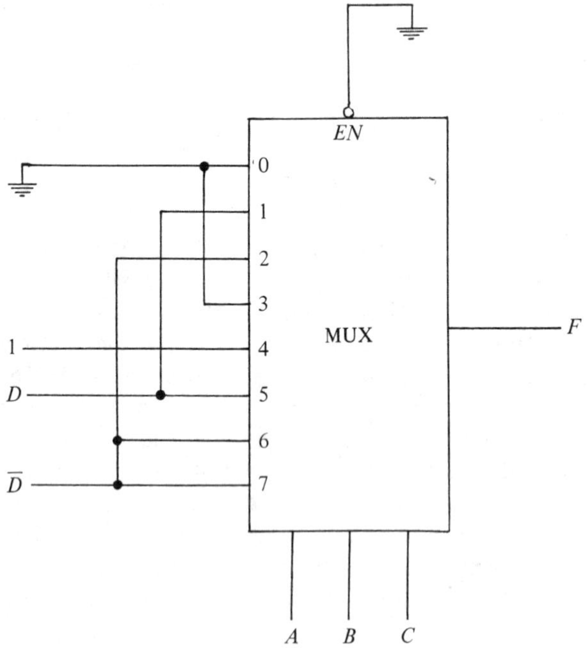

(b)

Figure 6.4. (a) Truth table of 4-variable logic function; (b) Realization using 8-to-1 line MUX.

which, for a NAND gate realization would require four 3-input NANDs and one 4-input NAND (assuming that complements of variables are available). This would require two separate IC packages—a triple 3-input NAND chip and a dual 4-input NAND chip could do the job; the MUX realization requires only one IC package. Note, however, that at current prices, the MUX realization would be slightly the more expensive.

Expanding Multiplexer Size. It was mentioned above that the largest commercially available MUX is 16-to-1. Larger MUXs can be constructed quite simply using standard IC packages as building blocks. For instance, a 64-to-1 MUX can be constructed using five smaller MUXs as shown in Figure 6.5.

The four 16-to-1 MUXs in Figure 6.5 are each connected to the same four select lines. Thus, a particular bit pattern on $s_3 s_2 s_1 s_0$ selects one input to each of the four 16-to-1 MUXs. The bit pattern on $s_5 s_4$ then selects one out of these four inputs. For example, suppose we wished to connect input I_{35} through to the output. This is achieved by applying the binary equivalent of 35 (i.e., 100011) to the select inputs as follows. The select inputs $s_3 s_2 s_1 s_0$ are set equal to the four least significant bits (i.e., 0011) so that input line number 3 in each 16-to-1 MUX is selected. The two most significant bits of binary 35 (i.e., 10) are applied to the select inputs $s_5 s_4$ so that the 4-to-1 MUX then selects the output of the MUX connected to I_{35}.

6.1.2. Decoders

In digital systems, decoding is a very common operation. Situations arise frequently in which different bit patterns indicate different actions that a system should undertake. To carry out these actions, the system has to be able to interpret or "decode" the various bit patterns. Most of the commercially available decoders take the form of an IC with n input lines and 2^n output lines. Usually the device has at least one enable input† and, usually also, when the decoder is not enabled, it has all its outputs high. When the decoder *is* enabled, whatever bit pattern is present on its n input lines is decoded by causing just one of the 2^n output lines to take on a low value (the remaining output lines stay high). Note that with n input lines there are 2^n possible binary bit patterns so that 2^n output lines are necessary for the decoding of all possible inputs.

Decoders can be employed in the realization of combinational logic functions in a very simple and straightforward way. To illustrate this fact, we have drawn up a circuit for a 3-to-8 line decoder in Figure 6.6. For simplicity of explanation, we have chosen a circuit which has all its outputs low when not enabled. When the enable input is low, all the outputs except one will be low; the location of the remaining output, which is high, is determined by the bit pattern

---

†More than one enable input can be provided by means of "spare" pins on the IC package; this gives additional flexibility to the device.

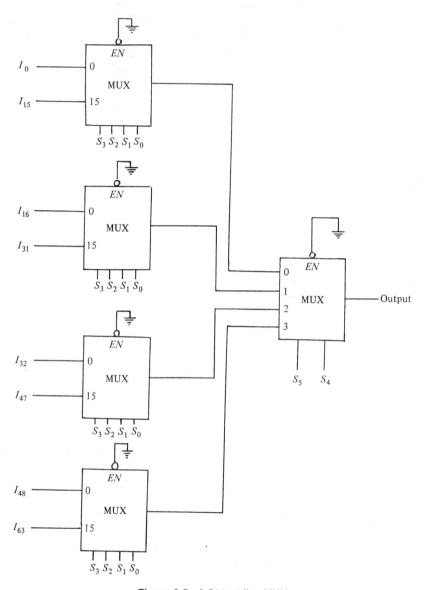

Figure 6.5. A 64-to-1 line MUX.

on the decoder input lines. For instance, if $A = B = C = 0$, only the top output will be high; if $A = B = 0$, $C = 1$, the second output down is high, and so on. It should now be clear to the reader that the circuit in Figure 6.6 actually makes available the full set of minterms associated with the variables A, B, and C; these minterms have been written alongside the outputs in Figure 6.6.

Because the decoder makes available all minterms in this way, realization of

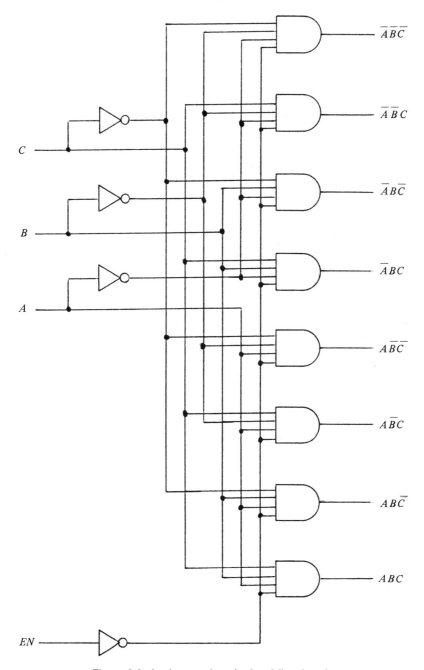

Figure 6.6. Implementation of a 3-to-8 line decoder.

combinational logic functions is quite direct and simple. For instance, if we had a decoder of the form shown in Figure 6.6 and wished to realize the logic function

$$F = \Sigma m(0,\ 1,\ 3,\ 5) \qquad (6.2)$$

we could achieve this by simply attaching a 4-input OR gate as shown in Figure 6.7.

Figure 6.7 draws attention immediately to two disadvantages of using decoders to realize combinational logic functions of this sort. First of all, the decoder (DX) provides all minterms and in this case, only half of them are used. Secondly, unlike the multiplexer, the decoder requires the attachment of a separate gate in order to realize a given logic function.

The first of these apparent disadvantages points to the situations in which the decoder is useful. There are many applications in which several functions of a set of logical variables are required simultaneously. A popular example concerns the logic required to convert binary-coded decimal (BCD) numbers into a form suitable for the seven-segment display commonly encountered in pocket calculators and digital watches. The seven-segment configuration is shown in Figure 6.8(a) and the truth table for the required logic is shown in Figure 6.8(b). As an example of how the truth table is drawn up, note that when the number zero is to be displayed, all segments of the display except g should be activated; this gives the first row of the truth table.

This is an example of a 4-variable problem with seven outputs. A decoder provides an efficient solution to this problem. A suitable arrangement showing two of the required outputs is depicted in Figure 6.9. It was mentioned earlier that most decoders have their outputs high when not enabled and assert a particular minterm by driving the corresponding output low. In Figure 6.9 we have assumed this type of decoder; the fact that minterms are asserted low is indi-

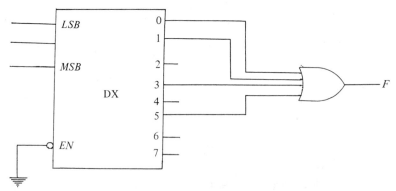

Figure 6.7. Decoder realization of the function $F = \Sigma m(0,1,3,5)$.

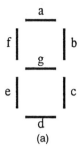

(a)

A	B	C	D	a	b	c	d	e	f	g
0	0	0	0	1	1	1	1	1	1	0
0	0	0	1	0	1	1	0	0	0	0
0	0	1	0	1	1	0	1	1	0	1
0	0	1	1	1	1	1	1	0	0	1
0	1	0	0	0	1	1	0	0	1	1
0	1	0	1	1	0	1	1	0	1	1
0	1	1	0	0	0	1	1	1	1	1
0	1	1	1	1	1	1	0	0	0	0
1	0	0	0	1	1	1	1	1	1	1
1	0	0	1	1	1	1	0	0	1	1

(b)

Figure 6.8. Seven-segment display: (a) Physical layout; (b) Truth Table.

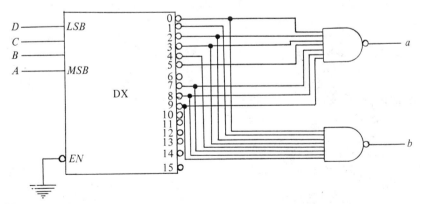

Figure 6.9. Decoder realization of logic functions for segments a and b in the seven-segment display.

cated by the little circles attached to each output line. Decoders of this type differ from the one shown in Figure 6.6 only in that they have NAND gates in place of the AND gates. It is for this reason that the OR operation in Figure 6.9 is carried out by NAND gates. The full set of seven outputs required for the display are, of course, available from the one decoder.

To return to the second disadvantage of DX realizations over MUX realizations (i.e., that a DX realization requires additional SSI gates) we should add the further point that the DX costs about twice as much as a MUX of the same size. By and large, a DX realization is only cheaper than a MUX realization for problems with four or more outputs.

Not all decoders have n input lines and 2^n output lines. For certain applications (a good example being the seven-segment display above) only a subset of the minterms is required and some commercially available decoders are available with n input lines and fewer than 2^n output lines. In the above 4-input example, only 10 output lines are required.

The Decoder as a Demultiplexer. In some applications, a serial data stream contains messages intended for different destinations. To send each message to the correct destination, a *demultiplexer* is required. A decoder is easily arranged as a demultiplexer as shown in Figure 6.10. The decoder inputs are used as selectors and the data stream is fed to the enable input. Suppose the first message in the stream is destined for output 2; this is arranged by setting $A = 1$, $B = 0$. If the next message is destined for output 1, A is set to 0 and B is set to 1. Larger demultiplexers are constructed from larger decoders in the obvious way.

Expanding Decoder Size. Limitations on the number of pins that can be attached to an IC package restrict the size of currently available decoders to a maximum size of 4-to-16. Larger decoders are easily constructed from standard MSI packages. A 5-to-32 line decoder is shown in Figure 6.11.

The manner in which this structure operates is quite simple. When $A = B = 0$, the upper 3-to-8 line DX is enabled and the inputs C, D, and E then determine which of the eight outputs will be asserted. Thus the upper 3-to-5 line DX provides all eight minterms commencing with $\overline{A}\,\overline{B}$. The other 24 minterms are similarly provided by the other 3-to-8 line decoders.

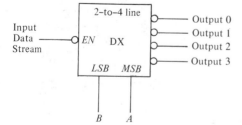

Figure 6.10. A decoder used as a demultiplexer.

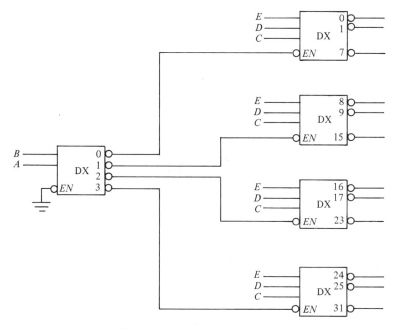

Figure 6.11. 5-to-32 line decoder.

Larger decoders can be constructed using the same approach. For instance a 6-to-64 line DX can be obtained by replacing the four 3-to-8 line DXs in Figure 6.11 by 4-to-16 line DXs.

6.1.3. Read-Only Memories (ROMs)

In general, computers need to be able to write data into memory and to read from it. There are, however, certain types of data that the computer must have available in memory and which it will never be required to change. For instance, the stored procedures for evaluating trigonometric functions never require change (always assuming, of course, that they are correct to begin with). Consequently, the computer only needs to *read* from memory containing such data—it will not be required to write into such memory. It is for the storage of data such as this that read-only memories (ROMs) are widely applied.

ROMs for storing programs are available with storage capacities of up to 1M bits. Smaller ROMs, which can be used in a range of different applications, are also available. In this section, we will consider the application of ROMs in the realization of combinational logic functions.

A ROM which can store up to 2^n words of m bits each has n input lines and m output lines. For simplicity, we will consider initially a very small ROM, with 3 input lines and 4 output lines. Figure 6.12(a) shows a block diagram of this ROM; the bit pattern applied to the input lines on the left defines an address

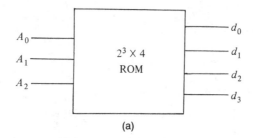

(a)

ADDRESS			DATA WORD			
A_2	A_1	A_0	d_3	d_2	d_1	d_0
0	0	0	1	0	0	1
0	0	1	1	1	0	0
0	1	0	0	1	1	0
0	1	1	0	0	1	0
1	0	0	1	1	1	0
1	0	1	1	0	1	1
1	1	0	0	0	0	0
1	1	1	1	1	1	1

(b)

Figure 6.12. (a) Block diagram of 8 × 4 ROM; (b) An example of data stored in 8 × 4 ROM.

and, for each input bit pattern applied, the data stored at the corresponding address can be read out from the output lines on the right. As an illustration, the table in Figure 6.12(b) contains a set of data that could be stored in the 2^3 × 4 ROM. The table also indicates the address at which each 4-bit data word is stored. Thus, in order to read out the data stored at address 011, the bit pattern $A_2A_1A_0 = 011$ is applied to the input lines; the data word stored at that address then appears at the output in the form $d_3d_2d_1d_0 = 0010$. The other data words stored in the ROM can be read out similarly.

The table in Figure 6.12(b) looks very much like a truth table and this observation gives an immediate indication of how ROMs are constructed. Each of the outputs of the ROM can be treated as a separate combinational logic function. For instance, the output variable d_3 takes on the value 1 or 0 depending on the values of the input variables A_2, A_1, A_0 and this could easily be represented by a sum-of-products logic function and realized as a two-level AND-OR structure. Note that the other three output variables could be realized in the same way and note also that all four output variables have the same set of inputs. Thus, the ROM can be considered as a logic circuit with four outputs and a common set of inputs. This is precisely the type of situation in which decoders can be used to obtain an economical realization. Consequently, read-only memories are constructed as combinational logic circuits using decoders and the same basic principles as those described in the previous section.

Recall that the decoder is a device that makes available at its output terminals the full set of minterms associated with the variables applied to its input terminals (see Figure 6.6). Realization of a logic function is then very simply achieved by applying the required set of decoder outputs to an OR gate as in Figure 6.7 (or if NAND logic is used the OR operation is carried out by a NAND gate as in Figure 6.9). Note that the NAND gates carrying out the OR operation in Figure 6.9 have quite a large number of inputs. In fact, the fan-in requirement of gates carrying out the OR operation in decoder realizations tends to go up very rapidly as the number of input variables increases. This is a direct consequence of the fact that there are 2^n minterms associated with n logic variables and a logic function of these variables can require the "ORing" of a large proportion of the minterms. Now note that ROMs are available with up to 14 inputs and it is immediately clear that decoder realizations of ROMs often have immense fan-in requirements for the gates carrying out the OR operation. And yet, ROMs *are* generally constructed using a decoder realization. This is made possible by the avoidance of discrete gates for carrying out the OR operation and the use of an array of switching elements instead.

The basic structure of the ROM is indicated in Figure 6.13 which shows how the eight data words listed in Figure 6.12(b) can be read from a ROM by applying the necessary address bits to the input terminals. The X's in the array on the right of Figure 6.13 represent switching elements that are turned on if the decoder output to which they are attached is activated. For instance, if the minterm $\overline{A_2}\,\overline{A_1}\,\overline{A_0}$ is asserted by the decoder, then the two switching elements in the top row of the array will be turned on. The switching elements are usually constructed using either bipolar transistors or field-effect transistors. The manner in which the required OR operations are achieved by the switching array can be seen by reference to Figure 6.14 which shows a circuit realization† of the column of switching elements providing the function d_3 in Figure 6.13. Note first of all that a switching transistor is supplied for every minterm, but that only those transistors in positions corresponding to X's in Figure 6.13 are actually connected to decoder outputs; the reasons unconnected transistors are also present will be discussed later. In this arrangement, the minterms are asserted "high" and it can be seen that the connected transistors carry out the required OR operation by first noting that if none of the connected minterms are asserted (i.e., if they are all "low") then the transistors in Figure 6.14 are all off and d_3 takes on a low value. If a connected minterm is asserted (by going "high"),

---

† The reader may wish to consult the section on bipolar transistor characteristics in the Appendix before proceeding further.

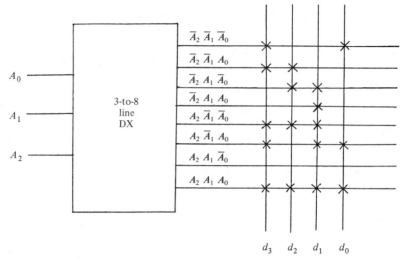

Figure 6.13. Internal structure of a ROM.

the transistor to which it is connected is turned on and connects d_3 to a high voltage as required; d_3 goes high if one or more of the five connected minterms goes high, as is required for the OR operation.

Large ROMs are normally used for storing fixed programs in a computer, but smaller ROMs are often used for realizing logic functions. The ROM contains a decoder and a set of OR gates that allow logic function realization and the complete system is contained in a single package. Thus, the ROM in Figure 6.13 can either be viewed as storing the eight data words listed in Figure 6.12(b) or as realizing the four logic functions that the variables d_0, d_1, d_2, and d_3 represent. So, given a problem requiring the realization of a combinational circuit with n inputs and m outputs, a $2^n \times m$ ROM can be used. The required sum of minterms for each output function is obtained by simply making the necessary connections in the switching array. The process of making these connections is known as "programming" the ROM. Note that most commercially available ROMs have 4-bit or 8-bit data outputs. For this reason, ROMs are usually only used for combinational logic realization in cases where a multiple-output function is required. Clearly much of a ROM's capability would be wasted in realizing a single-output logic function.

ROMs are available in three basic forms: the mask-programmed ROM, the programmable ROM (PROM) and the erasable PROM (EPROM). Mask-programmed ROMs have their data permanently inserted at the time of manufacture. As a typical case, consider again the example in Figure 6.12. The manner in which the data words in Figure 6.12(b) are stored is indicated by the circuit structure for bit d_3 shown in Figure 6.14. The construction of circuits of this sort is carried out using a series of masks, each controlling a different stage of

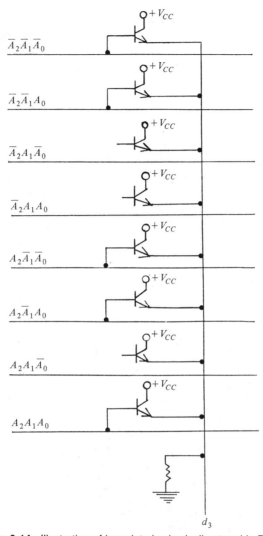

d_3

Figure 6.14. Illustration of how data is physically stored in ROM.

circuit construction. Note that the disposition of 1's and 0's in the memory of the ROM is governed entirely by the presence or absence of a connection between the transistor bases and decoder output lines. Thus, by making provision for transistors at every crosspoint in the switching array, the manufacturer only needs to change one mask (the one controlling the connections between transistor bases and decoder outputs) in producing ROMs (of the same size) which store different sets of data. Even so, changing just the one mask in the production process is quite an expensive business and so the use of mask-programmed

ROMs is restricted to situations in which a large number of ROMs (usually 1000 or more) are required, each storing exactly the same data. A typical example of such a situation concerns the storage of widely-used information. For instance, ROMs storing certain types of mathematical tables are available as off-the-shelf products.

Because of the expense associated with mask-programmed ROMs, there is a considerable market for ROMs that the user can program. Programmable ROMs (PROMs) are constructed in much the same way as the mask-programmed variety, the only difference being that all switching elements are constructed identically with each including a *fusible* link. For instance, returning once more to the example of Figure 6.12, a suitable PROM for storing the required data words would have an 8 × 4 switching array and, if the switching elements were bipolar transistors, each column of the switching array would have the appearance of the column depicted in Figure 6.14, *but with all transistors fully connected.* The PROM would, however, have fusible links between the transistor bases and decoder output lines. In normal operation, these links carry current in the usual way, but if they are subjected to a substantially higher current they "blow," i.e., go open-circuit. The user is able to progam the PROM by selectively blowing fusible links in the switching array. Thus, if Figure 6.14 were part of a PROM, the three disconnected transistors would have been put in that state by blowing the fusible links to which they were originally connected. A special device, known as a PROM programmer, is available which automatically blows the requisite links when fed (usually by means of a small computer) the address and bit pattern of each data word that is to be stored.

Once the fusible links in a PROM have been blown, they cannot be reconnected. Quite often, particularly when research or development work is being carried out, it is necessary to change the contents of a ROM and, if PROMs are being used, this means that a new PROM has to be used for each change. If many such changes are necessary, this can become quite expensive. For this reason the erasable PROM (EPROM) was developed. One form of EPROM is an MOS device† with a transparent lid. Programming of the EPROM leads to charge being stored at appropriate points in the device. Because of the insulating materials employed in the construction of MOS devices, the data represented by the stored charge is held by the EPROM for a period which is virtually permanent. The transparent lid allows the stored data to be erased by exposing the device to ultra-violet radiation. This radiation reduces the effectiveness of the insulating material holding the charge, and, as a consequence, the stored charge gradually leaks away. After exposure for a period of about 20 minutes, the EPROM has been "wiped clean" and is ready to be reprogrammed.

Expanding ROM Size. The size of ROMs available from manufacturers continues to grow, but regardless of this, there are always likely to be situations

---

† See Appendix on logic families.

in which a problem can be solved conveniently by connecting two or more ROMs together to create a larger ROM. Expansion can involve increasing the number of inputs, increasing the number of outputs, or a combination of both.

Output expansion can be achieved very simply: Figure 6.15 shows how two $2^8 \times 4$ ROM's can be connected together to form a $2^8 \times 8$ ROM. The manner in which this expanded ROM works should be quite obvious. Suppose data are stored at each of the available 2^8 addresses. Then, at each address, the upper ROM stores the four least-significant bits of the data and the lower ROM stores the four most-significant bits. This explains the operation of the structure in Figure 6.15 in terms of addressing data stored in the ROM, but it should be clear to the reader that the system could also be used as a means for realizing any combinational logic function with up to eight inputs and eight outputs.

At this point it is probably worthwhile to introduce a simplified notation for address and data buses which will be useful for the remainder of this chapter and for the next chapter. The diagram in Figure 6.16 is entirely equivalent to the diagram in Figure 6.15. Figure 6.16 has a much simpler appearance because the eight address lines are drawn as a single line; the fact that there are eight address lines is represented by the diagonal slash ($/$) and the number 8. A similar representation is used for the data lines. The term "bus" is often used to refer to a collection of lines that serve a common purpose. Thus, the eight address lines in Figure 6.16 are collectively termed the "address bus" and,

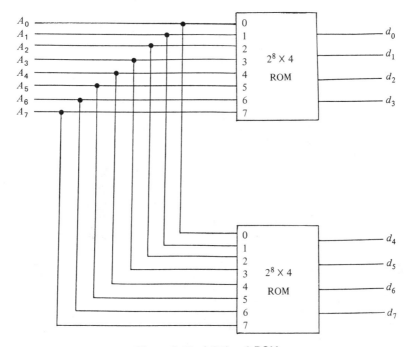

Figure 6.15. A 256 × 8 ROM.

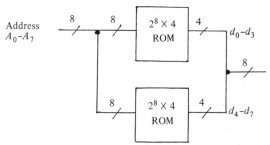

Figure 6.16. Block diagram of 256 × 8 ROM constructed from two 256 × 4 ROMs.

similarly, the eight data lines are termed the "data bus." The representation of buses as single lines in a circuit diagram will be used where practicable from now on.

Figure 6.17 shows how input expansion can be achieved with ROMs. In the figure, a set of four $2^8 \times 4$ ROMs have been connected together to form a $2^{10} \times 4$ ROM. Note that the two most significant bits of the address bus are applied to a 2-to-4 line decoder in order to enable one of the four ROMs. The remaining eight bits of the address then select the four bits of data stored at that address in the enabled ROM. These four bits of data appear on the data bus.

The reader might have noticed a slight ambiguity in the bus notation in relation to the manner in which the data buses in Figures 6.16 and 6.17 are represented. In both cases, the data buses of individual ROMs are shown connected together, but in Figure 6.16, two four-bit data buses join together to form an eight-bit data bus—they are *not* physically connected together. In Figure 6.17,

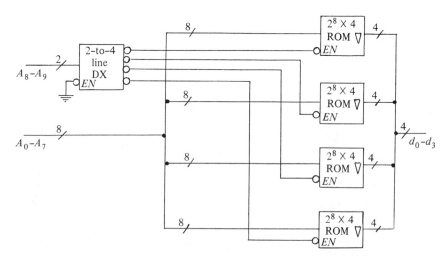

Figure 6.17. A 1024 × 4 ROM constructed from four 256 × 4 ROMs

on the other hand, the data buses from the four ROMs *are* physically connected together and, in a case such as this, special precautions have to be taken. The point is, when the decoder enables one of the ROMs, that particular ROM is required to output a data word onto the output bus and it is important that the other ROMs do not interfere with this process. This requirement can be met by providing each of the data lines of each ROM with a 3-state switch. As is explained in the Appendix on logic families, the 3-state switch can provide an output line with logic 1, or logic 0, and has a third, high-impedance state in which it isolates itself from the line. The fact that the ROM outputs in Figure 6.17 are driven by 3-state switches is indicated by the inverted triangle drawn next to each output. The presence of the 3-state switches allows three of the ROMs to isolate themselves from the output bus (when disabled by the decoder), leaving the fourth ROM (enabled by the decoder) to feed the required data word onto the output bus.

6.1.4. Programmable Logic Arrays

In a ROM, the input variables are fed to a decoder which makes available the 2^n possible minterms from which any desired logic function can be realized by ORing the appropriate minterms. For values of n up to 6 or so, realizing logic functions in this way is usually economically acceptable. However, because ROM realizations are obtained as sums of minterms, the ROM approach tends to become quite inefficient as n increases. The source of the inefficiency can be seen in the realization of the 6-variable function $H = AB + CD + EF$. To realize this function using a ROM, it would be necessary to expand the functions into a sum of minterms leading to an expression containing 37 minterms. In the ROM realization, all 37 minterms would have to be ORed to give the function H. And of course, if we used simple AND-OR logic instead of a ROM, the OR gate in the realization would require only three inputs. As the number of input variables is increased beyond 6, this kind of inefficiency in ROM realizations becomes much more pronounced (note again that an n-variable problem involves 2^n minterms). Clearly, for problems involving relatively small numbers of sums of products (i.e., relative to the total number of minterms), a much simpler realization can be obtained using AND-OR logic. The *programmable logic array* (PLA) is based upon AND-OR logic, but has a regular structure which can be programmed to meet the needs of an individual user in much the same way that a ROM can be programmed. We will use a simple example to illustrate the basic ideas involved.

Suppose we want to realize a 2-output, 3-variable problem defined by the following function:

$$F_1 = \overline{B}\,\overline{C} + A\overline{B} + BC$$
$$F_2 = A\overline{B} + B\overline{C}$$

(6.3)

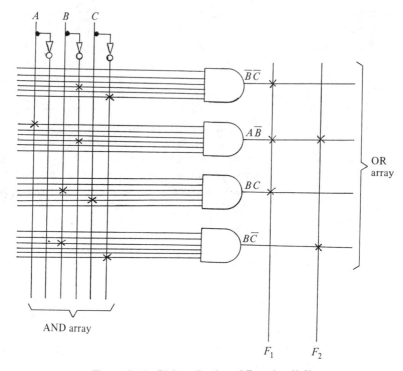

Figure 6.18. PLA realization of Equation (6.3)

For an n-variable problem, the PLA employs AND gates, each with $2n$ inputs so that a direct PLA realization of the problem defined by Equation (6.3) takes the form shown in Figure 6.18. The required inputs to the AND gates (marked by X's in the figure) are arranged in the process of programming the device. The programming may be carried out during manufacture (mask programming) or, as in PROM programming, by blowing fuses. PLAs which allow the latter form of programming are termed "field-programmable logic arrays" (FPLAs). Thus, in an FPLA, all possible AND-gate connections are provided and, in the process of programming, the unwanted connections are "blown." The connections for the OR operation are arranged in exactly the same way as for the PROM. Comparison of Figure 6.18 with Figure 6.13 highlights the only significant difference between the PLA and the ROM: the decoder in the ROM is replaced by a (programmable) set of AND gates in the PLA. In both devices, the OR operation is carried out in exactly the same way. The PLA, therefore, contains two switching arrays—the AND array and the OR array.

It should be clear to the reader that, because PLA realizations are based upon sums of products rather than sums of minterms, the techniques of combinational logic minimization described in Chapters 2 and 3 can be of value in reducing the size of PLA that is necessary for a given problem. In the problem described by Equation (6.3), the two logic functions have been reduced to their simplest sum-of-products form by means of K-maps. And yet, the circuit shown in Figure 6.18 does not represent the simplest PLA realization for this problem. The reason is that PLAs (of the field-programmable variety) are equipped with a third set of fuses, besides the fuses provided for the AND and OR arrays. To see why this is so, note the K-maps for the functions F_1 and F_2, shown in Figure 6.19.

Figure 6.19 points to a solution to the problem that requires one less AND gate than was used in the solution shown in Figure 6.18. This solution is obtained by realizing F_2 as before, and by using the function $\overline{F}_1$ in Figure 6.19 which, by use of an inverter, gives the required function F_1. Because simplifications of this kind are frequently possible, FPLAs are provided with inverters

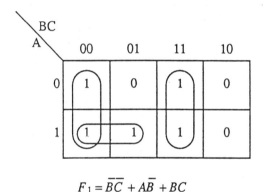

$$F_1 = \overline{B}\,\overline{C} + A\overline{B} + BC$$
$$\overline{F}_1 = B\overline{C} + \overline{A}\,\overline{B}C$$

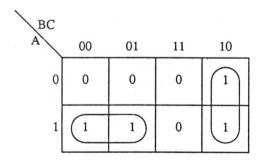

$$F_2 = A\overline{B} + B\overline{C}$$
$$\overline{F}_2 = \overline{A}\,\overline{B} + BC$$

Figure 6.19. K-maps for Equation (6.3)

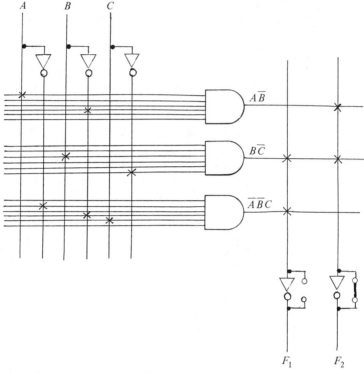

Figure 6.20. A more efficient PLA realization of Equation (6.3)

at the outputs. These inverters are short-circuited by fuses which can be blown during programming if an inverted output is required. This is illustrated in Figure 6.20, which depicts a PLA realization of F_1 and F_2 in which F_1 is obtained from the expression for $\overline{F}_1$ in Figure 6.19.

Notice that product terms common to more than one output (e.g., the term $\overline{BC}$ in this example) contribute to the simplification process. For problems with many inputs and outputs, minimization of PLA size is quite complex and we will not pursue it here. We simply point out these two general guidelines: (i) take advantage of products common to more than one output and (ii) check whether simplifications are available through use of the output inverters. The problem of PLA minimization is particularly important in VLSI design; for more details see [1]. In other applications, one is usually chiefly interested in minimizing the number of IC packages so that if a problem can be accommodated by an available PLA before any attempts at function minimization have been made, there is usually no point in attempting to carry out a minimization.

The switching arrays in a PLA are realized with either bipolar or MOS technology. In the bipolar case, the OR array has columns constructed exactly like the one depicted in Figure 6.14. The AND array is constructed similarly, so the reader should note that there are no "physical" AND gates of the type indicated in Figure 6.20. The AND function, like the OR operation, is realized directly by the array.

PLA size is specified in terms of the number of inputs, number of outputs and the number of products that can be accommodated. Thus, the $16 \times 48 \times 8$ PLA (a typical device) has 16 inputs, 8 outputs and the capacity to accommodate 48 product terms.

Expansion of PLAs is generally less straightforward than expansion of ROMs. Although output expansion can be achieved in exactly the same way as with a ROM, input expansion is more difficult, but is possible for certain types of problems (see [2]). Expansion of the number of product terms is also possible so long as device outputs are appropriately configured, e.g., in open-collector form (again see [2] for more details).

6.1.5. Other Programmable Devices

Besides PROMs and PLAs, there are currently several other types of programmable logic device available to the designer. One of these, called a PAL (*programmable array logic*), is really a special case of the PLA; it has the same basic AND/OR array structure, but in the PAL, only the AND array is programmable. Each OR gate in the PAL is fed from a fixed set of AND gates which are not accessible to any other OR gate. This means that, unlike the case of the PLA, there can be no "sharing" of minterms among OR gates. As a consequence, each logic function to be realized on a PAL can be minimized separately without any concern for terms that might be common to more than one function. PALs are less expensive than PLAs and are also easier to program; they are often used in preference to individual logic gates in cases where several logic functions have to be realized. For more details, see [3].

Other variations, built around the basic AND/OR array structure, are also available. An example is the *erasable programmable logic device* (EPLD) developed by Altera Corporation [4]. This device consists of a series of "macrocells," each containing, typically, a programmable logic array with other, selectable, devices, such as flip-flops, also being provided. For more details see [4].

One of the disadvantages of programmable arrays concerns the "rigidity" of the architecture imposed by the fixed interconnections involved. This rigidity results in only a small percentage (normally below 20%) of gates actually being used in a given application. One means of overcoming this inefficiency is available in the form of a *gate array* which typically consists of a vast array of 2-input NAND gates. Complex functions can be implemented on such arrays by appropriate interconnections (using feedback, where necessary, to create flip-flops). Gate utilization can be as high as 90% in some applications, but a major disadvantage of gate arrays is that they are not "field programmable." That is, the interconnections have to be implemented in the factory using mask programming.

In PALs and gate arrays, programming involves interconnecting individual gates. This is also required in EPLDs, although in the EPLD, provision for the interconnection of slightly higher-level devices such as flip-flops is also made. The subject of "configurable" logic devices is really in its infancy and it seems likely that there will be a trend toward the production of programmable structures in which the programming involves the interconnection of substantially higher-level devices—see, for example, the Xilinx devices [5].

6.2. ASM CHARTS AND DIGITAL-SYSTEM DESIGN

In the production of computer software, flowcharts are widely employed as a design aid. In the production of digital hardware, flowcharting is also very useful. The flowcharts employed in digital-system design are usually called *ASM charts*, where ASM stands for "algorithmic state machine." This terminology arises from the fact that in digital design the flowchart depicts the manner in which a system is required to move from state to state, usually according to some control scheme or algorithm.

The notation used in ASM charts is similar to that employed in flowcharts for computer software. Arrows are used to indicate the directions in which transitions are made from state to state. (Note that in synchronous systems these transitions are initiated at clock times.) Besides the arrows, there are three major components of ASM charts, depicted in Figure 6.21.

Transitions into a system state are always represented by an arrow leading to a rectangular box like the one shown in Figure 6.21(a). The name of the state is displayed within a circle located at the upper left of the box. Any actions that the system is required to carry out whenever it enters the state may be listed in the box.

In most systems of interest, some of the transitions from "current" state to "next" state depend not only on the nature of the current state but also on the current value of one or more system inputs. Typically, if the inputs satisfy some specified condition, the system will move from the current state to a particular next state; if the specified condition is not satisfied, the system will move to some other next state. This form of conditional branching is represented by means of the diamond-shaped box shown in Figure 6.21(b); the condition on which the branching depends is written within the box.

Sometimes, when a system is in a particular state, it is required to perform certain actions only if some specified condition is met at the time that the system is in that state. Such actions are listed in "conditional-output boxes" which appear in ASM charts as rectangular boxes with curved edges; one such box is shown in Figure 6.21(c). Conditional-output boxes always appear immediately

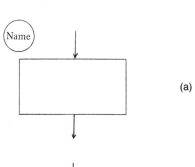

(a)

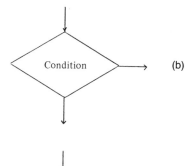

(b)

Figure 6.21. Major components of ASM charts; (a) state box; (b) conditional branch; (c) conditional output box

(c)

after a conditional branch point in the chart; such conditional branch points define the conditions under which the actions specified in the conditional-output boxes are to be carried out.

In the remainder of this chapter, we concentrate on two examples chosen to bring out the usefulness and convenience of ASM charts as well as provide some guidelines for general digital-system design. In the next chapter some computer aids will be presented.

6.2.1. A Traffic-Signal Controller

Figure 6.22 shows a traffic intersection for which a set of traffic signals must be installed. The signals will be required to control four directions of traffic flow: North to South (NS), South to North (SN), South to West (SW) and West to North (WN). Traffic using the intersection to move from North to West or from West to South is allowed to proceed whenever it is safe to do so. Note that when the SW signal is green, the SN signal can remain on green, but it is essential that the NS and WN signals be red. And when the WN signal is green, all three other signals are required to be red.

Figure 6.22 indicates that special lanes have been provided for the SW and

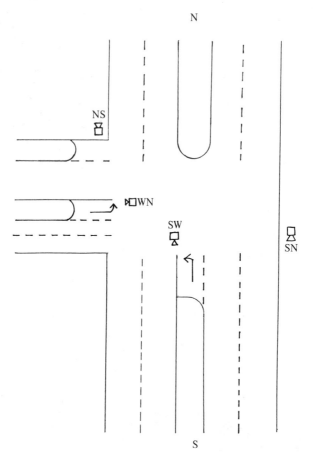

Figure 6.22. A traffic intersection.

WN traffic. A traffic sensor is located in each of these lanes to ensure that the SW and WN signals turn green only when there are vehicles waiting.

Statistical measurements of traffic flow have indicated that satisfactory results should be obtained if the signals are controlled according to the following sequence:

Step 1: NS and SN traffic is allowed to flow for 30 seconds on each cycle.

Step 2: Check for the presence of SW traffic. If there is none present, go to step 3; if there is some SW traffic waiting then SN and SW traffic should be allowed to flow for 15 seconds.

Step 3: Check for the presence of WN traffic. If there is none present, go to step 4; if there is some WN traffic waiting, it should be allowed to flow for 15 seconds.

Step 4: Restart the cycle by returning to step 1.

Although the problem has been stated in the form of a sequence of steps, it is still no more than a ''word description'' and is typical of the kind of specification often given to a design engineer. To carry out the design, the engineer must first of all ''translate'' the word description into a more formal and precise statement of the problem. The ASM chart can be of great assistance in this task.

In what follows, we will avoid unnecessary complications by ignoring the amber lights that traffic signals normally include. We here assume that the signals change immediately from green to red (and from red to green).

It is obvious that a system clock will be required and we will assume that a clock is available which produces short pulses every 15 seconds. Then, each time a clock pulse arrives, the control system will move to a new state.

To draw the ASM chart, we can pick any state as the starting state. In this case, considering the sequence of steps used to describe the required behavior of the system, it is most convenient to choose as the starting state the state in which NS and SN traffic is flowing. The ASM chart is shown in Figure 6.23. Note that this particular chart does not contain any conditional output boxes. Note also that the ASM chart is in many respects similar to the state-transition diagrams employed in earlier chapters. A major difference, of course, is that much more information is presented on an ASM chart and, as a consequence, the details of system operation are much more easily understood from inspection of the chart.

The chart indicates that the system has four states and that the sequence of state transitions in any cycle depends upon the values of the two inputs derived from the traffic sensors in the SW and WN lanes. The required outputs from the system are not explicitly shown in the ASM chart, although we could include them within the rectangular boxes denoting the system states. This would, however, be rather cumbersome, and we prefer to leave the ASM chart as it is. Figure 6.23 describes the required system control algorithm, displaying the manner in which the system is required to make transitions from state to state. Thus, we will first design a system which implements the required control algorithm and then add to it the logic circuitry that is necessary to provide the required outputs.

We will not, in this example, concern ourselves with problems of state minimization or state assignment, but instead proceed immediately with the arbitrary state assignment indicated in Figure 6.23 (the bit pattern assigned to each state has been marked at the top right of each rectangular box).

First we must decide on the type of flip-flop to be used, and, for simplicity of exposition, we choose the D flip-flop. Two flip-flops will be required and

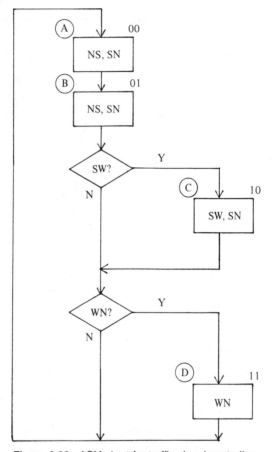

Figure 6.23. ASM chart for traffic signal controller.

we will, as usual, let the values of the flip-flop outputs define the system state. For the combinational circuitry required to drive the flip-flops from state to state, we could use discrete gates or any of the MSI devices mentioned earlier in this chapter. The use of discrete gates in situations such as this has been thoroughly discussed in earlier chapters, so we will here consider the use of MSI devices, starting with the multiplexer.

Multiplexer Implementation of Control Algorithm. A system containing n flip-flops can be controlled by n multiplexers each of size 2^n-to-1. Thus, for the problem in hand, we require two 4-to-1 MUXs. The control structure has the form shown in Figure 6.24 and our task now is to determine the MUX inputs that will cause the system to make its state transitions according to the ASM chart in Figure 6.23.

We commence with drawing up a state-transition table; this can be done di-

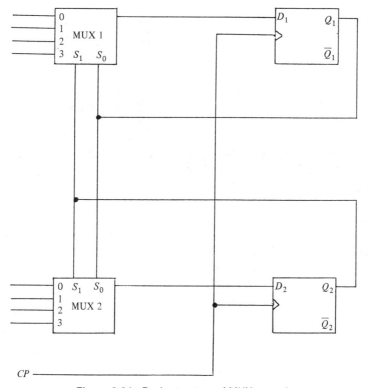

Figure 6.24. Basic structure of MUX control.

rectly from the ASM chart and the state-transition table for this problem is shown in Table 6.1. The required MUX inputs can now be obtained directly from the state-transition table.

The most important point to note here is that the system state is defined by the flip-flop outputs $Q_2^n Q_1^n$ and that these outputs also activate the select inputs on each multiplexer. Thus, when $Q_2^n = Q_1^n = 0$, we have D_1^n equal to the value

Table 6.1. State transition table for traffic signal controller.

Present State $Q_2^n Q_1^n$	Next state $Q_2^{n+1} Q_1^{n+1}$ Inputs ISW, IWN			
	0 0	0 1	1 0	1 1
A 0 0	0 1	0 1	0 1	0 1
B 0 1	0 0	1 1	1 0	1 0
C 1 0	0 0	1 1	0 0	1 1
D 1 1	0 0	0 0	0 0	0 0

of input 0 of MUX1 and D_2^n equal to the value of input 0 of MUX2. But the state-transition table tells us that with $Q_2^n = Q_1^n = 0$ we require $Q_2^{n+1} = 0$ and $Q_1^{n+1} = 1$ (regardless of the values of the inputs *ISW* and *IWN*). This can be achieved by setting $D_2^n = 0$ and $D_1^n = 1$ and hence by setting input 0 of MUX2 to 0 and input 0 of MUX1 to 1.

With the system in state 01 (i.e. $Q_2^n = 0$, $Q_1^n = 1$) input 1 of each multiplexer is selected. The state-transition table indicates that with the system in this state, Q_2^{n+1} is required to equal 1 if any of the following conditions on the system inputs is met: *ISW* = 0, *IWN* = 1; *ISW* = 1, *IWN* = 0; *ISW* = 1, *IWN* = 1. This can be achieved by setting $D_2^n = \overline{ISW}.IWN + ISW.\overline{IWN} + ISW.IWN = ISW + IWN$. And, in state 01, D_2^n is connected to input 1 of MUX2, so we are required to set this input to *ISW* + *IWN*. The remaining MUX inputs are determined similarly and are shown in Figure 6.25.

With the MUX inputs determined, the control algorithm implementation is completed. All that remains to be done to complete the system design is to determine the logic required to switch the traffic signals. The required logic circuitry is very simple and can be realized most easily using discrete gates. The inputs to these gates are the flip-flop outputs which determine the system state. The necessary logic circuitry is determined by noting the traffic signals that are required to be red or green in each system state. Using the convention that a 1 output is required for a green signal and a 0 for a red signal, a truth table representing required behavior can be drawn up as shown in Table 6.2; this gives the output circuitry shown in Figure 6.25.

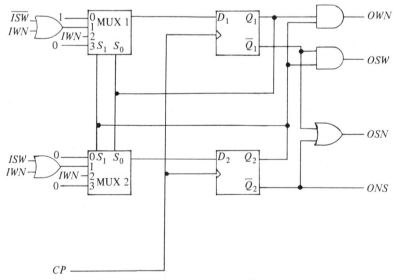

Figure 6.25. MUX implementation of traffic signal controller.

Table 6.2.   Truth table for traffic signal outputs.

Flip-flop inputs		System outputs			
Q_2	Q_1	ONS	OSN	OSW	OWN
0	0	1	1	0	0
0	1	1	1	0	0
1	0	0	1	1	0
1	1	0	0	0	1

ROM Implementation of Control Algorithm. The most direct and straightforward approach to the implementation of the control algorithm is by use of a ROM. The traffic signal problem demonstrates that, when using a ROM, design time is minimal and, as we shall see, the ROM implementation has further advantages in situations in which occasional changes in state-transition sequences are required.

For the traffic-signal problem, the basic structure is as shown in Figure 6.26. In this case, there is no need for combinational logic circuitry either at the ROM

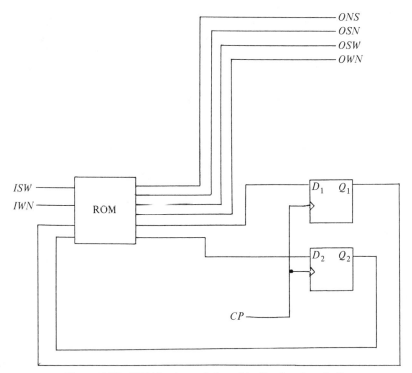

Figure 6.26. ROM implementation of traffic signal controller.

inputs or at the system outputs. The values of the system inputs (ISW and IWN) and the system state (represented by Q_1 and Q_2) define a ROM address and we simply have to program the ROM in such a way that for each ROM address the ROM output gives the correct system outputs and the correct flip-flop inputs.

Note that the ROM is required to have four inputs and six outputs so that a $2^4 \times 6$ ROM would be adequate. ROMs of this size are not available in standard packages but we will proceed with the example as if such ROMs are available and then discuss practicalities after the required ROM programming has been described.

For each 4-bit address in the $2^4 \times 6$ ROM, a 6-bit word is required that gives the four system outputs and the two flip-flop inputs. The four system outputs for each address are available directly from the truth table (Table 6.2) and the two flip-flop inputs are available from the state-transition table (Table 6.1). The complete ROM program is shown in Table 6.3.

To see how the inputs to the flip-flops are obtained, note that in Table 6.1 for $Q_2^n = Q_1^n = 0$ we require, for all four combinations of ISW and IWN, $Q_2^{n+1} = 0$ and $Q_1^{n+1} = 1$; hence we require $D_2^n = 0$ and $D_1^n = 1$. This gives the first two bits in each of the first four ROM data words. The first two bits of the remaining data words are obtained similarly.

The remaining bits of each data word are obtained directly from Table 6.2. For each system state the system outputs are defined by Table 6.2 and are independent of the system inputs. Thus, each set of system outputs appears in four consecutive rows of Table 6.3. This fact gives some indication of the re-

Table 6.3. Contents of ROM for traffic signal controller.

Address bits				Outputs (ROM data words)					
Q_2^n	Q_1^n	ISW	IWN	D_2^n	D_1^n	ONS	OSN	OSW	OWN
0	0	0	0	0	1	1	1	0	0
0	0	0	1	0	1	1	1	0	0
0	0	1	0	0	1	1	1	0	0
0	0	1	1	0	1	1	1	0	0
0	1	0	0	0	0	1	1	0	0
0	1	0	1	1	1	1	1	0	0
0	1	1	0	1	0	1	1	0	0
0	1	1	1	1	0	1	1	0	0
1	0	0	0	0	0	0	1	1	0
1	0	0	1	1	1	0	1	1	0
1	0	1	0	0	0	0	1	1	0
1	0	1	1	1	1	0	1	1	0
1	1	0	0	0	0	0	0	0	1
1	1	0	1	0	0	0	0	0	1
1	1	1	0	0	0	0	0	0	1
1	1	1	1	0	0	0	0	0	1

dundancy that is almost invariably present in a ROM realization of a logic function.

It was stated above that a $2^4 \times 6$ ROM is a non-standard arrangement. The nearest standard size that could be used in this problem is a $2^5 \times 8$ ROM. So, in practice we would have to use a ROM with five inputs and eight outputs. This does not create any difficulty; it simply means that only half the ROM addresses will be used and only six of the eight bits available at each address need be programmed. But it does, of course, indicate further redundancy in the final realization.

ROM Implementation of Modified Control Algorithms. It was stated earlier that the ROM offers advantages in situations in which occasional changes in state-transition sequences are required. To see this, consider again the traffic-signal problem, but assume that traffic patterns change to such an extent that a change in the control algorithm is warranted. Suppose that the necessary change involves reducing the time interval in which NS and SN traffic is allowed to flow so that checks are more frequently made for the presence of SW and WN traffic. The ASM chart in Figure 6.27 represents the situation in which the time

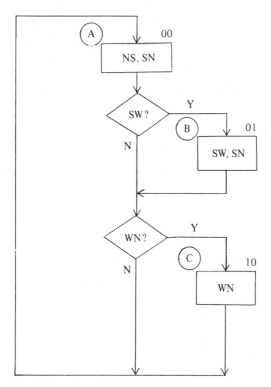

Figure 6.27. Modified ASM representation.

between checks has been halved. Notice that the number of system states has been reduced from 4 to 3. We still require two flip-flops, and this means that the system will have one unused state. We could treat this unused state as a don't-care state, but in dealing with a system such as a traffic-signal controller, it is far safer to recognize the possibility of some transient disturbance causing the system to enter the unused state and, in the state-transition table shown in Table 6.4, we have constrained the system to go from the unused state (state 11) to state 00. In addition, in the truth table for the output logic (Table 6.5) we have arranged for NS, SN traffic flow for the case where the system enters state 11.

The program for a $2^4 \times 6$ ROM to drive this system is shown in Table 6.6.

The advantage of ROM implementation is now evident. A change in the control sequence simply requires a change in the ROM program; the circuit structure remains unchanged. Thus, to make the system modifications, one simply has to replace one ROM with another. Contrast this with the MUX realization in which both the input logic and the output logic would require change, implying the likelihood of considerable rewiring. The advantage noted here should, of course, be weighed against the fact that multiplexers are considerably cheaper than ROMs and also that they do not need to be programmed.

PLA Implementation of Control Algorithm.   As in the case of the ROM, a PLA implementation allows changes in the state-transition sequence of a control algorithm to be made without the need for any changes in circuit structure. For the controller whose state transition sequence is described by Table 6.1, the required flip-flop inputs can be represented on K-maps as shown in Figure 6.28(a) and (b). The system outputs are described by Table 6.2 and can be represented in similar K-maps, as shown in Figure 6.28(c)–(f). Recall that efficient use of PLAs is achieved by arranging for individual product terms to be shared, where possible, by two or more outputs. This requires a rather unconventional use of K-maps, as shown in Figure 6.28. In this figure the 1 entries in each map have been looped in such a way as to maximize the sharing of

Table 6.4.   Modified state transition table.

Present State $Q_2^n Q_1^n$	Next state $Q_2^{n+1} Q_1^{n+1}$			
	Inputs ISW, IWN			
	0 0	0 1	1 0	1 1
0 0	0 0	1 0	0 1	0 1
0 1	0 0	1 0	0 0	1 0
1 0	0 0	0 0	0 0	0 0
1 1	0 0	0 0	0 0	0 0

Table 6.5. Modified truth table.

Flip-flop inputs		System outputs			
Q_2	Q_1	ONS	OSN	OSW	OWN
0	0	1	1	0	0
0	1	0	1	1	0
1	0	0	0	0	1
1	1	1	1	0	0

product terms among PLA outputs. Such action leads to the minimization of the total number of distinct product terms that have to be realized. For this problem, Figure 6.28 indicates that a solution exists which involves only seven distinct product terms.

The example demonstrates that in PLA implementations one is not concerned about minimizing the number of variables in a product, but rather one aims only to minimize the total number of products. The number of variables in any product is unimportant because, prior to the device being programmed, each AND gate is connected to every variable.

Note that further efficiencies might be gained by considering the complement of each required output (recall that the PLA can be programmed to provide the complement of one or more outputs). One would normally consider this pos-

Table 6.6. Modified contents ROM.

Address bits				Outputs (ROM data words)					
Q_2^n	Q_1^n	ISW	IWN	D_2^n	D_1^n	ONS	OSN	OSW	OWN
0	0	0	0	0	0	1	1	0	0
0	0	0	1	1	0	1	1	0	0
0	0	1	0	0	1	1	1	0	0
0	0	1	1	0	1	1	1	0	0
0	1	0	0	0	0	0	1	1	0
0	1	0	1	1	0	0	1	1	0
0	1	1	0	0	0	0	1	1	0
0	1	1	1	1	0	0	1	1	0
1	0	0	0	0	0	0	0	0	1
1	0	0	1	0	0	0	0	0	1
1	0	1	0	0	0	0	0	0	1
1	0	1	1	0	0	0	0	0	1
1	1	0	0	0	0	1	1	0	0
1	1	0	1	0	0	1	1	0	0
1	1	1	0	0	0	1	1	0	0
1	1	1	1	0	0	1	1	0	0

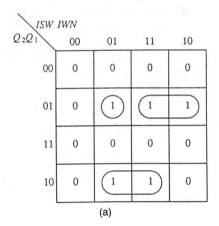

(a)

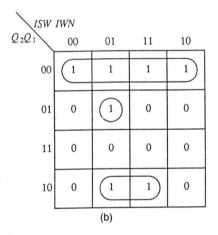

(b)

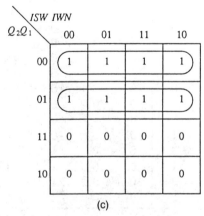

(c)

Figure 6.28. K-maps derived from Table 6.1. (a) D_2^n; (b) D_1^n; (c) ONS; (d) OSN; (e) OSW; (f) OWN.

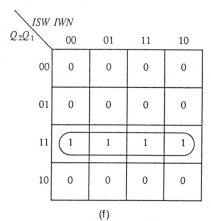

(d)

(e)

(f)

Figure 6.28. (*Continued*)

sibility only if the procedure outlined here led to a solution that required more product terms than were available on the PLA that one wished to use. Consideration of complementary outputs is left as an exercise.

It should now be clear that if the state-transition sequence of the control algorithm were altered (say, by changing from Table 6.1 to Table 6.4) the only physical change that would be required to the system would be the replacement of the PLA (programmed according to the K-maps in Figure 6.28) by another (programmed according to a new set of K-maps). This, too, is left as an exercise for the reader.

6.2.2. Selection of an 8-Bit Word from a Serial-Bit Stream

We will now consider a fairly simple example which involves an ASM chart with conditional output boxes and which also demonstrates the kinds of considerations that are the everyday concern of the digital-system designer.

For the purposes of this example we will assume that a mechanism is required which has access to a serial bit stream and which, upon receipt of a command signal, will read into a buffer the next eight bits that arrive in the serial stream. Moreover, the eight bits should be stored in the buffer in such a way that they can be read out in parallel, in the form of an 8-bit word. The mechanism is also required to set a flag when the 8-bit word is available for reading from the buffer. The time at which the word will be read is not given, but we are to assume that when the word is eventually read, the flag will be cleared by the reading mechanism.

The designer would normally set about a task of this sort by making some decisions on the kinds of hardware devices to be used. These decisions relate to what is commonly referred to as the *data part* of the problem; they are concerned with the choice of hardware devices to be used for handling *data*. Only when some decisions have been made regarding the data part of the problem is the designer in a position to set about the *control part* of the problem (i.e., that part of the problem concerned with the implementation of the control algorithm). In most digital-design problems, the first step taken is to distinguish between the control and data parts, and this will become clearer in Chapter 7. Note that we did not need to distinguish between the two in the traffic signal problem because the data part was trivial.

The data part of this problem is not very complex and, given that a source of clock pulses is available, the designer might decide that the easiest approach to the problem would be to feed the bit stream into a shift register (serial in/parallel out). On receipt of the command signal, a counter could then be set running which would count clock pulses up to eight whereupon the contents of the shift register could be transferred to a buffer and the required flag set to

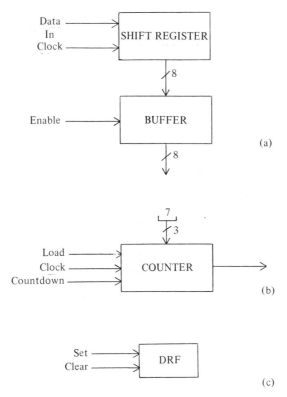

Figure 6.29. Hardware for data part of problem: (a) shift register and buffer; (b) counter; (c) flagging device for data register full.

indicate that the 8-bit word is available for reading. The basic idea is set out diagrammatically in Figure 6.29. In the figure, all the device inputs and outputs that are perceived as directly relevant to the problem have been displayed.

We will assume that the decision has been made that when the command signal arrives, the contents of the counter will be set to the number seven and the counter will then count down to zero. Reaching zero will signal that the required 8-bit word has been stored in the shift register. This is indicated in Figure 6.29(b).

In Figure 6.29(c), DRF represents a flagging device which will be set when the 8-bit word has been transferred to the buffer. (DRF stands for data register full).

Before proceeding to the control part of the problem, we should first have a look at manufacturers' data books to determine whether suitable devices exist for implementation of the data part as set out in Figure 6.29. For simplicity, we will make the decision that the devices we select should all be activated by the rising edge of the clock signal. An 8-bit serial in/parallel out shift register, which shifts data on the rising edge of the clock signal, is available as a 74164. A suitable 8-input, 8-output buffer is the 74377, which loads the data at its input on the rising edge of the clock (so long as its enable input ($\overline{G}$ in the data book) is held low).

A counter of the up/down variety will allow the countdown process to be implemented, but a 3-bit counter (indicated in Figure 6.29(b)) is not available as a standard package. Instead, a 4-bit up/down counter, such as the 74169, will have to be used. The databook indicates that in order to make the device count down, the up/down input must be set low. The databook also shows that when the 74169 counts down to zero, the carry output on the device, which is normally high, goes low for one clock period. This transition takes place immediately when the count reaches zero and hence can be used to signal that the required 8-bit word is available in the buffer. Two further points should be noted regarding the device: first, it will count down by one on each rising edge of the clock signal so long as the inputs $\overline{P}$ and $\overline{T}$ are both held low; and second, the device will load parallel data on a rising clock edge if the $\overline{load}$ input is set to zero.

For the flagging device in Figure 6.29(c) almost any set/clear flip-flop can be used and we select the straightforward JK flip-flop 7473, which comes in a dual package. This is again triggered on a rising clock edge.

Having established the devices we intend to use for the data part of the problem, we can now turn to the control part. An ASM chart for a suitable control algorithm is shown in Figure 6.30; the symbol ← should be read "takes the value".

In the chart there are only two state boxes, indicating that the control algorithm can be implemented using a single flip-flop. Recall that we have chosen to use a 7473 dual JK flip-flop package to provide the (single) flip-flop needed for the flagging device. Thus, it appears that we ought to be able to use the other flip-flop in the package to implement the control algorithm.

The state box representing state S_0 in the chart is empty, indicating that while in this state the system has no unconditional tasks to perform; it is simply waiting for the command signal and, when the signal arrives, the load input of the counter is to be set to 0. When the load input goes to 0 the counter is loaded with whatever bit pattern is present at its data inputs on the next rising clock edge. For this problem, we maintain the bit pattern 0111 permanently at the counter's data inputs. The need to load the counter as soon as the command signal arrives is indicated by a condition box; that the counter will be loaded with the number seven is understood (i.e., not displayed on the chart).

Once the counter has been loaded, the system moves to state S_1 and in this state we decrement the counter on each rising clock edge. This is achieved by holding the *count—enable* pin low. The system simply checks the value of the

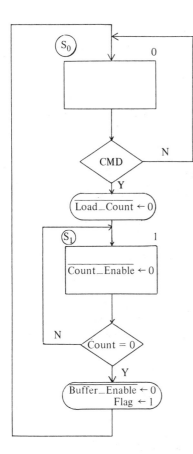

Figure 6.30. ASM chart for control algorithm.

counter, and repeatedly decreases the count by one until the value zero is reached, whereupon it is necessary to set the enable input on the buffer, $\overline{G}$, to zero (which causes the buffer to retain the eight bits that are in the counter on the next clock edge) and also to set the flag to indicate that the buffer now holds the required 8-bit word which can be read at any time.

One further point, which is not explicitly displayed on the chart, concerns the manner in which we deal with the enable inputs ($\overline{P}$ and $\overline{T}$) on the 74169. We arbitrarily choose to hold $\overline{T}$ permanently low and to use $\overline{P}$ as our count enable input. The ASM chart indicates that counting is required to take place with the system in state S_1 and, according to the state assignment marked on the chart, the flip-flop implementing the control algorithm will have its output at logic 1 when in state S_1. Thus, the complement of this output can be used to enable the counter.

The final circuit arrangement, in which the significant inputs and outputs are displayed, is shown in Figure 6.31. The reasoning behind this arrangement is illustrated by the waveform diagrams in Figure 6.32, and a description of the circuit operation is given below.

Before the operation of the circuit is described, it is pertinent to consider briefly the timing constraints involved. All storage devices (buffer, counter and flip-flops) are clocked with the same clock pulse and the data on their inputs must be valid for a small time before and after each rising edge of the clock in order to meet set-up and hold time requirements. One obvious constraint, therefore, is that data derived from external circuitry must be tailored to meet these set-up and hold-time requirements. This condition should create no difficulty if the external circuitry is synchronous. As regards set-up times for data being transferred within the circuit, we can avoid any problems by ensuring that the clock frequency is well below the maximum (see Section 4.5.4). The remaining constraint that we must consider is the one concerning hold times for data being transferred within the circuit. Fortunately, the propagation delay of storage devices is always substantially greater than the hold time† and this ensures that the hold time requirements will not be violated. To see this, note that the input data to any storage device only changes in response to changes in the outputs of other storage devices‡ and these latter outputs change after a propagation delay following the active clock edge. Since the propagation delay is greater than the hold time, the hold-time requirement is bound to be met. Note that the waveform diagram in Figure 6.32 ignores propagation delays.

The circuit in Figure 6.31 operates as follows. The shift register is permanently enabled to allow data to be shifted in on each clock edge. The state flip-flop is initially* in state S_0. When a CMD signal appears the load count input to the counter is set low (enabled) and the J_1 input to the state flip-flop is set high. On the next clock edge the counter is loaded, the flip-flop goes to state S_1, the load count input returns high and the count enable input goes low (enabled). The first bit of data enters the shift register.

At this point the counter holds "7". On each of the next seven rising clock edges, the count decreases by unity. When the count reaches zero, the carry output goes low, causing $\overline{G}$ to go low and causing K_1 and J_2 to go high. At this point all eight data bits are in the shift register. On the next rising edge the state flip-flop returns to S_0, the buffer is loaded and the flag flip-flop is set. When the system enters state S_0 the count enable input of the counter goes high (disabled). Notice that the counter actually counts down once too often and reaches 15 (1 less than 0). This is of no consequence for the problem in hand.

---

† For devices belonging to the same family.
‡ Bear in mind that we are discussing only data that is being transferred within the circuit.
*Ensuring that a sequential circuit always starts in a predetermined state can be arranged by suitable circuitry [6].

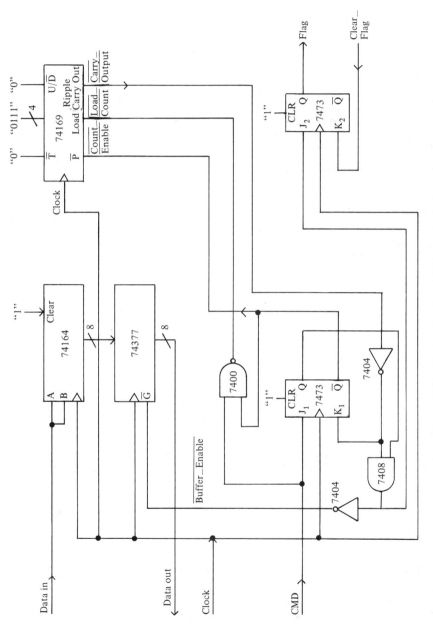

Figure 6.31. Final realization of 8-bit word selector.

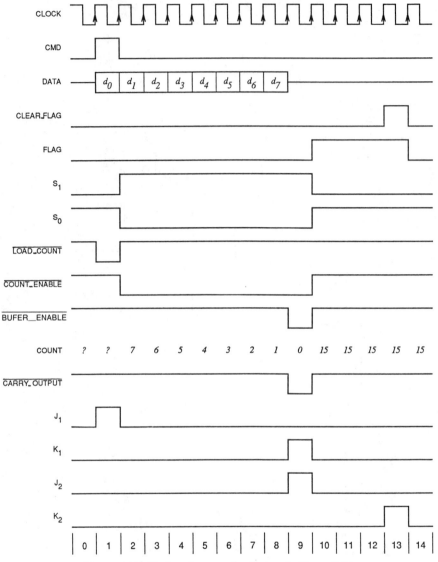

Figure 6.32. Timing diagrams for devices in Figure 6.31.

The flag flip-flop is now set, producing the flag signal. The external circuitry may now read the data in the buffer. After this has occurred the external circuit can send the clear flag signal for one clock cycle which will reset the flag flip-flop. It is assumed in this design that the external circuitry does not send CMD or clear flag signals at meaningless times.

REFERENCES

[1] R. K. Brayton, G. D. Hachtel, C. T. McMullen, A. L. Sangiovani-Vincentelli, *Logic Minimization Algorithms for VLSI Synthesis*, Kluwer, Boston, 1984.
[2] Peatman, J. B., *Digital Hardware Design*, McGraw-Hill, New York, 1980.
[3] *PAL Handbook*, Third Edition, Monolithic Memories, 1983.
[4] *Altera Data Book*, 1987.
[5] *The Programmable Gate Array Design Handbook*, Xilinx, 1986.
[6] D. Winkel, F. Prosser, *The Art of Digital Design*, Prentice-Hall, Englewood Cliffs, 1980, pp. 466–467.

Exercises

6.1. Use a 4-to-1 MUX to realize the logic function whose truth table is shown in Table E6.1. In your realization, connect the inputs A and B to the select lines S_1 and S_0 respectively.

Table E6.1.   Truth table of 3-variable logic function.

A	B	C	F
0	0	0	1
0	0	1	1
0	1	0	0
0	1	1	0
1	0	0	0
1	0	1	1
1	1	0	0
1	1	1	1

6.2. Repeat Exercise 6.1, but this time connect inputs B and C to select lines S_1 and S_0 (respectively).

6.3. Realize the function

$$F = AB + \overline{B}C$$

using a 4-to-1 MUX.

6.4. Realize the function

$$F = ABD + BC\overline{D} + ABC + \overline{B}\,\overline{C}D$$

using an 8-to-1 MUX.

6.5. Show how to construct a 16-to-1 MUX using two 8-to-1 and one 2-to-1 multiplexers.

6.6. Realize the BCD to 6311 code converter defined in Figure E2.24 by means of a 4-input decoder. Assume that minterms are asserted low so that NAND gates are required to carry out the "OR" operation. Note that 4-to-10 line decoders are commercially available for this kind of task. When a BCD number is applied at the inputs of such a decoder, the corresponding output goes low with all other outputs remaining high. If a 4-bit number which is not BCD is applied at the inputs, all outputs remain high.

6.7. Show how to construct a 2-to-4 line multiplexer using NAND gates only.

6.8. Show how to construct a 6-to-64 line decoder using four 4-to-16 line decoders and one 2-to-4 line decoder.

6.9. List the contents of a 16 × 4 ROM that will carry out the Binary to Gray code conversion listed in Table E6.9.

Table E6.9. Binary to Gray code conversion table.

A	B	C	D	W	X	Y	Z
0	0	0	0	0	0	0	0
0	0	0	1	0	0	0	1
0	0	1	0	1	0	0	1
0	0	1	1	1	1	0	1
0	1	0	0	0	1	0	1
0	1	0	1	0	1	1	1
0	1	1	0	1	1	1	1
0	1	1	1	1	0	1	1
1	0	0	0	0	0	1	1
1	0	0	1	0	0	1	0
1	0	1	0	1	0	1	0
1	0	1	1	1	1	1	0
1	1	0	0	0	1	1	0
1	1	0	1	0	1	0	0
1	1	1	0	1	1	0	0
1	1	1	1	1	0	0	0

6.10. List the contents of a 16 × 4 ROM that are required to carry out the conversion from BCD to 6311 code defined in Table E2.22. Explain how you would treat the unused entries in the ROM.

6.11. Show how you would use a 3-to-8 line decoder and eight $2^4 \times 4$ ROMs to create a $2^7 \times 4$ ROM.

6.12. Find a minimum PLA realization for the two-output function:

$$F_1 = \overline{A}\overline{B} + BC$$
$$F_2 = A\overline{B} + AC + \overline{A}B$$

6.13. Find a minimum PLA realization for the three-output function:

$$F_1 = \overline{A}B + A\overline{C}D$$

$$F_2 = \overline{A}\overline{B} + A(C + \overline{D})$$

$$F_3 = \overline{B} + B\overline{C}D$$

6.14. Figure E6.14 shows a road intersection for which a set of traffic signals is to be installed in the positions marked. The signals are required to control four directions of traffic flow: North to South (NS), South to North (SN), South to West (SW) and East to West (EW). Traffic using the intersection to move from East to North or from North to West are allowed to make their moves whenever they consider it safe to do so. Note that a special lane has been provided for traffic wishing to move from South to West. A traffic sensor has been embedded in this lane to ensure that the SW traffic signal will only turn green when there are vehicles waiting. A similar sensor has been embedded in the East-to-West one-way street.

Statistical measurements of traffic flow have indicated that satisfactory results

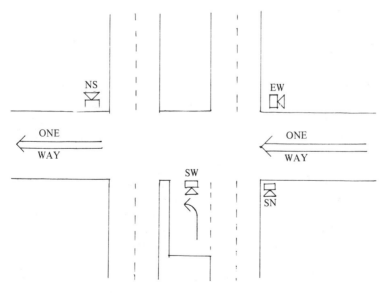

Figure E6.14. A traffic intersection.

should be obtained if the traffic signals are controlled according to the following sequence:

Step 1: The NS and SN signals are green for 40 seconds with the other signals held at red.

Step 2: Check for the presence of SW traffic. If there is none, go to step 3. If there is some SW traffic waiting, then set the NS signal to red and allow the SW and SN traffic to flow for 20 seconds.

Step 3: Check for the presence of EW traffic. If there is none, return to step 1. If there is EW traffic waiting, then set all signals to red except EW and allow EW traffic to flow for 20 seconds before returning to step 1.

You are to proceed as follows:

(i) Construct an ASM chart that describes the required behavior of a controller for this traffic signal system.

(ii) Then design three separate systems, each system designed to control and operate the traffic signals in the required manner. The three systems are to be based on different MSI devices; the devices to be used are

(a) multiplexers
(b) read-only memory
(c) programmable logic array.

In each case use D flip-flops as the sequential devices.

Assume that there are no amber lights in the traffic signal system (i.e., transitions are made directly from red to green and from green to red). Assume also that a source of clock pulses with a period of 20 seconds is available.

6.15. Repeat Exercise 6.14 for the case in which the NS and SN signals are held at green for only 20 seconds before checks are made for the presence of SW and EW traffic.

6.16. A machine dispenses candy bars at 10¢ each and will accept 5¢ or 10¢ coins. Any other coins that are inserted in the machine are returned to the customer. A synchronous digital system is required to control and operate the machine. Assume that suitable sensors are available to detect when a coin is inserted into the machine and also to distinguish between 5¢, 10¢ and other coins. Assume also that a suitable source of clock pulses is available.

The machine is required to indicate that it is ready for use by displaying the words ''INSERT COIN''. While displaying these words, the machine checks, on the rising edge of each clock pulse, to see if a coin has been inserted. If no coin has been inserted it remains in this state. If a coin has been inserted, it checks to see if it is a 10¢, 5¢ or other coin. Depending on which of the possible outcomes occurs, the digital system is required to behave as follows:

(i) If the coin is neither a 10¢ nor a 5¢ coin, the digital system is required to move into a state which causes the machine to return the coin to the customer. Following this, on the next clock pulse, the digital system is required to return the machine to the "ready for use" state.

(ii) If the coin is a 10¢ piece, the digital system is required to move into a state which causes the machine to dispense a candy bar. Following this, on the next clock pulse, the digital system is required to return the machine to the "ready for use" state.

(iii) If the coin is a 5¢ piece, the machine is required to move to a state in which it displays the words "NEXT COIN". While in this state, the machine checks, on the rising edge of each clock pulse, to see if another coin has been inserted. If a coin has been inserted, it checks to see if it is a 5¢ or other coin. Depending on which of the possible outcomes occurs, the digital system is required to behave as follows:

  (a) If the coin is not a 5¢ piece, the digital system is required to move into a state where it returns the inserted coins to the customer. Following this, on the next clock pulse, the digital system is required to return the machine to the "ready for use" state.

  (b) If the coin is a 5¢ piece, the digital system is required to move into the state which causes the machine to dispense a candy bar. Following this, on the next clock pulse, the digital system is required to return the machine to the "ready for use" state.

You are required to proceed as follows:

(i) Construct an ASM chart that describes the required behavior of the digital system. In drawing up this chart you should assume that the digital system will always go to the same state when the machine is required to return coins to the customer. With this assumption your chart should have four states.

(ii) Design three separate systems that could be used to control the dispensing machine. The three systems should be based on different MSI devices; the devices to be used are:

  (a) multiplexers
  (b) read-only memory
  (c) programmable logic array.

In each case use D flip-flops as the sequential devices.

6.17. Repeat Exercise 6.16 on the assumption that the price of candy bars has increased to 15¢. In this case, the machine is required to give out change if two 10¢ pieces are inserted. Keep the required number of flip-flops down to two by using the idea of conditional outputs.

7

REGISTER-TRANSFER LANGUAGES IN DIGITAL SYSTEM DESIGN

7.1 INTRODUCTION

This chapter introduces top-down design and shows how register-transfer languages can be used as a major design aid when the top-down approach is applied. In the design of any given system, the top-down approach commences with a specification of system requirements. At this level of description of the system (which we call the "top" level), details of required input and output behavior of the system are given, but details of the actual implementation are left until later. Design proceeds from the top-level description to the next level down by decomposing the overall design problem into a number of subproblems, each of which constitutes an easier design task than the overall system design. There are usually many different ways in which a given design can be decomposed into subproblems and it is the role of the designer to decide which way is best. The subproblems that result from this decomposition are subsystem design problems whose inputs and outputs are (or should be) well-defined. Thus each subsystem-design problem can be treated in the same way as was the overall system-design problem; that is, each subsystem-design problem can be decomposed into further subproblems. As the design process moves from the top level through various levels of decomposition, so the amount of detail regarding the types of devices to be employed in the final system realization steadily increases. Ultimately the final design is accomplished.

A *register-transfer language* (RTL) allows the writing-down of formal statements that provide clear and unambiguous descriptions of the design decisions that are made at each level of the top-down process. This is very important in the design of large and complex systems in which different subsystems are designed by different designers because it gives members of the design team a common language with which to communicate and ensures that the interfaces between the subsystems are well-defined and clearly understood. It is also very useful in the design of smaller systems because it provides a record of all the decisions made during the design process; this record can be consulted if problems are experienced when the system has finally been constructed.

The application of a register-transfer language in top-down design is illustrated in this chapter by means of one fairly lengthy (but not particularly complex) design example. We feel that this one example should provide an adequate illustration of the method and we hope that it will motivate the reader to adopt this kind of approach for digital-system design.

A compiler for our RTL is provided at the end of this chapter. The compiler collates all the information regarding the design and carries out a range of checks for design errors. For instance, it will check to see that register dimensions are not exceeded. It also reports to the user on the connections made to every pin on each IC package used and points out any pins that have not been assigned connections.

In order that a compiler listing could be accommodated in this book, the RTL had to be kept down to the very barest essentials. Nevertheless, this "bare-bones" RTL is sufficient to illustrate the main points that we wish to emphasize.

RTLs are commonly used as an aid to system analysis in conjunction with a system simulator. In top-down design, such usage allows the checking (by simulation) of the correctness of each major step in the top-down process. We do not have the space to include a simulator listing in this book. The interested reader might like to consult [1] where the topic is covered in more detail.

7.2. DESIGN OF A BINARY MULTIPLIER

Multiplication in binary can be carried out in exactly the same way as multiplication is carried out in the decimal system. Suppose, for instance, that we wanted to multiply the number 1100 (the 'multiplicand') by the number 1011 (the 'multiplier'). The required procedure is illustrated in Figure 7.1. We commence by multiplying the multiplicand by the least-significant digit of the multiplier (1 in this case) and write the result (the 'first partial product') immediately below the horizontal line drawn beneath the multiplier. We then multiply the multiplicand by the second least-significant digit (again 1 in this case) and write the result immediately below the first partial product (but shifted one digit to the left). The procedure continues in the obvious way and the final result is given by adding up the set of partial products.

We intend to design a system that will use this procedure to carry out the multiplication of any two 4-bit numbers. It can be seen from Figure 7.1 that the procedure can be implemented in the form of a "shift-and-add" algorithm. In terms of Figure 7.1, the way we intend to carry out this implementation is as follows. The first partial product (equal to the multiplicand) is stored in a register which, for convenience, we will refer to as the "accumulator". The second partial product (equal to the multiplicand shifted one digit to the left) is

```
    1100
    1011
    1100
    1100
    0000
    1100
 10000100
```

Figure 7.1. Shift-and-add example.

then added to the contents of the accumulator. The third partial product is equal to zero and so need not be added to the accumulator. The fourth partial product (equal to the multiplicand shifted three digits to the left) is then added to the accumulator. The accumulator then contains the complete product.

For the data part of the problem, the choice of hardware devices appears quite straightforward. We will need two 4-bit registers, one to store the multiplier and one to store the multiplicand. A further register is also required to act as the accumulator. Since the product of two 4-bit numbers consists of up to 8 binary digits, it might appear that an 8-bit register is required for the accumulator. However, because of the way that the shift-and-add algorithm works, it is possible to realize the data part of the problem using just three 4-bit registers and one flip-flop.

The reason an 8-bit register is not required can be seen in Figure 7.1: the first partial product is determined by the least-significant digit of the multiplier and, once this digit has been used to determine the first partial product, it is no longer required. Thus, after formation of the first partial product, the storage space holding the least-significant digit of the multiplier can be overwritten. Each time a partial product is formed, a digit of the multiplier can be over-written and this eliminates any need for an 8-bit register.

The algorithm we shall use can be stated as below (some explanatory remarks are made following the statement of the algorithm). The notation $REG\langle 0:m \rangle$ denotes a register named REG with $m + 1$ storage spaces numbered from 0 to m.

The storage devices are as follows:

$A\langle 0:3 \rangle$ will contain the multiplicand;
$B\langle 0:3 \rangle$ will contain (initially) the multiplier†;
$C\langle 0:3 \rangle$ will be used in the accumulation of the product;
OVR is a flip-flop that stores an overflow flag obtained from the adder.

In addition, we choose to use a counter to keep track of the steps of the algorithm and to use a flip-flop (called "Done") to flag the completion of the task.

---

† The algorithm is developed on the assumption that $A\langle 3 \rangle$ and $B\langle 3 \rangle$ contain the least significant digits of multiplicand and multiplier respectively, and that $A\langle 0 \rangle$ and $B\langle 0 \rangle$ contain the most significant digits.

Algorithm

Step 1: Set the counter to 3; set *Done* = 0; clear *C*; clear *OVR*. Move multiplicand into *A*; move multiplier into *B*.

Step 2: **if** $B\langle 3 \rangle$ = 1 **then** load *C* with the result of adding *C* and *A* **and** load *OVR* with the carry of the adder.

Step 3: Shift contents of *B* right one bit; shift contents of *C* right one bit, moving $C\langle 3 \rangle$ into $B\langle 0 \rangle$; set $C\langle 0 \rangle$ equal to *OVR*; decrement counter by 1.

Step 4: Clear *OVR*; **if** counter = 0 **then** *Done* = 1 **else** goto Step 2.

Step 1 of the algorithm simply initializes the contents of the storage devices and of the counter.

Step 2 indicates that addition of a partial product to the accumulator is only necessary for the nonzero digits in the multiplier. Note also that the addition of two 4-bit numbers in a 4-bit adder can lead to a 5-bit outcome and, in order to take care of this fact, the carry output is fed to the flip-flop *OVR*.

In Step 3, the required shift operations are carried out. In terms of the multiplication detailed in Figure 7.1, after the first partial product is added into register *C*, *C* contains 1100. Register *B* contains 1011 and the final digit in this 4-bit word is no longer required. The contents of *B* are now shifted one to the right and the right-hand digit in *C* is now moved into $B\langle 0 \rangle$. Simultaneously, the remaining contents of *C* are shifted one bit to the right and the output of the flip-flop *OVR* (which equals 0 at this juncture) is fed into $C\langle 0 \rangle$. This leaves the contents of *B* reading 0101 and those of *C* reading 0110.

In Step 4 it is necessary to clear *OVR* because we have not specified any action in Step 2 on occasions when $B\langle 3 \rangle$ = 0. On such occasions, no addition is required and so no carry digit can occur; it is important to clear *OVR* in case it is holding a carry digit from a previous addition operation. The full sequence of operations, showing how the contents of registers *B* and *C* change is given in Figure 7.2: when the counter reaches 0, the contents of registers *C* and *B* give the required product.

7.2.1. A First-Level RTL Description

Now that we are confident that the algorithm will work, we can express it formally in a register-transfer language (RTL). Expressed in our own RTL, the algorithm appears as in Figure 7.3. The reader should note that the algorithm has been defined in the RTL as a *module* with the clear implication that the hardware system we are designing has the potential for use in a larger system. As we proceed, it will become clear that the RTL bears some similarities to the Pascal programming language. In Figure 7.3, the module we are considering is named "multiplier" and has an associated parameter list which describes the full set of terminals (inputs and outputs) that the system is required to have.

Step	counter	C	B	OVR	DONE
1	4	0000	1011	0	0
2	4	1100	1011	0	0
3	3	0110	0101	0	0
4	3	0110	0101	0	0
2	3	0010	0101	1	0
3	2	1001	0010	1	0
4	2	1001	0010	0	0
2	2	1001	0010	0	0
3	1	0100	1001	0	0
4	1	0100	1001	0	0
2	1	0000	1001	1	0
3	0	1000	0100	1	0
4	0	1000	0100	0	1

Figure 7.2. Expanded example of shift-and-add algorithm.

Thus the module has four terminals to read in the 4-bit multiplier and another four to read in the multiplicand. It also has eight terminals to allow reading out of the 8-bit product and three further terminals, one to receive the start command, one to receive clock pulses and one to output a flag to indicate when the multiplication operation has been completed. Within the multiplier, a number of registers are required; this requirement has already been identified in our preliminary example and the register list in Figure 7.3 shows the necessary dimensions in each case. Note that in cases in which no dimension is stated (as with *OVR* in the register list here) the compiler assumes a 1-bit register. Note also that, at this stage, we are not concerned with specific types of device and represent all devices in terms of registers and terminals only. Thus, the term *register* is a general description here and this is why *counter* appears in the register list. The main point here, then, is that the RTL description in Figure 7.3 is intended to be independent of technology and device type. The description represents one stage in a "top-down" approach to the design of the multiplier. Since specific details have been avoided as much as possible in Figure 7.3, any design engineer, given this RTL description, would be able to realize the multiplier using whatever available devices are suitable for the task.

The system will have four states and these are listed in line 3 for the convenience of the RTL compiler.

We now come to the body of the RTL description. The first statement (on line 5) should be read "the product terminals are connected to the concatenation of registers *C* and *B*". Basically this is a statement which says that the product will ultimately be available from registers *B* and *C* with the most-significant bits provided by *C* and the least-significant bits provided by *B*.

Line 6 of the RTL description contains the label *Step1* and indicates entry into the first state of the control algorithm. In this state, the system waits for the externally applied start pulse. The statement **on** *Start* **do** indicates actions that have to be carried out when *Start* takes the logic value 1. Clearly, the **on. . .do** statement plays a similar role in this RTL to the role played by the

```
1          module multiplier(Multiplier<0:3>, Multiplicand<0:3>,
                                Product<0:7>, Start, Done, clock);

2          register A<0:3>, B<0:3>, C<0:3>, OVR, counter<0:2>;

3          state Step1, Step2, Step3, Step4;

4          begin
5              Product ← C @ B;
6              Step1:
7                  on Start do begin
8                      counter ← 4%4;
9                      A ← Multiplicand;
10                     B ← Multiplier;
11                     OVR ← 0;
12                     C ← 0;
13                     goto Step2
14                 end else
15                     goto Step1;

16             Step2:
17                 begin
18                     on B<3> do begin
19                         add(C, A, OVR);
20                     end;
21                     goto Step3
22                 end;

23             Step3:
24                 begin
25                     shiftright(B, C<3>);
26                     shiftright(C, OVR);
27                     counter ← counter - 1;
28                     goto Step4
29                 end;

30             Step4:
31                 begin
32                     OVR ← 0;
33                     on counter = 0 do begin
34                         Done ← 1;
35                         goto Step1
36                     end else
37                         goto Step2
38                 end
39         end { multiplier }
40     $
```

Figure 7.3. First level RTL description of the multiplier.

if. . .then statement in Pascal. A major difference between the RTL and Pascal is also evident at this point. When the *Start* pulse arrives, a number of operations are required to be carried out simultaneously (or very nearly so—they must at least be all carried out within a single clock period). Thus, the statements listed in lines 8 through 13 of the RTL description represent hardware operations that are to be carried out simultaneously; this contrasts with ordinary Pascal where statement after statement is executed in a strictly sequential fashion.

Line 8 indicates that the input to *counter* should be permanently connected to the constant 4, and that the constant must be a 4-bit value (i.e., the construct employed here has the general meaning *value % size*).

Before we move on to consider *Step2* in the RTL description, we mention a few points of interest. Note that statements 8 through 12 specify data transfers and that statement 13 is a control statement specifying a change of state. Note also that this RTL allows an **else** statement for ease of code writing. In this case the **else** statement provides a simple means of stating that when the system is in the first state (*Step1*), it is required to wait for the arrival of the start pulse. Finally note that there is considerable flexibility regarding the allowable duration of the start pulse. It must, of course, be long enough to set the multiplier going; the only other restriction is that it should not extend beyond the time taken to complete the multiplication operation—if it did, the system would restart itself as soon as it had completed the task.

Once in *Step2*, we state that if $B\langle 3 \rangle$ is equal to 1, we have to perform an addition operation. We do not go into any details about how the addition will be carried out because we are employing a form of top-down design and details such as this can be left until later.† Our bare-bones RTL does not contain any standard notations for the various addition operations possible, so here we simply use the non-standard operator "add(C, A, OVR)" which indicates the addition of C to A with the result stored in C, and the carry bit fed to register OVR. Finally, note that regardless of the value of $B\langle 3 \rangle$, the system is required to go to *Step3* next; when $B\langle 3 \rangle$ has the value 1, the **goto** statement is executed simultaneously with the addition operations.

On entering *Step3*, another "nonstandard" operation is encountered. The basic language does not cater for operations such as shift right. If needed, a simulator could easily be organized to carry out the shift right operation. Line 25 of Figure 7.3 states that register B is to shift right one bit, and place the value of the least significant bit in register C (i.e., $C\langle 3 \rangle$) into the vacated bit position of B (i.e., into bit $B\langle 0 \rangle$). Similarly, line 26 of Figure 7.3 states that register C is to shift right one bit, and place the value held in register OVR into the vacated bit position (i.e., into $C\langle 0 \rangle$).

The remainder of the listing in Figure 7.3 is quite straightforward and the reader should have no difficulty establishing that the listing properly describes the shift-and-add procedure illustrated in Figure 7.2.

With the RTL description completed, a simulator could be used to check that the system does indeed perform its required functions (see [1] for example). In this book we do not have the space to include a listing for a simulator and so

---

† Note, however, that if we were intending to use a simulator to check this description, we would have to specify the type of addition intended (e.g., 1's complement, 2's complement, etc.). The ISPL system [1] is one such practical simulator that can handle this kind of specification.

we must here restrict our use of the RTL description to that of a design aid in the process of top-down design.

Note that our system is so far entirely independent of technology and device type. We must now move to a lower-level description of system behavior by making decisions about the types of device that will be used in the final system realization. As a first step in moving toward this lower-level description it is useful to collect all the information regarding the various registers in the system in the form of a table. For our multiplier example, this information has been collected, directly from the RTL description, in Table 7.1.

Table 7.1 lists the types of operations that must be carried out by each register and also indicates the connections that must be made between registers (and to the controller) so that data and control signals can be passed in the required

Table 7.1. Specification of register/device characteristics.

Name	Line Number	Operation	Source/ Destination
A	9	Load	Controller
	9	Input Data	Multiplicand<0:3>
	19	Output Data	add input #2
B	5	Output Data	Product<4:7>
	10	Load	Controller
	10	Input Data	Multiplier<0:3>
	18	Output Data	Controller
	25	Shiftright	Controller
	25	Shiftin Data	C<3>
C	5	Output Data	Product<0:3>
	12	Clear	Controller
	19	Output Data	add input #1
	19	Input Data	add output
	19	Load	Controller
	26	Shiftright	Controller
	26	Shiftin Data	OVR
OVR	11	Clear	Controller
	19	Input Data	Carryout of add
	19	Load	Controller
	26	Output Data	C_shiftin
	32	Clear	Controller
counter	8	Load	Controller
	8	Input Data	4 bits of constant 4
	27	Decrement	Controller
	33	= 0 ?	Controller
Multiplicand	9	Output Data	A<0:3>
Multiplier	10	Output Data	B<0:3>
Product	14	Input Data	C<0:3> and B<0:3>
Start	7	Output Data	Controller
Done	34	set (implicitly to 1)	Controller
add	19	Input Data 1	C<0:3>
	19	Input Data 2	A<0:3>
	19	Output Data	C<0:3>
	19	Output Carryout	OVR

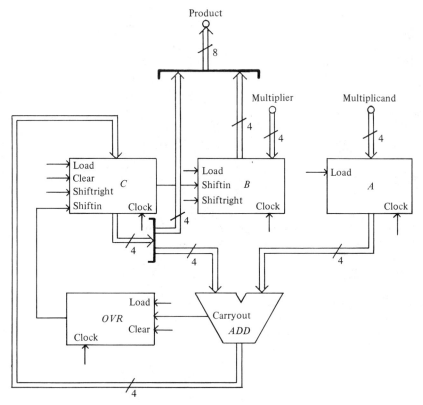

Figure 7.4. Data part of multiplier.

manner.† With the required connections within the system established, block diagrams for the data part and the control part of the problem can be drawn (Figure 7.4 and 7.5 respectively).‡

A Note on System Timing. Before we discuss the selection of devices, we should devote some attention to the manner in which the clock signal will govern system behavior. In order to see why, let us assume that we arrange our system so that the controller and all the registers respond to the rising edge of the clock.

---

†Table 7.1 was drawn up by simply scanning the RTL description and noting the significance of every appearance of each of the registers and terminals in the description.

‡Note that in Figures 7.4 and 7.5 we have employed a bus notation which differs from that used earlier in the book. We feel that this notation adds greater clarity to the representation of more complex digital systems. The reader should have no difficulty in interpreting the notation, which is used throughout this chapter.

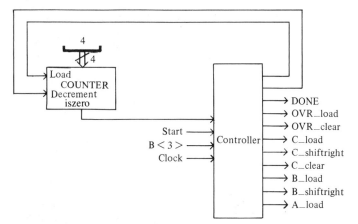

Figure 7.5. Control part of multiplier.

Now, in the RTL description in Figure 7.3, the four distinct steps of the control algorithm are clearly defined. Each of these steps represents a different state of the controller and, as the controller moves from state to state, it is required to produce control signals that will initiate the various actions required at each step. Thus, when the controller perceives the start signal, it is required to produce signals that will cause the various data transfers listed in lines 8 through 12. The controller will respond to the start signal on a rising clock edge (call it rising clock edge number 1), but there will be a propagation delay before the control signals appear at the controller outputs. As a consequence, the registers will only receive the control signals some time after the rising clock edge has passed. It follows that the registers will not respond to the data transfer signals until the next rising clock edge (i.e., rising clock edge number 2).

When rising clock edge number 2 occurs, not only will the *Step1* data transfers take place, but also the controller will respond to the rising edge by moving to *Step2*, thereby producing (if $B\langle 3 \rangle$ is a 1) the control signals to carry out the actions stated in line 19. Note that, once again, these control signals will appear at the controller outputs after a propagation delay and that the registers will only respond to the control signals when rising clock edge number 3 occurs.

The manner in which the system operates can be summarized as follows: the controller generates control signals at the start of a clock cycle and the registers respond to these signals at the start of the next clock cycle.

It is not difficult to see that this mode of operation will allow correct realization of the system described in Figure 7.3. In general, however, when using an RTL to describe a system in which all devices respond to a rising clock edge, the mode of operation must always be borne in mind. As an example, suppose we had the section of RTL description below, with A and B representing 4-bit registers:

Step10:
　begin
　　　　B ← A;
　　　　A ← B;
　　　　on B⟨3⟩ do begin
　　　　　　　．
　　　　　　　．
　　　　　　　．
　　　　end
　end

    The statements $B \leftarrow A$ and $A \leftarrow B$ imply that the contents of registers A and B are to be interchanged. The statement **on** $B\langle 3\rangle$ **do begin** will be followed by a set of actions that are to be carried out if $B\langle 3\rangle$ is a 1. Now note that the system will move into *Step10* on a rising clock edge (call it rising clock edge i) and that it will be rising clock edge $i + 1$ that causes A and B to interchange their contents. The test on the value of $B\langle 3\rangle$ will take place at the time of arrival of rising clock edge $i + 1$ and it will therefore take place before registers A and B have had time to interchange their contents. Thus, the test will be made on the value of $B\langle 3\rangle$ before *Step10* was entered.

    So long as considerations such as this are borne clearly in mind, the RTL can be freely used in situations where all devices respond to a rising clock edge.

    An alternative approach is to use the idea of a two-phase clock where the controller responds to the rising edge of the clock pulse and the registers respond to the trailing edge of the pulse. Inverters can be used in the clock line, where necessary, to cause registers to respond to the trailing edge (recall how this is done in the master-slave flip-flop). In the two-phase clock scheme, both the generation of control signals and the response of registers to the control signals take place in the same clock cycle. This approach can, however, lead to complications and is difficult to implement in our simple RTL. Thus, in this chapter we restrict our attention to the case where all devices respond to a rising clock edge.

    Now that we have established the mode of operation that we want our system to follow, we should check whether this imposes any specific requirements on the incoming signal *Start* and also how it will affect the setting of the flag *Done* when the multiplication is complete.

    Clearly, the *Start* signal must satisfy the set-up and hold times of the controller. We will assume that the *Start* signal is supplied to the controller by a flip-flop that is triggered by the system clock (this is a typical method of synchronizing external inputs with the system clock). With this assumption, it follows that the *Start* signal will arrive at the controller one flip-flop propagation delay after the rising edge of the system clock. It will therefore have to be held for a whole clock period in order to satisfy the set-up and hold times at the controller. The flip-flop supplying the *Start* signal could be cleared on the next clock edge because the flip-flop propagation delay will be sufficient to meet the hold time requirement. The *Start* signal could be held for a longer period, but must be cleared before the multiplication operation is complete.

The flag *Done* will be set one clock cycle after the final values are available on the Product output and will remain set only for one clock cycle. This is because we have associated no storage device with this signal. It is again assumed that the external logic will correctly interpret this signal by sampling it on a rising clock edge.

We are now in a position to identify the types of device necessary to realize the final system.

Device Selection. The process of device selection depends upon the resources available to the designer. In a large organization, the designer may have access to an online database which contains details of all the devices available to the organization. In other circumstances the designer will have to rely on manufacturer's data sheets and catalogs. In either case, the designer draws upon the available resources in order to attempt to match the required characteristics of registers (listed in Table 7.1) with the characteristics of available devices.

For example, Table 7.1 tells us that register A is required to have four input pins, four output pins and a load pin to control the load operation of the register. Consultation of manufacturers' data sheets shows that the 74379 quad D flip-flop is a prime candidate for implementation of this function.

The 74379 has the required 4 input pins along with 4 output pins for reading out the stored 4-bit word. It also has a clock pin and a load pin which enables loading on the next rising clock edge. In addition, there are 4 pins that allow reading out the complement of each of the stored bits which are not needed for our design. It very frequently happens in a digital-system design that some of the pins on a selected device are not required for implementation of the function being realized. In such circumstances, the unused pins have to be taken care of in the appropriate manner. However, the problem of assigning suitable connections to unused pins is an item of detail whose consideration is more suited to a lower level in the (top-down) design process. Thus, we shall return to this matter later.

We experienced no difficulty in locating, within manufacturers' databooks, a device that can be used to provide exactly the behavior required of register A. Indeed, the reader would have little difficulty finding (within a 7400 series catalog) a suitable device for each of the registers listed in Table 7.1. This is because the multiplier we have chosen as our design example is really quite a simple system. In the design of larger and more complex systems, it frequently happens that no device can be found (in manufacturers' catalogs) that will provide the required behavior for a register. In such circumstances, it is necessary to introduce (into the design process) a further level, at which required register behavior is realized by constructing a suitable device from components that *are* available. This is a very important feature of the top-down design process and we wish to illustrate its implementation here. In order to do this, we shall ignore the fact that the required characteristics of registers *B* and *C* can be provided by the 74195 shift register and will proceed as if no suitable device were available for these registers. Thus, the actual implementation of registers *B* and *C* will not be considered at this level in the (top-down) design process and we simply proceed with the process of selecting devices for the remaining registers in Table 7.1.

Register *OVR* can be implemented by means of a 7474 dual D flip-flop. Only one of the two flip-flops in the package will actually be required to realize *OVR*, but design of the multiplier is not yet complete and some use could possibly be found at a later stage for the other flip-flop. For the counter we can use a 74169 in a similar fashion to that in which it was employed in the example of Section 6.2.2.

None of the remaining items in column 1 of Table 7.1 is a register; that is, none is an information storage device. *Multiplier* and *Multiplicand* are data inputs; *Product* is a data output; *Start* is a control input and *Done* is a control output.

The final item in column 1, viz "Add", is simply a 4-bit adder and is available as a 7483.

7.2.2. A Second-Level RTL Description

For purposes of illustration, we have proceeded thus far on the assumption that no suitable devices are available for implementation of registers *B* and *C*. At this point in the design process then, we have selected devices for all registers whose characteristics match those of components which are available (in manufacturer's data sheets). No such match exists for the remaining registers (in this case registers *B* and *C*) and the selection of components for these registers is deferred until the next design level.

Before the next design level is begun, a new RTL description should be produced, giving details of how the selected devices are to carry out the required operations. This description will incorporate details of the interconnection scheme for the various devices. Some schemes exist for achieving this automatically, e.g., DAA [2], but these require vast computing resources. With our bare-bones RTL scheme this work has to be done by the user. Although our RTL scheme does not provide a great deal of automation in the design process, it *does* constrain the designer to follow the basic rules of top-down design.

To obtain the second level RTL description, we return to the first-level description and "fill out" the statements in Figure 7.3 to accommodate the devices selected for the various registers.

The registers in Figure 7.3, at the new level of description, are now defined as modules, just as the multiplier itself was defined as a module at the previous level of description.

The new level of description is shown in Figure 7.6. Note that line 2 in Figure 7.3 has been replaced by lines 2 through 11 in Figure 7.6. Lines 2 through 6 specify the types of devices that we intend to use†, including any that still have to be designed (in this case we still have to design a device‡ with the characteristics of registers B and C, and this we have called module *Shifter* in line 3). Lines 7 through 11 show how many of each device type are required, by associating register names with each type. For instance, we require one 74379 corresponding to register A and two *Shifters* corresponding to registers B and C, and so on.

The parameter lists associated with each device in lines 2 through 6 of Figure 7.6 detail the terminals that we wish to use on each of the selected devices. For instance, with device 74379 we wish to use 4 input pins, 4 output pins, a load-pin and a clock pin.

The keyword **external** following a module declaration indicates that a detailed description of the module is to be found elsewhere. Either it can be found in a databook (or database) or it will become available at the next level of design (as is the case with the module *Shifter*).

Lines 3 and 4 of Figure 7.3 appear (unchanged) as lines 12 and 13 in Figure 7.6. Line 5 of Figure 7.3 appears as line 14 in Figure 7.6 and has undergone one small change. At this lower level of description, we specify that the output pins of registers B and C are to be used to provide the product and this is done by appending __out to each of the register names. We use the underscore (__) character to separate the component name from the set of terminals being referenced on the component. Note that since *Product* is a set of terminals and not a component, then we do not (indeed, cannot) use the underscore form of reference for this item.

Lines 6 and 7 in Figure 7.3 appear (unchanged) as lines 15 and 16 in Figure 7.6. Lines 8 through 12 in Figure 7.3 do change and appear as lines 17 through 21 in Figure 7.6. Lines 17 through 19 state that the counter and registers A and B are to be loaded (via their respective *load*-control pins) with the data which is assumed to be available at their inputs when the start signal arrives.¶ Similarly lines 20 and 21 indicate the necessity to clear registers *OVR* and C.

In *Step2*, line 28 of Figure 7.6, which states "**activate** C__load", implies

---

† The M preceding each device number is there to indicate that some further modification will be required at the next level of detail (e.g. to account for unused input pins on the devices selected).
‡ We can use the same device to realize both B and C because their characteristics only differ to the extent that C requires a clear pin and B does not.
¶ Table 7.1 shows that the *counter* and registers A and B are only required to load data from a single source and this implies that their data inputs can be permanently connected to the constant 0100, the *Multiplicand* and the *Multiplier* respectively.

```
1          module multiplier(Multiplier<0:3>, Multiplicand<0:3>,
                            Product<0:7>, Start, Done, clock);

2             module M74379(in<0:3>, out<0:3>, load, clock);
                 external;
3             module Shifter(in<0:3>, out<0:3>, load, shiftright,
                            shiftin, clear, clock);
                 external;
4             module M7474(in, out, load, clear, clock);
                 external;
5             module M74169(in<0:3>, load, decrement, iszero, clock);
                 external;
6             module M7483(in1<0:3>, in2<0:3>, out<0:3>, carryout);
                 external;

7             component M74379  A;
8             component Shifter B, C;
9             component M7474   OVR;
10            component M74169  counter;
11            component M7483    Adder;

12            state Step1, Step2, Step3, Step4;

13            begin
14                   Product ← C_out @ B_out;
15                   Step1:
16                       on Start do begin
17                           activate counter_load;
18                           activate A_load;
19                           activate B_load;
20                           activate OVR_clear;
21                           activate C_clear;
22                           goto Step2
23                       end else
24                           goto Step1;

25                   Step2:
26                       begin
27                           on B_out<3> do begin
28                               activate C_load;
29                               activate OVR_load
30                           end;
31                           goto Step3
32                       end;

33                   Step3:
34                       begin
35                           activate B_shiftright;
36                           activate C_shiftright;
37                           activate counter_decrement;
38                           goto Step4
39                       end;

40                   Step4:
41                       begin
42                           activate OVR_clear;
43                           on counter_iszero do begin
44                               activate Done;
45                               goto Step1
```

Figure 7.6. Second level RTL description of the multiplier.

```
46                              end else
47                                  goto Step2
48                      end;

49                      A_in ← Multiplicand;
50                      B_in ← Multiplier;
51                      C_in ← Adder_out;
52                      Adder_in1 ← C_out;
53                      Adder_in2 ← A_out;
54                      OVR_in ← Adder_carryout;
55                      B_shiftin ← C_out<3>;
56                      C_shiftin ← OVR_out;
57                      counter_in ← 4 % 4;
58                      B_clear ← 0
59                      A_clock ← clock;
60                      B_clock ← clock;
61                      C_clock ← clock;
62                      OVR_clock ← clock;
63                      counter_clock ← clock
64          end { multiplier }
65      $
```

Figure 7.6. (*Continued*)

that the addition operation $C + A$ is to be carried out because it is understood
(see Figure 7.4) that a permanent connection exists between the outputs of registers C and A and the inputs to the *Adder*. Similarly, line 29 of Figure 7.6
indicates that the carry output of the *Adder*, i.e., *Adder_carryout*, is to be
loaded into register *OVR*.

Step3 in Figure 7.6 follows directly from *Step3* in Figure 7.3. The only significant difference is that in the second level RTL description the required operations are expressed in terms of the actual application of control signals to
device terminals.

In *Step4* the one significant point to note is that the variable *Done*, which
represents an output terminal of the multiplier, has to take on the value 1 at the
completion of the multiplication process. *Done* will return to 0 upon the return
to *Step1*.

The remaining statements in the description, viz, 49 through 63, simply define the permanent connections within the data part of the system. Line 57
indicates that the input to *counter* should be permanently connected to the constant 4. Lines 59 through 63 indicate the connection of the clock to those devices which require it.

7.2.3. A Third-Level RTL Description

At the completion of the second-level description, we have identified the device
types that we intend to use for four of the registers. For each of these devices,
there still remains the problem of specifying connections to the inputs so far
unused. In addition, of course, we still have to carry out the design of registers
B and C.

```
1          module M74379(in<0:3>, out<0:3>, load, clock);

2            module D74379(in<0:3>, out<0:3>, outcomp<0:3>,
                        load, clock);
               external;

3            component D74379 temp;

4            begin
5                temp_in ← in;
6                out ← temp_out;
7                temp_clock ← clock;
8                temp_load ← load
9            end { M74379 }
10     $
```

Figure 7.7a. RTL description of the 74379 device.

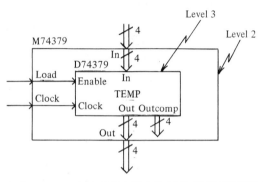

Figure 7.7b. Block diagram representation of second level description of 74379 device.

We will commence the third level of the design process by completing the interconnection details for the four registers whose device types have already been selected.

Completion of the Description of Register A. Figure 7.7(a) shows the final specification for register A which is realized by means of a 74379 chip. Line 1 gives the module name as it appeared in the second-level description (line 2 of Figure 7.6). In the second-level description, the parameter list contained only the terminals of the 74379 that were pertinent to the problem in hand. Line 2 of Figure 7.7(a) lists the full set of pins (other than the power-supply pins) for the 74379.† The keyword **external** indicates that full information on the 74379 is not contained in our description, but is to be found elsewhere. Here, our only concern is to ensure that terminals on the 74379 that

---

†The D preceding the device number in line 2 indicates that at this level we are dealing with the complete device. It is included because the compiler expects the first symbol of a module name to be an alphabetic character. All D devices are commercially available and their internal descriptions need not be given.

were not included in the second-level description are now properly accounted for.

In line 3, the fact that we are concerned with only the one 74379 device is indicated and the device has been given the name *temp*.

To appreciate the significance of lines 5 through 8 requires reference to Figure 7.7(b). The outer box in the figure represents the second level of description (i.e., the M74379). The inner box represents the device we are now using to create the M74379. This device (the D74379) has the connections *in*, *out*, *clock* and *load* in common with the M74379, the only difference being that the load operation will be carried out using the enable pin on the actual 74379 device. The fact that the enable is active "low" will be accounted for when we design the controller. Figure 7.7(b) indicates also that the complementary outputs on the D74379 are not required for the M74379.

Completion of the Specification for Register Counter.

The final specification for the register *counter* is shown in Figure 7.8(a). For reasons that are explained below, an inverter is required in the realization of the M74169. We have chosen to obtain this inverter from a 7404 Hex inverter package, whose full set of input and output pins are listed in line 3 of Figure 7.8(a). The meaning of lines 1 through 6 should not require further explanation. Lines 7 through 12 detail connections that are common to M74169 and D74169 (see Figure 7.8(b)). Note that line 9 indicates that a signal from the controller to decrement the counter is fed to the enableP pin. The datasheet on the 74169 shows that this signal should be a "low" and that it will have the desired effect so long as the enableT and Up/Down pins of the device are also set low; this is accounted for in lines 13 and 14.

An inverter is required between the *ripplecarryout* of the D74169 and the *iszero* terminal on the M74169 (refer again to Figure 7.8(b)). The reason for this is that the 74169 produces a 0 on the *ripplecarryout* when the contents of the counter reach zero. Referring back to the first-level RTL description (Figure 7.3), we see from line 33 of the description

$$\text{on } counter = 0 \text{ do begin}$$

that the actions to be carried out once the count reaches 0 depend upon the *counter* = 0 signal being "on". Throughout our RTL description we have assumed that "on" corresponds to "positive", so that a 1 is required from *M*74169 to indicate that the count has reached zero.

Lines 7 through 12 of the description show the interconnection of the various control signals and the inverter. Lines 13 and 14 of the description specify two pins on the *D*74169 that should be permanently connected to 0.

```
1        module M74169(in<0:3>, out<0:3>, load, decrement, iszero, clock);

2            module D74169(in<0:3>, out<0:3>, load, clock, updown,
                               enableT, enableP, ripplecarryout);
                  external;

3            module D7404(in1, out1, in2, out2, in3, out3, in4, out4,
                               in5, out5, in6, out6);
                  external;

4            component D74169 temp;
5            component D7404 inverter;

6            begin
7                temp_in ← in;
8                temp_load ← load;
9                temp_enableP ← decrement;
10               temp_clock ← clock;
11               inverter_in1 ← temp_ripplecarryout;
12               iszero ← inverter_out1;
13               temp_enableT ← 0;
14               temp_updown ← 0
15           end { M74169 }
16       $
```

Figure 7.8a. RTL description of the 74169 device.

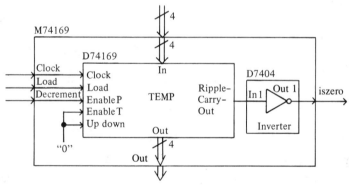

Figure 7.8b. Block diagram representation of second level description of 74169 device.

Completion of the Specification for Device "Add".

Figure 7.9(a) details the final specification for device *add*. It should be clear to the reader that the only extra measure taken for this device at this level is to set the *carryin* terminal to 0 (see Figure 7.9(b)).

Completion of the Specification for Register OVR.

The final specification for register *OVR* is shown in Figure 7.10(a). This specification appears quite complex, especially when it is recalled that our original intention was to use a single-delay flip-flop (the 7474) for register *OVR*. The reason for the complexity here lies in the fact that simple flip-flops do not have load pins and, without proper care, this can lead to timing problems.

```
1           module M7483(in1<0:3>, in2<0:3>, out<0:3>, carryout);

2             module D7483(in1<0:3>, in2<0:3>, out<0:3>,
                           carryin, carryout);
              external;

3             component D7483  plus;

4             begin
5                 plus_in1 ← in1;
6                 plus_in2 ← in2;
7                 out ← plus_out;
8                 carryout ← plus_carryout;
9                 plus_carryin ← 0
10            end { M7483 }
11        $
```

Figure 7.9a. RTL description of the 7483 device.

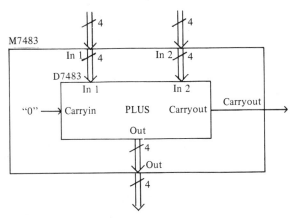

Figure 7.9b. Block diagram representation of second level description of 7483 device.

Recall that our design approach is based upon the idea that on a given rising clock edge (call it rising clock edge i) the controller begins to produce control signals for the implementation of data transfers between registers *at the time of rising edge $i + 1$*. These control signals arrive at the registers well before the arrival of rising clock edge $i + 1$, but they have no effect on the contents of the register until the clock edge arrives so long as they are fed to synchronous inputs such as load or enable.

Since an ordinary flip-flop has neither load nor enable inputs, we require some means of instructing the 7474 to "load" on the next rising clock edge. It might be thought that the simple arrangement shown in Figure 7.10(b) would provide a solution (for "active high" load signals). The load signal will arrive at the AND gate after some propagation delay following the rising edge of the clock and when it arrives, the clock signal will still be high, causing a rising edge at the clock input of the 7474. However, at this time, the 7474 may not

```
1          module M7474(in, out, clear, load, clock);

2              module D7474(in1, out1, outcomp1, clock1, clear1, preset1,
                              in2, out2, outcomp2, clock2, clear2, preset2);
                   external;

3              module D7402(in1a, in1b, out1, in2a, in2b, out2,
                              in3a, in3b, out3, in4a, in4b, out4);
                   external;

4              module D7404(in1, out1, in2, out2, in3, out3, in4, out4,
                              in5, out5, in6, out6);
                   external;

5              module D7410(in1a, in1b, in1c, out1, in2a, in2b, in2c, out2,
                              in3a, in3b, in3c, out3);
                   external;

6              component D7474 flipflop;
7              component D7402 orgate;
8              component D7404 inverter;
9              component D7410 andgate;

10             begin
11                 inverter_in1 ← clear;
12                 andgate_in1a ← inverter_out1;
13                 andgate_in1b ← load;
14                 andgate_in1c ← in;
15                 orgate_in1a ← clear;
16                 orgate_in1b ← load;
17                 flipflop_in1 ← orgate_out1;
18                 inverter_in2 ← clock;
19                 flipflop_clock1 ← inverter_out2;
20                 andgate_in2a ← flipflop_out1;
21                 andgate_in2b ← clock;
22                 andgate_in2c ← 1;
23                 flipflop_in2 ← flipflop_out1;
24                 flipflop_clock2 ← andgate_out2;
25                 out ← flipflop_out2;
26                 clear1 ← 1;
27                 clear2 ← 1;
28                 preset1 ← 1;
29                 preset2 ← 1
30             end { M7474 }
31         $
```

Figure 7.10a. RTL description of the 7474 device.

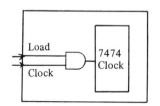

Figure 7.10b. An infeasible approach to the loading of the 7474 device.

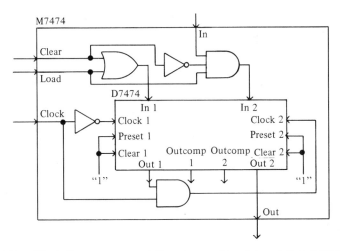

Figure 7.10c. Block diagram representation of second level description of 7474 device.

have the correct data established at its input and so an alternative configuration (inevitably more complex) must be sought.

A suitable circuit arrangement is shown in Figure 7.10(c). This and similar configurations are often used in complex chips to prevent spurious clocking of registers when an enable signal changes.

Note that with this configuration, we will be realizing register *OVR* using both of the D flip-flops in the 7474 package.

Consider first the circuitry associated with flip-flop number 2 (call it FF_2) in Figure 7.10(c). This is the flip-flop that generates the output for the M7474 and so we need to check that it will load and clear correctly. Note first that if input *clear* is a 1, the 3-input AND gate will have a 0 output and this will indeed clear FF_2 on the next rising clock edge. If, on the other hand, the input *load* is a 1 (and we assume that in this circumstance *clear* will be a 0†) then the input to FF_2 will be the value of input *in* and this will be transferred to the output on the next rising clock edge.

Thus, to verify that the circuit will operate correctly, all we need to do now is ensure that FF_2 is clocked at the correct time. In the circuit of Figure 7.10(c) this has been achieved by using the idea of a two-phase clock. FF_1 is clocked with the inverse of the clock waveform and hence responds to the trailing edge of the clock pulse. By the time the trailing edge occurs, the controller will have settled to its required state so that the signals *clear* and *load* will be at their

---

†Ensuring that this is so belongs to the control part of the problem and will be dealt with after completion of the data part.

correct levels. If either is at level 1, the input to FF_1 will be a 1 and, after the trailing edge of the clock, the output will go to 1. This ensures that FF_2 will be clocked on the next rising clock edge, because of the way the output of FF_1 is "gated" with the clock signal.

The reader should now have no difficulty in interpreting the RTL description in Figure 7.10(a). Standard chips have been chosen for the AND and OR gates, with inverters being available from the 7404 package already employed in the realization of register *counter*.

Design of Shifter (for Registers B and C).   Table 7.1 lists the required functions of registers B and C. Both registers are required to be able to load a 4-bit quantity, their contents must be accessible for reading in parallel, and it has to be possible to shift their contents one bit to the right. In addition, it must be possible to clear the contents of register C. Obviously the two registers are very similar in function and so, for economy, we will design a single device that can be used for both.

We have already noted that a shift register exists that might be used to implement the functions of registers B and C (the 74195), but we are here attempting to demonstrate the basic principles of RTL-based top-down design and the design of devices capable of implementing the functions required of registers B and C provides a convenient illustration.

As a starting point, we note that the shift-right operation can be specified using our RTL (in terms of an arbitrary 4-bit register X) as

$$X\langle 1:3 \rangle \leftarrow X\langle 0:2 \rangle$$

$$X\langle 0 \rangle \leftarrow shiftin$$

The first statement indicates that the entries 1 through 3 in X are to be replaced by entries 0 through 2 and the second statement indicates that entry 0 in X is to receive the *shiftin* bit.

The two statements indicate that the shift right operation can be carried out on register X by reading the three bits $X\langle 0:2 \rangle$ and feeding them back to the $X\langle 1:3 \rangle$ input terminals. If, in addition, the *shiftin* bit is presented to the $X\langle 0 \rangle$ input terminal, then implementation of the load operation would complete the task. This is illustrated in Figure 7.11.

Now note that in *Step1* of Figure 7.3, register B is required to be loaded with the *Multiplier* and in *Step2*, register C is to be loaded with the output of the adder. According to the first- and second-level RTL descriptions these are the only load operations to be carried out on the two registers. In *Step3*, both B and C are required to undergo a shift-right operation; we have just seen that this can be implemented by means of feedback and a load operation. With the use of this implementation, the full set of operations to be carried out by registers B and C can be accomplished by the structure shown in Figure 7.12.

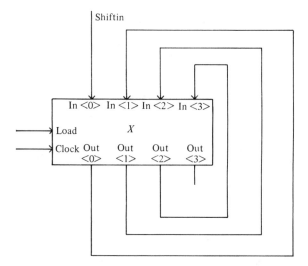

Figure 7.11. A method of implementing the shift-right operation.

The idea behind Figure 7.12 stems from the fact that registers B and C are each required to carry out load operations from two different sources at different steps in the multiplication process. One is the load operation specified in the first- and second-level RTL descriptions and the other is the load operation we have just introduced for carrying out the shift-right operation. A multiplexer can be used for selecting the correct source for the two load operations. The *shiftright* signal can be used as the selector signal for the multiplexer because, when it is asserted, the multiplexer will select input 1 and, with the *shiftright* signal also connected to the *load* terminal of register X (through the OR gate), the register will load from the appropriate source.

We have assumed that the controller never asserts the *shiftright* and *load* signals at the same time so that, when the "external" load signal is asserted in Figure 7.12, the *shiftright* signal is low and the external data will be fed to register X through input 0 of the multiplexer. The requirement for a clear input (recall that register C has to be cleared in *Step1*) can also be handled using the multiplexer. This can be achieved because most multiplexers have a strobe input which, when fed a logic 1, causes all the multiplexer outputs to take on the value 0 irrespective of the select signal or data inputs. By connection of the *clear* signal to the *load* pin of X through the OR gate as shown in Figure 7.12 and by the additional connection of the *clear* signal to the strobe input on the multiplexer, register X will be cleared when the *clear* signal takes the value 1. The controller is, of course, assumed to assert one and only one of the inputs to the 3-input OR gate at any given time. The problem of ensuring that suitable control signals are available constitutes the control part of the problem and it will be discussed after the completion of the data part.

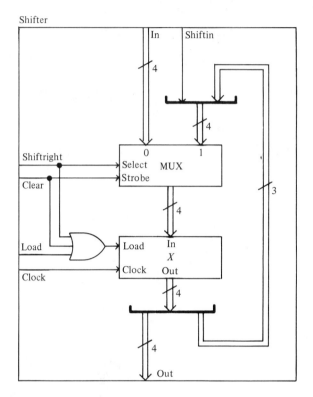

Figure 7.12. Block diagram of the Shifter device.

Device Selection. Figure 7.12 indicates that the devices we have to select for register *Shifter* are a multiplexer and the register *X*.

For register *X*, the 74379 (selected earlier for register *A*) has the required characteristics. As before, we will not require the complemented output of the device and so we can use the 74379 as in Figure 7.7. For the multiplexer, a quad 2-to-1 line MUX is needed and the 74157 is a suitable device. In this application, all input and output pins of the 74157 will be required, so we declare this as a D74157 (in line 3 of Figure 7.13(a)).

Selection of the 74379 for register X enforces us to modify slightly the design of the shifter depicted in Figure 7.12. This modification is necessary because the load pin on the 74379 is activated by a logic 0 and the arrangement in Figure 7.12 assumes that a logic 1 is required to initiate the load operation. This situation can be rectified by simply replacing the OR gate in Figure 7.12 by a NOR gate. The resulting arrangement is shown in Figure 7.13(b) which indicates that a 7427 chip is to provide the NOR gate. This is shown more explicitly in the RTL description in Figure 7.13(a) where the NOR gate is declared in line

```
1          module Shifter(in<0:3>, out<0:3>, load, shiftright,
                             shiftin, clear,clock);

2              module D74379(in<0:3>, out<0:3>, outcomp<0:3>, load, clock);
                  external;

3              module D74157(in0<0:3>, in1<0:3>, out<0:3>, select, strobe);
                  external;

4              module D7427(in1a,in1b,in1c,out1,in2a,in2b,in2c,out2,
                             in3a,in3b,in3c,out3);
                  external;

5              component D74379 X;
6              component D74157 MUX;
7              component D7427 gate1;

8              begin
9                    MUX_in0 ← in;
10                   MUX_in1 ← shiftin @ X<0:2>;
11                   X_in ← MUX_out;
12                   MUX_select ← shiftright;
13                   MUX_strobe ← clear;
14                   out ← X_out;
15                   X_load ← gate1_out;
16                   gate1_in1a ← shiftright;
17                   gate1_in1b← clear;
18                   gate1_in1c← load;
19                   X_clock ← clock;
20           end { Shifter }
21       $
```

Figure 7.13a. RTL description of the Shifter device.

4 as device D7427. The 7427 chip contains three 3-input NOR gates and only one of them is used here.

In line 10 of Figure 7.13(a) the symbol @, representing concatenation (and used earlier in Figure 7.3), has been employed.

Recall that register *Shifter* has been designed to implement both register *B* and register *C*. For these two registers, we have not yet specified the connection required for the *clear* pin. Rather than go to a further level in our RTL description in order to specify this connection (as we should do strictly) we simply point out that the *clear* pin on register *C* will be connected to the controller (so that *C* can be cleared in *Step1* of the algorithm) and the *clear* pin on register *B* will be connected to logic 0 (because there is no requirement to clear *B*).

The data part of the specifications has now been completed. All necessary devices have been selected and the interconnection scheme has been specified. We must now turn to the design of the control part.

7.2.4. Design of the Controller

The first-level RTL description of the multiplier (Figure 7.3) was drawn up on the assumption that the multiplication algorithm should involve four distinct

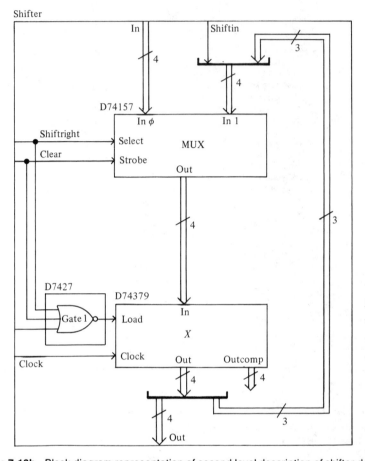

Figure 7.13b. Block diagram representation of second level description of shifter device.

steps. No further steps were introduced at lower levels of the description, so we infer that the controller should have four distinct states. We commence the design of the controller by drawing up a state-table description.

The second-level RTL description (Figure 7.6) contains all the information we need to draw up the state table for the controller (lower-level descriptions are concerned with the internal workings of individual devices). As a first step, we identify all the inputs to the controller (apart from the clock). These inputs are given in Figure 7.6 by the expressions appearing between the keywords **on** and **do.** Thus, Figure 7.6 tells us that the controller requires inputs *Start*, *B_out* $\langle 3 \rangle$, and *counter__iszero* (from lines 16, 27, and 43 respectively). This information allows us to fill out the first four columns of the state table shown in Table 7.2.

The outputs of the controller are determined by identifying the control signals

Table 7.2. Controller state table.

Current state	Start	B_out<3>	counter_is_zero	Next state	counter_load	A_load	B_load	C_load	OVR_load	C_clear	OVR_clear	B_shift	C_shift	counter_decrement	Done
Step1	0	x	x	Step1	1	1	0	0	0	0	0	0	0	1	0
Step1	1	x	x	Step2	0	0	1	0	0	1	1	0	0	1	0
Step2	x	0	x	Step3	1	1	0	0	0	0	0	0	0	1	0
Step2	x	1	x	Step3	1	1	0	1	1	0	0	0	0	1	0
Step3	x	x	x	Step4	1	1	0	0	0	0	0	1	1	0	0
Step4	x	x	0	Step2	1	1	0	0	0	0	1	0	0	1	0
Step4	x	x	1	Step1	1	1	0	0	0	0	1	0	0	1	1

required from the controller to the various devices in the data part of the multiplier. These control signals all appear in Figure 7.6 following the keyword **activate**. Thus the controller is required to have 11 distinct outputs and these are represented in the state table by the 11 (right-hand) columns labelled *counter__load* through *Done* in Table 7.2. The entries in these columns are determined from the fact that in three cases, the controller is required to output a 0 in order to initiate a particular action; these cases are *counter__load*, *counter__decrement* and *A__load*. In the other eight cases, the required signal is a 1.

The only remaining task is setting up the state table to specify the "next-state" entries. This is achieved by scanning lines 15 through 48 in Figure 7.6 and, for each state in turn, noting the state labels that appear after the keyword **goto**; each of these state labels is entered in the "next-state" column of the state table in the row corresponding to the appropriate input conditions. Thus, in Table 7.2, the first row indicates that when the controller is in state *Step1* and when *Start* is 0, the next state will be *Step1* (note that the other two inputs have no effect on this). This information is obtained from lines 16, 23 and 24 of Figure 7.6. Similarly lines 16 and 22 contain the information we need to complete row 2 of Table 7.2; these lines tell us that when the controller is in *Step1* and *Start* is 1, the next state is *Step2*. The remaining rows of the state table are completed in a similar fashion.

Several of the output columns in Table 7.2 are identical, implying that the controller is required to provide identical signals to different devices in the data part of the system. For instance, the controller is required to provide identical output signals to *B__load* and *C__clear*. Obviously there is no need to provide

Table 7.3. Reduced state table for controller.

	C S $u t$ $r a$ $r t$ $e e$ n t	S t a r t	B _ o u t $<$ 3 $>$	c i $o s$ $u z$ $n e$ $t r$ $e o$ r _	N S $e t$ $x a$ $t t$ e	Z < 0 >	Z < 1 >	Z < 2 >	Z < 3 >	Z < 4 >
A	00	0	x	x	00	0	0	0	0	0
B	00	1	x	x	01	1	0	1	0	0
C	01	x	0	x	11	0	0	0	0	0
D	01	x	1	x	11	0	1	0	0	0
E	11	x	x	x	10	0	0	0	1	0
F	10	x	x	0	01	0	0	1	0	0
G	10	x	x	1	00	0	0	1	0	1

where the correspondence between the new outputs and the previous outputs is given by:

$Z<0>$	B_Load, C_clear
$\overline{Z<0>}$	counter_load, A_Load
$Z<1>$	C_load, OVR_load
$Z<2>$	OVR_clear
$Z<3>$	B_shiftright, C_shiftright
$\overline{Z<3>}$	counter_decrement
$Z<4>$	Done

and the state encoding is given by:

Step1	00
Step2	01
Step3	11
Step4	10

a separate controller output for each of these and the state table can be simplified by merging the two columns B__load and C__clear to form a single column which we will call $Z\langle 0 \rangle$ (see Table 7.3). Now note that the columns counter__load and A__load have identical entries and that these are simply the complements of the entries in columns B__load and C__clear. Consequently, the control signals required for counter__load and A__load can be obtained from the controller output $Z\langle 0 \rangle$ by use of an inverter.

Thus we see that a single controller output, which we have called $Z\langle 0 \rangle$, can be used to provide control signals for four devices in the data part of the problem. Further simplifications are also possible. Device inputs C__load and OVR__load can be fed from the same controller output which we will call $Z\langle 1 \rangle$.

And similarly the device inputs *B__shiftright* and *C__shiftright* can be fed from a single controller output that we have called $Z\langle 3 \rangle$. *Counter__decrement* can be obtained by inverting $Z\langle 3 \rangle$.

Taking all these factors into account, we obtain a simplified state table which has only 5 output columns, as shown in Table 7.3. Table 7.3 also indicates a state assignment (arbitrarily chosen) that has been made for the four controller states.

Controller Implementation.   In Chapter 6, several methods of implementing a controller were described. For simplicity here we will use a ROM. With this choice we do not have to concern ourselves with optimal state assignment because different assignments will not affect the size of the ROM required. This is why an arbitrary state assignment was made in Table 7.3.

Figure 7.14 shows a block diagram of the controller using a ROM realization. The fact that the controller has four states implies that we will require two flip-flops to hold the state information. These flip-flops make up what is commonly called the *state sequence register (SSR)* and this is indicated in Figure 7.14 along with the ROM which is seen to require 5 inputs and 7 outputs. Note that the outputs $Z\langle 0 \rangle$ through $Z\langle 4 \rangle$ of Table 7.3 are assigned to the output pins *out* $\langle 0 \rangle$ through *out* $\langle 4 \rangle$ of the controller in Figure 7.14, with $\overline{Z\langle 0 \rangle}$ and $\overline{Z\langle 3 \rangle}$

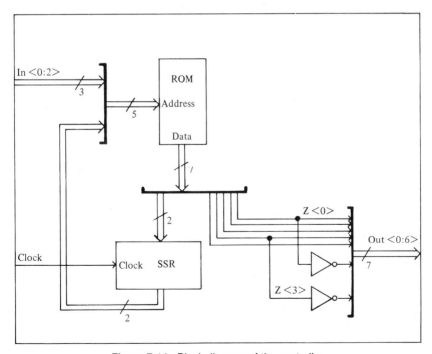

Figure 7.14. Block diagram of the controller.

```
1      module controller(in<0:2>, out<0:6>, clock);

2         module ssr(in<0:1>, out<0:1>, clock);

3            module D7474(in1, out1, outcomp1, clock1, clear1, preset1,
                          in2, out2, outcomp2, clock2, clear2, preset2);
                external;

4            component D7474 temp;

5            begin
6                temp_in1 @ temp_in2 ← in;
7                out ← temp_out1 @ temp_out2;
8                temp_clock1 ← clock;
9                temp_clock2 ← clock;
10               temp_clear1 ← 1;
11               temp_clear2 ← 1;
12               temp_preset1 ← 1;
13               temp_preset2 ← 1
14           end; { ssr }

15        module M74S188(in<0:4>, out<0:6>);

16           module D74S188(in<0:4>, out<0:7>, enable);
                external;

17           component D74S188 fsm;

18           begin
19               fsm_in ← in;
20               out ← fsm_out<0:6>;
21               fsm_enable ← 0
22           end; { M74S188 }

23        module D7404(in1, out1, in2, out2, in3, out3, in4, out4,
                        in5, out5, in6, out6);
              external;

24        component ssr      SSR;
25        component M74S188 PROM;
26        component D7404 inverter;

27        begin
28            PROM_in<0:2> ← in;
29            PROM_in<3:4> ← SSR_out;
30            SSR_in ← PROM_out<5:6>;
31            SSR_clock ← clock;
32            out<0:4> ← PROM_out<0:4>;
33            inverter_in1 ← out<0>;
34            inverter_in2 ← out<3>;
35            out<5> ← inverter_out1;
36            out<6> ← inverter_out2
37        end { controller }
38   $
```

Figure 7.15a. RTL description of controller.

Address	Row	Data	Address	Row	Data
00000	A	0000000	10000	F	0100100
00001	A	0000000	10001	G	0000101
00010	A	0000000	10010	F	0100100
00011	A	0000000	10011	G	0000101
00100	B	0110100	10100	F	0100100
00101	B	0110100	10101	G	0000101
00110	B	0110100	10110	F	0100100
00111	B	0110100	10111	G	0000101
01000	C	1100000	11000	E	1000010
01001	C	1100000	11001	E	1000010
01010	D	1101000	11010	E	1000010
01011	D	1101000	11011	E	1000010
01100	C	1100000	11100	E	1000010
01101	C	1100000	11101	E	1000010
01110	D	1101000	11110	E	1000010
01111	D	1101000	11111	E	1000010

Figure 7.15b. Contents of ROM for controller implementation.

assigned to the controller output pins $out\langle 5 \rangle$ and $out\langle 6 \rangle$ respectively. Note also that the SSR is driven by an external clock signal (specified in line 1 of Figure 7.3).

Our next task is to select the two devices making up the controller, i.e., the ROM and the SSR. The ROM we require must have at least 5 inputs and 7 outputs (i.e., a 32 × 7 ROM). From inspection of manufacturer's data sheets we determine that a 74S188 (32 × 8) 256-bit TTL ROM will suit our task. The extra output on this ROM will not be used. The SSR can be realized using a 7474 dual D flip-flop. We also require a 7404 to supply the two inverters needed to realize $\overline{Z\langle 0 \rangle}$ and $\overline{Z\langle 3 \rangle}$. The RTL description of these three devices is given in Figure 7.15(a).

Lines 2 through 14 of Figure 7.15(a) describe the implementation of the SSR. Note that in line 2 the inputs and outputs of the module *ssr* are described in terms of a 2-bit vector rather than in terms of individual inputs to each of the flip-flops in the 7474 package. We have done this because we feel that it is more logical to think of the transfer of state information in terms of a single entity, rather than in terms of two separate bits of information. The relationship between the inputs of module *ssr* and the two input terminals of the 7474 package is then expressed in line 6 in the single transfer statement

$$temp\_in\,1 \,@\, temp\_in\,2 \leftarrow in;$$

Note that *temp* is the name given to component *D7474* in line 4. The symbol @ is the concatenation operator and the transfer statement above states that *temp__in1* and *temp__in2* are to be treated as a 2-bit terminal with the following

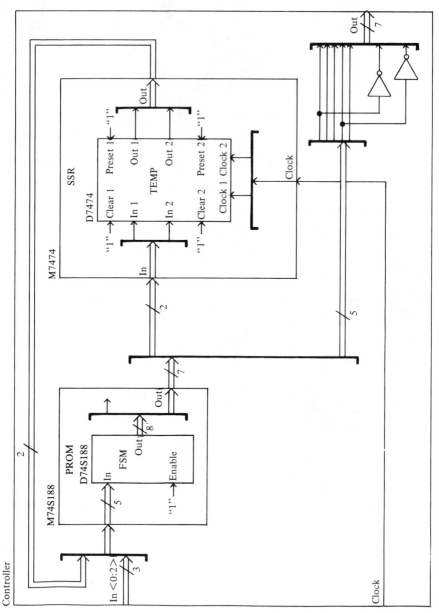

Figure 7.15c. Block diagram of second-level description of controller.

```
1          module multiplier(Multiplier<0:3>, Multiplicand<0:3>,
2                                    Product<0:7>, Start, Done, clock);

3              module M74175(in<0:3>, out<0:3>, load, clock);
4                  external;
5              module Shifter(in<0:3>, out<0:3>, load, shiftright,
6                                    shiftin, clear, clock);
7                  external;
8              module M7474(in, out, load, clear, clock);
9                  external;
10             module M74169(in<0:3>, load, decrement, iszero, clock);
11                 external;
12             module M7483(in1<0:3>, in2<0:3>, out<0:3>, carryout);
13                 external;
14             module controller(in<0:2>, out<0:6>, clock);
15                 external;

16             component M74175      A;
17             component Shifter     B, C;
18             component M7474       OVR;
19             component M74169      counter;
20             component M7483       Adder;
21             component controller  Control;

22             begin
23                     Product ← C_out @ B_out;
24                     A_in ← Multiplicand;
25                     B_in ← Multiplier;
26                     C_in ← Adder_out;
27                     Adder_in1 ← C_out;
28                     Adder_in2 ← A_out;
29                     OVR_in ← Adder_carryout;
30                     B_shiftin ← C_out<3>;
31                     C_shiftin ← OVR_out;
32                     counter_in ← 4 % 4;
33                     Control_in<0> ← Start;
34                     Control_in<1> ← B_out<3>;
35                     Control_in<2> ← counter_iszero;
36                     A_load ← Control_out<5>;
37                     B_load ← Control_out<0>;
38                     C_load ← Control_out<1>;
39                     counter_load ← Control_out<5>;
40                     C_clear ← Control_out<0>;
41                     OVR_load ← Control_out<1>;
42                     OVR_clear ← Control_out<2>;
43                     B_shiftright ← Control_out<3>;
44                     C_shiftright ← Control_out<3>;
45                     counter_decrement ← Control_out<6>;
46                     Done ← Control_out<4>;
47                     B_clear ← 0;
48                     A_clock ← clock;
49                     B_clock ← clock;
50                     C_clock ← clock;
51                     OVR_clock ← clock;
52                     counter_clock ← clock;
53                     Control_clock ← clock
54             end { multiplier }
55     $
```

Figure 7.16. Final RTL description of multiplier.

414 LOGIC DESIGN WITH PASCAL: COMPUTER-AIDED DESIGN TECHNIQUES

individual connections:

$$temp\_in\ 1\ \leftarrow\ in\langle\,0\,\rangle;$$

$$temp\_in\ 2\ \leftarrow\ in\langle\,1\,\rangle;$$

Line 7 of Figure 7.15(a) has a similar meaning, indicating that *temp_out1* and *temp_out2* are connected, respectively, to *out*⟨ 0 ⟩ and *out*⟨ 1 ⟩ of module *ssr*. Lines 8 and 9 specify that the clock input to the SSR is connected to each of the clock inputs of the 7474 package, i.e., the two flip-flops share the same clock source. Lines 10 through 13 specify the connections needed for the clear and preset pins of the 7474. These pins will not play any role in the operation of the controller, and by setting them all high (rather than leaving them unconnected or "floating") we avoid any possible problems through noise pickup.

The ROM connections are specified in lines 15 through 22 of Figure 7.15(a). Line 20 expresses the fact that only seven of the ROM outputs are to be used; the eighth will be left unconnected.

Lines 28 through 36 detail the connections required between the inputs and the outputs of the controller and the ROM and between the ROM and the SSR. Lines 33 through 36 detail the connections of *out*⟨ 0 ⟩ and *out*⟨ 3 ⟩ (corresponding to $Z\langle 0 \rangle$ and $Z\langle 3 \rangle$ of Table 7.3) to inverters to derive the signals *out*⟨ 5 ⟩ and *out*⟨ 6 ⟩ respectively (corresponding to $\overline{Z\langle 0 \rangle}$ and $\overline{Z\langle 3 \rangle}$ in Table 7.3).

Figure 7.15(b) shows the ROM contents which are derived directly from the state table given in Table 7.3. The column headed "ROW" has been included for ease of comparison—it indicates the row in the state table to which each address and data entry corresponds.

The controller design is now completed. Figure 7.15(c) is a block diagram of the controller. Figure 7.16 gives the completed RTL description of the multiplier, detailing all the data and control connections between the modules we have defined above.

REFERENCES

[1] M. R. Barbacci, G. Barnes, R. Cattell, D. P. Siewiorek, *The Symbolic Manipulation of Computer Descriptions: ISPS Primer and Reference Manual*, Research Report, Dept. of Computer Science, Carnegie-Mellon Univ., Pittsburgh, 1977.
[2] T. J. Kowalski, *An Artificial Intelligence Approach to VLSI Design*, Kluwer Academic Publishers, Boston, 1985.

Exercises

7.1. *Project.* Write a Pascal program which will read the *connect* file and produce an equivalent function array (for the data-part description of each module) suitable for input to the combinational-logic packages of Chapter 3.

7.2. *Project.* Write a Pascal program which will read the *connect* file and produce a state table description for the control part description of each module. The state-table description must be in a format suitable for input to the state-minimization and state assignment packages of Chapter 5.

7.3. *Project.* Design and implement an online database which will act as an assistant when performing device selection. Note that the database must be expandable, so that new modules can be added quickly and simply. You are required to design and implement a "front-end" to enable the user to make enquiries and additions.

7.4. *Project.* Write a program which will produce the equivalent of Table 7.1 using the method outlined in Section 7.2.1. Note that this will require the use of the database built in Exercise 7.3. (*Note:* This may require the design of a suitable expert system).

Appendix 7-A

DESCRIPTION OF THE DIGITAL-DESIGN LANGUAGE

7-A.1. INTRODUCTION

The development of our RTL was motivated by two principal aims. The first was to make available a language suitable to teach hardware design as a systematic discipline based on certain fundamental concepts clearly and naturally reflected in the language. The second was to develop a language which is simple enough not to require the constant use of a manual, even if the language is not used frequently.

This Appendix is written in the same style as the Pascal Report [1].

7-A.2. NOTATION, TERMINOLOGY, AND VOCABULARY

According to traditional Backus-Naur form [2], syntactic constructs are denoted by English words enclosed between the angle brackets ⟨ ⟩. These words also describe the meaning of the construct, and are used in the accompanying description of the semantics. Possible repetition of a construct is indicated by enclosing the construct within the metabrackets { }. The symbol ⟨ *empty* ⟩ denotes the null sequence of symbols.

The basic vocabulary of the RTL consists of basic symbols classified into letters, digits, and special symbols.

```
<letter> ::= A | B | C | D | E | F | G | H | I | J | K | L | M |
             N | O | P | Q | R | S | T | U | V | W | X | Y | Z |
             a | b | c | d | e | f | g | h | i | j | k | l | m |
             n | o | p | q | r | s | t | u | v | w | x | y | z

<digit> ::= 0 | 1 | 2 | 3 | 4 | 5 | 6 | 7 | 8 | 9
```

<special symbol> ::= @ | & | | | <- | : | ; | , | $ | (|) | % |

    < | > | _ | **module** | **component** | **terminal** |

    state | **begin** | **end** | **goto** | **activate** | **on** |

    do

The construct

/* <any sequence of symbols not containing "*/"> */

may fall between any two identifiers, numbers, or special symbols. It is a *comment* and may be removed from the text without altering its meaning.

7-A.3. IDENTIFIERS AND NUMBERS

Identifiers serve to denote types and variables. Their association must be unique within their scope of validity, i.e., within the module in which they are declared.

<identifier> ::= *<letter>* { *<letter or digit>* }

<letter or digit> ::= *<letter>* | *<digit>*

Numbers may be in hexadecimal, octal, decimal or binary notation.

<number> ::= *<hexadecimal number>* | *<decimal number>* | *<octal number>* |
    <binary number>

<hexadecimal number> ::= **0H** *<hexadecimal string>* |
    0h *<hexadecimal string>*

<hexadecimal string> ::= *<hexadecimal digit>* { *<hexadecimal digit>* }

<hexadecimal digit> ::= A | B | C | D | E | F | a | b | c | c | e | f |
    <digit>

<decimal number> ::= *<digit>* { *<digit>* }

<octal string> ::= *<octal digit>* { *<octal digit>* }

<octal number> ::= **0O** *<octal string>* | **0o** *<octal string>*

<octal digit> ::= 0 | 1 | 2 | 3 | 4 | 5 | 6 | 7

<binary number> ::= **0B** *<binary string>* | **0b** *<binary string>*

<binary string> ::= *<binary digit>* { *<binary digit>* }

<binary digit> ::= 0 | 1

Examples:

1   298   0Hffe0   0ha9e1   0O357   0o743   0b00100   0B110011

7-A.4. TYPE DEFINITIONS

There are two simple types of variables in our RTL description: terminal and state. A type declaration determines the operations which can be performed on a variable of that type, and associates an identifier with the type.

7-A.4.1. Terminal Types

The terminal type defines a set of connection points local to a module.

<terminal> ::= **terminal** *<port list>* ;

<port list> ::= *<port variable>* { , *<port variable>* }

<port variable> ::= *<identifier>* { <range> }

<range> ::= < *<number>* : *<number>* >

7-A.4.2. State Types

A state type defines a set of identifiers associated with the states of a sequential machine. These variables must, at a later stage of design, be converted to binary values which can be loaded into a state sequence register in the controller, or implemented via some other suitable scheme (this is determined by the designer).

<state declaration> ::= **state** *<identifier list>* ;

<identifier list> ::= *<identifier>* { , *<identifier>* } ;

7-A.5. STRUCTURED TYPES

A structured type is characterized by the type(s) of its elementary parts and by its structuring method. Our RTL supports only a limited set of structuring primitives: arrays of terminals, and modules.

7-A.5.1. Array Types

An array type is applicable only to terminal types, and is a structure consisting of a fixed number of terminals. The elements of the array are designated by indices (which must be constant numbers). Only 1-dimensional arrays are supported in the RTL. See ⟨ *port list* ⟩ of Section 7-A.4.1 for the syntax of the declaration.

Examples:
   a<0:7>, fred<15:0>

7-A.5.2. Module Types

A module definition defines the set of terminals (or connection ports) through which a particular type of component may communicate, as well as defining the internal operation of a component of that type. It associates an identifier with the module type.

<module> : := **module** *<identifier>* (*<port list>*) *<module body>* ;

<module body> : := **external** | *<block>*

Examples:

See the main text of Chapter 7 for detailed examples of declarations of modules.

7-A.6. DECLARATION OF TERMINALS AND COMPONENTS

Terminal declarations consist of a list of identifiers, some of which may have array dimension details associated with them.

<terminal declaration> : := **terminal** *<port list>* ;

Component declarations consist of a module type identifier followed by a list of identifiers denoting the new components.

<component declaration> : := **component** *<component body>* ;

<component body> : := *<component instance>* { ; *<component instance>* }

<component instance> : := *<module identifier>* *<identifier>* { , *<identifier>* }

<module identifier> : := *<identifier>*

7-A.7. DENOTATIONS OF VARIABLES

Denotations of variables either designate a terminal variable or a port terminal variable.

<variable> : := *<terminal variable>* | *<port terminal variable>*

7-A.7.1. Terminal Variables

A terminal variable is specified by either its identifier, or by its identifier and a range specifier itemizing a subset of the terminal array. The indices of the subrange must lie within the bounds declared in the definition of the terminal identifier.

<terminal variable> : := *<identifier>* { *<subrange specifier>* }

<subrange specifier> : := < *<number>* { : *<number>* } >

7-A.7.2. Port Terminal Variables

A port terminal variable is specified by a module variable followed by a terminal variable. The terminal identifier must correspond with ports defined for the module type.

<port terminal variable> : := *<module identifier>* _ *<terminal variable>*

7-A.8. EXPRESSIONS

Expressions are constructs denoting rules of combination for terminals. Expressions consist of operands (i.e., constants and variables) and operators. The rules of composition specify operator precedences according to the three operators used. The *not* operator has the highest precedence, followed by the *and* operator, followed by the *or* operator.

<factor> ::= <variable> { <concat op> <variable> } | <number> |
(<expression>) | ~ <factor>

<concat op> ::= @

<term> ::= <factor> | <term> <and op> <factor>

<and op> ::= &

<expression> ::= <term> | <expression> <or op> <term>

<or op> ::= |

Examples:

Factors:

x

0Hffe9

(a & b)

~x

c<3>

f<5:7>

D7400_in1

D74111_in<15:0>

Terms:

x & y

x<1:3> & y<5:7>

divide_out & (error1 | error2)

Expressions:

in1 | in3

subtract_out<3:5> | out<0:2>

7-A.8.1. Operators

Both operands of the *and* and *or* operators must refer to variables of the same length, i.e., if either operand references a 1-dimensional terminal array, then the number of bits specified in each reference must be the same. If the two operands are both *n*-bit quantities, then the result produced by the operator is also an *n*-bit quantity.

Examples:

    terminal a, b, x<0:15>, y<1:16>;
    module check(in<7:0>, out<7:0>); external;

    a & b
    x & y
    x<3> & a
    x<0:7> & y<16:9>
    check_in & x<0:7>
    a & check_in<0>

7-A.9. STATEMENTS

Statements denote hardware interconnections. All statements are said to be "executed" in parallel. Statements may be prefixed by a label which can be referenced by a goto statement.

<statement> ::= *<unlabelled statement>* | *<state identifier>* : *<unlabelled statement>*

<state identifier> ::= *<identifier>*

<unlabelled statement> ::= *<transfer statement>* | *<goto statement>* | *<activate statement>* |

<on statement> | *<compound statement>* | *<empty>*

7-A.9.1. Transfer Statements

A transfer statement denotes the connection of the hardware specified by the right-hand side expression to the terminals specified on the left-hand side. The number of bits specified by the left- and right-hand sides must be the same, or the right-hand side must be a single bit expression.

<transfer statement> ::= *<variable>* { @ *<variable>* } <- *<expression>*

Examples:

terminal a<0:7>, b<0:7>, c<0:7>, x, y, z;

x <- y | z

c <- a & b

a<0:1> @ c<5:6> <- b<3:6>

7-A.9.2. Goto Statements

A goto statement indicates that the controller is to change state, the new state being the state defined by the state label.

<goto statement> : := **goto** *<state label>*

<state label> : := *<identifier>*

The following restrictions hold concerning the applicability of state labels:

1. The scope of the state label is the module within which it is defined. It is not possible to transfer control directly into another module via a goto statement.
2. Every label must be specified in a state declaration in the heading of the module in which the label is used.
3. If state labels are defined in a module, there must be more than one label defined; that is, controllers must have more than one state. (If a controller has only one state, it can be realized with combinational logic).

7-A.9.3. Activate Statements

The activate statement specifies that the controller is to assert the signal specified by the variable whenever the stated conditions are satisfied (i.e., when the controller is in the specified state and stated conditions are also satisfied).

<activate statement> : := **activate** *<variable>*

The variable must refer to a single bit terminal, and must be qualified by a ⟨ *state identifier* ⟩.

7-A.9.4. On Statements

The on statement specifies that a statement be executed only on condition that the expression is true. If it is false, then no statement is to be executed, or the statement following the symbol **else** is to be executed.

<on statement> : : = **on** <expression> **do** <statement> |

                        on <expression> **do** <statement> **else** <statement>

The expression between the symbols **on** and **do** must be a single-bit expression.

7-A.9.5. Compound Statements

The compound statement specifies that the statements of which it is comprised are to be treated as though they were a single statement, with each statement executed concurrently.

<compound statement> ::= **begin** <statement> { ; <statement> } **end**

7-A.10. MODULE DECLARATIONS

Module declarations serve to define new types of hardware devices and to associate identifiers with them so that they can be used to instantiate components.

<module declaration> ::= <module heading> <module body>

<module body> ::= **external** I <block>

<block> ::= <module declaration part> <component declaration part>

            <terminal declaration part> <state declaration part>

                <statement part>

The *module heading* specifies the identifier naming the module and the formal port identifiers.

<module heading> : : = **module** <identifier> (<port list>) ;

The *module body* may contain a description of the implementation of the module, or it may contain the keyword **external**. The appearance of the keyword **external** specifies that the details of the module implementation (or specification) appear elsewhere, perhaps in an online data base.

The *module declaration part* contains all the module type definitions local to the module.

<module declaration part> : : = <empty> | <module declaration>

The *component declaration part* instantiates one (or more) hardware devices of the type given by the module identifier and associates a name with each instantiation. These components are local to the module.

<component declaration part> : : = <empty> | <component declaration>

The *terminal declaration part* contains all terminal declarations local to the module declaration.

<terminal declaration part> : : = *<empty>* | *<terminal declaration>*

The *state declaration part* contains all the state declarations local to the module declaration.

<state declaration part> : : = *<empty>* | *<state declaration>*

The *statement part* specifies the connections to be made to implement the desired hardware algorithm.

<statement part> : : = *<compound statement>*

All identifiers introduced in the module declaration part, the component declaration part, the terminal declaration part and the state declaration part are **local** to the module declaration which defines the **scope** of these identifiers. They are not known outside their scope. The identifier introduced in the module heading to name the module is globally defined, and not known inside the module declaration. The port list introduced in the module heading introduces identifiers which are both globally and locally defined; they can be referenced locally by their name alone, or can be referenced globally when preceded by the component name followed by the symbol __. Identifiers which appear in more deeply nested module definitions are not visible outside their defining module definition.

7-A.11. SYNTAX GRAPH REPRESENTATION

An alternative description for our RTL is given in the syntax diagrams following the references below. An introduction to syntax diagrams is given in [2].

REFERENCES

[1] K. Jensen, N. Wirth, *PASCAL User Manual and Report*, Springer-Verlag, Berlin, 1975.
[2] N. Wirth, *Algorithms + Data Structures = Programs*, Prentice-Hall, 1976.

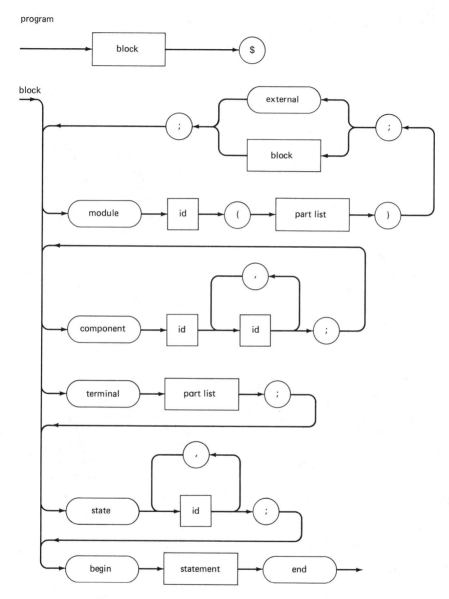

Figure 7-A.1. RTL syntax diagram.

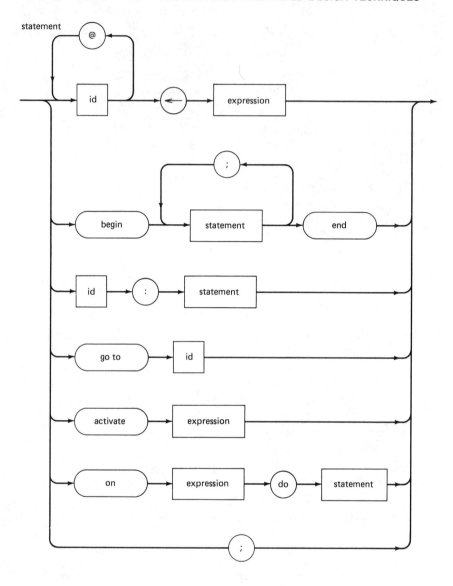

Figure 7-A.1. RTL syntax diagram (*Continued*).

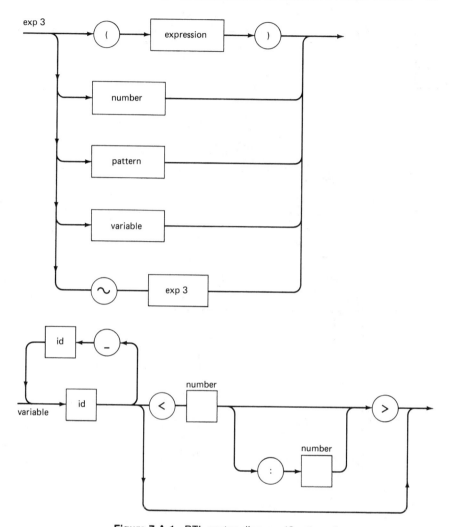

Figure 7-A.1. RTL syntax diagram (*Continued*).

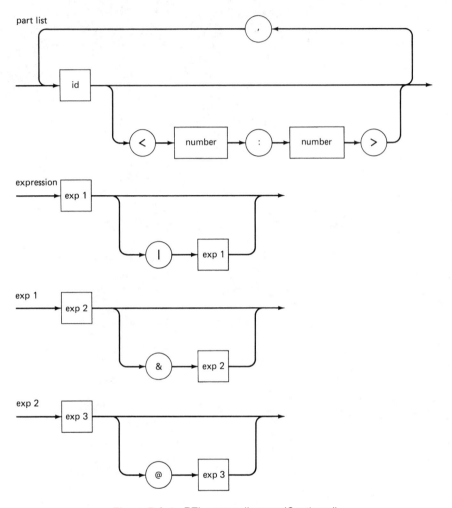

Figure 7-A.1. RTL syntax diagram (*Continued*).

Appendix 7-B

COMPILER LISTING

program ddl(input, output, listing, connect);   *ddl*

const
  norw = 12; {*no of reserved words*}
  txmax = 50; {*length of identifier table*}
  pmax = 32; {*no. of bits in pattern – machine dependent*}
  al = 16; {*length of identifiers*}
  errormax = 20; {*maximum number of error messages allowed*}

type
  symbol = (nul, ident, number, larrow, rarrow, lparen, rparen, percent,
    pattern, orsy, andsy, concat, notsy, gotosy, actsy, onsy,
    dosy, semicolon, tdef, dollar, comma, colon, beginsy,
    xfer, sdef, cdef, endsy, modulesy, comment,
    endcomment, externsy, elsesy);
  object = (termdef, statedef, module);
  carriertype = (pointype, vectortype);
  symset = **set of** symbol;
  palfa = **packed array** [1..pmax] **of** char;
  nalfa = **packed array** [1..al] **of** char;
  nodep = ˆ node;
  node =
    record
      len: integer; {*length of this expression*}
      rptr: nodep; {*right branch*}
      case ntype: symbol **of**
              notsy, andsy, orsy, concat, xfer, onsy, semicolon, gotosy, actsy: (
                lptr: nodep
              );
              pattern: (
                pattn: palfa
              );
              ident: (
                tablep: integer;
                regs, regf: integer
)
    end;
  pair =
  record
    left, right: integer
  end;

429

```
pairlist = array [1..pmax] of pair;
sizelist = array [1..pmax] of integer;
useset = set of (Input, Output);
tblentry = record
   name: nalfa;
   typ: carriertype;
   nlen: integer; {length of name}
   gather: nodep;
   lvl: integer;
   usage: useset;
   case kind: object of
     module:
                            (nargs, argindex: integer);
             termdef, statedef:
                            (reglen, freg, lreg: integer)
   end;


var
   ch: char; {last character read}
   sym: symbol; {last symbol read}
   id: nalfa; {last identifier read}
   num: integer; {last number read}
   pat: palfa; {last pattern read}
   plen: integer; {length of last pattern read}
   cc: integer; {character count}
   ll: integer; {linelength}
   lineno: integer; {current line number}
   kk: integer;
   line: array [1..81] of char;
   blankid: nalfa;
   word: array [1..norw] of nalfa;
   wsym: array [1..norw] of symbol;
   ssym: array [char] of symbol;
   expbegsys, statbegsys, declbegsys: symset;
   argtable, table: array [0..txmax] of tblentry;
   level: integer; {static nesting level}
   errors: integer; {error count}
   warnings: integer; { warning count }
   listflag: boolean; {set if listing reqd}
   xplainflag: boolean; {set if explanation req in listing}
   warnflag: boolean; {set if warnings to be shown}
   stateflag: boolean; {set for state machine descriptions}
   expflag: boolean; {set if expressions are allowed}
   nodealloc: integer; {number of nodes allocated}
   nodecount: integer; {count of the number of nodes in use}
   nodeuse: integer; {no. of nodes used}
   nfree, pfree, ifree: nodep; {list of free nodes}
   listing, connect: text;
   termcount: 0..txmax; {current temporary terminal number}

procedure comperror(n: integer);
{ Report error to output. Print on listing file, if required. }

procedure writemessage(var f: text; err: integer);
   begin { writemessage }
   if not (err in [1,2,3,4,5,6,7,8,9,10,
                         11,12,13,14,15,16,17,18,19,
                         20,21,22,23,24,25,26,27,
```

comperror

writemessage

```
                    30,31,33,34,35,36,37,39,
                    40,42,44,47,48,
                    50]) then
writeln(f, 'error number:', err:3)
else case err of
            1:
              writeln(f, ' identifier symbol expected');
            2:
              writeln(f, ' undeclared identifier');

            3:
              writeln(f, ' module type identifier expected');
            4:
              writeln(f, ' number expected');
            5:
              writeln(f, ' ; or , expected');
            6:
              writeln(f, ' error in expression');
            7:
              writeln(f, ' statement expected');
            8:
              writeln(f, ' identifier multiply defined');
            9:
              writeln(f, ' undeclared state identifier');
            10:
              writeln(f, ' expressions not permitted in structural description');
            11:
              writeln(f, ' "begin" expected');
            12:
              writeln(f, ' "end" expected');
            13:
              writeln(f, ' <- expected');
            14:
              writeln(f, ' illegal character');
            15:
              writeln(f, ' declaration out of order');
            16:
              writeln(f, ' pattern too long');
            17:
              writeln(f, ' index out of range');
            18:
              writeln(f, ' illegal symbol');
            19:
              writeln(f, ' "$" expected');
            20:
              writeln(f, ' error in declaration part');
            21:
              writeln(f, ' single bit terminals must follow ACTIVATE');
            22:
              writeln(f, ' ) expected');
            23:
              writeln(f, ' variables used with ACTIVATE must be 1 bit long');
            24:
              writeln(f, ' > expected');
            25:
              writeln(f, ' "do" expected');
            26:
              writeln(f, ' error in terminal access');
```

```
                  27:
                  writeln(f, ' ACTIVATE statements cannot be unconditional');
                  30:
                  writeln(f, ' number too large');
                  31:
                  writeln(f, ' specified length should be greater than 1');
                  33:
                  writeln(f, ' state labels not permitted in structural description');
                  34:
                  writeln(f, ' left side of transfer statement incorrect');
                  35:
                  writeln(f, ' expressions have incompatible length');
                  36:
                  writeln(f, ' cannot access module identifiers');
                  37:
                  writeln(f, ' "goto" not permitted in structural description');
                  39:
                  writeln(f, ' conditional expressions must be 1 bit in length');
                  40:
                  writeln(f, ' conditional expression missing');
                  42:
                  writeln(f, ' : expected');
                  44:
                  writeln(f, ' malformed pattern');
                  47:
                  writeln(f, ' number or unique pattern expected');
                  48:
                  writeln(f, ' multiply defined state');
                  50:
                  writeln(f, ' "goto" statement appears with no current state')
        end

      end; { writemessage }

  begin { comperror }
    if listflag then begin
      writeln(listing, ' ': cc + 7, '^^');
      write(listing, ' E -');
      writemessage(listing, n)
    end;
    write(lineno: 5, ':');
    writemessage(output, n);
    errors := errors + 1;
    if errors > errormax then begin
      if listflag then
              writeln(listing, 'Too many errors. Execution terminated.');
      writeln('Too many errors. Execution terminated.');
      halt
    end
  end; { comperror }

  function topattern(n, f, l: integer): boolean;                  topattern
  { convert decimal number n to a binary bit pattern. }
  { save only the bits f to l in the pattern      }
  { return true if it succeeds             }

  var
    i, k: integer;
```

```
begin { topattern }
  topattern := true;
  for i := 1 to pmax do
    pat[i] := '0';
  if n = 0 then
    plen := 1
  else if n = 1 then begin
    plen := 1;
    pat[pmax] := '1'
  end else begin
    if n < 0 then begin
            if f = 1 then
                pat[1] := '1';
                n := n + maxint + 1
    end;
    i := pmax;
    k := pmax;
    while n <> 0 do begin
            if (k >= f) and (k <= l) then begin
              if odd(n) then
                pat[i] := '1'
              else
                pat[i] := '0';
              i := i - 1
            end;
            k := k - 1;
            n := n div 2
    end;
    plen := l - f + 1
  end
end; { topattern }


function tonumber(var n: integer; f, l: integer): boolean;                 tonumber
{ convert a pattern in variable 'pat' to a decimal number. }
{ return false if dontcares appear.                        }
{ convert only bits f to l of the pattern                  }

var
  i: integer;
  success: boolean;

begin { tonumber }
  success := true;
  n := 0;
  for i := f to l do
    if pat[i] = '?' then
            success := false;
  if success then
    { pattern is unique - no dontcares }
    for i := l downto f do
            if n >= 0 then
            n := n * 2 + (ord(pat[i]) - ord('0'))
            else if success then begin
              success := false;
              comperror(30)
            end;
  tonumber := success
end; { tonumber }
```

```
procedure getch;                                                          getch
{ get a character from the input. The characters are line buffered }
{ for speed of access. }

begin { getch }
 if cc = ll then begin
  if eof(input) then begin
          if listflag then
             writeln(listing, '*** Program incomplete');
          writeln('*** Program incomplete');
          halt
  end;
  ll := 0;
  cc := 0;
  lineno := lineno + 1;
  if listflag then
          write(listing, ' ', lineno: 5, ' ': 3);
  while not eoln(input) do begin
          ll := ll + 1;
          read(ch);
          if listflag then
            write(listing, ch);
          if ll <= 81 then
            line[ll] := ch
  end;
  if listflag then
          writeln(listing);
  ll := ll + 1;
  read(line[ll])
 end;
 cc := cc + 1;
 ch := line[cc]
end; { getch }


procedure getsym;                                                        getsym
{ convert character sequences to compiler symbols. }

var
 i, j, k: integer;
 zeroseen: boolean;

procedure makepattern(c: char);                                   makepattern
{ convert a character sequence to a bit pattern. This will }
{ handle binary, octal, or hexadecimal constants. No more }
{ than "pmax" bits may be stored. This is MACHINE DEPENDENT.}

var
 range: set of char;
 base, i, inc, bits: integer;
 overflow: boolean;

begin { makepattern }
 sym := pattern;
 plen := 0;
 zeroseen := false;
 range := ['0', '1', '?'];
 base := 2;
 bits := 1;
```

```
if (c = 'H') or (c = 'h') then begin
        range := ['0'..'9', 'A'..'F', 'a'..'f', '?'];
        bits := 4;
        base := 16
end else if (c = 'O') or (c = 'o') then begin
        range := ['0'..'7', '?'];
        bits := 3;
        base := 8
end;
getch;
overflow := false;
while ch in range do begin
        if not overflow then begin
        if plen + bits - 1 > pmax then
          { too many bits in pattern }
          overflow := true
        else begin
          { make space for next pattern }
          if plen > 0 then
            for i := pmax - plen - (bits - 1) to pmax - bits do
                pat[i] := pat[i + bits];
          case base of
            2:
                    pat[k] := ch;
            8:
                    begin
                      if ch <> '?' then
                       inc := ord(ch) - ord('0');
                      for i := pmax downto pmax - 2 do
                       if ch = '?' then
                         pat[i] := ch
                       else begin
                        pat[i] := chr(inc mod 2 + ord('0'));
                        inc := inc div 2
                       end
                    end;
            16:
                    begin
                      if ch <> '?' then
                       if ch in ['A'..'F'] then
                        inc := ord(ch) - ord('A') + 10
                       else if ch in ['a'..'f'] then
                        inc := ord(ch) - ord('a') + 10
                       else
                        inc := ord(ch) - ord('0');
                      for i := pmax downto pmax - 3 do
                       if ch = '?' then
                        pat[i] := '?'
                       else begin
                        pat[i] := chr(inc mod 2 + ord('0'));
                        inc := inc div 2
                       end
                    end
          end; { case }
          plen := plen + bits
        end
        end;
        getch
```

```
        end; { while }
        if overflow then begin
                comperror(30);
                plen := 0
        end
end; { makepattern }

procedure setoptions;                                                setoptions
{ set options specified in description file }

var
i: integer;
oldlistflag: boolean;

        procedure switch(var flag: boolean);                             switch
        begin { switch }
                getch;
                if ch in ['+', '-'] then begin
                flag := ch = '+';
                getch
                end
        end; { switch }

begin { setoptions }
oldlistflag := listflag;
getch;
while ch in ['L', 'l', 'X', 'x', 'W', 'w', 'S', 's', 'E', 'e'] do begin
        case ch of
        'L', 'l':
          switch(listflag);
        'X', 'x':
          switch(xplainflag);
        'W', 'w':
          switch(warnflag);
        'S', 's':
          switch(stateflag);
        'E', 'e':
          switch(expflag);
        end;
        if ch = ',' then
                getch
end;
if xplainflag then
        listflag := true;
if listflag and not oldlistflag then begin
        write(listing, ' ', lineno: 5, ' ': 3);
        for i := 1 to ll do
          write(listing, line[i]);
        writeln(listing)
end
end; { setoptions }

begin {getsym}
repeat
  while (ch = ' ') or (ord(ch) = 9) do { handle TAB in funny manner }
        getch;
  if ch in ['A'..'Z', 'a'..'z'] then begin { reserved word or identifier}
        k := 0;
        id := blankid;
```

```
            repeat
             if k < al then begin
              k := k + 1;
              id[k] := ch
             end;
             getch
             until not (ch in ['A'..'Z', 'a'..'z', '0'..'9', '_']);
             plen := k;
             i := 1;
             j := norw;
             repeat
              k := (i + j) div 2;
              if id <= word[k] then
               j := k - 1;
              if id >= word[k] then
               i := k + 1
             until i > j;
             if i - 1 > j then
              sym := wsym[k]
             else
              sym := ident
 end else if ch in ['0'..'9'] then begin {number or pattern}
            k := pmax;
            plen := 0;
            num := 0;
            sym := number;
            zeroseen := false;
            for i := 1 to pmax do
             pat[i] := '0';
            if ch = '0' then begin
             getch;
             zeroseen := true
            end;
            if ch in ['H', 'h', 'O', 'o', 'B', 'b'] then
             makepattern(ch)
            else if ch in ['0'..'9', 'D', 'd'] then begin
             if ch in ['D', 'd'] then begin { pattern type }
             getch;
             zeroseen := false
            end;
            if ch in ['0'..'9'] then begin { decimal no. }
             repeat
              if num >= 0 then
                      num := num * 10 + (ord(ch) - ord('0'))
              else
                      comperror(30);
              getch
             until not (ch in ['0'..'9']);
             if zeroseen and (num = 0) then
              plen := 1
             else if (num = 1) and not zeroseen then begin
              { unique pattern of all 1's assumed }
              for i := 1 to pmax do
                      pat[i] := '1';
              plen := 1
             end
            end else
             comperror(44)
```

```
                end else if zeroseen then
                plen := 1
                else
                comperror(44)
        end else if ch = '<' then begin
                getch;
                if ch = '−' then begin
                sym := xfer;
                getch
                end else
                sym := larrow
        end else begin
                sym := ssym[ch];
                if sym = comment then begin
                getch;
                if ch = '$' then
                  setoptions;
                while ssym[ch] <> endcomment do
                getch
                end else if sym = nul then
                comperror(14);
                getch
        end
    until not (sym in [comment, nul])
end; { getsym }


procedure nextif(fsy: symbol; err: integer);
{ skip to next symbol if cuurent symbol is acceptable; }
{ else report an error. }


begin { nextif }
  if fsy = sym then
    getsym
  else
    comperror(err)
end; { nextif }


procedure skip(fsys: symset);
{skip input until relevant symbol found}


begin { skip }
  while not (sym in fsys) do
    getsym
end; { skip }


procedure find(fsys: symset; err: integer);
{symbol of fsys expected; if not then error and search for fsys}


begin { find }
  if not (sym in fsys) then begin
    comperror(err);
    repeat
        getsym
    until sym in fsys
  end
end; { find }
```

nextif

skip

find

findorskip

```
procedure findorskip(s1, s2: symset; n: integer);
{ if current symbol not in the set S1 then report an error }
{ and skip to any symbol in the sets S1 or S2. }

begin { findorskip }
  if not (sym in s1) then begin
    comperror(n);
    skip(s1 + s2)
  end
end; { findorskip }
```

stopifnot

```
function stopifnot(fsy: symbol): boolean;
{used to stop repeat statements; stop if sym<>fsy else getsym and repeat}

begin { stopifnot }
  if sym <> fsy then
    stopifnot := true
  else begin
    stopifnot := false;
    getsym
  end
end; { stopifnot }
```

newnode

```
function newnode(typ: symbol; lp, rp: nodep; l: integer): nodep;
{ allocate a new node of the desired type. If none are on }
{ the free list, then dynamically allocate new space. }

var
  x: nodep;
begin { newnode }
  if nfree <> nil then begin
    x := nfree;
    nfree := x^.rptr
  end else begin
    case typ of
            andsy:
              new(x, andsy);
            orsy:
              new(x, orsy);
            notsy:
              new(x, notsy);
            xfer:
              new(x, xfer);
            actsy:
              new(x, actsy);
            gotosy:
              new(x, gotosy);
            onsy:
              new(x, onsy);
            concat:
              new(x, concat);
            semicolon:
              new(x, semicolon)
    end;
    nodealloc := nodealloc + 1
  end;
  nodeuse := nodeuse + 1;
  nodecount := nodecount + 1;
```

```
with x^ do begin
  len := l;
  ntype := typ;
  lptr := lp;
  rptr := rp
end;
newnode := x
end; { newnode }
```

```
function newident(tp, st, fin: integer): nodep;
{ allocate a new identifier node, taking the details from }
{ the symbol table entry at "tp". }
```
newident

```
var
  x: nodep;

begin { newident }
  if ifree <> nil then begin
    x := ifree;
    ifree := x^.rptr
  end else begin
    new(x, ident);
    nodealloc := nodealloc + 1
  end;
  nodecount := nodecount + 1;
  nodeuse := nodeuse + 1;
  with x^ do begin
    len := abs(st − fin) + 1;
    ntype := ident;
    rptr := nil;
    tablep := tp;
    regs := st;
    regf := fin
  end;
  newident := x
end; { newident }
```

```
function newpattern(l: integer; p: palfa): nodep;
{ allocate a node containing a specified bit pattern. }
```
newpattern

```
var
  x: nodep;

begin { newpattern }
  if pfree <> nil then begin
    x := pfree;
    pfree := x^.rptr
  end else begin
    new(x, pattern);
    nodealloc := nodealloc + 1
  end;
  nodeuse := nodeuse + 1;
  nodecount := nodecount + 1;
  with x^ do begin
    ntype := pattern;
    len := l;
    pattn := p;
    rptr := nil
  end;
  newpattern := x
end; { newpattern }
```

```
procedure dspsenode(var p: nodep);                                          dspsenode
{ return a node to the appropriate free list for reuse later. }


begin { dspsenode }
  if p <> nil then begin
    with p^ do
            case ntype of
              notsy, andsy, orsy, concat, xfer, onsy, semicolon, actsy, gotosy:
                begin
                  rptr := nfree;
                  nfree := p
                end;
              pattern:
                begin
                  rptr := pfree;
                  pfree := p
                end;
              ident:
                begin
                  rptr := ifree;
                  ifree := p
                end
            end;
    p := nil;
    nodecount := nodecount − 1
  end
end; { dspsenode }


procedure dspsetree(var p: nodep);                                          dspsetree
{ return the nodes of a tree structure to their free lists. }


begin { dspsetree }
  if p <> nil then
    with p^ do
            if ntype in [orsy, concat, xfer, andsy, onsy, semicolon, notsy, gotosy, actsy] then begin
              dspsetree(lptr);
              dspsetree(rptr)
            end;
    dspsenode(p)
end; { dspsetree }


function copytree(p: nodep): nodep;                                         copytree
{ return a complete copy of a tree structure. }


begin { copytree }
  copytree := nil;
  if p <> nil then
    with p^ do begin
            case ntype of
              xfer, andsy, orsy, concat, onsy, semicolon, notsy,
              actsy, gotosy:
                copytree := newnode(ntype, copytree(lptr), copytree(rptr), len);

              ident:
                copytree := newident(tablep, regs, regf);

              pattern:
                copytree := newpattern(len, pattn)
            end
    end
end; { copytree }
```

```
procedure pnumber(var f: text; n: integer);
{ print a number to file "f" without leading blanks. }
```

```
var
  l: integer;

begin { pnumber }
  if n < 10 then
    l := 1
  else if n < 100 then
    l := 2
  else if n < 1000 then
    l := 3
  else if n < 10000 then
    l := 4
  else
    l := 5;
  write(f, n: l)
end; { pnumber }
```

```
procedure ptree(var f: text; p: nodep);
{ print a linearized version of a tree structure }
{ to the file "f". }
```

```
var
  i: integer;
  brackets: boolean;
  range: symset;

begin { ptree }
  if p <> nil then
    with p^ do
            case ntype of
            andsy, orsy, concat:
              begin
              range := [ident, pattern, notsy, concat];
              if ntype = orsy then
                      range := range + [orsy, andsy];
              brackets := not (lptr^.ntype in range);
              if brackets then
                      write(f, '(');
              ptree(f, lptr);
              if brackets then
                      write(f, ')');
              if ntype = concat then
                      write(f, '@')
              else if ntype = orsy then
                      write(f, '|')
              else
                      write(f, '&');
              if ntype = orsy then
                      range := range + [orsy];
              brackets := not (rptr^.ntype in range + [andsy]);
              if brackets then
                      write(f, '(');
              ptree(f, rptr);
              if brackets then
                      write(f, ')')
              end;

            xfer:
              begin
                ptree(f, lptr);
```

```
    write(f, ' <- ');
    ptree(f, rptr)
  end;


notsy:
 begin
  write(f, '^');
  brackets := not (lptr^.ntype in [ident, pattern]);
  if brackets then
          write(f, '(');
  ptree(f, lptr);
  if brackets then
          write(f, ')')
 end;


actsy:
 begin
  write(f, 'activate ');
  ptree(f, lptr)
 end;


gotosy:
 begin
  write(f, 'goto ');
  ptree(f, lptr)
 end;


onsy:
 begin
  write(f, 'on ');
  if lptr = nil then begin
          if (rptr^.ntype <> actsy) and (rptr^.ntype <> gotosy) then begin
            writeln('COMPILER ERROR: ptree found nil in "on" condition');
            write('rptr: ');
            ptree(f, rptr);
            writeln;
            halt
            end else
            write(f, '*AnyInput*')
    end else
          ptree(f, lptr);
  write(f, ' do ');
  if rptr^.ntype = colon then begin
            writeln(f, ' {');
            ptree(f, rptr);
            writeln(f);
            writeln(f, '}')
    end else
          ptree(f, rptr)
 end;


semicolon:
 begin
  ptree(f, lptr);
  if rptr <> nil then begin
          writeln(f, ';');
          ptree(f, rptr)
  end
 end;
```

```
      pattern:
        begin
          write(f, '0B');
          for i := pmax − len + 1 to pmax do
                  write(f, pattn[i]);
          write(f, '%');
          pnumber(f, len)
        end;

    ident:
      with table[tablep] do begin
        if kind = statedef then
              write(f, '#');
        write(f, name:nlen);
        if kind = termdef then begin
              if typ <> pointype then begin
              write(f, '<');
              pnumber(f, regs);
              if len > 1 then begin
                write(f, ':');
                pnumber(f, regf)
              end;
              write(f, '>')
            end
        end
      end
    end {case}
end; { ptree }


procedure markusage(p: nodep);                              markusage
{ record the use of each variable in a tree structure. }
{ This is recorded as: for Input to the module and/or }
{ for Output from this module. }


procedure markit(p: nodep; use: useset);                    markit
{ recursively traverse a tree structure and mark the variables. }


begin { markit }
    if p <> nil then begin
        if p^.ntype in [orsy, andsy, concat, xfer, onsy, semicolon,
                          notsy, gotosy, actsy, ident] then
        with p^ do case ntype of
        xfer:
                begin
                  markit(lptr, [Output]);
                  markit(rptr, [Input])
                end;

        ident:
                table[tablep].usage := table[tablep].usage + use;

        notsy:
                markit(lptr, use);

        gotosy, actsy:
                markit(lptr, [Output]);
```

```
        onsy:
                begin
                  markit(lptr, [Input]);
                  markit(rptr, [])
                end;

        semicolon:
                begin
                  markit(lptr, []);
                  markit(rptr, [])
                end;

        orsy, andsy, concat:
                begin
                  markit(lptr, use);
                  markit(rptr, use)
                end;

              end
            end
  end; { markit }

begin { markusage }
  if p <> nil then
    markit(p, [])
  end; { markusage }


procedure unjoin(var y: sizelist; var ny: integer; var x: pairlist; npairs, max: integer);
{            Given a vector with range 1..max, and npairs subranges, produce the }
{            ordered list of sizes of subranges formed.                          }

var
  i, nyl, nyr: integer;
  yl, yr: set of 1..pmax;

begin { unjoin }
  yl := [1];
  yr := [max];
  for i := 1 to npairs do
    with x[i] do begin
            yl := yl + [left];
            yr := yr + [right];
            if left > 1 then
              yr := yr + [left − 1];
            if right < max then
              yl := yl + [right + 1]
    end;
  ny := 0;
  nyl := 1;
  nyr := 1;
  repeat
    while not (nyl in yl) do
            nyl := nyl + 1;
    while not (nyr in yr) do
            nyr := nyr + 1;
    ny := ny + 1;
    y[ny] := nyr − nyl + 1;
```

unjoin

```
      yl := yl - [nyl];
      yr := yr - [nyr]
   until nyr >= max
end; { unjoin }
```

```
function dissect(var x: nodep; size: integer): nodep;
{ Traverse a transfer statement, producing a new statement }
{ comprising only the first "size" bits. The statement is }
{ modified so that subsequent "dissect"s will return new }
{ transfer statements. Used to remove concatenation operators. }

var
   p: nodep;
   f, s, i: integer;

begin { dissect }
   p := nil;
   if x <> nil then
      with x^ do begin
            if size > len then
            size := len;
            case ntype of
            xfer, andsy, orsy, notsy:
               p := newnode(ntype, dissect(lptr, size), dissect(rptr, size), size);
            concat:
               if lptr^.len > 0 then begin
               i := size - lptr^.len;
               p := dissect(lptr, size);
               if i > 0 then
                        p := newnode(concat, p, dissect(rptr, i), size)
               end else
               p := dissect(rptr, size);
            ident:
               begin
               s := regs;
               if regs > regf then begin
                        f := s - size + 1;
                        regs := f - 1
               end else begin
                        f := regs + size - 1;
                        regs := f + 1
               end;
               p := newident(tablep, s, f)
               end;
            pattern:
               begin
               p := newpattern(size, pattn);
               if len > size then
                        with p^ do
                        for i := 1 to size do
                        pattn[pmax - size + i] := x^.pattn[pmax - len + i]
               end
            end;
            len := len - size
      end;
   dissect := p
end; { dissect }
```

dissect

```
function rmconcat(p: nodep): nodep;                                    rmconcat
{ remove the concatenation operator from the left–hand }
{ size of a transfer statement. }


var
  ny, npairs, max, i: integer;
  y: sizelist;
  x: pairlist;
  r, s: nodep;


procedure formpairlist(p: nodep; offset: integer; var max: integer);      formpairlist

  begin { formpairlist }
  if p <> nil then
          with p^ do
          case ntype of
            notsy, xfer, andsy, orsy, concat:
              begin
                      formpairlist(lptr, offset, max);
                      if ntype = concat then
                        formpairlist(rptr, offset + lptr^.len, max)
                      else
                        formpairlist(rptr, offset, max)
              end;
            pattern, ident:
              begin
                      npairs := npairs + 1;
                      with x[npairs] do begin
                      left := offset + 1;
                      right := offset + len;
                      if max < right then
                        max := right
                      end
              end
          end
  end; { formpairlist }

begin { rmconcat }
  npairs := 0;
  max := 0;
  formpairlist(p^.lptr, 0, max);
  unjoin(y, ny, x, npairs, max);
  s := nil;
  for i := 1 to ny do begin
    r := dissect(p, y[i]);
    if s = nil then
          s := r
    else
          s := newnode(semicolon, r, s, 0)
  end;
  dspsetree(p);
  rmconcat := s
end; { rmconcat }


procedure collect(p, cond: nodep);                                      collect
  { Place transfer statement p on the collection list of the }
  { identifier appearing on the left–hand side of the statement }
```

function isreversed(p: nodep): boolean;   *isreversed*
{ *Returns true if the bit ordering of the lhs of a transfer statement* }
{ *was in reverse order to its declared ordering.   * }

begin { *isreversed* }
  isreversed := false;
  if p <> **nil then**
          with p^ **do**
            with table[tablep] **do**
              isreversed := (freg > lreg) **and** (regs < regf) **or** (freg < lreg) **and** (regs > regf)
end; { *isreversed* }

procedure reverse(**var** p: nodep);   *reverse*
{ *reverse the bit ordering of a statement or an expression* }

var
  i: integer;
  temp: char;

begin { *reverse* }
  if p <> **nil then**
          with p^ **do**
            case ntype **of**
              xfer, andsy, orsy, concat:
              begin
                      reverse(lptr);
                      reverse(rptr)
              end;

              notsy:
                reverse(lptr);

              ident:
                if len > 1 **then begin**
                      i := regs;
                      regs := regf;
                      regf := i
                end;

              pattern:
                for i := 1 **to** len **div** 2 **do begin**
                      temp := pattn[pmax – i + 1];
                      pattn[pmax – i + 1] := pattn[pmax – len + i];
                      pattn[pmax – len + i] := temp
                end
            end { *case* }
end; { *reverse* }

begin { *collect* }
  { *p is always an xfer statement* }
  if p <> **nil then**
    with p^ **do begin**
          if isreversed(lptr) **then**
            reverse(p);
          if cond <> **nil then**
            p := newnode(onsy, copytree(cond), p, p^.len);
          with table[lptr^.tablep] **do begin**

```
            if gather = nil then
              gather := p
            else
              gather := newnode(semicolon, p, gather, 0);
              markusage(gather)
            end;
            if xplainflag then begin
              write(listing, ' ', '*': 5, ' ': 3);
              ptree(listing, p);
              writeln(listing)
            end
      end
end; { collect }
```

procedure separate(tp: integer);   *separate*
{ Scan the symbol table and produce the transfer }
{ statements for each terminal. This involves }
{ determining the complete set of connections to }
{ each subfield of each terminal. }

```
var
  p, q: nodep;
  i, npairs, ny: integer;
  x: pairlist;
  y: sizelist;
```

procedure formpairlist(p: nodep);   *formpairlist*
{ determine the subfield range of indices and the number of subfields. }

```
begin { formpairlist }
  if p <> nil then
          with p^ do
          if not (ntype in [semicolon, onsy, xfer]) then begin
            writeln('COMPILER ERROR: illegal arg type to formpairlist');
            halt
          end else
          case ntype of
          semicolon:
            begin
                    formpairlist(lptr);
                    formpairlist(rptr)
            end;

          onsy:
            formpairlist(rptr);

          xfer:
            with lptr^ do begin
                    npairs := npairs + 1;
                    with x[npairs], table[tp] do begin
                    if freg > lreg then
                      left := freg − regs + 1
                    else
                      left := regs − freg + 1;
                    right := left + len − 1
                    end
            end
          end { case }
end; { formpairlist }
```

```
function fitslhs(p: nodep): boolean;
{ return TRUE if the lhs is a single terminal or it starts }
{ at the first bit position of the declared terminal index. }

begin { fitslhs }
  with p^, table[tp] do
            if typ = pointype then
              fitslhs := true
            else
              fitslhs := freg = regs
end; { fitslhs }
```

fitslhs

```
procedure printname(var f: text; tp: integer);
{ print the declared terminal name and its dimensions. }

begin { printname }
  with table[tp] do begin
            write(f, name:nlen);
            if reglen > 1 then begin
              write(f, '<');
              pnumber(f, freg);
              write(f, ':');
              pnumber(f, lreg);
              write(f, '>')
            end
  end
end; { printname }
```

printname

```
procedure writename(var f: text; tp: integer);
{ print a comment on the connect file giving the }
{ terminal declaration and its usage. }

begin { writename }
  with table[tp] do begin
            write(f, 'terminal ');
            printname(f, tp);
            write(f, ' Usage = [');
            if usage = [] then begin
              write(f, '**UNUSED**');
              warnings := warnings + 1;
              if warnflag then begin
                write(' w - ');
                printname(output, tp);
                writeln(' used for neither Input nor Output')
              end;
              if listflag then begin
                write(listing, ' w - ');
                printname(listing, tp);
                writeln(listing, ' used for neither Input nor Output')
              end
            end else begin
              if Input in usage then
                write(f, 'Input ');
              if Output in usage then
                write(f, 'Output')
            end;
            write(f, ']')
  end
end; { writename }
```

writename

```
function generate(var p: nodep; when: nodep; size: integer): nodep;
{ generate equations for each of the subfields of the }
{ terminal declaration. }

var
q, cond, lhs, rhs: nodep;
lhsize: integer;

procedure walk(var p: nodep; when: nodep);
{ a recursive procedure to walk the tree }
{ and produce the transfer statements. }

var
          x: nodep;

begin { walk }
          if p <> nil then
          with p^ do
          case ntype of
            semicolon:
                    begin
                    walk(lptr, when);
                    walk(rptr, when);
                    if lptr = nil then begin
                    x := rptr;
                    dspsenode(p);
                    p := x
                    end
                    end;
            onsy:
                    begin
                    walk(rptr, lptr);
                    if rptr = nil then
                    dspsetree(p)
                    end;
            xfer:
                    if fitslhs(lptr) then begin
                    lhsize := lptr^.len;
                    x := dissect(rptr, size);
                    if (lhs <> nil) and (when = nil) then begin
                    { unconditioned assignment occurs when }
                    { a previous assignment occurred.    }
                    if listflag then begin
                    write(listing, ' E – conflict with usage of ');
                    ptree(listing, lhs);
                    writeln(listing)
                    end;
                    write(' E – conflict with usage of ');
                    ptree(output, lhs);
                    writeln;
                    errors := errors + 1;
                    dspsetree(x)
                    end else begin
                    if when <> nil then
                    x := newnode(andsy, copytree(when), x, size);
                    if cond = nil then
                    cond := copytree(when)
```

```
                                else
                                  cond := newnode(orsy, copytree(when), cond, 1);
                                if rhs = nil then
                                  rhs := x
                                else
                                  rhs := newnode(orsy, x, rhs, size);
                                if lhs = nil then
                                  lhs := dissect(lptr, size)
                                else begin
                                  x := dissect(lptr, size);
                                  dspsetree(x)
                                end
                                end;
                                if lhsize = size then
                                  dspsetree(p)
                                end
                      end { case }
        end; { walk }


   begin { generate }
     cond := nil;
     lhs := nil;
     rhs := nil;
     walk(p, when);
     q := nil;
     if lhs <> nil then begin
                q := newnode(xfer, lhs, rhs, 0);
                dspsetree(cond)
     end;
     generate := q
   end; { generate }


  begin { separate }
   p := table[tp].gather;
   if errors = 0 then begin
     writeln(connect);
     write(connect, ' { ');
     writename(connect, tp);
     writeln(connect, ' }');
     if p <> nil then
                with table[tp] do begin
                npairs := 0;
                formpairlist(p);
                unjoin(y, ny, x, npairs, reglen);
                for i := 1 to ny do begin
                  q := generate(p, nil, y[i]);
                  if q <> nil then begin
                    ptree(connect, q);
                    writeln(connect);
                    dspsetree(q)
                  end else begin
                    if listflag then begin
                          write(listing, ' W – unused subfields of ');
                          printname(listing, tp);
                          writeln(listing)
                    end;
                    warnings := warnings + 1;
```

```
            if warnflag then begin
                    write(' W – unused subfields of ');
                    printname(output, tp);
                    writeln
                end
                end;
                if freg < lreg then
                    freg := freg + y[i]
                else
                    freg := freg – y[i]
                end
            end
    end;
    if p <> nil then
        dspsetree(p);
    table[tp].gather := nil
    end; { separate }
```

function position(id: nalfa; tx: integer): integer;   *position*
```
{ seach symbol table for presence of id.   }
{ return 0 if unsuccessful, else table index }
var
  i: integer;

begin { position }
  table[0].name := id;
  i := tx;
  while table[i].name <> id do
    i := i – 1;
  position := i
end; { position }
```

function rdnum(**var** x: integer): boolean;   *rdnum*
```
{ read a symbol and convert it to a number. }
{ return TRUE if successful. }

begin { rdnum }
  x := 0;
  rdnum := sym in [number, pattern];
  if not (sym in [number, pattern]) then
    comperror(4)
  else begin
    if sym = number then begin
            x := num;
            getsym
    end else if sym = pattern then begin
            if not tonumber(x, 1, plen) then
            comperror(47);
            getsym
    end
  end
end; { rdnum }
```

function expression(fsys: symset; tx: integer): nodep;   *expression*
```
{ parse an expression and return a tree structure. }
{ this routine handles the OR expression. }
{ returns 'nil' if an error occurs. }
```

```
var
  L: nodep;

  function variable(fsys: symset): nodep;                            variable
  { parse a variable }
  { returns 'nil' if an error occurs. }

  var
    p: nodep;
    errcount: integer;
    i: integer;

    function inrange(x, y, l: integer): boolean;                     inrange
    { check if variable dimensions lie within declared dimensions. }

    begin { inrange }
            inrange := (l >= x) and (l <= y) or (l >= y) and (l <= x)
    end; { inrange }

  begin { variable }
  errcount := errors;
  variable := nil;
  p := nil;
  i := position(id, tx);
  if (i = 0) or (table[i].lvl <> level) then
          findorskip([], fsys, 2)
  else
          with table[i] do
            if kind in [module, statedef] then
            findorskip([], fsys, 36)
            else begin
            getsym;
            p := newident(i, freg, lreg);
            if sym = larrow then
              with p^ do begin
                    if typ = pointype then
                    findorskip([], fsys + [rarrow], 26)
                    else begin
                    getsym;
                    if rdnum(i) then begin
                      if not inrange(freg, lreg, i) then
                      comperror(17);
                      regs := i;
                      regf := i;
                      len := 1;
                      if sym = colon then begin
                      getsym;
                      if rdnum(i) then begin
                              if not inrange(freg, lreg, i) then
                              comperror(17);
                              regf := i;
                              len := abs(regs - i) + 1;
                              if len > pmax then
                              comperror(16)
                    end
                  end
                end
```

```
                    end;
                    nextif(rarrow, 24)
              end;
           if (errors > errcount) and (p <> nil) then
              dspsenode(p)
           end;
   variable := p
   end; { variable }


   function exp(s: symbol; L, R: nodep): nodep;
   { return a node of type "s" given (possibly) two operands. }
   { returns 'nil' if an error occurs. }


   var
     x: nodep;

   begin { exp }
     x := nil;
     if (L <> nil) and (R <> nil) then
              if L^.len <> R^.len then
                comperror(35)
              else
                x := newnode(s, L, R, L^.len);
     exp := x;
     if x = nil then begin
              dspsetree(L);
              dspsetree(R)
     end
   end; { exp }


   function exp1(fsys: symset): nodep;
   { parse AND expressions }
   { returns 'nil' if an error occurs. }


   var
     L: nodep;

   function exp2(fsys: symset): nodep;
   { parse CONCAT expressions }
   { returns 'nil' if an error occurs. }


   var
         L, R, x: nodep;

         function exp3(fsys: symset): nodep;
         { parse highest precedence items: variable, numbers, NOT, (). }
         { returns 'nil' if an error occurs. }


         label
           1;

         var
           x: nodep;
           notfound: boolean;

         procedure setsize(var x: nodep);
         { read the size of a constant number or pattern. }
```

exp

exp1

exp2

exp3

setsize

```
begin { setsize }
getsym;
            if sym <> number then
            find(fsys, 4)
            else begin
            x`.len := num;
            if num > pmax then
                        comperror(16);
            getsym
            end
         end; { setsize }



begin { exp3 }
 x := nil;
 notfound := false;
 exp3 := nil;
 while sym in expbegsys do begin
1:
   case sym of
     notsy:
                begin
                 if not expflag then
                  comperror(10);
                 getsym;
                 notfound := not notfound;
                 goto 1
                end;
         ident:
                x := variable(fsys);
         pattern:
                begin
                 x := newpattern(plen, pat);
                 getsym;
                 if sym = percent then
                  setsize(x)
                end;
         number:
                if topattern(num, 1, 32) then begin
                 x := newpattern(plen, pat);
                 getsym;
                 if sym = percent then
                  setsize(x)
                end;
         lparen:
                begin
                 if not expflag then
                  comperror(10);
                 getsym;
                 x := expression(fsys + [rparen], tx);
                 nextif(rparen, 22)
                end
   end;
   if not (sym in fsys) then begin
    dspsetree(x);
    findorskip(fsys, [lparen], 6)
   end
```

```
            end;
            if notfound and (x <> nil) then
                x := newnode(notsy, x, nil, x^.len);
            exp3 := x
            end; { exp3 }

    begin {exp2}
            x := nil;
            R := nil;
            L := exp3(fsys + [concat]);
            if sym <> concat then
                exp2 := L
            else begin
            getsym;
            R := exp2([concat] + fsys);
            if (L <> nil) and (R <> nil) then
                x := newnode(concat, L, R, L^.len + R^.len);
            exp2 := x;
            if x = nil then begin
                dspsetree(L);
                dspsetree(R)
            end
            end
    end; { exp2 }

    begin {exp1}
    L := exp2(fsys + [andsy]);
    if sym <> andsy then
            exp1 := L
    else begin
        if not expflag then
        comperror(10);
            getsym;
            exp1 := exp(andsy, L, exp1([andsy] + fsys))
    end
    end; { exp1 }

    begin {expression}
    L := exp1(fsys + [orsy]);
    if sym <> orsy then
        expression := L
    else begin
        if not expflag then
        comperror(10);
        getsym;
        expression := exp(orsy, L, expression([orsy] + fsys, tx))
    end
    end; { expression }

procedure statedescription(indx: integer);                        statedescription
{ print details of the finite state machine controller }
{ to the connect file. }

begin { statedescription }
    with table[indx] do
    if errors = 0 then begin
        writeln(connect);
                write(connect, name:nlen);
```

```
        writeln(connect, ´:´);
            if usage = [] then begin
            warnings := warnings + 1;
            if warnflag then
                writeln(´ w – state ´, name:nlen, ´ is not used´);
            if listflag then
                writeln(listing, ´ w – state ´, name:nlen, ´ is not used´);
            end else if gather = nil then begin
            if listflag then
                writeln(listing, ´ E – state ´, name:nlen, ´ no next state´);
            writeln(´ E – state ´, name:nlen, ´ no next state´);
            errors := errors + 1
    end else begin
            ptree(connect, gather);
            writeln(connect)
    end
  end
end; { statedescription }


procedure block(tx, argptr: integer; fsys, stopsy: symset);          block
{ parse the body of a ´block´. }


var
  i, ntable: integer;

procedure newentry(var entry: tblentry; nme: nalfa; idlen: integer; k: object);    newentry
{ fill in a new symbol table entry. }

  begin { newentry }
            with entry do begin
            name := nme;
            typ := pointype;
            nlen := idlen;
            gather := nil;
            lvl := level;
            kind := k;
            usage := [];
            if k = module then begin
              nargs := 0;
              argindex := 0
            end else begin
              reglen := 1;
              freg := 0;
              lreg := 0
            end
    end
  end; { newentry }


function enter(var entry: tblentry): integer;                        enter
{ add a name to the symbol table. Flag multiply defined names. }


var
  i: integer;

begin {enter object into table}
  i := position(entry.name, tx);
  with table[i] do
```

```
    if (i > 0) and (level = lvl) then begin
            enter := 0;
            comperror(8)
    end else begin
            tx := tx + 1;
            entry.lvl := level;
            table[tx] := entry;
            usage := [];
            enter := tx
    end
end; { enter }


procedure modifyarg(var entry: tblentry; m, a: nalfa; nm, na: integer);
{ concatenate the component name string and the accessed }
{ terminal name string, separated by the ´_´ character. }


var
    i: integer;


begin { modifyarg }
    entry.nlen := nm + na + 1;
    if entry.nlen > al then
            entry.nlen := al;
    entry.name := m;
    if nm < al then
            entry.name[nm + 1] := ´_´;
    na := al – (nm + 1);
    for i := 1 to na do
            entry.name[nm + 1 + i] := a[i]
end; { modifyarg }


procedure putsemicolon;
{ help the user by adding missing semicolons. }


begin { putsemicolon }
    if sym <> semicolon then begin
            if listflag then begin
              writeln(listing, ´ ´: cc + 7, ´^´);
              writeln(listing, ´ w – ; inserted before this item´)
            end;
            warnings := warnings + 1;
            if warnflag then
              writeln(lineno: 5, ´: w – ; inserted´)
    end else
            getsym
end; { putsemicolon }


function declbody(fsys: symset; fob: object): integer;
{ process the body of a terminal declaration or a module }
{ argument declaration. }


    var entry: tblentry;
            baseofargs: integer;


            function pair: boolean;
            { parse the dimensions of a terminal. }
```

modifyarg

putsemicolon

declbody

pair

```
          begin { pair }
           pair := false;
           with entry do
             if rdnum(freg) then
               if sym = colon then begin
               getsym;
               if rdnum(lreg) then begin
                       pair := true;
                       if freg = lreg then
                         comperror(31)
               end
               end else
                 comperror(42)
          end; { pair }
```

```
          procedure getrest;                                         getrest
          { parse the information after the variable name. }
```

```
          begin { getrest }
           getsym;
           if (sym = larrow) and (fob <> statedef) then
             with entry do
               if sym = larrow then begin
                       getsym;
                       typ := vectortype;
                       if pair then begin
                       reglen := abs(freg – lreg) + 1;
                       if reglen > pmax then
                         comperror(16)
                       end;
                       nextif(rarrow, 24)
               end
           end;
```

```
procedure declaration;                                         declaration
{ add the declaration to the symbol table. }
```

```
var
          i: integer;
```

```
begin { declaration }
          i := enter(entry);
          { NB. if i=0 then nothing appears in the visible symbol table }
          getrest;
          table[i] := entry
```

```
end; { declaration }
```

```
begin { declbody }
 baseofargs := tx;
 getsym;
 repeat
          if sym <> ident then
            comperror(1)
          else begin
            if fob = module then
              newentry(entry, id, plen, termdef)
```

```
              else
                newentry(entry, id, plen, fob);
              declaration
        end;
              find([comma, semicolon, rparen] + fsys, 5)
        until stopifnot(comma);
        if fob = module then
              nextif(rparen, 22);
        putsemicolon;
        find(fsys, 20);
        declbody := tx − baseofargs
        end; { declbody }
```

```
procedure statement(fsys: symset; cond, curstate: nodep);                statement
{ parse a statement. }
```

```
var
  i: integer;
  x: nodep;
```

```
function mkterm(p: nodep): nodep;                                        mkterm
{ make an assignment to a temporary terminal }
```

```
var
          lhs: nodep;
          i, j: integer;
          n: nalfa;
          entry: tblentry;
```

```
begin { mkterm }
          mkterm := nil;
          if termcount > txmax then begin
            writeln(' FATAL ERROR: Too many temporary terminals used(', txmax: 4, ')');
            if listflag then begin
              write(listing, ' FATAL ERROR: ');
              writeln(listing, ' Too many temporary terminals used(', txmax: 4, ')')
            end;
            halt
          end;
          n := 'TEMP        ';
          j := termcount;
          termcount := termcount + 1;
          for i := 7 downto 5 do begin
          n[i] := chr(j mod 10 + ord('0'));
          j := j div 10
          end;
          newentry(entry, n, 8, termdef);
          i := enter(entry);
          if i > 0 then begin
            lhs := newident(i, 0, 0);
            with table[i] do begin
            gather := newnode(xfer, lhs, copytree(p), 1);
            markusage(gather);
            if xplainflag then begin
              write(listing, ' ', '*': 5, ' ': 3);
              ptree(listing, gather)
            end
          end
        end;
```

```
              if xplainflag then
                 writeln(listing);
              mkterm := lhs
              end
  end; { mkterm }

  procedure transfer(fsys: symset; cond: nodep);                        transfer
  { parse a transfer statement. }

  var

              L, R, x, y, z, oncond: nodep;
              rmANDnode, isconcatenated, xferOK: boolean;
              i: integer;

              function checklhs(p: nodep; var iscat, xok: boolean): boolean;   checklhs
              { check for concatenation on the left hand side. }

              var
              x: boolean;

              procedure walk(p: nodep; var x: boolean);                 walk
              { a recursive procedure to check for concatenation }

              begin { walk }
                if (p <> nil) and x then
                  with p^ do
                           if ntype in [ident, concat] then begin
                              if ntype = concat then begin
                              iscat := true;
                              walk(lptr, x);
                              walk(rptr, x)
                              end
                           end else
                              x := false
              end; { walk }

              begin { checklhs }
              x := p <> nil;
              xok := x;
              iscat := false;
              walk(p, x);
              checklhs := x
              end; { checklhs }

  begin { transfer }
              x := nil;
              R := nil;
              L := expression(fsys + [xfer], tx);
              if sym <> xfer then
                comperror(13)
              else begin
                if L <> nil then
                  if not checklhs(L, isconcatenated, xferOK) then begin
                    comperror(34);
                    dspsetree(L)
                  end else if not xferOK then begin
                    comperror(40);
                    dspsetree(L)
```

```
    end;
getsym;
R := expression(fsys, tx);
if (L <> nil) and (R <> nil) then
  if (L^.len <> R^.len) and (R^.len <> 1) then
   comperror(35)
  else begin
    { enforce matching number of bits on left and right }
    { hand sides of the transfer command. }
    if L^.len <> R^.len then
          if R^.ntype = pattern then begin
          for i := pmax – L^.len + 1 to pmax – 1 do
            R^.pattn[i] := R^.pattn[pmax];
            R^.len := L^.len
          end else begin
            y := nil;
            if R^.ntype <> ident then
             R := mkterm(R);
            for i := 1 to L^.len do
             if y = nil then
               y := R
             else
               y := newnode(concat, copytree(R), y, i);
             R := y
          end;
    x := newnode(xfer, L, R, L^.len);
    markusage(x);
    if isconcatenated then
          x := rmconcat(x);
    rmANDnode := false;
    { generate the condition on the transfer }
    if (curstate <> nil) and (cond <> nil) then begin
          oncond := newnode(andsy, curstate, cond, 1);
          rmANDnode := true
    end else if cond = nil then
          oncond := curstate
    else
      oncond := cond;
    z := oncond;
    if xferOK and (x <> nil) then begin
          if x^.ntype = semicolon then begin
          if oncond <> nil then
            if oncond^.ntype in [andsy, orsy] then
             z := mkterm(z);
          while x^.ntype = semicolon do begin
            collect(x^.lptr, z);
            y := x^.rptr;
            dspsenode(x);
            x := y
          end
          end;
          collect(x, z)
    end;
    if rmANDnode then
          dspsenode(oncond)
  end
end;
```

```
      if x = nil then begin
        dspsetree(L);
        dspsetree(R)
      end
end; { transfer }
```

```
procedure statelabel(fsys: symset; cond, curstate: nodep; identry: integer);
{ parse the body of statements after a state label. }
```
statelabel

```
var
      x: nodep;
```

```
begin { statelabel }
      getsym;
      if sym <> colon then
        findorskip([colon], fsys, 42)
      else begin
        if curstate <> nil then
          comperror(48);
        getsym;
        x := newident(identry, 0, 0);
        statement(fsys, cond, x);
        dspsenode(x)
      end
end; { statelabel }
```

```
procedure onstatement(fsys: symset);
{ parse the "on .. do .." statement. }
```
onstatement

```
var
      x, y: nodep;
```

```
begin { onstatement }
      getsym;
      y := nil;
      x := expression(fsys + [dosy], tx);
      if x <> nil then
        if x^.len <> 1 then begin
          comperror(39);
          dspsetree(x)
        end;
      nextif(dosy, 25);
      if cond <> nil then begin
        y := newnode(andsy, x, cond, 1);
        statement(fsys + [elsesy], y, curstate);
        dspsenode(y)
      end else
        statement(fsys + [elsesy], x, curstate);
      if sym = elsesy then begin
        getsym;
        x := newnode(notsy, x, nil, 1);
        if cond <> nil then begin
          y := newnode(andsy, x, cond, 1);
          statement(fsys, y, curstate);
          dspsenode(y)
        end else
          statement(fsys, x, curstate)
```

```
          end;
          dspsetree(x)
end; { onstatement }


procedure gotostatement;                                          gotostatement
{ parse the goto statement. Save the next state information }
{ in the symbol table entry for the current state. }


var
          i: integer;


          procedure storestate(var p: nodep; cond: nodep; identry: integer);    storestate
          { store next state information in the symbol table entry "identry". }


          var
          hit: boolean;
          x: nodep;


          procedure match(p: nodep);                              match
          { check if we already have an entry for the same next state. }
          { if so, then OR rthe conditions together. }


          begin { match }
            if (p <> nil) and not hit then
              with p^ do
                      case ntype of
                      semicolon:
                        begin
                         match(lptr);
                         match(rptr)
                        end;
                      onsy:
                        begin
                         match(rptr);
                         if hit then
                                  lptr := newnode(orsy, cond, lptr, 1)
                        end;
                      actsy:
                        ;
                      gotosy:
                        hit := lptr^.tablep = identry
                      end { case }
          end; { match }

          begin { storestate }
          hit := false;
          match(p);
          if not hit then begin
            x := newident(identry, 0, 0);
            x := newnode(gotosy, x, nil, 0);
            x := newnode(onsy, cond, x, 0);
            markusage(x);
            if xplainflag then begin
              write(listing, ' ', '*': 5, ' ': 3);
              ptree(listing, x);
              writeln(listing)
            end;
```

```
              if p = nil then
                p := x
              else
                p := newnode(semicolon, x, p, 0)
              end
           end; { storestate }

   begin { gotostatement }
          getsym;
          if sym <> ident then
            comperror(1)
          else begin
            i := position(id, tx);
            if (i > 0) and (table[i].lvl = level) then
              if curstate <> nil then
                storestate(table[curstate^.tablep].gather, copytree(cond), i)
              else
                comperror(50)
            else
              comperror(2);
            getsym
          end
   end; { gotostatement }
```

```
   procedure actstatement(fsys: symset);                          actstatement
   { parse the "activate .. do .." statement. }

   var
          i: integer;
          y: nodep;

          procedure storeact(var p: nodep; cond, actid: nodep);     storeact
          { save the activate statement in the output specification }
          { of the current state of the finite state machine controller. }

          var
            x: nodep;

          begin { storeact }
          x := newnode(actsy, actid, nil, 0);
          x := newnode(onsy, cond, x, 0);
          markusage(x);
          if xplainflag then begin
            write(listing, ' ', '*': 5, ' ': 3);
            ptree(listing, x);
            writeln(listing)
          end;
          if p = nil then
            p := x
          else
            p := newnode(semicolon, x, p, 0)
          end; { storeact }

   begin { actstatement }
          getsym;
          if sym <> ident then
            comperror(1)
```

```
          else begin
            y := expression(fsys, tx);
            if y^.ntype <> ident then
              comperror(21)
            else if y^.len <> 1 then
              comperror(23)
            else if (curstate = nil) and (cond = nil) then
              comperror(27)
            else begin
            i := y^.tablep;
            if (i > 0) and (table[i].lvl = level) then
              if curstate <> nil then
                      storeact(table[curstate^.tablep].gather, copytree(cond), y)
              else
                      comperror(50)
            else
              comperror(2)
            end
          end
  end; { actstatement }

begin { statement }
  while sym = semicolon do
          getsym;
  if sym in statbegsys + [ident] then
          case sym of
            ident:
            begin
            i := position(id, tx);
            if table[i].kind = statedef then
                      if table[i].lvl = level then begin
                        statelabel(fsys, cond, curstate, i);
                        if not stateflag then begin
                          comperror(33);
                          skip(fsys)
                        end
                      end else
                        comperror(9)
            else
                      transfer(fsys, cond)
            end;

            beginsy:
            begin
            getsym;
            x := cond;
            if cond <> nil then
                      if cond^.ntype in [andsy, orsy] then
                        x := mkterm(cond);
            statement([semicolon, endsy] + fsys, x, curstate);
            while sym in [semicolon] + statbegsys do begin
                      if sym <> semicolon then
                        putsemicolon;
                      statement(fsys + [semicolon, endsy], x, curstate)
            end;
            while sym = semicolon do
                      getsym;
            nextif(endsy, 12)
            end;
```

```
                    gotosy:
                      if not stateflag then begin
                        comperror(37);
                        getsym;
                        skip(fsys)
                      end else
                      gotostatement;

                    actsy:
                      actstatement(fsys);

                    onsy:
                      onstatement(fsys)
                  end;
          findorskip(fsys, [], 7)
        end; { statement }

        procedure moduledecl(fsys: symset);                     moduledecl
        { parse a module description. }

        var
         i, idindex: integer;
         entry: tblentry;
         isexternal: boolean;

        begin { moduledecl }
         getsym;
         idindex := 0;
         if sym <> ident then
                  comperror(1)
         else begin
                  writeln(connect);
                  writeln(connect, ' {$Module:', id, ' }');
                  newentry(entry, id, plen, module);
                  idindex := enter(entry);
                  getsym
         end;
         level := level + 1;
         if sym = lparen then
           table[idindex].nargs := declbody(fsys + [rparen], module)
         else
                  putsemicolon;
         isexternal := sym = externsy;
         if isexternal then
                  getsym
         else
                  block(tx, argptr, fsys, [semicolon, dollar]);
         level := level − 1;
         if not isexternal then
                  { only print the terminals of modules which have a local description. }
                  for i := idindex + 1 to tx do
                    with table[i] do
                      if kind = termdef then begin
                      if errors = 0 then
                              separate(i);
                      dspsetree(gather);
                      gather := nil
                      end;
```

```
writeln(connect, ' {$EndModule:', table[idindex].name, ' }');
if table[idindex].nargs > 0 then begin
        { move args to argument stack }
        table[idindex].argindex := argptr;
  for i := idindex + 1 to idindex + table[idindex].nargs do begin
            argtable[argptr] := table[i];
            argptr := argptr + 1;
            if argptr > txmax then begin
            writeln(' argument stack overflow (', txmax:3, ' items');
            halt
            end
        end
end;
tx := idindex;
if sym <> dollar then begin
        putsemicolon;
        find(fsys, 20)
end
end; { moduledecl }


procedure compdecl(fsys: symset);                                compdecl
{ parse the declaration of a component. }


var
  i, k, otx: integer;
  entry: tblentry;


begin { compdecl }
getsym;
if sym <> ident then
        findorskip([], fsys + [semicolon], 1)
else begin
        i := position(id, tx);
        with table[i] do
        if i = 0 then
          find(fsys + [semicolon], 2)
        else
          if kind <> module then
            find(fsys + [semicolon], 3)
          else begin
          getsym;
          repeat
                if sym <> ident then
                  findorskip([], fsys + [comma, semicolon], 1)
                else begin
                if nargs > 0 then
                  { declare each argument as <componentname>_<argname> }
                  for k := argindex to argindex + nargs - 1 do begin
                  entry := argtable[k];
                  entry.kind := termdef;
                  modifyarg(entry, id, argtable[k].name, plen, argtable[k].nlen);
                  otx := enter(entry)
                  end;
                getsym;
                find([comma, semicolon] + fsys, 5)
                end
          until stopifnot(comma)
          end
```

```
      end;
      putsemicolon;
      find(fsys, 20)
    end; { compdecl }

begin { block }
  ntable := tx + 1;
  repeat
    while sym = modulesy do
            moduledecl(fsys + [externsy, dollar]);
    while sym = cdef do
            compdecl(fsys);
    if sym = tdef then
            i := declbody(fsys, termdef);
    if sym = sdef then begin
            if not stateflag then
              comperror(33);
            i := declbody(fsys, statedef)
    end;
    if sym in declbegsys then
            comperror(15)
    else
            findorskip([beginsy, dollar], fsys, 11)
  until sym in statbegsys + [dollar];
  if sym <> dollar then begin
    nextif(beginsy, 11);
    repeat
            repeat
             repeat
              statement(fsys + [semicolon, endsy], nil, nil)
             until not (sym in statbegsys)
            until stopifnot(semicolon);
            nextif(endsy, 12);
            if not (sym in stopsy) then
             findorskip([], fsys, 18)
    until sym in declbegsys + stopsy + [beginsy];
    for i := ntable to tx do
            with table[i] do
            if kind = termdef then begin
             if errors = 0 then
               separate(i);
             dspsetree(gather);
             gather := nil
            end;
            writeln(connect);
            writeln(connect, ' {$StateTable } ');
            for i := ntable to tx do
             with table[i] do
               if kind = statedef then begin
                if errors = 0 then
                        statedescription(i);
                dspsetree(gather);
                gather := nil
    end;
            writeln(connect, ' {$EndStateTable } ')
  end
end; { block }
```

procedure init;   *init*
{ *set up all the initial values.* }

procedure initsymtab;   *initsymtab*
{ *initialize the symbol tables.* }

```
begin { initsymtab }
 for ch := 'A' to ';' do
         ssym[ch] := nul;

 {must have dictionary words in lexicographic order}
 word[1] := 'activate    ';
 word[2] := 'begin       ';
 word[3] := 'component    ';
 word[4] := 'do          ';
 word[5] := 'else        ';
 word[6] := 'end         ';
 word[7] := 'external     ';
 word[8] := 'goto        ';
 word[9] := 'module       ';
 word[10] := 'on          ';
 word[11] := 'state       ';
 word[12] := 'terminal     ';

 wsym[1] := actsy;
 wsym[2] := beginsy;
 wsym[3] := cdef;
 wsym[4] := dosy;
 wsym[5] := elsesy;
 wsym[6] := endsy;
 wsym[7] := externsy;
 wsym[8] := gotosy;
 wsym[9] := modulesy;
 wsym[10] := onsy;
 wsym[11] := sdef;
 wsym[12] := tdef;

 ssym['|'] := orsy;
 ssym['^'] := notsy;
 ssym['$'] := dollar;
 ssym['('] := lparen;
 ssym[')'] := rparen;
 ssym['<'] := larrow;
 ssym['>'] := rarrow;
 ssym['@'] := concat;
 ssym[';'] := semicolon;
 ssym[','] := comma;
 ssym['{'] := comment;
 ssym['}'] := endcomment;
 ssym[':'] := colon;
 ssym['%'] := percent;
 ssym['&'] := andsy
end; { initsymtab }

begin { init }
 initsymtab;
 expbegsys := [ident, pattern, number, lparen, notsy];
```

```
    statbegsys := [beginsy, onsy, gotosy, actsy];
    declbegsys := [tdef, modulesy, sdef, cdef];
    cc := 0;
    ll := 0;
    ch := ' ';
    level := 0;
    errors := 0;
    warnings := 0;
    lineno := 0;
    for kk := 1 to al do
      blankid[kk] := ' ';
    nodecount := 0;
    nodeuse := 0;
    nodealloc := 0;
    nfree := nil;
    pfree := nil;
    ifree := nil;
    termcount := 0;
    listflag := false;
    warnflag := true;
    xplainflag := false;
    stateflag := false;
    expflag := false;
    rewrite(listing, 'listing');
    rewrite(connect, 'connect')
  end; { init }


begin { main }
  init;
  getsym;
  repeat
    block(0, 0, declbegsys + statbegsys, [dollar]);
    if sym <> dollar then
      comperror(19)
  until sym = dollar;
  if errors > 0 then
    { delete file if errors in source }
    rewrite(connect);
  if listflag then begin
    writeln(listing);
    writeln(listing, 'Number of errors detected:   ', errors);
    writeln(listing, 'Number of warnings:       ', warnings);
    writeln(listing, 'Number of nodes unrecovered: ', nodecount);
    writeln(listing, 'Number of nodes allocated:   ', nodealloc);
    writeln(listing, 'Number of nodes used:       ', nodeuse)
  end;
  if errors > 0 then begin
    writeln;
    writeln('Number of errors detected: ', errors)
  end
end. { main }
```

Appendix 7-C

WORKED EXAMPLES

7-C.1. INTRODUCTION

This appendix serves to demonstrate the use of the compiler for our RTL language. We introduce the "compiler options" through the study of one example module description.

The implementation of the compiler is based on the techniques outlined in Chapter 5 of Wirth [1], and interested readers are referred to this reference if any modifications and/or extensions are contemplated. Detailed discussions of individual procedures and functions are not undertaken in this book.

In the discussions below, we will assume that the file *output* is associated with the screen of the terminal from which the compiler is executed, and that the file *input* is associated with the keyboard of the controlling terminal. We will further assume that there exists some mechanism by which the input description file can be associated with the file *input* (e.g., with the UNIX operating system the input file can be "piped" into the compiler program).

All listings appear in the file *listing* and all terminal connections in the file *connect*.

7-C.2. BASIC USAGE

We will use the RTL description of the device Shifter (shown in Figure 7.13(a)) to illustrate some of the features of the RTL compiler. The description of Shifter given below is basically the same as that given in Figure 7.13(a), but it is presented here in the form that a user would type it into the computer on an ASCII terminal. Thus there are no boldface characters and the symbol " ← " is shown here as the compound symbol " <- ".

```
module Shifter(in<0:3>, out<0:3>, load, shiftright, shiftin, clear, clock);

    module D74379(in<0:3>, out<0:3>, outcomp<0:3>, load, clock);
        external;

    module D74157(in0<0:3>, in1<0:3>, out<0:3>, select,strobe);
        external;
```

```
module D7427(in1a,in1b,in1c,out1,in2a,in2b,in2c,out2,in3a,in3b,in3c,out3);
    external;

component D74379 X;
component D74157 MUX;
component D7427 gate1;

begin
      MUX_in0 <- in;
      MUX_in1 <- shiftin @ X_out<0:2>;

      X_in <- MUX_out;
      MUX_select <- shiftright;
      MUX_strobe <- clear;
      out <- X_out;
      X_load <- gate1_out1;
      gate1_in1a <- shiftright;
      gate1_in1b <- clear;
      gate1_in1c <- load;
      X_clock <- clock;
    end { Shifter }
$
```

If this description is placed in a file and presented as input to the RTL compiler, then the following text appears on the output. (For UNIX systems, this text appears on the screen; other operating systems may have this text appear in a special file).

```
w - X_outcomp<0:3> used for neither Input nor Output
w - gate1_in2a used for neither Input nor Output
w - gate1_in2b used for neither Input nor Output
w - gate1_in2c used for neither Input nor Output
w - gate1_out2 used for neither Input nor Output
w - gate1_in3a used for neither Input nor Output
w - gate1_in3b used for neither Input nor Output
w - gate1_in3c used for neither Input nor Output
w - gate1_out3 used for neither Input nor Output
```

Observe that the compiler prints nine lines of warning information (indicated by the character ''w'' at the start of each line; errors start with ''E''). The first line states that the complemented output of the 74379 has not been used in the description. The compiler warns the user of all terminals that are left unconnected. In this case it was the intention of the designer to leave the complemented output of the 74379 unconnected. The remaining eight lines of the above output warn the user that two of the NOR gates in the 7427 package are unused, as was intended in this case. As we shall soon see, we can elect to have the warning messages suppressed if we so desire, but turning warning messages off should only be contemplated in well-understood descriptions.

As well as this information, the RTL compiler creates a file which contains information concerning every connection to each terminal in the description. This file is named ''connect'', and the contents of it for the ''shifter'' description are reproduced below.

```
{$Module:Shifter            }

{$Module:D74379             }
{$EndModule:D74379              }

{$Module:D74157             }
{$EndModule:D74157              }

{$Module:D7427          }
{$EndModule:D7427           }

{ terminal X_in<0:3>  Usage = [Output] }
X_in<0:3> <- MUX_out<0:3>

{ terminal X_out<0:3>  Usage = [Input ] }

{ terminal X_outcomp<0:3>  Usage = [**UNUSED**] }

{ terminal X_load  Usage = [Output] }
X_load <- gate1_out1

{ terminal X_clock  Usage = [Output] }
X_clock <- clock

{ terminal MUX_in0<0:3>  Usage = [Output] }
MUX_in0<0:3> <- in<0:3>

{ terminal MUX_in1<0:3>  Usage = [Output] }
MUX_in1<0:3> <- shiftin@X_out<0:2>

{ terminal MUX_out<0:3>  Usage = [Input ] }

{ terminal MUX_select  Usage = [Output] }
MUX_select <- shiftright

{ terminal MUX_strobe  Usage = [Output] }
MUX_strobe <- clear

{ terminal gate1_in1a  Usage = [Output] }
gate1_in1a <- shiftright

{ terminal gate1_in1b  Usage = [Output] }
gate1_in1b <- clear

{ terminal gate1_in1c  Usage = [Output] }
gate1_in1c <- load

{ terminal gate1_out1  Usage = [Input ] }

{ terminal gate1_in2a  Usage = [**UNUSED**] }

{ terminal gate1_in2b  Usage = [**UNUSED**] }

{ terminal gate1_in2c  Usage = [**UNUSED**] }

{ terminal gate1_out2  Usage = [**UNUSED**] }

{ terminal gate1_in3a  Usage = [**UNUSED**] }

{ terminal gate1_in3b  Usage = [**UNUSED**] }

{ terminal gate1_in3c  Usage = [**UNUSED**] }

{ terminal gate1_out3  Usage = [**UNUSED**] }
```

```
{$StateTable }
{$EndStateTable }

{ terminal in<0:3>  Usage = [Input ] }

{ terminal out<0:3>  Usage = [Output] }
out<0:3> <- X_out<0:3>

{ terminal load  Usage = [Input ] }

{ terminal shiftright  Usage = [Input ] }

{ terminal shiftin  Usage = [Input ] }

{ terminal clear  Usage = [Input ] }

{ terminal clock  Usage = [Input ] }
{$EndModule:Shifter            }
```

The first point to observe is that there are a large number of lines containing text between the delimiters { }. These can be treated as comments, and serve to:

(i) list every terminal in the description, giving both its declared size and its usage within the defining module—either as an Input or an Output or both or neither (i.e., "**UNUSED**");

(ii) produce the state table description of the controller, for those modules which are defined as using a controller (via the use of **state** declarations, state labels, and **goto** statements);

(iii) preserve some of the structure of the original description by showing the start and end of each module declaration in the description.

The first and last lines of the description state that this is the definition of the module *Shifter*, by placing the words *$Module:Shifter* immediately after the opening comment delimiter ({), and *$EndModule:Shifter* immediately before the closing comment delimiter (}). Lines 2 through 7 indicate the presence, in the description, of modules D74379, D74157, and D7427. These modules have been declared as externally defined so no further detail is given here. The remaining lines of text relate to the terminal connections used to realize the Shifter module.

Terminal declarations appear as comments, with the first word of the comment being "terminal". For example, consider the first terminal comment and connection statement:

```
{ terminal X_in<0:3> Usage = [Output] }

X_in<0:3> <- MUX_out<0:3>
```

The first line tells us that there is a terminal *X_in*, that it is four bits in size, that the bits are numbered 0 through 3 (MSB to LSB), and that it appears on the left-hand side of at least one connection statement. The fact that *X_in* appears on the left-hand side of a connection statement implies that data has to be transferred to it and hence that it will be used as an output. The second line is a collection of all the connection statements in which X_in occurs on the left-hand side. In this case, there is only one such statement and this expresses the fact that $MUX\_out\langle 0:3 \rangle$ is connected to $X\_in\langle 0:3 \rangle$.

The fact that $MUX\_out\langle 0:3 \rangle$ occurs on the right-hand side of a connection statement implies that it acts as an input (data has to be transferred *from* $MUX\_out\langle 0:3 \rangle$) and further down the listing, there is a comment statement indicating that $MUX\_out\langle 0:3 \rangle$ is an input. There is no connection statement following this terminal comment because the connection of $MUX\_out\langle 0:3 \rangle$ to $X\_in\langle 0:3 \rangle$ has already been indicated. Thus, to avoid duplication of this sort, connection statements are listed only for output terminals.

Some terminals act as neither input nor output. Consider, for example, the third terminal comment in the above listing:

```
{ terminal X_outcomp<0:3> Usage = [**UNUSED**] }
```

This line tells us that there exists a terminal $X\_outcomp$, that it is four bits in size, that the bits are numbered 0 through 3 (MSB to LSB), and that it appears on neither the right-hand side nor the left-hand side of any transfer statement, i.e., it is unused in the Shifter module.

Terminal comments and the connections to terminals are listed until the comment line {*$StateTable* }. In the general case, the comment line {*$StateTable* } would be followed by information concerning required state transitions, but module Shifter has only a single state so that state transitions do not apply in this case. Thus, the comment line {*$StateTable* } is followed immediately by {*$EndStateTable* }. These two comment lines may appear redundant here, but they would ease the task of interpretation for any program developed to carry out further processing on the information presented in the listing. An example is given later which includes the listing of state transition information.

All terminal comment lines up to the comment {*$StateTable* } refer to terminals associated with the connections to terminals on the components within the module, i.e., the components X, MUX, and *gate1*. The terminal comments and connections to terminals listed after the line {*$EndStateTable* } are concerned with connections to the terminal ports of the module Shifter itself. The reader should have no difficulty interpreting these.

7-C.3. COMPILER OPTIONS

A number of options are available to the user when using the compiler. For example, the compiler can produce a listing of the input file, along with the line numbers. Compiler options appear as comments in the input file, and must be of the form

```
{$<letter>[+|-], ... }
```

Table 7-C.1 details the full set of options available. We will give a detailed explanation of each in following sections.

Table 7-C.1. User Options with RTL Compiler.

Option	Explanation
l+	turn listing on
l-	turn listing off (default)
w+	print warning messages to *input* file (default)
w-	suppress warning messages to *input* file
x+	generate listing file with expansion of transfer statements
x-	suppress listing file with expansion of transfer statements (default)
s+	allow state declarations and goto statements
s-	generate error message if state declarations and goto statements are present (default)
e+	allow Boolean expressions in transfer statements
e-	generate error message if a Boolean expression appears in a transfer statement (default)

7-C.3.1. Listing Option

To obtain a complete listing of the input file, we would place the comment
{*$l*+} as the first line in the file. In the case of the Shifter description, this
results in the following output, which appears in the file *connect:*

```
1    {$l+}
2    module Shifter(in<0:3>, out<0:3>, load, shiftright,
3                           shiftin, clear,clock);
4
5        module D74379(in<0:3>, out<0:3>, outcomp<0:3>, load, clock);
6           external;
7
8        module D74157(in0<0:3>, in1<0:3>, out<0:3>, select,strobe);
9           external;
10
11       module D7427(in1a,in1b,in1c,out1,in2a,in2b,in2c,out2,
12                          in3a,in3b,in3c,out3);
13          external;
14
15       component D74379 X;
16       component D74157 MUX;
17       component D7427 gate1;
18
19       begin
20             MUX_in0 <- in;
21             MUX_in1 <- shiftin @ X_out<0:2>;
22             X_in <- MUX_out;
23             MUX_select <- shiftright;
24             MUX_strobe <- clear;
25             out <- X_out;
26             X_load <- gate1_out1;
27             gate1_in1a <- shiftright;
```

```
   28               gate1_in1b <- clear;
   29               gate1_in1c <- load;
   30               X_clock <- clock;
   31        end { Shifter }
   32     $
w - X_outcomp<0:3> used for neither Input nor Output
w - gate1_in2a used for neither Input nor Output
w - gate1_in2b used for neither Input nor Output
w - gate1_in2c used for neither Input nor Output
w - gate1_out2 used for neither Input nor Output
w - gate1_in3a used for neither Input nor Output
w - gate1_in3b used for neither Input nor Output
w - gate1_in3c used for neither Input nor Output
w - gate1_out3 used for neither Input nor Output

Number of errors detected:        0
Number of warnings:               9
```

Selected parts of a description can be printed by bracketing them with the comments $\{\$l+\}$ and $\{\$l-\}$.

7-C.3.2 Warning Option

Warnings are, by default, printed on the terminal. The user can request that warnings not be sent to the terminal by inserting the comment $\{\$w-\}$ at the beginning of the file. The user is cautioned to take care to ensure that warnings are suppressed only in those cases in which it is absolutely safe; otherwise errors may be introduced into the design. Similar to the use of the listing option, warnings can be selectively suppressed by bracketing lines of description between the comments $\{\$w-\}$ and $\{\$w+\}$.

7-C.3.3. State Option

When a design is complete, i.e., when the lowest-level RTL description of a given system has been obtained, the description should contain no explicit references to system states. That is, there should be no references to state-type variables (i.e., state declarations or goto statements) in the final description. The example given in the body of this chapter is illustrative of this fact. At the higher levels of description, the use of state types is important, but their presence in a description indicates that further steps are necessary before a design is complete. Error messages are printed if state types are present unless the user takes specific action. The error messages can be avoided by inserting the comment $\{\$s+\}$ at the start of the file. In addition, error messages can be selectively avoided by bracketing lines of code with the comments $\{\$s+\}$ and $\{\$s-\}$.

7C-3.4. Expression Option

The compiler will also pick out certain types of expressions that should not be present in a final description. The types of expressions involved are those that include the logical operators AND(&), OR(|), or NOT(^). These operators are sometimes used in RTL descriptions (an example of the use of the AND operator is given below) but the final (lowest level) description should have all such operators replaced by device interconnections. Error messages are generated if any of the logical operators are present. These messages can be avoided by placing the comment {$e+} at the start of the file. And, as with the other options, error messages can be selectively avoided by bracketing lines of code with the comments {$e+} and {$e−}.

7C-3.5. Explanation Option

The explanation option allows the user to expand statements for clarification of meaning. An example is given below. The user can obtain an explanation for a group of statements by bracketing with the comments {$x+} and {$x−}, or an explanation for the whole file by placing the comment {$x+} at the start of the file.

The following, rather contrived, example illustrates the use of the explanation option. The comments e+, s+ at the beginning have been inserted to avoid unwanted output from the *listing* file.

```
 1    {$e+,s+,x+}
 2    module interesting(a, b, c<0:3>);
 3
 4    terminal x, y;
 5    state s0, s1;
 6
 7    begin
 8        s0:
 9        begin
10            a @ b <- c<1:2>;
 *    on #s0 do b <- c<2>
 *    on #s0 do a <- c<1>
11            x @ y <- b @ a;
 *    on #s0 do y <- a
 *    on #s0 do x <- b
12                c<1:3> <- 0
13                goto s1
 *    on #s0 do c<1:3> <- 0B000%3

w - ; inserted before this item
 *        on *AnyInput* do goto #s1
14            end;
15
16        s1:
17        begin
18            on c<3> do
19                c<0:2> <- (a & x) @ c<3:2>;
 *    on #s1&c<3> do c<0:2> <- (a&x)@c<3:2>
20            goto s0
 *    on *AnyInput* do goto #s0
21        end
22    end
23    $
```

```
Number of errors detected:       0
Number of warnings:              1
```

There are a number of points to note from the listing file for the module "interesting". Lines which begin with the symbol * are produced by the use of the *x* option, i.e., they constitute the explanation produced from the preceding line of input description by the compiler. For example, line 10 of the listing

$$a \ @ \ b \ <- \ c<1:2>;$$

is expanded into two transfer statements, one for *a* and one for *b*:

```
on #s0 do b <- c<2>;

on #s0 do a <- c<1>;
```

The two transfer statements are now conditioned by on statements to show that the transfers are performed on the condition that the system is in state *s0* (we precede the variable *s0* by the # symbol to show that it is a state output from the controller). Note also that terminal *a* (the most significant bit of the concatenated terminal set *a@b*) is connected to the terminal $c\langle 1 \rangle$ (the most significant bit of the terminal set $c\langle 1:2 \rangle$); and *b* is connected to terminal $c\langle 2 \rangle$.

The transfer statement on line 12 and the goto statement on line 13 are not separated by a semicolon (;); the compiler recognizes that this is a common error and assumes that the semicolon can be taken as present. This is shown by the warning message:

```
w - ; inserted before this item
```

Line 12 assigns the constant 0 to the terminals $c\langle 1:3 \rangle$. Since it is common to connect terminal sets to either 1 or 0, the compiler will expand the 1 or 0 to the binary bit pattern of 0's or 1's of the appropriate length, in this case a binary bit pattern of 0's of length 3 (recall from Appendix A that *0B* means "binary"):

```
c<1:3> <- 0B000%3
```

Line 19 is a transfer statement which is executed on the condition that the system is in state *s1* and on the condition that $c\langle 3 \rangle$ is *TRUE*. The compiler collects these conditions together to form the single on statement

```
on #s1&c<3> do c<0:2> <- (a&x)@c<3:2>
```

The compiler also generates data for a state-table description of the controller's operation. Line 13 states that if the system is in state *s0* then the next state is to be state *s1*, and line 20 states that if the system is in state *s1* then the next state is to be state *s0*. The compiler recognizes that these goto statements are not conditioned by any input terminal values, and generates the separate statements

```
on *AnyInput* do goto #s0

on *AnyInput* do goto #s1
```

The fact that one warning message was printed and no errors were detected is given by the last two lines in the output.

The file *connect* containing the details of connections to each of the terminals for module "interesting" is as follows:

```
{$Module:interesting    }

{ terminal x  Usage = [Input Output] }
x <- #s0&b

{ terminal y  Usage = [Output] }
y <- #s0&a

{$StateTable }

s0:
on *AnyInput* do goto #s1

s1:
on *AnyInput* do goto #s0
{$EndStateTable }

{ terminal a  Usage = [Input Output] }
a <- #s0&c<1>

{ terminal b  Usage = [Input Output] }
b <- #s0&c<2>

{ terminal c<0:3>  Usage = [Input Output] }
c<0> <- (#s1&c<3>)&a&x
c<1:2> <- #s0&0B00%2 | (#s1&c<3>)&c<3:2>
c<3> <- #s0&0B0%1
{$EndModule:interesting    }
```

Two points need to be brought out from an examination of the contents of the connection description file (*connect*). First, note that the state table description appears between the comments {*$StateTable*} and {*$EndStateTable*}. Thus, the first two lines of the state table description

```
s0:

on *AnyInput* do goto #s1
```

state that, with the controller in state *s0*, the next clock pulse should cause the controller to go into state *s1* regardless of the value of any of the terminals. Similarly, the remaining two lines of the state table description state that, if the controller is in state *s1*, the next clock pulse should cause the controller to go into state *s0* regardless of the value of any of the terminals.

Second, the transfer statements associated with terminal $c\langle 0:3\rangle$ (which appear in lines 12 and 19 of the listing file) are collected together after the line beginning { *terminal* $c\langle 0:3\rangle$ . . . } in the connection description file. We see that the terminal set $c\langle 0:3\rangle$ is used (in part) for both input and output. For our purposes here, its use as an output is the most significant. In line 12, we see that with the system in state *s0*, $c\langle 1:3\rangle$ is used as an output and in line 19, with the system in state *s1*, $c\langle 0:2\rangle$ is used as an output. The compiler takes note of this and lists information about the required connections at the end of the file *connect*. In particular note that $c\langle 1:2 \rangle$ is required to be connected to different terminals when the system is in states $s0$ and $s1$. In practice, this requirement would be realized by means of a multiplexer.

REFERENCE

[1] N. Wirth, *Algorithms + Data Structures = Programs*, Prentice-Hall, 1976.

Appendix

LOGIC FAMILIES

A.1. TRANSISTOR-TRANSISTOR LOGIC (TTL)

TTL is currently the most widely used logic family and is the one on which the 7400 series of integrated circuits is based. TTL was developed from an earlier family, diode-transistor logic (DTL) and, for ease of presentation, we will explain the basic structure of DTL first. As a preamble, we will review briefly the characteristics of diodes and transistors.

A.1.1. Characteristics of Diodes and Transistors

Diodes are devices that allow current to flow in one direction (from anode to cathode) but prohibit the flow of current in the opposite direction. The standard symbol for a diode is shown in Figure A1(a). Silicon diodes are constructed from p-type and n-type silicon with the junction between the two types (the pn junction) providing the required behavior. Typical characteristics of a silicon diode are shown in Figure A1(b). This figure shows that the silicon diode will start to conduct when v_d is 0.6V (this is usually called the *cut-in voltage*). The figure also shows that no matter what current the diode is carrying, the voltage v_d will not go much above 0.7V. Note that these voltages represent typical values and that fluctuations in the manufacturing process imply that characteristics are subject to some variability. This variability is not very great, however, and in analyzing circuits involving silicon pn-junction diodes it is usual practice to assume a cut-in voltage of 0.6V and a conducting voltage of 0.7V under "normal" operating conditions.

The circuit shown in Figure A.2 includes an npn transistor and can be used to carry out the logical inversion operation (i.e., converting logic 0 to logic 1 and vice-versa). To see how this circuit can be used as an inverter, we should first examine the behavior of the base current I_B as a function of the base-emitter voltage V_{BE}. It turns out that if I_B is plotted against V_{BE}, a curve very similar to the diode characteristic in Figure A.1(b) is obtained. That is, with $V_{BE} <$ 0.6V, no base current flows and the transistor is said to be *cut-off*. When the

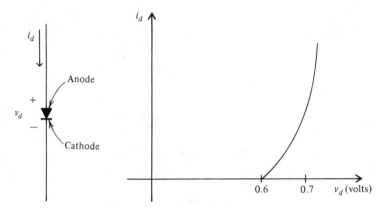

Figure A.1. The diode (a) Circuit symbol (b) Typical characteristics

base-emitter junction is forward biased beyond 0.6V, the base current I_B rises very rapidly with only a small increase in V_{BE}. In the whole range of transistor operation, the voltage V_{BE} does not go much above 0.7V.

From the behavior of I_B with V_{BE} we can see that if the input voltage V_i in the circuit of Figure A.2 is set to a value less than 0.6V (say 0V) the transistor will be cut off. In this condition, no collector current flows, so there is no voltage drop across R_C and consequently, $V_0 = 5V$. Thus we see that an input voltage of 0V leads to an output of 5V and if we identify logic 0 with 0V and logic 1 with 5V, we can interpret this behavior as the conversion of logic 0 into logic 1.

For the circuit to operate as a true inverter, it must also convert logic 1 into logic 0 (i.e., an input of 5V should lead to an output of 0V). It turns out that however hard we try, we will not be able to arrange for an input voltage of 5V to cause the output voltage to go down as low as 0V. The best we can do is to

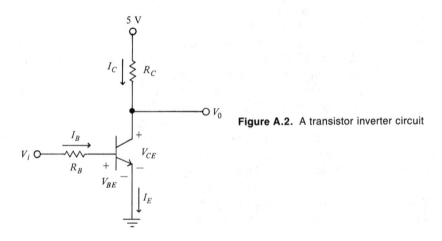

Figure A.2. A transistor inverter circuit

choose the values of R_B and R_C so that an input voltage of 5V will cause the transistor to go into saturation. With the transistor saturated $V_0 = V_{CE(sat)} = 0.2V$.

This example illustrates the manner in which npn transistors are employed as digital switches. In the "off" state, the transistor is in cut-off and in the "on" state, the transistor is in saturation. Logic 0 is identified with $V_{CE(sat)}$ and logic 1 is identified with a positive voltage sufficient (when applied to the base) to drive a transistor into saturation.

In what follows, transistors will occasionally be seen to be operating in a state somewhere in between cut-off and saturation. When operating in this way, a transistor is said to be operating in the *active region* of its characteristic.

A.1.2. The DTL NAND Gate

The basic DTL gate is a NAND, having the form shown in Figure A.3. In analyzing the behavior of a gate belonging to any logic family, we assume that inputs are derived from gates of the same type and that the output also feeds to a gate of the same type. Thus a low input to the circuit in Figure A.3 is assumed to be 0.2V i.e., the collector-emitter voltage of a saturated transistor. A high input is taken as the supply voltage, 5V in this case.

Then, if one or more of the inputs in the circuit of Figure A.3 is low, the voltage at point A in the figure is equal to the low-input level (0.2V) plus the voltage across a conducting diode (i.e., 0.7V). Thus the voltage at point A is 0.9V. The two diodes D_1 and D_2 have been inserted in the circuit to ensure that

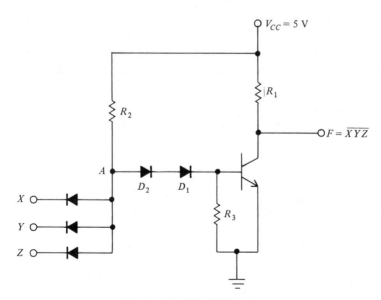

Figure A.3. DTL NAND gate

a voltage of 0.9V at point A is insufficient to turn on the output transistor; this ensures that one or more low inputs produce a high output, as is required for NAND operation. The cut-in voltage for the transistor, and for each of the diodes, is assumed to be 0.6V, so that the voltage at point A would have to reach 1.8V before the output transistor would start to turn on. Since point A is at 0.9V with one or more low inputs, this indicates that for low inputs, the circuit should be able to operate satisfactorily in the presence of noise spikes of up to 0.9V.

With all inputs high (at 5V) the output transistor goes into saturation. In this circumstance, the voltage at point A is equal to the voltages across the conducting diodes D_1 and D_2 (each 0.7V) plus the voltage across the base-emitter diode of the transistor (also taken as 0.7V) giving 2.1V in all. With 2.1V at point A, and 5V at each input, the input diodes are all substantially reverse-biased. From the point of view of noise immunity, it can be seen that in this state, an input would have to fall as low as 1.5V before the corresponding input diode began to turn on. Thus, in this state, the circuit can withstand noise spikes of up to 3.5V.

In summary, when one or more inputs to the circuit are low, the output transistor is off giving a high output and in this state the noise immunity is 0.9V. When all inputs are high, the output transistor is saturated, giving a low output and in this state the noise immunity is 3.5V.

Noise Margin.   Noise margin is one of several figures of merit used to compare performance of different logic families. It is defined as the maximum-amplitude noise pulse that will not change the state of a given gate. In the case of the DTL NAND gate we have seen that in one state the gate can withstand noise pulses of up to 0.9V and in the other state it can withstand noise pulses of up to 3.5V. Thus, 0.9V is the maximum-amplitude noise pulse that will *not* change the state of the gate, so that the noise margin for the DTL NAND gate is 0.9V.

A.1.3. The TTL NAND Gate

The TTL NAND gate, depicted in Figure A.4, looks considerably more complex than the DTL NAND gate but, as is explained below, the TTL circuit is really no more than a modified form of the DTL circuit, the modifications having been made to produce a gate which can operate at higher speeds.

Notice first that the 5 diodes in the DTL circuit have all been replaced by pn junctions located within transistors T_1 and T_2. Transistor T_1 has 3 emitters (multi-emitter transistors are easy to construct with today's technology) and the three emitter-base junctions replace the three input diodes in the DTL gate. The diode D_2 in Figure A.3 is replaced by the base-collector junction of T_1 in Figure A.4 and the diode D_1 in Figure A.3 is replaced by the base-emitter junction of T_2 in Figure A.4.

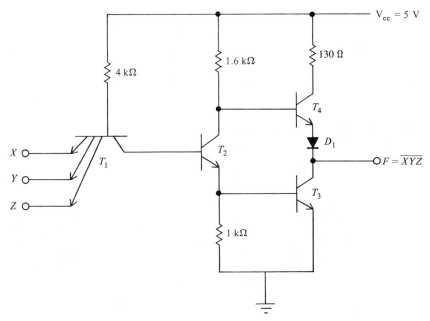

Figure A.4. A TTL NAND gate

Transistor T_4 and diode D_1 are present in the TTL circuit simply to speed up the turn-off time of transistor T_3 and we shall discuss this below. First, however, it is useful to observe how the operation of the TTL circuit is basically the same as that of the DTL circuit.

If any input is low (0.2V) the corresponding base-emitter junction is forward-biased and the base of T_1 is therefore at 0.9V. This ensures that T_3 is off because, for T_3 to be on, the voltage at the base of T_1 has to be at least 1.8V (i.e. the sum of the cut-in voltages for the base-collector junction of T_1 and the base-emitter junctions of T_2 and T_3). With all inputs high, the voltage at the base of T_1 rises above 1.8V and causes the transistors T_2 and T_3 to saturate.

Thus, the basic mechanisms causing the output transistor to turn off and to saturate in the DTL and TTL circuits are essentially the same. There is one significant difference, however, because the base-collector junction of T_1 in Figure A.4 does not act solely as a replacement for the diode D_2 in Figure A.3. As the following discussion shows, T_1 helps speed up the process undergone by transistors T_2 and T_3 when they make the transition from saturation to cutoff.

Note that when the output is low, the collector of T_1 has a voltage of 1.4V (the sum of the voltages across the forward-biased base-emitter junctions of T_2 and T_3) and that the base-collector junction of T_1 is also forward-biased, causing the voltage on the base of T_1 to be at 2.1V. In this situation, all inputs are high. If one or more inputs now drop to a low level, the voltage at the base of T_1

drops to 0.9V causing the base-collector junction of T_1 to be reverse-biased, thus placing T_1 in its active region. The resulting collector current, drawn from the base of T_2, results in rapid removal of the excess charge accumulated in the base of T_2 due to saturation. In DTL, no such mechanism exists, and a longer time is required to remove the stored charge, indicating that the output transistor in the DTL gate takes longer to turn off than does the output transistor in the TTL gate.

Before we examine the mechanism by which transistor T_4 and diode D_1 in Figure A.4 contribute to the speeding up of the turn-off time of the gate, it is appropriate here to introduce another figure of merit for logic gates, viz, propagation delay.

Propagation Delay. The propagation delay for a logic gate is the *average* time taken for a signal to propagate from input to output when a change of state is initiated at the input. Note that propagation delay is defined as an "average" value. The reason for this is that the time taken for a low-to-high transition in a given type of gate is usually different from the time taken for a high-to-low transition.

This is illustrated in Figure A.5 for a TTL NAND gate in which all inputs are held high except one, whose voltage level changes according to Figure A.5(a). The voltage V_{th} is a threshold voltage that is used as a basis for propagation delay measurements. (For TTL, $V_{th} = 1.5V$). The symbols t_{PHL} and t_{PLH} used in Figure A.5(b) are employed in manufacturers' data books. t_{PHL} represents the time taken for an input signal causing a high-to-low transition at the output to bring about the transition. Similarly, t_{PLH} represents the time taken for an input signal causing a low-to-high transition at the output to bring about the transition.

The gate propagation delay is defined by

$$Propagation\ delay = \tfrac{1}{2}(t_{PHL} + t_{PLH})$$

This definition is employed for gates in other logic families, the only difference being in the choice of V_{th}.

Figure A.5(c) indicates the effects of increased capacitive loading on the TTL NAND gate. Large capacitive loads occur when the gate has a high fan-out and also if the gate output is connected to a device that is located some distance away (printed-circuit-board wiring adds a capacitance of roughly 100pF per meter). In either case, in making the low-to-high transition, the output transistor (T_3 in Figure A.4) has to come out of saturation and charge the load capacitance to the high-voltage level. Obviously, the larger the load capacitance, the larger t_{PLH} will be.

Note that Figure A.5(c) shows t_{PHL} virtually unchanged from its value in Figure A.5(b). The reason for this is that when T_3 goes into saturation it pro-

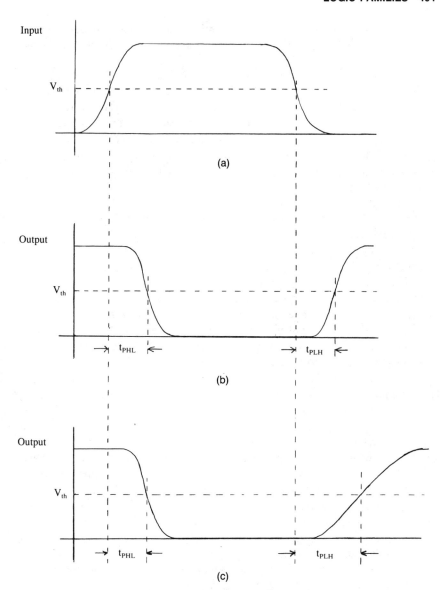

Figure A.5. Input and output waveforms illustrating propagation delay (a), (b), (c)

vides a very low output impedance (typically about 10Ω) and the load capacitance is able to discharge very rapidly. Thus, t_{PHL} is largely determined by other factors (which we need not go into here).

The main cause for concern, then, is t_{PLH}. Obviously, t_{PLH} could be reduced by giving transistor T_3 a low load resistance (when T_3 turns off, the load capacitance has to charge up through the load of T_3). However, a low load resistance connected to T_3 would cause T_3 to draw a heavy current whenever it went into saturation (implying high power dissipation). As is explained below, the presence of diode D_1 and transistor T_4 in the load circuit of T_3 allows the load capacitance to charge up through a low resistance while, in addition, preventing T_3 from drawing a heavy current when saturated.

The effects of D_1 and T_4 on the basic TTL NAND gate of Figure A.4 can be seen by first considering the case where all inputs are high. T_2 and T_3 are then saturated and the output F is low. The voltage at the base of T_4 is 0.9V (given by the sum of the base emitter voltage of T_3 (0.7V) and the collector-emitter voltage of T_2 (0.2V)). The presence of the diode D_1 ensures that this voltage is insufficient to turn on T_4. With T_3 saturated, a voltage of 1.4V would be required at the base of T_4 to start it conducting. (The figure of 1.4V is given by the collector-emitter voltage of T_3 (0.2V) plus the cut-in voltages of D_1 and the base-emitter diode of T_4). Thus, with all inputs high, T_4 is off and prevents T_3 from drawing a heavy current through the 130Ω resistor. (T_3 draws its current from whatever device to which the TTL gate is connected).

When one or more inputs go low, transistors T_2 and T_3 turn off. The output level cannot rise instantaneously because of the capacitive load but, with T_2 turned off, the voltage at the base of T_4 rises to a sufficiently high level for T_4 to turn on and briefly saturate. The capacitive load now draws current through D_1 and T_4 with T_4 operating in the emitter-follower configuration and hence offering a low impedance output (typically 70Ω). Although this is a low value, it is still seven times larger than the value of the output impedance when the output goes low so that the capacitive load still has a much greater effect on t_{PLH} than on t_{PHL}. The (typical) values usually quoted in databooks, for a fanout of 10, are $t_{PLH} = 11$ns and $t_{PHL} = 7$ns. The fact that t_{PLH} is nowhere near seven times as large as t_{PHL} indicates that capacitive loading is only one of several factors affecting propagation delay.

The output arrangement in Figure A.4 is referred to as a *totem-pole output*, obviously because of the way T_4 is located vertically above T_3.

We have seen how the totem-pole improves the switching speed of the TTL NAND gate without significantly increasing power consumption. The totem-pole arrangement does, however, lead to another problem: during switching, the off transistor turns on faster than the on transistor turns off. As a consequence, each time switching takes place, both transistors are on together for a short time creating a low-impedance path between the 5V supply and ground. This results in current spikes on the supply line. This effect is substantially more marked in the low-to-high transitions at the output. It is important that these current spikes be prevented from spreading over the power supply system as noise and a simple remedy is to connect decoupling capacitors between V_{cc} and ground. As a rule of thumb, for every eight or so IC packages use one ceramic capacitor whose value is in the range of $0.047\mu F$ to $0.1\mu F$.

A.1.4. The TTL Family

The TTL NAND gate that lies at the heart of the 7400 series differs in only one minor detail from the circuit shown in Figure A.4. The difference is illustrated in Figure A.6, which shows the multi-emitter transistor T_1 with a set of clamping diodes attached to its inputs. These diodes serve to limit any negative excursions of input signals (which can occur due to high-frequency signals causing "ringing") and thereby to protect T_1. Under normal operation, the diodes are reverse-biased, but if a negative voltage of 0.6V or greater arrives at one of the inputs, the corresponding diode starts to conduct and restricts the negative voltage to one diode drop.

The 74L00 Series (Low-Power TTL).   The 74L00 series is a low-power version of the 7400 series. The same basic circuitry is employed, but all resistor values are increased in order to reduce power consumption. The increase in resistor values does, of course, also lead to an increase in propagation delay.

Since decreasing power consumption generally leads to an increase in propagation delay, it follows that a good figure-of-merit for comparing logic families (and different versions of the same family) is the product of propagation delay

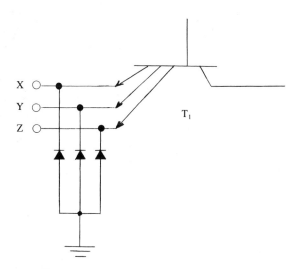

Figure A.6. Input to a 7400 series NAND gate

Table A.1.   Performance comparison of TTL family.

TTL type	Gate propagation delay (ns)	Power Dissipation (mW)	Speed-power (pJ)
Standard	10	10	100
Low-power	33	1	33
High-speed	6	22	132
Schottky	3	19	57
Low-power Schottky	9.5	2	19

and power consumption. This figure-of-merit, which is termed the *speed-power product*, is formed by taking the product of the propagation delay in ns and the power dissipation in mW. The speed-power product therefore has units of pico-joules (pJ).

A comparison of the performance of standard TTL and low-power TTL (along with the performance of other types) is given in Table A.1.

The 74H00 Series (High-Speed TTL).   This series is a high-speed version of standard TTL. The circuitry is again much the same except that smaller resistor values are employed. Reducing the resistor values has the effect of re-ducing the time constants associated with the resistors and stray capacitance. This in turn has the effect of reducing switching times, but this is achieved, of course, at the expense of increased power consumption.

An additional difference between this series and standard TTL is that the emitter-follower transistor T_4 in Figure A.4 is replaced by a Darlington pair. The Darlington-pair configuration (which is illustrated below in connection with Schottky TTL) has a substantially lower output impedance than does the emit-ter-follower and therefore provides a further reduction in t_{PLH}. The performance of high-speed TTL is summarized in Table A.1.

Schottky TTL—the 74S00 Series.   In surveying the principles of opera-tion of the basic TTL NAND gate in Figure A.4, we have seen how TTL has a major advantage over DTL in that transistor T_1 speeds up the removal of excess charge from saturated transistors as they are turned off. The idea behind Schottky TTL is to avoid the problem of removing excess charge by preventing transistors from going into saturation. This can be achieved by means of the *Schottky diode*.

The Schottky diode, sometimes called a Schottky barrier diode, is formed by means of a metal-semiconductor junction; the property that makes it useful in this context is that the voltage across it, when conducting, is very low, typically 0.3V. This is a useful property because when a transistor is in saturation it has

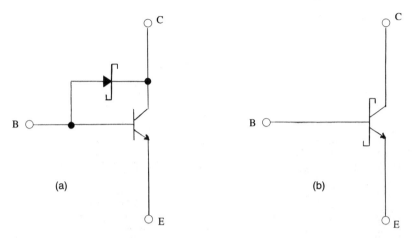

Figure A.7. (a) Clamping the collector-base voltage of a transistor using a Schottky diode; (b) Symbol of resulting Schottky transistor.

$V_{CE} = 0.2$V and $V_{BE} = 0.7$V, implying that the collector-base junction is forward-biased by 0.5V. It follows that connecting a Schottky diode between base and collector of a transistor, as shown in Figure A.7(a), can prevent the collector-base voltage from exceeding 0.3V and thereby prevent the transistor from going into saturation.

The manufacture of transistors with Schottky diodes attached as shown in Figure A.7(a) is quite straightforward and the resulting devices are known as Schottky transistors; they are given the symbol shown in Figure A.7(b).

The Schottky TTL NAND gate is illustrated in Figure A.8. The basic structure here is not greatly different from that shown in Figure A.4. The main point of departure concerns the use of two extra transistors. T_5 has been added to the totem-pole arrangement to form, with T_4, a Darlington pair which helps reduce t_{PLH}, as was discussed in relation to the 74H00 series. The other extra transistor is T_6, whose presence allows T_3 to turn off more rapidly. Clamping diodes are also shown connected to each of the inputs.

All transistors except T_4 in Figure A.8 are Schottky transistors. T_4 is not provided with a clamping diode because it never saturates.

As shown in Table A.1, Schottky TTL has twice the speed of high-speed TTL and uses less power. As a consequence, the 74H00 series can be considered obsolescent.

The 74LS00 Series (Low-Power Schottky).   This is a low-power version of Schottky TTL. The lower power dissipation is achieved by increasing the resistor values, and this leads also to an increase in propagation delay.

As is shown in Table A.1, low-power Schottky provides virtually the same propagation delay as the basic 7400 series, but with one-fifth the power dissi-

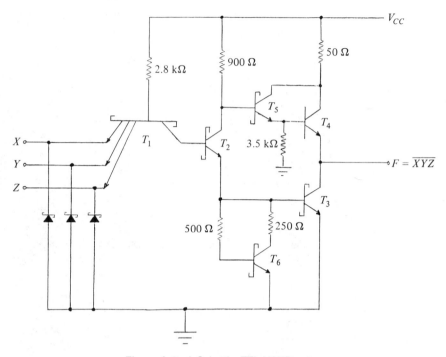

Figure A.8. A Schottky TTL NAND gate

pation. As a consequence, the 74LS00 series is currently the most widely used form of TTL.

The Tri-State Gate. Situations frequently arise in digital design requiring that the outputs of two or more gates feed to a common bus. In such circumstances, only one gate will be required to feed data onto the bus at any given time and it is obviously important that the other gates connected to the bus do not interfere with this process. Standard TTL gates, with the totem-pole output arrangement, cannot be used in such an application. It is possible, however, to modify TTL gates with a totem-pole output so that they *can* be connected to a common bus. The basic idea underlying the modification is illustrated in Figure A.9(a).

The circuit in Figure A.9(a) is a basic TTL inverter with a small amount of extra circuitry providing an enable input. When *EN* is high, the extra circuitry draws no current and the gate operates as a normal inverter. When *EN* goes low, however, diode D_2 begins to conduct so that the voltage at the base of T_4 is 0.7V and T_4 is turned off. In addition *EN* provides a low input to T_1, which causes transistors T_2 and T_3 to be turned off also. Thus, with *EN* low, both transistors in the totem-pole are off and the output is virtually open-circuited. The very high impedance created at the output of the gate when *EN* is low

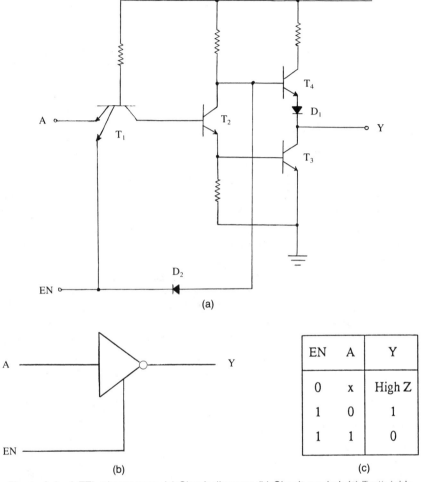

Figure A.9. A TTL tristate gate: (a) Circuit diagram; (b) Circuit symbol; (c) Truth table.

EN	A	Y
0	x	High Z
1	0	1
1	1	0

allows two or more gates of this type to feed a common bus. Any individual gate can feed data onto the bus so long as the other gates are in the high-impedance state.

The circuit symbol and truth table for the gate in Figure A.9(a) are shown in Figures A.9(b) and A.9(c). The name of the gate obviously comes from the ability of its output to assume three distinct states.

Non-inverting tri-state gates, called tri-state buffers, are also available, and are also intended for use in driving a common bus.

The Open-Collector Gate. In addition to the tri-state gates, the TTL family has another type of gate, the open-collector, that can also be used for feeding a common bus. This device gets its name from the fact that its circuitry is the same as that of an ordinary TTL gate, but with the upper half of the totem-pole output missing; that is, the collector of the lower transistor in the totem-pole is left open-circuit. When the outputs of two or more open-collector TTL gates are connected to a common load resistor, the connection creates the wired-AND function. This arrangement is often used to drive a common bus.

A.2. MOS TRANSISTOR LOGIC

A.2.1. The MOSFET

The behavior of the transistors employed in TTL is determined by the flow of two types of charge carrier, namely electrons and holes. It is for this reason that such transistors are known as *bipolar* devices. MOS transistors, on the other hand, are *unipolar* devices; that is, their behavior results from the flow of only one type of charge carrier. As an example, consider the structure shown in Figure A.10. Here are shown two n-type regions located on a p-type substrate. Terminals called the source and drain are attached to the n-type regions. A further terminal, the gate, is attached to a metal layer which is insulated from the substrate by a layer of silicon dioxide. This arrangement is the reason for the device being called a *MOS (metal-oxide semiconductor) transistor*. If the gate voltage is negative or zero (with respect to the substrate) a very high impedance exists between source and drain (typically $10^{10} \, \Omega$) and the device is OFF. If the gate voltage is increased positively from zero, a threshold voltage is reached (typically 1.5V) at which conduction becomes possible. Conduction becomes possible at this point because, when the positive voltage on the gate

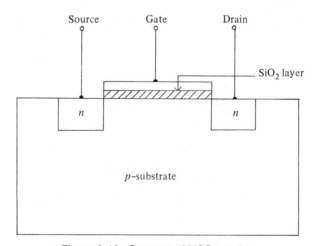

Figure A.10. Structure of MOS transistor.

is large enough, it is able to attract negative charges (electrons) to the edge of the p-type substrate in contact with the SiO_2 layer. This effect creates an n-type *channel* that connects the n-type regions at the source and drain and, with the drain held at a positive voltage with respect to the source, the n-type charge carriers flow from source to drain. In this conducting state, the device is ON and has a resistance between source and drain usually of about $1k\Omega$.

Note that the behavior of the device is controlled by the *voltage* at the gate. This is in contrast to the bipolar transistor whose behavior is controlled by the *current* in the base. The voltage at the gate of the device in Figure A.10 leads to an electric field that determines the presence or absence of a conducting channel. Consequently devices of this type are known as *field-effect transistors* (FETs). Thus, the device in Figure A.10 is normally referred to as an *n-channel MOSFET*. It is also possible to construct p-channel MOSFETs that operate on a similar principle. The p-channel MOSFET has an appearance similar to the device shown in Figure A.10. The only difference is that the n-type and p-type materials are interchanged and, of course, a negative voltage is necessary on the gate to create the p-channel. Both of these MOSFETs are known as *enhancement* type because increasing the gate voltage increases the current flow. Another type of MOSFET, the *depletion* type, is constructed in a fashion similar to the enhancement type; the only difference is that a conducting channel is built into the device. Thus, an n-channel MOSFET of depletion type would look like the device in Figure A.10, but with the addition of a thin n-type layer immediately beneath the SiO_2 layer. With 0V on the gate, the device would conduct readily, and hence would be in the ON state. A negative voltage on the gate would drive away some of the charge carriers in the n-channel and a sufficiently large negative voltage would leave the channel completely depleted of charge carriers (hence the name "depletion" type); in this state the device would be OFF.

In this section, we will confine our discussion to MOSFETs of the enhancement type. A variety of symbols are in use for representation of MOSFETs. Three of the most common are shown in Figure A.11. Each of the symbols in the figure represents an n-channel MOSFET of the enhancement type. In Figure A.11(a), the device is shown with four terminals. In most applications, the substrate is connected to the source and devices are manufactured with this connection made internally; Figures A.11(b) and (c) represent devices with this internal connection. The broken vertical line between drain and source in Figures A.11(a) and (b) is intended to indicate that a conducting path does not exist between the two terminals without the presence of a suitable voltage at the gate (this emphasizes the fact that the MOSFET is of enhancement type). Figure A.11(c) is just a simplified form of Figure A.11(b) and we shall use this simplified form in what follows. Note that similar symbols exist for p-channel enhancement MOSFETs; the only difference is that the arrow in each symbol points in the opposite direction.

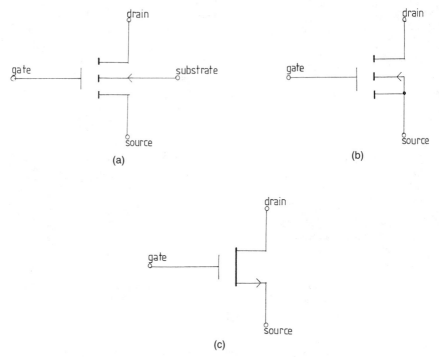

Figure A.11. Symbols for n-channel MOSFET.

A.2.2. MOSFET Logic Circuitry

There are three basic types of MOSFET logic circuits: (i) those based solely upon *n*-channel MOSFETs (and referred to as NMOS circuits), (ii) those based solely upon p-channel MOSFETs (PMOS circuits) and (iii) those which use particular mixtures of both n-channel and p-channel devices (which are known as complementary MOS, or CMOS, circuits).

A major advantage of MOSFET logic is that a resistor can be created by connecting a MOSFET in such a way that it is permanently ON (the usual method of achieving this will be explained later). The normal MOSFET structure provides a resistance of approximately 1kΩ when in the ON state; other values of resistance can be obtained by modifying the device geometry. These facts allow logic circuits to be built on a chip using only one type of component, the MOSFET. The fact that actual resistors need not be built onto the chip leads to a considerable improvement in packing density (i.e. gates per chip) to be achieved in comparison to other logic families. Of the three types of MOS logic, NMOS allows the greatest packing density and has therefore found greatest favor in LSI and VLSI systems. PMOS also allows a greater packing density

than CMOS but has the disadvantages of being both twice as slow as NMOS†
and allowing only half the packing density of NMOS. Although CMOS has the
disadvantages of being the most complex type (from the point of view of fabrication) and of allowing the least packing density, it does have the advantages
of offering higher speed and much lower power dissipation than the other two.
As a consequence, CMOS has found wide application in SSI and MSI. Since
NMOS and CMOS have found the widest applications, we will concentrate on
these two types in the discussion that follows. The reader should note, in addition, that PMOS circuitry is essentially the same as NMOS circuitry except
that opposite voltage polarities are employed.

Before we proceed with our discussion of NMOS and CMOS we point out
one other advantage that is common to all forms of MOSFET logic. MOSFETs
have a very high input impedance (because of the insulation between gate and
substrate), typically 10^{12} Ω. As a consequence they draw very little current and
this provides MOSFET logic with a very high fan-out capability, typically 50
or more.

NMOS Logic Gates.   The basic logic functions NOT, NAND and NOR are
all very easily realized using MOS devices. An NMOS inverter is shown in
Figure A.12. Note first of all that the circuit consists simply of two NMOS
transistors. Transistor T_2 has its gate connected directly to the $+5V$ supply, so
that T_2 is permanently in the ON state and thereby behaves like a resistor. Be-

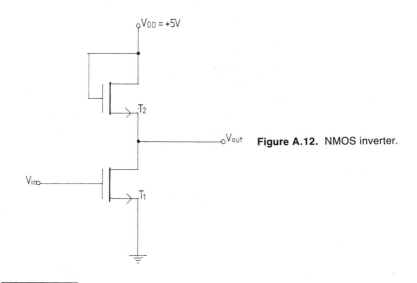

Figure A.12. NMOS inverter.

---

† This is because the charge carrier in PMOS is the hole, which has lower mobility than the electron, which carries the charge in NMOS.

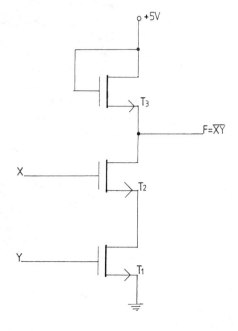

Figure A.13. NMOS NAND gate.

cause of this the behavior of the NMOS inverter is very similar to that of the bipolar transistor inverter depicted in Figure A.2. With V_{in} at logic 0 (i.e., at a voltage below the threshold voltage) transistor T_1 is OFF so that very little current flows and V_{out} goes high. With V_{in} at logic 1 (i.e., approximately +5V) transistor T_1 turns ON, thereby entering a low-resistance state. Thus, in this state, both T_1 and T_2 are ON and, if the two transistors were identical, this would lead to an output voltage of approximately 2.5V (by potential divider action). With V_{in} at logic 1 we require a logic 0 at the output (i.e., a voltage less than 1.5V, the threshold voltage). In order to achieve this with the structure in Figure A.1, the ON resistance of T_2 has to be substantially larger than that of T_1. This can be achieved by constructing T_2 so that it has a narrower channel than T_1.

An NMOS NAND gate is depicted in Figure A.13. The principle of operation is very similar to that of the inverter circuit in Figure A.12. If either X or Y or both are at logic 0, very little current flows in the circuit and the output F is at logic 1. If both X and Y are at logic 1, all three transistors are conducting and, with T_3 having a much higher ON resistance than the other two transistors, the output F is at logic 0.

Figure A.14 shows an NMOS NOR gate. If both X and Y are set at logic 0, very little current flows and F is at logic 1. If, on the other hand, either X or Y or both are at logic 1, a conducting path exists from T_3 to the earth, and the high ON resistance of T_3 ensures that F is at logic 0.

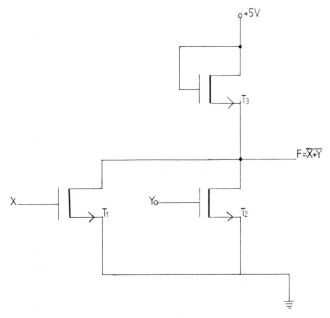

Figure A.14. NMOS NOR gate.

CMOS Logic Gates.   It was stated earlier that CMOS circuitry consumes far less power than NMOS or PMOS. The reason for this can be seen from examination of the operation of the basic CMOS gates. The CMOS inverter is depicted in Figure A.15. The circuit involves one p-channel MOSFET and one n-channel MOSFET. If the input X is at logic 1, the n-channel MOSFET (T_1) is ON because its gate-source voltage is approximately V_{DD} and hence above threshold. The p-channel MOSFET, on the other hand, is OFF, because its gate-source voltage is approximately zero and hence below threshold. With T_1 ON and T_2 OFF, the output is at logic 0. When the input X goes to logic 0, the two transistors each change state. T_1 now turns OFF because its gate-source voltage is approximately zero and T_2 turns ON because its gate-source voltage is approximately $-V_{DD}$ (note that a negative voltage is required to turn on a p-channel device). Thus, if the input goes low, the output goes high, as required.

Since the two transistors in Figure A.15 are never both on simultaneously, the circuit draws very little current and hence consumes very little power. For a similar reason the other basic CMOS gates consume very little power. The CMOS configurations for two-input NAND and NOR gates are shown in Figures A.16(a) and (b) respectively. In the NAND gate, if both of the inputs are high, the n-channel devices are ON and the p-channel devices are OFF; thus

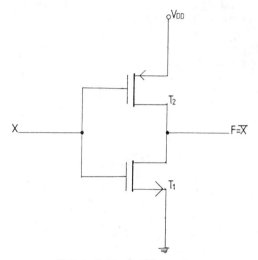

Figure A.15. CMOS inverter.

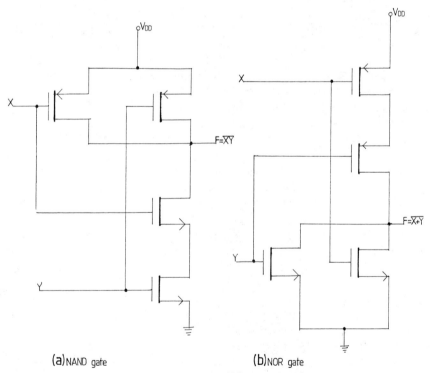

(a)NAND gate   (b)NOR gate

Figure A.16. CMOS gates: (a) NAND gate; (b) NOR gate.

Table A.2. Typical characteristics of IC logic families.

Logic family	Noise immunity (V)	Fan-out	Gate propagation delay (ns)	Power dissipation (mW)	Speed-power product (pJ)
7400 series	0.4	10	10	10	100
74S00 series	0.4	10	3	19	57
74LS00 series	0.4	20	9.5	2	19
CMOS	3	50	25	0.05	1.25
ECL	0.2	25	2	25	50

the output is low. If any input goes low, the n-channel device to which it is connected will turn OFF and the p-channel device to which it is connected will turn ON; the output will then be high.

For the NOR gate, in Figure A.16(b), if both inputs are low, the two p-channel devices will be ON and the n-channel devices will be OFF, giving a high output. If any input goes high, this will result in a p-channel device being turned OFF and an n-channel device being turned ON, thus giving a low output.

Note that in both circuits in Figure A.16 a conducting path never exists from the V_{DD} terminal to earth. This results in the very low power consumption of approximately 10nW per gate at low frequencies. The power consumption does increase with frequency, however, because of the inevitable charging and discharging of load (and other stray) capacitances. However, the power consumption of CMOS does not approach that of low-power Schottky TTL until switching frequencies reach as high as 500kHz.

In addition to its low power consumption, CMOS has several other advantages. First of all, it can operate with a wide range of power-supply voltages (3V–15V), which implies that power-supply regulation is unimportant with CMOS. Second, it has a relatively high noise immunity (approximately 30% of the supply voltage), and third, a high fan out capability. The one disadvantage, in comparison to other logic families, is its relatively high propagation delay (see Table A.2).

A degree of compatibility among CMOS integrated circuits has been achieved through the 4000 series which is produced by a number of manufacturers. One other series worth noting is the 74C00 series, which is pin-compatible (but *not* electrically compatible) with the 7400 TTL series. The main use of the 74C00 series is in the production of low-power versions of existing TTL circuits.

A.3. CONCLUDING REMARKS

We have reviewed the basic attributes of logic families based upon TTL and MOSFETs. Of the various types considered, two have become industry standards for SSI and MSI. The first of these is low-power Schottky TTL, which has the lowest speed-power product of the TTL family (see Table A.1); the second is CMOS, which is slower than low-power Schottky but offers various advantages, particularly very low power consumption and high fan-out. For LSI and VLSI, NMOS and PMOS have advantages over CMOS in terms of packing density and simplicity of fabrication. NMOS has further advantages over PMOS, higher speed and packing density, and so is the most widely used for larger-scale integration.

Another family that we should mention, because of its high speed, is *emitter-coupled logic (ECL)*. This is a bipolar family which achieves its speed by employing a configuration that avoids transistor saturation (but without the need for the artifice of Schottky clamping). ECL is about 50% faster than the fastest TTL family (the 74S00 series) and hence is the automatic choice if speed is at a premium. For more details on ECL, see [1].

Table A.2. contains a comparison of the main performance parameters of the more important logic families.

REFERENCE

[1] M. M. Mano, *Digital Design*, Prentice-Hall, Englewood Cliffs, N.J., 1984.

INDEX